The Robot in the Garden

Telerobotics and Telepistemology in the Age of the Internet

Edited by Ken Goldberg

The MIT Press   Cambridge, Massachusetts   London, England

First MIT Press paperback edition, 2001

© 2000 Massachusetts Institute of Technology

Chapter 18, "The Film and the New Psychology" by Maurice Merleau-Ponty is reprinted from Maurice Merleau-Ponty, *Sense and Non-Sense* (Paris: Editions Gallimard, 1996). © Editions Gallimard, 1996.

This book was set in Garamond 3 and Bell Gothic by Graphic Composition, Inc.

Printed and bound in the United States of America.

Library of Congress Cataloging-in-Publication Data

The Robot in the garden : telerobotics and telepistemology in the age of the Internet / edited by Ken Goldberg.

    p. cm.—(Leonardo (Series) (Cambridge, Mass.))

    Includes bibliographical references and index.

    ISBN 0-262-07203-3 (alk. paper), 0-262-57154-4 (pb)

    1. Robotics. 2. Knowledge, Theory of. I. Goldberg, Ken. II. Series.

TJ211 .R537 2000
121—dc21
                                                      99-059405

To the memory of M. G. and M. G.

Contents

Information, Abstracts, and Examples can be found online at:
http://mitpress.mit.edu/telepistemology

Series Foreword

*Editorial Board: Roger F. Malina, Denise Penrose,
and Pam Grant Ryan*

We are living in a world in which the arts, sciences, and technology are becoming inextricably integrated strands in a new emerging cultural fabric. Our knowledge of ourselves expands with each discovery in molecular and neurobiology, psychology, and the other sciences of living organisms. Technologies not only provide us with new tools for communication and expression, but also provide a new social context for our daily existence. We now have tools and systems that allow us as a species to modify both our external environment and our internal genetic blueprint. The new sciences and technologies of artificial life and robotics offer possibilities for societies that are a synthesis of human and artificial beings. Yet these advances are being carried out within a context of increasing inequity in the quality of life and in the face of a human population that is placing unsustainable burdens on the biosphere.

The Leonardo series, a collaboration between the MIT Press and Leonardo/International Society for the Arts, Sciences, and Technology (ISAST), seeks to publish important texts by professional artists, researchers, and scholars involved in Leonardo/ISAST and its sister society, Association Leonardo. Our publications discuss and document the promise and problems of the emerging culture.

Our goal is to help make visible the work of artists and others who integrate the arts, sciences, and technology. We do this through print and electronic publications, prizes and awards, and public events.

To find more information about Leonardo/ISAST and to order our publications, go to the Leonardo Online Web site at <http://www.mitpress.-mit.edu/e-journals/Leonardo/home.html> or send e-mail to <leo@mit-press.mit.edu>.

Acknowledgments

On August 15, 1994, my colleagues and I were beta testing a web page we'd linked to an old IBM robot arm and camera, allowing remote users to excavate for buried objects in a sandbox. An email arrived from a stranger named Don Patterson: "I don't believe that this is real. It would be easy, at least conceptually, to entirely fake this site." Patterson's comment came as a surprise, but he was absolutely correct: It would be "conceptually easy" to fake the site. Could anyone know the difference? This dilemma has a rich history: philosophers have studied skepticism for centuries. The word *telepistemology* does not exactly roll trippingly off the tongue, but it captures the subclass of epistemology that is the subject of this book.

I'd like to thank Bert Dreyfus, who encouraged this project from the beginning, for his many insights and intellectual generosity. Bert introduced me to Jeff Malpas, who edited my first prospectus for the book, and to Michael Idinopulos, who spent a year as a post-doc in the role of assistant editor. Michael's keen intelligence, rigor, and tact were essential to this project; it has been a true pleasure working with him.

I am fortunate to have a superb editor at MIT Press. Doug Sery trusted his instincts and shepherded this book through each stage with charm and confidence. He and Roger Malina, editor of the *Leonardo* series, were instrumental in selecting top-notch reviewers. I am honored to have worked with the contributors to this volume. Their professionalism, brilliant writing, and intellectual generosity set the highest standards.

The following friends and colleagues provided feedback and advice at the early stages of my thinking on this subject: Steve Antonson, John Canny, David Gibson, Adele Goldberg, Ann Goldberg, Eduardo Kac, Chine Lanzmann, Peter Lunenfeld, Lev Manovich, Michael Naimark, Eric Paulos, David Pescovitz, Debra Pughe, Sue Spaid, and Richard Wallace provided feedback and ideas at the early stages of my thinking on this subject.

Telepistemology is central to a series of net art projects I've developed in collaboration with some extraordinary artists and engineers: George Bekey, Erich Berger, Karl Bohringer, Florian Brody, John Canny, Billy Chen, Judith Donath, Bob Farzin, Lind Gee, Steven Gentner, Gil Gershoni, Sarah Hahn, Adam Jacobs, Gregory Kuhn, Woj Matusik, Rosemary Morris, Randall Packer, Mark Pauline, Eric Paulos, Joe Santarromana, Carl Sutter, Richard Wallace, and Jeff Wiegley.

I am also grateful for the advice I've received from Ruzena Bajcsy, George Bekey, Shawn Brixey, Brian Carlisle, Catharine Clark, John Craig, Elizabeth Daley, Erik Davis, Steve Dietz, Jim Gibson, Michael Grey, Kate Hayles, Selma Holo, David Hunt, Jon Ippolito, Reena Jana, Caroline Jones, Marc Lafia, Jean-Claude Latombe, Susan Miller, Leo Marx, Matt Mason, Howard Moraff, Christos Padadimitriou, Mark Pesce, Larry Rinder, David Ross, Itsuko Sakane, Shankar Sastry, Julia Scher, Tom Sheridan, Leonard Shlain, Gerfried Stoker, Hal Varian, Paul Wright, Heidi Zuckerman-Jacobson, and my students and colleagues at UC Berkeley.

An attempt to explore beyond one's area of expertise risks being viewed as folly, trespass, or both. But as Philip Rieff said: "You only live once, if then." I thank my entire family for their love and encouragement, and my wife Tiffany Shlain, best friend and digital diva, who continues to teach me the value of proximity.

Contributors

Ken Goldberg is associate professor of industrial engineering and computer science and founder of the Art, Technology, and Culture Colloquium at UC Berkeley. In 1994, Goldberg led the team that developed the first robot on the Internet. His net art installations have been exhibited in the Interactive Media Festival, Ars Electronica Center, Walker Center, Kwangju Biennale, and in the 2000 Biennial at the Whitney Museum of American Art. Goldberg has taught at the SF Art Institute and was selected as one of 3 artist groups to represent the United States at the ICC Biennale '99 in Tokyo.

Goldberg received his Ph.D. in 1990 from the School of Computer Science at Carnegie Mellon University. His primary research area is geometric algorithms for feeding, sorting, and fixturing industrial parts. Goldberg serves on the Advisory Board of the IEEE Society of Robotics and Automation and has given invited lectures on telerobotic art at MIT Media Lab, CMU, Stanford, NYU, NY School of Visual Arts, IBM, Interval, and Xerox. Goldberg won the National Science Foundation Young Investigator Award in 1994, NSF Presidential Faculty Fellow in 1995, and the Joseph Engelberger Award in 2000.

Albert Borgmann has an M.A. in German literature from the University of Illinois (Urbana) and a Ph.D. in philosophy from the University of Munich (Germany). Since 1970 he has taught at the University of Montana. His special area is the philosophy of society and culture with particular emphasis on technology. Among his publications are *Technology and the Character of Contemporary Life* (University of Chicago Press, 1984), *Crossing the Postmodern Divide* (University of Chicago Press, 1992), and *Holding on to Reality: the*

Nature of Information at the Turn of the Millennium (University of Chicago Press, 1999).

Thomas J. Campanella is an urbanist, historian, and cultural critic. He writes on a wide variety of subjects related to cities, landscape, and the changing built environment. His work often bridges scholarship and journalism, and has appeared in *Salon, Wired, Harvard Design Magazine, Landscape Journal, Orion,* and other publications. Campanella holds graduate degrees from Cornell and MIT, where he recently completed a Ph.D. in the Department of Urban Studies and Planning. He is currently a Fulbright fellow in Hong Kong, where he is working on a book about the transformation of the Chinese landscape in the Deng Xiaoping era.

John Canny is a professor in the Computer Science Division at UC Berkeley. His MIT Ph.D. in 1987 was the ACM dissertation winner that year, and he became one of the first Packard Foundation Fellows in 1988. He has since worked in robotics, computational geometry and algebra, graphics, and HCI. He directs the 3DDI project (3D Direct Interaction), which is an MIT-University of California collaboration supported by BMDO and ONR. His goal for the next decade or so is to nurture a human-centered approach to computing.

Judith Donath is assistant professor of Media Arts and Sciences at the MIT Media Lab, where she is the director of the Sociable Media Group. Her research focuses on the social side of computing, synthesizing knowledge from fields such as graphic design, urban studies and cognitive science to create novel and intuitive mediated environments.

Donath is the creator of numerous projects that address the problem of design for social interaction, such as *Visual Who* (a visualization of activity and affiliations in a virtual community), *Portraits in Cyberspace* (a participatory art show), and *The Electric Postcard* (a popular web/email amalgamation). She received her doctoral and master's degrees in media arts and sciences from MIT, her bachelor's degree in history from Yale University, and has worked professionally as a designer and builder of educational software and experimental media.

Hubert Dreyfus is philosophy professor in the Graduate School at the University of California, Berkeley. He received his Ph.D. at Harvard University and has taught at Brandeis University and MIT. His publications include: *What Computers (Still) Can't Do,* third edition, MIT Press (translated into ten languages); *Being-in-the-World: A Commentary on Division I of Being and Time;* (with Paul Rabinow) *Michel Foucault: Beyond Structuralism and Hermeneutics;* (with Stuart Dreyfus) *Mind over Machine;* and last year (with Charles Spinosa and Fernando Flores) *Disclosing New Worlds: Entrepreneurship, Democratic Action, and the Cultivation of Solidarity.* As his publications suggest, Dreyfus thinks of himself as an applied philosopher reflecting on the bearing of the work of existential phenomenologists such as Martin Heidegger and Maurice Merleau-Ponty on current cultural developments such as the attempt to create artificial intelligence, and the effect of the Internet and various technologies that facilitate action at a distance on everyday human interactions. Dreyfus is currently working on a second edition of *Being-in the-World,* which will expand his Heidegger Commentary to include Division II of *Being and Time.*

Alvin Goldman is regents' professor of philosophy and research scientist in cognitive science at the University of Arizona. His most recent book is *Knowledge in a Social World* (Oxford University Press, 1999), which develops an objectivist approach to social epistemology, covering science, law, democracy, information technology, and issues in the theory of speech and argumentation. His earlier book, *Epistemology and Cognition* (Harvard University Press, 1986), explored individual epistemology with special attention to the interface between epistemology and cognitive science. He is well known for his development of a causal theory of knowing and a reliabilist approach to knowledge and justification. In addition to epistemology, he has worked on the theory of action and on topics in the philosophy of mind, especially folk psychology and consciousness.

Goldman received his B.A. from Columbia College and his Ph.D. (1965) from Princeton University. He has spent most of his teaching career at the University of Michigan and the University of Arizona, with visiting appointments at the University of Pittsburgh and Yale University. He has been a fellow of the Guggenheim Foundation, the National Science Foundation, the Center for Advanced Study in the Behavioral Sciences, and the National Humanities Center. He served as president of the Pacific Division of the

American Philosophical Association and president of the Society for Philosophy and Psychology.

Oliver Grau is a new-media art historian. He teaches at Humboldt-University of Berlin and is doing research in the history and theory of virtual reality (financed by the Deutsche Forschungsgemeinschaft DFG) within an international network. He is author of *Die Sehnsucht im Bild zu sein: Zur Kunstgeschichte der Virtuellen Realität* (forthcoming 2000).

Involved in various exhibitions and festivals, he has published and lectured widely on the subhistory of media art in Europe, Asia and North and South America. Grau spent one year in Italy courtesy of the *Deutscher Akademischer Austauschdienst* (DAAD). He works and publishes primarily on the history of immersion, critical theory, body criticism, and the aesthetics of the sublime.

Marina Gržinić was born in Rijeka (Croatia), and has lived and worked in Ljubljana, Slovenia, since 1976. She holds a Ph.D. from the Faculty of Philosophy, Ljubljana, and works as researcher at the Institute of Philosophy at the ZRC SAZU (Scientific and Research Center of the Slovenian Academy of Science and Art) Ljubljana, and as a freelance critic and curator. Gržinic has written several books, including: *Ljubljana, Ljubljana* (with Ales Erjavec, 1991), *In Line for Virtual Bread: Time, Space, the Subject, and New Media in the Year 2000* (1996), *Fiction Reconstructed: New Media, Video, Art, Post-Socialism, and the Retro-Avant-Garde: Essays in Theory, Politics, and Aesthetics* (1997).

Together with Aina Smid, Gržinic has produced more than 30 video art projects, numerous installations, a CD-ROM (*Artintact 4,* ZKM, 1997), and a net.art site, *Axis of Life* (http://lois.kud-fp.si/quantum.east/). Gržinic and Smid have presented and exhibited their media works in more than 100 video festivals in Europe and throughout the world. They have received several major awards for their video productions, including: first prize at the Videonale Bonn in 1992, the *Deutscher Videokunst Preis* at ZKM Karlsruhe, first prize at the *1. Festival International de Video y Artes Electronicas,* Buenos Aires, 1996. They participated in the exhibitions *Europe, Europe: A Hundred Years of Avant-garde in Central and East Europe in Bonn,* 1994 and *I and the Other (Ik + De Ander)* at the Beurs van Berlage, Amsterdam 1994. They also presented a selection of their video works at the Museum of Modern Art (MOMA) Video Viewpoints program, New York, in 1994.

Blake Hannaford received the B.S. degree in engineering and applied science from Yale University in 1977, and the M.S. and Ph.D. degrees in electrical engineering from the University of California, Berkeley, in 1982 and 1985, respectively. Before graduate study, he held engineering positions in digital hardware and software design, office automation, and medical image processing. At Berkeley he pursued thesis research in multiple target tracking in medical images and the control of time-optimal voluntary human movement. From 1986 to 1989 he worked on the remote control of robot manipulators in the Man-Machine Systems Group in the Automated Systems Section of the NASA Jet Propulsion Laboratory, Caltech. He supervised that group from 1988 to 1989.

Since September 1989, Hannaford has been at the University of Washington in Seattle, where he has been associate professor of electrical engineering since 1993. He was awarded the National Science Foundation's Presidential Young Investigator Award and the Early Career Achievement Award from the IEEE Engineering in Medicine and Biology Society. His currently active interests include haptic displays on the internet, surgical biomechanics, and biologically based design of robot manipulators. He is the founding editor of *Haptics-e, The Electronic Journal of Haptics Research* (www.haptics-e.org). His lab URL is http://rcs.ee.washington.edu/BRL.

Michael Idinopulos received a B.A. from the University of Chicago and a Ph.D. in philosophy from the University of California, Berkeley. In his doctoral dissertation, entitled *Perceptual Content,* he defended a robust view of perceptual content, advocating it as a solution to central problems in epistemology, the philosophy of mind, and cognitive science. He spent 1998–1999 at UC Berkeley's ALPHA Lab working on this book, co-developing a telerobotic web site, and studying telepistemological questions surrounding robotics and the Internet. He works in New York for McKinsey & Company, a management consulting firm.

Martin Jay is Sidney Hellman Ehrman Professor and chair of the history department at the University of California, Berkeley. He has taught European intellectual history there since 1971, when he got his doctorate from Harvard. Among his books are *The Dialectical Imagination* (Boston: Little, Brown, 1973, and Berkeley: University of California Press, 1996); *Marxism and Totality* (Berkeley: University of California Press, 984); *Adorno* (Cambridge, Mass.: Harvard University Press, 1984); *Permanent Exiles* (New York: Columbia University Press, 1985); *Fin-de-Siecle Socialism* (New York: Routledge, 1989); *Force Fields* (New York: Routledge, 1993); *Downcast Eyes* (Berkeley: University of California, 1993); *Cultural Semantics* (Amherst: University of Massachusetts Press, 1998).

A fellow of the American Academy of Arts and Sciences and winner of Guggenheim, National Endowment of the Humanities, American Council of Learned Societies, and Rockefeller Foundation fellowships, he has been an associate of St. Antony's College, Oxford; Clare Hall, Cambridge, and the Stanford University Humanities Center. Since 1987, he has written a biannual column for *Salmagundi.* He is currently writing a book on the history of the concept of "experience" in Western thought.

Eduardo Kac is an artist and writer who investigates the philosophical and political dimensions of communications processes. Equally concerned with the aesthetic and the social aspects of verbal and nonverbal interaction, Kac examines linguistic systems, dialogic exchanges, and interspecies communication. His pieces, which often link virtual and physical spaces, propose alternative ways of understanding the role of communication processes in shaping consensual realities. Internationally known in the 1980s as a pioneer of Holopoetry and Telepresence Art, in the 1990s Kac created the new categories of Biotelematics (art in which a biological process is intrinsically connected to computer-based telecommunications work) and Transgenic Art (new art form based on the use of genetic engineering techniques to transfer synthetic genes to an organism or to transfer natural genetic material from one species into another, to create unique living beings).

Kac works with electronic and photonic media, including telepresence, holography, computers, video, robotics, and the Internet, as well as biological systems, such as animals, plants, bacteria, and organic tissue. His work has been exhibited widely in the United States, Europe, and South America. Kac's works belong to the permanent collections of the Museum of Modern Art in New York, the Museum of Holography in Chicago, and the Museum of Modern Art in Rio de Janeiro, Brazil, among others. He is a member of the editorial board of the journal *Leonardo,* published by MIT Press. In 1995 he received the Shearwater Foundation Holography Award for his body of work in the medium. In 1998 he received the Leonardo Award for Excellence. His anthology "New Media Poetry: Poetic Innovation and New Technologies" was published in 1996 as a special issue of the journal *Visible Language,* of which he was a guest editor. Writings by Kac on electronic art and literature as well as articles about his work have appeared in books, newspapers, magazines, and journals in more than twenty countries. Eduardo Kac is a Ph.D. research fellow at the Centre for Advanced Inquiry in Interactive Arts (CAiiA) at the University of Wales, Newport, United Kingdom. He is an assistant professor of art and technology at the School of the Art Institute of Chicago and has received numerous grants and awards for his work. The 88-page book *Teleporting An Unknown State,* published by Kibla, in Maribor, Slovenia (ISBN 961–6304-00–3) documents Kac's work in telepresence, telematics, and biology. Kac can be contacted at: ekac@artic.edu. His work can be seen at: http://www.ekac.org.

Machiko Kusahara is associate professor at Kobe University Graduate School of Science and Technology. She is the author of many writings in Japanese and in English including *Alife and Automata* (Art@Science, Springer 1997), *Signed by Artist* (Cyberart, Springer 1997), and *Flora and Fauna* (Fleshfactor, Springer 1997). She is also widely known as a curator and researcher in media art since 1985. After working in the field of computer graphics since 1983, in 1989 and 1992 she published seventeen laserdiscs of historical computer graphics animation. She was involved in founding of Tokyo's NTT InterCommunication Center, Tokyo Metropolitan Museum of Photography, and Digital Image. She curated exhibitions internationally and served as a jury member in major international competitions. She works and publishes primarily in the interdisciplinary area between art, culture, science, and technology with a background in art, computer science, and history of science. Currently her research focuses on the correlation between culture and digital technology such as network, artificial life, and digital entertainment. She is also a committee member of the Virtual Reality Society of Japan, Multimedia Contents Association, Japan Science, and Technology Corporation among others. Kusahara taught media art theory and practice in the Tokyo Institute of Technology Faculty of Art from 1994 to 1998.

Jeff Malpas is professor of philosophy and head of School at the University of Tasmania in Hobart, Australia. He is the author of *Donald Davidson and the Mirror of Meaning* (Cambridge, 1992), *Place and Experience* (Cambridge, 1999), and many scholarly articles. He is also the editor of a number of collections including (with Robert Solomon) *Death and Philosophy* (Routledge, 1998). In 1998–1999 he was a Humboldt Research Fellow at the University of Heidelberg.

Lev Manovich is an artist, a theorist, and a critic of new media. He has published more than forty articles, which have been translated into many languages and reprinted in eighteen countries. In his writings, Manovich places new media within the larger context of modern visual culture, relating it to the histories of art and cinema. Manovich was born in Moscow where he studied fine arts and architecture and participated in the underground art shows. Moving to New York in 1981, he began working in computer animation in 1984 at Digital Effects, one of the first commercial companies devoted to producing 3D animation for television and film. Manovich received an M.A. in experimental psychology from New York University (1988) and a Ph.D. in visual and cultural studies from the University of Rochester (1993). He is now an assistant professor in the Department of Visual Arts, University of California, San Diego, where he teaches studio and theory classes in new media. Currently he is working on a book entitled *The Language of New Media* for the MIT Press. His articles and projects are available at http://jupiter.ucsd.edu/~manovich.

Eric Paulos is a Ph.D. graduate student in the electrical engineering computer science department at the University of California, Berkeley. His research interests revolve around robotics and internet based personal telepresence, particularly the physical, aural, visual, and gestural interactions between humans and machines and various permutations of those interactions. Since developing *Mechanical Gaze* in 1995, he has been involved in the design of numerous web and internet based telepresence systems. Most notable are small human-sized helium filled tele-operated blimps (Space Browsers), the first internet accessible tele-laboratory (Legal Tender), and the first lethal control of internet connected machines. His current work focuses on Personal Roving Presence devices (PRoPs) designed to allow a remote user to explore and interact freely within a distant space. He is also the director of the Experimental Interaction Unit (EIU) founded to research and address various interaction dilemmas.

Paulos received his B.S. and M.S. in computer science from UC Berkeley. He has also collaborated extensively with Mark Pauline of Survival Research Laboratories (SRL) since 1994. Eric's work has been exhibited internationally, including the InterCommunication Center (ICC) in Japan, Ars Electronica in Austria, SIGGRAPH, the Dutch Electronic Art Festival (DEAF) in Rotterdam, a performance for the opening of the Whitney Museum's 1997 Biennial Exhibition, and an event for the inauguration of the ZKM Center for Art and Media Technology in Karlsruhe, Germany. In 1999 he was awarded Honorable mention in the Interactive Art category at Ars Electronica.

Catherine Wilson is professor of philosophy at the University of British Columbia. She is the author, most recently, of *The Invisible World* (Princeton University Press, 1995) which won the Honorable Mention in the AAUP's annual competition in the philosophy category for its year. She works and publishes primarily in the history and philosophy of science of the seventeenth and eighteenth century but has recently become interested in problems concerning naturalism in ethics and the role of fictions and representations in human behavior. She is currently editing a collection of Leibniz essays and a collection of essays on political philosophy and the history of ethics entitled *Civilization and Oppression.*

Wilson holds graduate degrees from Oxford (1974) and Princeton (1977) where she specialized in philosophical logic, linguistic theory, and theory of perception. She spent one year in the UK as the recipient of an NEH fellowship and two years in Germany courtesy of the Alexander von Humboldt Foundation. She has taught at the University of Oregon and the University of Alberta and has been a visitor to Notre Dame University. She is currently the editor of *History of Philosophy Quarterly.*

The Robot in the Garden

1

Introduction: The Unique Phenomenon of a Distance

Ken Goldberg

Every day the urge grows stronger to get hold of an object at very close range by way of its likeness, its reproduction.
— WALTER BENJAMIN, 1936

Some of our most influential technologies, the telescope, telephone, and television, were developed to provide knowledge at a distance. *Telerobots,* robots controlled at a distance, were developed in the 1950s to facilitate *action* at a distance. Specialists use telerobots to actively explore environments such as Mars, the Titanic, and Chernobyl. Military personnel increasingly employ reconnaissance drones and telerobotic missiles. At home, we have remote controls for the garage door, the car alarm, and the television (the latter a remote for the remote).

The Internet dramatically extends our scope and reach. As "real world" documentary-style shows are increasingly in demand on television, thousands of webcameras are being set up by amateurs to continuously transmit live scenes from their street corners, offices, and bedrooms. The Internet offers not only new ways of viewing, but also new ways of exhibiting. The bi-directional structure of the Internet also offers a new means for action. Telerobotic devices can be directly controlled from the Internet. From his or her desktop, anyone on the Internet can now stack blocks in a distant laboratory, or—as the title of this book suggests—tend a distant garden.

Access, agency, authority, and authenticity are central issues for the new subject of *telepistemology:* the study of knowledge acquired at a distance. One of the great promises of the Internet is its potential to increase our access to remote objects. The distributed nature of the Internet, designed to ensure reliability by avoiding centralized authority, simultaneously increases the potential for deception. Many Internet cameras and telerobotic systems have been revealed as forgeries, providing unsuspecting users with prerecorded images masquerading as live footage. The capacity for deception is inherent to the Internet and is particularly vivid in the context of telerobotics.

Are we being deceived? What can we know? What should we rely on as evidence? These are the central questions of epistemology, the philosophical study of knowledge, dating back to Aristotle, Plato, and the ancient Skeptics. The inventions of the telescope and microscope in the seventeenth century moved epistemology to the center of intellectual discourse for Descartes, Hume, Locke, Berkeley, and Kant. Although epistemology has lost primacy within philosophy, each new invention for communication or measurement forces us to recalibrate our definition of knowledge.

This is particularly true of the Internet, which provides widespread access to remote agency without relying on a trusted institutional authority. As the Internet extends our reach, it leaves us increasingly vulnerable to error, deception and forgery. In McLuhan's terms it simultaneously extends and amputates.[1] Hal Foster[2] traces this bipolar "dis/connection" through the writings of Benjamin,[3] Mcluhan, Debord,[4] and Haraway.[5]

"Now, at the close of the twentieth century," Hubert Dreyfus writes in chapter 3, "new tele-technologies . . . are resurrecting Descartes's doubts." Telepistemology asks: To what extent can epistemology inform our understanding of telerobotics and to what extent can telerobotics furnish new insights into classical questions about the nature and possibility of knowledge?

Artists have always been concerned with how representations provide us with knowledge.[6] Telerobotics, like photography and cinema, is a mode of representation. As such, it has aesthetic implications; a variety of artworks that incorporate telerobotics have appeared on the Internet. But as we have noted, representations can misrepresent. If Orson Welles's *War of the Worlds* was the defining moment for radio, what will be the defining moment for the Internet? How will artistic strategies be shaped by telerobotics and what is its potential as an artistic medium?

In the past six years, I have been exploring telepistemological questions about perception, knowledge, and agency in a series of Internet projects. The title of this book refers to the *Telegarden,* a telerobotic art installation on the Internet where remote users direct a robot to plant and water seeds in a real garden located in the Ars Electronica Museum in Austria.[7,8]

1. M. McLuhan, *Understanding Media* (Cambridge, Mass.: MIT Press, 1964).

2. H. Foster, *The Return of the Real* (Cambridge, Mass.: MIT Press, 1996.)

3. W. Benjamin, *Illuminations,* trans. Harry Zohn (New York: Schocken Books, 1969).

4. G. Debord, *The Society of the Spectacle,* Zone Books, 1969.

5. D. Haraway, "A Manifesto for Cyborgs," *Socialist Review* 80 (1995).

6. L. Shlain, *Art and Physics: Parallel Visions in Space, Time, and Light,* Quill Press, 1991, and L. Shlain, *The Alphabet v. The Goddess: The Conflict Between World and Image* (New York: Viking Press, 1998).

7. http://telegarden.aec.at.

8. G. Hardin, "The Tragedy of the Commons," *Science* 162 (1968): 1243–1248; P. Lunenfeld, "Technofornia," *Flash Art,* 1996; W. Mitchell, "Replacing Place," in *The Digital Dialectic,* ed.

Figure 1.1. The Telegarden (1995–1999), Ars Electronica Center, Austria, http://telegarden.aec.at. (K. Goldberg, J. Santarromana, G. Bekey, S. Gentner, R. Morris, C. Sutter, J. Wiegley, and E. Berger). Photo: R. Wedemeyer.

This volume includes sixteen original chapters by leading contemporary figures in philosophy, art, history, and engineering, with a postscript by Maurice Merleau-Ponty. In bringing together diverse perspectives on the fundamental philosophical issues surrounding this new technology, our aim is to identify critical points of reference.

This book focuses on telerobotics (TR) rather than virtual reality (VR). Although Gibson's term "cyberspace" encompasses both, the distinction is vital: VR is simulacral, TR is distal.[9] Michael Benedikt's *Cyberspace: First*

P. Lunenfeld (Cambridge, Mass.: MIT Press, 1999). R. Winters, "Planting Seeds of Doubt," *Time Digital,* 8 March 1999.

9.   K. Goldberg, "Virtual Reality in the Age of Telepresence" *Convergence* 4, no. 1 (March 1998): 33–37.

Steps,[10] published by The MIT Press in 1991, initiated a decade of dialogue about the theoretical implications of virtual reality.[11] Three years later, the World Wide Web provided the basis for Internet telerobotics, which led to the present volume. Another book, co-edited with Roland Siegwart and due out in the Fall of 2000, will collect technical papers on twelve specific Internet telerobot projects.[12]

We will not attempt to cover the general category of unreliable textual information on the Internet, of which there is no shortage. We focus on the subcategory of information that arises from live interaction with remote physical environments. Accordingly, we will not explicitly address "softbots": information-gathering systems that remain wholly within the confines of software.

Nor is this book intended as a treatise on social constructivism, the passionate debate about the fundamental existence of scientific entities such as fields, quarks, and photons. Our focus is less on ontological or metaphysical issues of existence than on the practical epistemic grounds for knowledge. The two are of course related: A scientific realist who firmly believes in the existence of quarks can still be interested in how we know their properties. And the social constructivist, convinced of the constructed nature of the

10.   M. Benedikt, *Cyberspace: First Steps* (Cambridge, Mass.: MIT Press, 1991).

11.   P. Levy, *Becoming Virtual: Reality in the Digital Age,* Plenum Press, 1998; M. Heim, *Virtual Realism* (Oxford: Oxford University Press, Oxford, 1997); M. Poster, "Theorizing Virtual Reality: Baudrillard and Derrida," in *Cyberspace Textuality,* ed M. L. Ryan (Bloomington: Indiana University Press, 1999); J. Steuer, "Defining Virtual Reality: Dimensions Determining Telepresence," in *Communication in the Age of Virtual Reality,* ed. F. Biocca and M. R. Levey (Hillsdale, N.J.: Lawrence Erlbaum), pp. 33–56. See also A. Feenberg and A. Hannay, eds., *Technology and the Politics of Knowledge* (Bloomington: Indiana University Press, 1995). For edited collections of critical theory on new media, See L. Hershman, ed., *Clicking In* (Bay Press, 1996); A. Kroker and M. Kroker, eds., *Digital Delirium* (St. Martin's Press, 1997); C. Sommerer and L. Mignonneau, eds., *Art @ Science* (Springer Verlag, 1998); and the very recent P. Lunenfeld, ed., *The Digital Dialectic* (Cambridge, Mass.: MIT Press, 1999).

12.   Examples include: G. Bekey, Y. Akatsuka, and S. Goldberg, 1998, "Digimuse: An Interactive Telerobotic System for Viewing of three-dimensional art objects," *IROS* 1998; P. Saucy and F. Mondada, "Khep-on-the-web: One year of access to a mobile robot on the Internet," *IROS* 1998; R. Simmons, "Xavier: An Autonomous Mobile Robot on the Web"; Taylor and Dalton, "A Framework for Internet Robotics," IROS 1998; Siegwart, Wannaz, Garcia, and Blank, "Guiding Mobile Robots Through the Web," all included in *Workshop on Web Robots, IEEE/RSJ International Conference on Robots and Systems* (IROS), organized by Roland Siegwart, 1998.

Figure 1.2. NASA's Sojourner telerobot on Mars (1997)
(http://mpfwww.jpl.nasa.gov/rovercom/pix.html)

quark model, can nonetheless be interested in what we can know about this model. No one would deny the existence of constructed models on the Internet that are patently false, but this should not be construed as an argument for constructivism.

The twenty chapters in this book are organized into three sections: (1) Philosophy, (2) Art, History, and Critical Theory, and (3) Engineering, Interface, and System Design. The remainder of this Introduction provides definitions and an overview of the issues raised.

What Is a Telerobot?

A robot can be broadly defined as a mechanism controlled by a computer. A telerobot is a robot that accepts instructions from a distance, generally from a trained human operator. The human operator thus performs live actions in a distant environment and through sensors can gauge the consequences. Telerobotic systems date back to the need for handling radioactive materials in the 1940s, and are now being applied to exploration, bomb disposal, and surgery. In the summer of 1997, the film *Titanic* included scenes with undersea telerobots, and NASA's Mars Sojourner telerobot successfully completed a mission on Mars. T. Sheridan's *Telerobotics, Automation, and Human*

Figure 1.3. Black-and-white digital image of a coffee pot in the Trojan Room student lounge at Cambridge University, 1993. http://www.cl.cam.ac.uk/coffee/coffee.html (Q. Stafford-Frazier and P. Jardetzky)

Supervisory Control provides an excellent review of research issues in telerobotics.[13]

The Internet makes telerobotics accessible to a rapidly growing audience. Text-based Internet interfaces to soda machines were demonstrated as early as 1980. The first Internet camera was set up by researchers at Cambridge University to monitor the status of a coffeepot. In August 1994, my collaborators and I set up the first Internet telerobot.[14] A digital camera and air jet were mounted on a robot arm so that anyone on the Internet could view and excavate for artifacts in a sandbox located in our laboratory at the University of Southern California.

In September 1994, Ken Taylor at the University of Western Australia demonstrated a remotely controlled six-axis telerobot on the Internet.[15] In

13. T. Sheridan, *Telerobotics, Automation, and Human Supervisory Control* (Cambridge, Mass.: MIT Press, 1992). See also T. Sheridan, "Musings on Telepresence and Virtual Presence" *Presence* 1 (1992): 1.

14. K. Goldberg, M. Mascha, S. Gentner, J. Rossman, N. Rothenberg, C. Sutter, and J. Wiegley, "Beyond the Web: Manipulating the Real World," *Computer Networks and ISDN Systems Journal* 28, no. 1 (December 1995).

15. B. Dalton and K. Taylor, "A Framework for Internet Robotics" *IROS* 1998. (See note 12.)

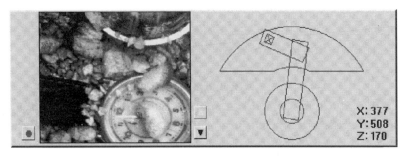

Figure 1.4. User interface for the *Mercury Project* at the University of Southern California, August 1994. The first robot on the Internet, it allowed visitors to excavate for buried objects in a sandbox.

October 1994, Eduardo Kac and Ed Bennett exhibited a telerobotic artwork combining telephone and Internet control. Later that Fall, Richard Wallace demonstrated a telerobotic camera and Mark Cox put up a system that allows Internet users to remotely schedule photos from a robotic telescope. The early Internet telerobots designed by John Canny and Eric Paulos are described in chapter 15. Two internationally sponsored technical workshops on Internet telerobotics were recently organized. Examples of Internet telerobotic projects are available online at http://mitpress.mit.edu/telepistemology.

Chapter 2 focuses on Internet webcameras. Thomas J. Campanella of MIT's Urban Studies and Planning Program describes these as "points of contact between the virtual and the real-spatial anchors in a placeless sea." Campanella characterizes the distributed ability to set up such cameras as a "grassroots phenomenon" realized by thousands of volunteers. The grassroots metaphor also applies to the subject of many of these cameras: the local landscape. Citing Leo Marx's influential literary analysis,[16] Campanella characterizes the relationship between the machine and the garden as one of the central dialectics in American history. Our ambiguity toward the juxtaposition of robot and garden is compounded by telepistemic concerns that our "live" images may not in fact be live. Campanella suggests that careful correlation of image illumination with time of day, accounting for

16. L. Marx, *The Machine in the Garden: Technology and the Pastoral Ideal in America* (Oxford: Oxford University Press, 1964).

differences in time zones, can provide evidence of liveness. "The most reliable means of checking the veracity of our telepresent landscape may well be the sun itself—the most ancient of our chronographic aids."

Philosophy

In this section, five authorities consider telerobotics and telepistemology from the perspective of philosophy. Although the role of mediation in technology has been a fixture of philosophy since the seventeenth century,[17] the Internet forces a reconsideration. As the public gains access to telerobotic instruments previously restricted to scientists, questions of mediation, knowledge, and trust take on new significance for everyday life. Telepistemology, once a theoretical curiosity, becomes a practical problem. As Michael Idinopulos writes in chapter 17, "Skepticism is often treated as a . . . 'philosophical' issue with no real consequences for everyday life. . . . This view is deeply and importantly mistaken."

We can divide telepistemological issues into technical and moral categories. Technical telepistemology is concerned with skeptical questions: Do telerobotics and the Internet really provide us with knowledge? To what extent is telerobotic experience equivalent to proximal experience? Moral telepistemology asks: How should we act in telerobotically mediated environments? What is the impact of technological mediation on human values? Both of these categories are addressed in this section.

Agency is the ability to perform actions, to intervene as we observe. Ian Hacking[18] provides a superb account of the optical distortions and limitations of early microscopes, noting that perception achieved with a microscope is fundamentally different than perception with the "naked eye." Hacking cites George Berkeley's *New Theory of Vision* (1710), according to which our sense of vision is acquired not just by passive looking but by intervening in the world. When looking through a microscope, our ability to actively manipulate a cell as we watch gives us confidence in what we are seeing. Agency plays an analogous role for telepistemology in telerobotics.

In chapter 3, Hubert Dreyfus, an authority on Heidegger, Merleau-Ponty, and the limits of artificial intelligence, notes that Cartesian episte-

---

17. R. Descartes (1641), in *Meditations on First Philosophy,* ed, J. Cottingham (New York: Cambridge University Press, 1996).

18. I. Hacking, *Representing and Intervening* (Cambridge: Cambridge University Press, 1983).

mology arose in response to seventeenth-century developments in optics and biology. Instruments such as the telescope and the microscope challenged our claims to scientific knowledge and launched a new spirit of doubt and skepticism. Descartes applied this skepticism to human sense organs, treating them as transducers of mediated knowledge whose accuracy was always in question. Dreyfus reviews how philosophers have worked during three hundred years to refute Descartes's mediated conception of the senses— most recently with a phenomenological appeal to embodied perception. As in the seventeenth century, we are now experiencing a rapid increase in the extent to which our knowledge is technologically mediated. Dreyfus suggests that advances in Internet telerobotics may reinvigorate the notion that our knowledge of the world is fundamentally indirect, provoking further advances and refutations.

Catherine Wilson, author of *The Invisible World* (1995)[19] a historical and philosophical analysis of the microscope, traces our mistrust of instrument-mediated knowledge even further, to the Greek idea that all representations are ignoble. In chapter 4, Wilson points out that as eighteenth-century philosophers developed theories of landscape in response to the locomotive, twentieth-century phenomenologists developed theories of immediate experience in response to the telephone and radio. These theories privilege everyday objects over the "opaque" and "inscrutable" workings of industrial machines such as hydroelectric plants. Wilson acknowledges that "there are ever fewer gardens . . . and there are ever more robots," but points out that contemporary technologies such as Internet telerobotics function "not to replace the natural world, but to display it . . . like windows and telescopes." Tele-technologies can enhance our respect for and understanding of distant cultures. But Wilson cautions that our primitive association of distance with fiction can also become an excuse for violence.

In chapter 5, Albert Borgmann also addresses moral telepistemology, although he disagrees with Wilson on several points. Borgmann, author of *Information and Reality at the Turn of the Millenium,*[20] begins by characterizing technical differences between proximal space and mediated space. Borgmann uses the terms "continuity" and "repleteness" to describe the hori-

19. C. Wilson, *The Invisible World* (Princeton, N.J.: Princeton University Press, 1995).

20. A. Borgmann, *Information and Reality at the Turn of the Millennium* (Chicago: University of Chicago Press, Chicago, 1999).

zontal and vertical dimensions of richness that are lacking in telerobotic experience. Applying a notion of continuity different than Wilson's, Borgmann claims there is a sharp contrast between the suppleness of natural experience and the brittleness of computer mediated experience.

Why then do we increasingly seek out the latter? Borgmann notes that in the age of hunting and gathering, sugars and fats were desirable but rare and scattered, requiring great effort for their collection. When technology made sugars and fats easily and abundantly available, "we retained our desires but lost the tempering circumstances." Borgmann argues that the Internet has played an analogous role with information: Our curiosity remains but we are losing the attentiveness and stamina needed to identify and extract knowledge.

Jeff Malpas, author of *Place and Experience,*[21] argues in chapter 6 that "mediated knowledge" is a contradiction: Knowledge is inextricably bound up with physical location. He attacks the "Cartesian-Lockean" view of experience, according to which all our knowledge of the world is mediated. It is this view, he argues, which leads to the mistaken idea that technological mediation is a natural extension of ordinary experience.

Alvin Goldman's chapter can be read as a response to the skepticism of Dreyfus and Malpas towards telerobotically mediated knowledge. One of the foremost figures in contemporary epistemology,[22] Goldman has developed a theory that knowledge can be defined in terms of reliable causation. In chapter 7 he argues that this reliabilist account can be extended to cover telerobotically acquired knowledge. Developing a famous example from D. M. Armstrong, Goldman suggests that using a telerobotic device is like using a thermometer: It gives us knowledge if it reliably causes us to adopt true beliefs. Thus, a webcam or telerobot provides knowledge if it produces true beliefs and would not, in any relevant alternative situation, produce false ones. But as Goldman points out, telerobotic scenarios may alter the standard analysis of relevant alternatives in terms of "near neighborhoods." Telerobotic scenarios also make a particularly strong case for contextualism—the view that the criteria for knowledge depend on the consequences of error: what is at stake in knowing.

21.   J. Malpas, *Place and Experience* (Cambridge: Cambridge University Press, 1999).

22.   A. Goldman, *Epistemology and Cognition* (Cambridge, Mass.: Harvard University Press, 1986); and A. Goldman, *Knowledge in a Social World* (Oxford: Clarendon Press, 1999).

Epistemologists consider our knowledge of propositions, the sorts of things that can be asserted, believed, doubted, and denied, for example, "Jupiter has 16 moons." Consider a proposition P. According to Plato's classical definition of knowledge, I know that P if and only if 1) I believe that P, 2) this belief is justified, and 3) P is true. This tripod of conditions for knowledge is the cornerstone of classical epistemology.

Suppose, for example, that I visit the Telegarden, which claims to allow users to interact with a real garden in Austria by means of a robotic arm. The page explains that by clicking on a "Water" button users can water the garden. Let P be the proposition "I water the distant garden." Suppose that when I click the button, I believe P. Furthermore I have good reason for believing P: A series of images on my computer screen shows me the garden before and after I press the button, revealing an expected pattern of moisture in the soil. And suppose P is true. Thus, according to the definition above, all three conditions are fulfilled and we can say that I know that I watered the distant garden.

Forty years ago, epistemologists exposed a fundamental flaw in Plato's definition. Edmund Gettier constructed cases of justified true belief that should not be considered knowledge.[23] We can adapt his argument to the case of the telerobotic garden as follows. Let P' be the proposition that I do *not* water a distant garden. Suppose now that when I click the button, I believe P' and that I have good reasons: An expert engineer informed me about Internet forgeries, how the garden could be an elaborate forgery based on prestored images of a long-dead garden. Now suppose that there is in fact a working Telegarden in Austria but that the water reservoir happens to be empty on the day I click on the water button. So P' is true. But should we say that I know P'? No. But I believe P', I have good reasons, and P' is true. Although epistemologists have developed new ways to define knowledge that can exclude P', the problem of justification is challenged by cases involving forgery. A clever programmer can set up a telerobotic forgery cheaply and easily. A number of supposedly live Internet cameras have been exposed as forgeries. If forgery sheds light on the nature of authenticity, the Internet provides an ample supply of illumination.[24]

23.   E. Gettier, "Is Justified True Belief Knowledge?" *Analysis* 23 (1963): 121–123.

24.   N. Goodman, "Art and Authenticity," in *Languages of Art* (Indianapolis: Hackett Publishing, 1976).

Does it matter whether a telerobotic site is real or not? Perhaps not to the majority of casual net surfers, but to those who spend enough time to care, to patiently interact with a purported telerobotic site, discovering the site to be a forgery can be as traumatic as the discovery by a museum curator of a forgery among one of the Rembrandts in the museum's permanent collection.

Art, History, and Critical Theory

The word *media* is derived from the Latin for "middle": Mediated experience, in contrast to immediate experience, inserts something in the middle, between source and viewer. The authors in this section address the aesthetic implications of telerobotic mediation.

In chapter 8, historian and critical theorist Martin Jay considers the time delay between reality and appearance that is inherent to telescopic vision and to telerobotic devices on the Internet. Jay traces the implications of this delay back to the 1676 discovery of the finite speed of light by Danish astronomer Ole Roemer. This "astronomical hindsight" has ontological and epistemological implications ranging from Benjamin's notion of starlight as *Memento Mori* to Nietzsche's anticipation of a breakdown of the fundamental concept of the "present" as grounded in the Aristotelian/Lockean/Berkeleyan/Cartesian notion of atemporal eyesight. Analyzing Baudrillard's reference to the finite speed of light,[25] Jay argues that the supposedly "pure simulacra" of virtual reality are in fact parasitic on prior corporeal experience and that telerobotic systems have the potential to transmit attenuated indexical traces from their distant sources.

Lev Manovich, artist and new media critic, begins chapter 9 by analyzing how the index is subverted in cinema. The ability to record and edit images into spatial and temporal montage allows film to "overcome its indexical nature, presenting a viewer with scenes that never existed in reality." Cinema does not rely on the viewer's willing suspension of disbelief; computers are now used to carefully engineer undeniable illusion.[26] Some films, such as

25. J. Baudrillard, "Fatal Strategies," in *Selected Writings,* ed. Mark Poster (Stanford: Stanford University Press, 1988).

26. For an in-depth discussion of phenomenology in film, see V. Sobchack, *The Address of the Eye: A Phenomenology of Film Experience* (Princeton, N.J.: Princeton University Press, 1992).

Blow Up, Capricorn One, Blade Runner, The Truman Show, and *The Matrix,* incorporate this process into their subject matter. Although sports is an area where live broadcasts are highly valued and deception is prosecuted, the recent success of professional wrestling on television suggests that sports viewers may be developing an increased appetite for irony.

Manovich considers virtual reality as the culmination of a trend toward deception that goes back to Potemkin's eighteenth-century construction of false facades in Czarist Russia. He describes *teleaction,* the ability to act over distances in real time, as a "much more radical technology than virtual reality." Citing Bruno Latour's definition of power as "the ability to mobilize and manipulate resources across space and time," Manovich notes that telerobotic systems not only represent reality but allow us to act on it. Now that Internet telerobotic systems deliver teleaction to a broad audience, it is vital to reconsider the relationship between objects and their signs. Television allowed objects to be transformed instantly into signs; telerobotics allows us, through signs, to instantly touch the objects they represent.

> The boundaries between what is seen and what is staged are increasingly blurry. . . . The crucial issue may not be the camera but a gnawing sense that the world itself, knowable only through imprecise perceptions, is a tissue of uncertainties, ambiguities, fictions masquerading as facts and facts as tenuous as clouds.
> — V. GOLDBERG[27]

Artists were among the first to use telerobotics to explore this "gnawing sense" of uncertainty. There is a rich history of Communications Art from Moholy-Nagy to Nam Jun Paik, Roy Ascott, and Douglas Davis. Much of this "telematic" artwork was based on telephone and satellite technology; contemporary artists are now incorporating telerobotics into their work. An (incomplete) list includes: Robert Adrian, Maurice Benayoun, Erich Berger, Shawn Brixey, Susan Collins, Peter Coppin, Elizabeth Diller, Ken Feingold, Scott Fisher, Masaki Fujihata, Kit Galloway, Greg Garvey, Emily Hartzell, Lynn Hershman, Perry Hobermann, Natalie Jeremijenko, Eduardo Kac, Knowbotic Research, Richard Kriesche, Tina Laporte, Rafael Lozano-

27. V. Goldberg, review of Jeff Wall Photography, *New York Times,* 16 March 1997.

Paulos, Simon Penny, Sherry Rabinowitz, Michael Rodemer, Julia Scher, Ricardo Scofidio, Paul Sermon, Joel Slayton, Nina Sobell, Stelarc, Gerfried Stoker, Survival Research Laboratories, Rirkrit Tiravanija, Victoria Vesna, Richard Wallace, Peter Weibel, Norman White, and Steve Wilson.

> Why there is any aesthetic difference between a deceptive forgery and an original work challenges a basic premise on which the very functions of collector, museum, and art historian depend.
> — NELSON GOODMAN[28]

In two recent articles, David Hunt[29] and David Pescovitz[30] survey examples of telerobotic art, including *Refresh,* an Internet-based art installation by Diller and Scofidio[31] that juxtaposes a live webcamera with recorded videos staged by professional actors. Each image is accompanied with a fictional narrative making it difficult to distinguish which is the live webcamera.[32]

Brazilian-born artist Eduardo Kac has exhibited projects involving telerobotics since 1986. In chapter 10, Kac describes four of his art projects, including *Rara Avis,* a critique of exoticism where a telerobotic wooden bird was placed into a cage with 30 zebra finches. Visitors on the Internet access cameras inside the avatar's head to achieve the rare bird's eye view from inside the cage. In Kac's *Ornitorrinco* project, real-time video was inserted into a false Internet interface, forcing bird and human participants to navigate through a complex network of true and fictitious projections. Kac's *Telepresence Garment* placed the artist into a sealed rubber bag where his movements and voice were contained and controlled by an external human "master" transmitting instructions from a remote art gallery.

28. N. Goodman, "Art and Authenticity," in *Languages of Art* (Indianapolis: Bobbs-Merrill, zp1968).

29. D. Hunt, "Telepresence Art," *Camerawork Journal,* 1999.

30. D. Pescovitz, "Be There Now: Telepresence Art Online," *Flash Art* 32, no. 205: 51–52.

31. www.diacenter.org

32. In Paris, the Cartier Foundation for Contemporary Art hosted an exhibition involving Internet telecameras from June 29 to November 30, 1999. See www.fondation.cartier.fr.

In chapter 11, new media art curator and critic Machiko Kusahara reviews the work of five artists who use telerobotics. By allowing users to affect the real world by means of actions at a distance, these artists create a tension between "here and there." Some, such as Lynn Hershman Neeson, use this dichotomy to simultaneously represent multiple points of view, so that the user is at once both the observer and the observed. Others, such as Masaki Fujihata, use telerobotics to establish a sense of human community and cooperation despite physical separation. Others emphasize the limits of telerobotics; Ken Feingold shows how it can lead to alienation and Stelarc goes further by illustrating how telerobotics has the potential for inflicting physical pain.

Artist and critic Marina Gržinić considers the aesthetic implications of time-delay in chapter 12. Often seen as an aggravating and problematic aspect of the Internet, Gržinić defends time-delay as a potential resource for representing space and time. As Walter Benjamin suggested in the context of photography, shortening the "exposure time" can drain the essence from an image. Citing Baudrillard,[33] Gržinić notes the absence of aura in the sterile television images of recent bombings in Iraq and Serbia. In contrast, the inherent time delay between a viewer's request on the Internet and the resulting image functions in a way analogous to exposure time, giving the viewer time to consider and invigorating the image with meaning. Time-delay thus emerges as an aesthetic and telepistemological asset, leading to a deeper view of imaging technology and the world it seeks to capture.

In chapter 13, art historian Oliver Grau considers how a Gnostic desire to transcend the limitations of the physical body provides an early referent for contemporary interest in telerobotics. Grau focuses on *telepresence*— the superclass of immersive technologies that often make use of helmets, goggles, and 3-D projections.[34] Grau sees the realist illusions of renaissance

33. J. Baudrillard, *The Gulf War Did Not Take Place*, trans. Paul Patton (Sydney: Power Publications).

34. M. Minsky, "Telepresence" *Omni* 2, no. 9: 48; J. Steuer, "Defining Virtual Reality: Dimensions Determining Telepresence," in *Communication in the Age of Virtual Reality*, ed. F. Biocca and M. R. Levy (Hillsdale, N.J.: Lawrence Erlbaum, 1995), pp. 33–56. Immersive telepresence is not feasible at current Internet speeds. See also T. Campanella's discussion of telepresence in chapter 2 of this volume.

art and the panoramas of the nineteenth century as early examples of tele-presence technology. Robots and their precursors—golems, puppets, and androids—provide a different strategy for transcending the body. Grau discusses how Simon Penny's newest art project combines these themes of bodily rejection, illusion, and automata. Grau concludes by citing Ernst Cassirer and Paul Valéry on the relationship between distance and aesthetic contemplation.

Engineering, Interface, and System Design

The third section provides perspectives from engineers and designers. Blake Hannaford, professor of engineering and an authority on telerobotics, pro-vides a historical overview of telerobotics research in chapter 14. Focusing on the issues of time delay, control, and stability, Hannaford reviews the 1950s work of R. Goertz, who developed mechanical teleoperators to handle radioactive materials at Los Alamos. As mechanical linkages were replaced by electrical signals, kinematics and dynamics were incorporated into effi-cient computer control algorithms for telerobotic systems. When control is attempted over long distances, for example on the Internet, variable time delays introduce the potential for system instabilities. Hannaford describes several of the techniques proposed to compensate, such as Sheridan's *Supervisory Control,* and Conway and Volz's *Time Clutch.* The distortions inher-ent to telerobotics pose fundamental questions of telepistemology that are further compounded on the Internet, where the user may not know or trust the engineers who designed the system.

In chapter 15, computer scientists John Canny and Eric Paulos address computer-mediated communication from Cartesian and phenomenological perspectives. The current Cartesian model for teleconferencing ignores the role of the body and breaks communication into separate channels for video, text, and audio. The results are often stilted and unsatisfying. Canny and Paulos propose an alternative model based on a phenomenological integra-tion of physical cues and natural responses; they have designed a range of "tele-embodiment" devices to facilitate believable interactions over the In-ternet from helium-filled blimps equipped with cameras and wireless trans-ceivers to ground-based telerobots. As issues of trust and intimacy arise in their experiments, Canny and Paulos conjecture that future telepresence systems will be "anti-robotic." Rather than automatons blindly repeating orders, "social machines" and toys of the future will express a wide range of behaviors including emotions. Telepistemology may help us to better understand not only what can be conveyed online, but also what is essential to hugs and handshakes.

In chapter 16, Judith Donath, director of the MIT Media Lab's Sociable Media Group, addresses skepticism in our knowledge of other minds. This question has long been of interest to philosophy (the problem of other minds) and cognitive science (the Turing Test, Joseph Weizenbaum's ELIZA and now Internet "chatterbots" such as Richard Wallace's ALICE).[35] As Canny and Paulos point out, technology that mediates our interaction with other people—chat rooms, email, video conferencing, etc.—generally restricts the range of social cues that guide our behavior. Our ability to recognize online deception has important implications. Unless we know who we are communicating with, we do not know how to behave. Consistent with Wilson's point in chapter 4, Donath suggests that as telerobotics enables remote agency, it may desensitize us to those whose identity, and even humanity, remains hidden from view.

In chapter 17, Michael Idinopulos uses telepistemological considerations to draw normative conclusions about telerobotic interface design on the Internet. Drawing on Descartes, Berkeley, and contemporary philosophers Donald Davidson and Richard Rorty, he distinguishes between "causal" and "epistemic" mediation: Knowledge is always mediated causally (by the events that produce it), but it is mediated epistemically only if it is the product of inference. Skepticism—the central problem in epistemology—challenges knowledge that is epistemically mediated. If knowledge from a distance is the goal of telerobotic devices, then epistemic immediacy should be the goal of interface design. This may be achieved by interfaces that allow the user to "cope skillfully" in the remote environment—to interact instinctively and unreflectively with distant objects, rather than treating them as theoretical entities to be inferred from evidence on a video screen.[36] Like eyeglasses, telescopes, and microscopes, telerobotic devices should mediate our knowledge causally, but not epistemically. When we visit a telerobotic web site, we should not see the interface itself. We should see through the interface to the distant environment beyond.

35. R. Wallace designed ALICE, a sophisticated Internet chatterbot: http://www.alicebot.org.

36. H. Dreyfus and S. Dreyfus, *Mind Over Machine: The Power of Human Intuition and Expertise in the Era of the Computer* (New York: Free Press, 1986).

As a postscript, we reprint Merleau-Ponty's 1945 essay, *The Film and the New Psychology*.[37] Merleau-Ponty describes how both Gestalt psychology and phenomenology reject the Cartesian dichotomy between mind and body. Rather than analyzing each sensation separately, phenomenology recognizes that humans respond as "beings thrown into the world and attached to it by a natural bond." Merleau-Ponty applies this model of perception to cinema, the new medium of his time. For example, Pudovkin's cinematic sequences using the face of Mosjoukin are cases of temporal Gestalt. Merleau-Ponty's essay provides a precedent where "modes of [philosophy] correspond to technical methods" and recalls Kant's remark that in knowledge, imagination serves the understanding, whereas in art, understanding serves the imagination.

As we race forward, throwing overboard the values that used to provide ballast, we struggle to maintain our hold on the slippery thing we call knowledge. What will be the form and status of knowledge as we accelerate into a new millennium? As Walter Benjamin foresaw in 1936, we have an increasing urge to view and manipulate distant objects through their images. Tele-technologies, always useful for science, are increasingly relevant to politics and to our daily lives. It is in this context that telepistemology, the study of knowledge acquired at a distance, may help us to stay on course.

37.   M. Merleau-Ponty, "The Film and the New Psychology," (1945) in *Sense and Non-Sense*, trans. H. Dreyfus and P. Dreyfus (Evanston, Ill.: Northwestern University Press, 1964). Chapter 18 of this volume.

2

Eden by Wire: Webcameras and the Telepresent Landscape

Thomas J. Campanella

Hello, and welcome to my webcam; it points out of my window here in Cambridge, and looks toward the centre of town. . . .[1]

Wake up to find out that you are the eyes of the World.[2]

The sun never sets on the cyberspatial empire; somewhere on the globe, at any hour, an electronic retina is receiving light, converting sunbeams into a stream of ones and zeros. Since the popularization of the Internet several years ago, hundreds of "webcameras" have gone live, a globe-spanning matrix of electro-optical devices serving images to the World Wide Web. The scenes they afford range from the sublime to the ridiculous—from toilets to the Statue of Liberty. Among the most compelling are those webcameras trained on urban and rural landscapes, and which enable the remote observation of distant outdoor scenes in real or close to real time. Webcameras indeed constitute something of a grassroots global telepresence project. William J. Mitchell has described the Internet as "a worldwide, time-zone-spanning optic nerve with electronic eyeballs at its endpoints."[3] Webcameras are those eyeballs. If the Internet and World Wide Web represent the augmentation of collective memory, then webcameras are a set of wired eyes, a digital extension of the human faculty of vision.

Before the advent of webcameras, the synchronous observation of remote places (those farther than the reach of mechano-optical devices such as telescope or binoculars) was impossible for the average person—even the computer literate. To watch the sun set over Victoria Harbor in Hong Kong would have required physically being in Hong Kong, unless you happened tune in to a live television broadcast from the harbor's edge (an unlikely event, as sunsets generally do not make news). Now it is possible to log into one of several webcameras in that city and monitor the descendent sun even as the morning's e-mail is read (figure 2.1). We can, at the same time, watch the sun rise over Chicago, or stream its noonday rays over Paris, simply by opening additional browser windows and logging into the appropriate sites. As little as a decade ago, this would have been the stuff of science fiction.

Of course, remote observation through a tiny desktop portal will never approach the full sensory richness of a sunset over the South China sea; *telepresence* is an ambitious term. Webcameras may not cure seasonal affective disorder; yet, there is something magical—even surreal—about watching

1.   Caption on Sam Critchley's CamCam page, a webcamera site in Cambridge, UK (http://www.pipex.net/~samc/).

2.   Lyrics from the Grateful Dead anthem "Eyes of the World," by Robert Hunter.

3.   William J. Mitchell, *City of Bits: Space, Place, and the Infobahn* (Cambridge: MIT Press, 1995), 31.

Figure 2.1. View of harbor and the Hong Kong Convention and Exhibition Centre from webcamera at Pacific Place. Courtesy Hong Kong Tourist Association (http://www.hkta.org).

the far-off sun bring day to a city on the far side of the planet. That we can set our eyes on a sun-tossed Australian street scene, from the depths of a New England winter night, is oddly reassuring—evidence that the home star is burning bright and heading toward our window.

The Abnegation of Distance

Webcameras enable us to select from hundreds of destinations, and observe these at any hour of the day or night. The power to do so represents a quantum expansion of our personal space-time envelope; webcameras are a relatively simple technology, yet they are changing they way we think about time, space and geographic distance. As byte-sized portals into far-off worlds, webcameras demonstrate effectively how technology is dwindling the one-time vastness of the earth.

The story of technology is largely one of abnegating distance—time expressed in terms of space. For most of human history, communication in real time was limited to the natural carrying range of the human voice, or the distance sound-producing instruments (drums, horns, bells, cannon, and the like) could be heard. Visual real-time communication over wide areas could be achieved using flags, smoke signals or, as Paul Revere found effective, a lantern in a belfry. However, such means were restricted by atmospheric conditions and intervening topography. Asynchronous messages—using the earlier innovations of language, writing, and printing—could conceivably be carried around the globe by the fifteenth century; but doing so took years. Transportation and communications remained primitive well into the nineteenth century, effectively limiting the geographic "footprint" of the average person to the proximate landscape of his birth. The space-time envelope of the typical peasant, for example, was restricted to the fields and byways of her village and surrounding countryside; that of the medieval townsman by the ramparts of the city in which he lived. Travel, even between settlements, was costly and dangerous; those who took to the roads were often criminals and outcasts from society. Indeed, the etymological source of the word *travel* is the Old French *travailler* or "travail"—to toil and suffer hardship.

It was not until about 1850 that technology began to profoundly alter the spatial limits of the individual, collapsing distance and expanding the geography of daily life. The development of the locomotive and rail transport in this period had the greatest impact on notions of time and space. The railroad destroyed the tyranny of vastness and the old spatial order; it was a technology that, as Stephen Kern has put it, "ended the sanctuary of remoteness."[4] Once-distant rural towns suddenly found themselves within reach of urban markets, if they were fortunate enough to be positioned along the new "metropolitan corridor" (towns bypassed, conversely, often found themselves newly remote, a particularly tough fate for places previously well-served by canal or stage).[5] Rail transport also brought about a new temporal order: Countless local time zones made the scheduling of trains a logistical nightmare, and eventually led to the adoption of a uniform time standard in the United States.[6]

Subsequent advances in transportation technology—fast steamers, the Suez Canal and eventually the airplane—osculated the great distances separating Europe, Asia, and America. Circumnavigation of the globe itself, a

4. Stephen Kern, *The Culture of Time and Space* (Cambridge: Harvard University Press, 1983), 213.

5. See John R. Stilgoe, *Metropolitan Corridor: Railroads and the American Scene* (New Haven: Yale University Press, 1983).

6. Kern, 12–14. November 18, 1883, the day the new national standard was imposed, became known as "the day of two noons."

dream of ages, became reality not long after Jules Verne's *Around the World in Eighty Days* was published in 1873. Inspired by the novel, American journalist Nellie Bly became, in 1890, the first to circle the earth in less than the vaunted eighty days.[7] In the following two decades, this figure—and the scale of the globe itself—progressively shrank. A journey to China—once an impossibility for all but the most intrepid seafarers—had become, by 1936, a two-day flight by Pan American "China Clipper." With the arrival of commercial jet aviation in the 1960s, traversing the earth was reduced to a day's travel and a middle-class budget.

The abnegation of distance by electricity was somewhat less romantic, but no less profound. Innovations such as the telegraph, "wireless" and radio neutralized distance by making communication possible irrespective of space and intervening geography. Immediate, synchronous, real-time communication could take place via "singing wires" or even thin air. The first electric telegraph line linked Baltimore and Washington in 1844, and two decades later the first transatlantic cable went into operation—the alpha segment of today's global telecommunications network. Marconi discovered that telegraphic signals could be transmitted via electromagnetic waves, and in 1902 succeeded in sending the first transatlantic wireless message. The telephone, which spanned the United States by 1915, brought the power of distant synchronous communication into the kitchen. It made the electronic abnegation of space routine, and prompted predictions of home-based work and "action at a distance" as early as 1914.[8]

The more recent development of the networked digital computer has further neutralized distance and geography. The globe-spanning Internet, described as a "fundamentally and profoundly antispatial" technology, has in effect cast a great data net over the bumps, puddles, and irregularities of the physical world. The "cyberspace" of the Net operates more or less independently of physical place, terrain, geography and the built land-scape.[9] This was partly by design: The origins of the Internet may be traced to ARPANET, a Cold War initiative of the United States Department of Defense intended to create a multinodal knowledge-sharing infrastructure

7. Kern, 213.

8. "Action at a Distance," *Scientific American* 77 (1914): 39.

9. Mitchell, *City of Bits,* 8.

that could withstand nuclear attack; if any one part of the system was destroyed by an ICBM—for example New York or Washington—data would simply re-route itself around the blockage.

If the Net and the "mirror world" of cyberspace is spatially abstract, webcameras can be interpreted as mediating devices—points of contact between the virtual and the real, or spatial "anchors" in a placeless sea.[10] Webcameras open digital windows onto real scenes within the far-flung geography of the Internet. The networked computer enables the exchange of text-based information with distal persons or machines; webcameras add to that a degree of real-time *visual* knowledge. As Garnet Hertz put it, webcameras constitute an attempt "to re-introduce a physical sense of actual sight into the disembodied digital self."[11] In a rudimentary way, they make us *telepresent,* in places far removed from our bodies.

Varieties of Telepresence

The term *telepresence,* like its cousin *virtual reality,* has been applied to a wide range of phenomena, and often inaccurately. It was coined in 1980 by Marvin Minsky, who applied it to teleoperation systems used in remote object-manipulation applications. As Jonathan Steuer has defined it, telepresence is "the experience of presence in an environment by means of a communication medium." Put another way, it is the mediated perception of "a temporally or spatially distant real environment" via telecommunications. Telepresence is reciprocal, involving both the observer and the observed. In other words, the observer is telepresent in the remote environment, and the observed environment is telepresent in the physical space in which the observer is viewing the scene.[12]

The genealogy of visual synchronicity begins with the development of simple optical devices to augment sight, such as the telescope, binocular, microscope, the *camera lucida,* and the *camera obscura (asynchronous* co-presence, on the other hand, can be traced back to scenic depictions by primitive cave painters, though its modern roots lie with the discovery of

10.   The term is from David Gelernter's *Mirror Worlds* (New York: Oxford University Press, 1991).

11.   Garnet Hertz, "Telepresence and Digital/Physical Body: Gaining a Perspective" (http://www.conceptlab.com/interface/theories/reality/index.html).

12.   Jonathan Steuer, "Defining Virtual Reality: Dimensions Determining Telepresence," *Journal of Communications* 42 (Autumn 1992): 75–78.

photography and the later development of the stereoscope. This latter technology provided an illusion of a third dimension, dramatically increasing the sense of immersion into the photographic scene; by the turn of the century, stereoscopic cards were immensely popular, and depicted such exotic landscapes as the Pyramids of Giza).[13]

Synchronous visual co-presence *by means of electricity* was a dream long before it became reality. One fanciful depiction, published in an 1879 edition of *Punch,* imagined an "Edison Telephonoscope" enabling family members in Ceylon to be telepresent in a Wilton Place villa.[14] The first experiments in transmitting still images via telegraph took place in the 1840s, with Alexander Bain's proposal for a transmission system based on the electrochemical effects of light. Twenty years later, Abbe Caselli devised a similar system that used rotating cylinders wrapped with tin foil to transmit and receive photographs and handwritten notes.[15] As early as the 1880s, photographs had been transmitted via radio signal in England; by 1935, Wirephotos enabled the rapid transmission of photographs around the globe.[16]

The electrical transmission of *live* images was first explored by the German physicist Paul Nipkow in the 1880s. Nipkow understood that the electrical conductivity of selenium—itself discovered in 1817—changed with exposure to light, and that all images were essentially composed of patterns of light and dark. Based on this principle, he devised an apparatus to scan (using a rotating, perforated "Nipkow disk") a moving image into its component patterns of light and dark, and convert this into electrical signals using selenium cells. The signals would then illuminate a distal set of lamps, projecting the scanned image on a screen. Nipkow's ideas, which remained theoretical, provided the basis for the early development of television, which by the 1920s was transmitting live images overseas.

Until the advent of the Net, television remained the closest thing to telepresence most people would ever experience. Even with the development

13. Don Gifford, *The Farther Shore: A Natural History of Perception* (New York: Atlantic Monthly Press, 1990), 31.

14. See Mitchell, *City of Bits,* 32, 46.

15. Brad Fortner, "Communication Using Media," see printout.

16. Gifford, *The Farther Shore,* 26.

of videoconferencing technology in the last decade, access to the hardware and software required to experience even basic telepresence was limited to a privileged few. Proprietary videoconferencing systems were costly and required specialized installation and service. The arrival of the World Wide Web, by providing inexpensive and ready access to a global computer network, made telepresence a reality for anyone with a modem, a PC, and a video camera. The World Wide Web, enabling webcameras as well as simple desktop videoconferencing applications such as CUSeeMe, brought telepresence to the grassroots.

Admittedly, webcamera technology as it exists today affords only the most basic variety of telepresence. The simple observation of distal scenes, even in real time, hardly satisfies most definitions of telepresence. David Zeltzer has argued that a sense of "being in and of the world"—real or virtual—requires no less than a "'bath' of sensation," and this can be achieved only when we are receiving a high-bandwidth, multisensory stream of information about the remote world—something hardly provided by most webcamera sites.[17] According to Held and Durlach, "high telepresence" requires a transparent display system (one with few distractions), high resolution image and wide field of view, a multiplicity of feedback channels (visual as well as aural and tactile information, and even environmental data such as moisture level and air temperature), and a consistency of information between these. Moreover, the system should afford the user dexterity in manipulating or moving about the remote environment, with high correlation between the user's movements and the actions of the remote "slave robot."[18] Sheridan similarly proposed three "measurable physical attributes" to determine telepresence: extent of sensory information received from the remote environment; control of relation of sensors to that environment (the ability of the observer to modify his viewpoint); and the ability to modify the telepresent physical environment.[19]

With sluggish images appearing in a tiny box on a desktop, webcameras hardly constitute full sensory immersion in a distal world, let alone mobility and engagement in that world. While it is true that some of the more so-

17.   David Zeltzer, "Autonomy, Interaction, and Presence," *Presence* 1: 128.

18.   Richard M. Held and Nathaniel I. Durlach, "Telepresence," *Presence* 1: 109–111.

19.   Thomas B. Sheridan, "Musings on Telepresence and Virtual Presence," *Presence* 1: 120–122.

phisticated webcameras sites offer a modicum of telerobotic interactivity, these tend to be clumsy and difficult to use—particularly when a number of users are fighting for the controls.[20] Webcameras afford what might be described as "low telepresence" or "popular telepresence." But their limitations are at least partially compensated by the vast extent of the webcam network, which itself can be seen as enabling remote-world mobility simply by providing such a wide range of geographic destinations (figure 2.2).

Coffee Pot to Deep Space

The accessibility of the Net and the simplicity of webcamera technology produced, in less than a decade, a network of independent cameras spanning the globe. As networking technology evolved, it was discovered that a sensory device affixed to a server could distribute real-time visual information to a large number of people. In 1991 a pair of Cambridge University computer scientists, Quentin Stafford-Fraser and Paul Jardetzky, attached a recycled video camera to an old computer and video frame-grabber, and aimed it at a coffee pot outside a computer lab known as the Trojan Room. They wrote a simple client-server program to capture images from the camera every few minutes and distribute them on a local network, thus enabling people in remote parts of the building to check if there was coffee available before making the long trek downstairs.[21] Later served over the Internet (and still in operation) the Trojan Room Coffee Cam became the Internet's first webcamera.

Inspired by Coffee Cam, Steve Mann—at the time a graduate student at the MIT Media Lab—devised a wireless head-mounted webcamera unit in the early 1990s that fed a chain of images via radio to a fixed base station and server. His "experiment in connectivity" enabled anyone logged into his website to simultaneously share his field of vision, or trace his movements in

20.   For a collection of examples see http://mitpress.mit.edu/telepistemology. Some of the better known telerobotic webcamera sites include the Keio Mt. Fuji Server (http://www.flab.mag.keio. ac.jp/fuji/); the Virtual Artists' Rundle Street VA RoboCam in Adelaide, Australia (http://robocam. va.com.au/); the SchoolNet Robotics Webcam at Carleton University (http://webcam.engsoc. carleton.ca/); the EyeBot Project (http://www.dma.nl/eyebot/); the Interactive Model Railroad (http://rr-vs.informatik.uni-ulm.de/rr/); and the Light on the Net Project (http://light.softopia. pref.gifu.jp/), which enables the user to turn on or off a panel of lights in real time.

21.   Quentin Stafford-Fraser, "The Trojan Room Coffee Pot: A (non-technical) Biography." (http:// www.cl.cam.ac.uk/coffee/qsf/coffee.html).

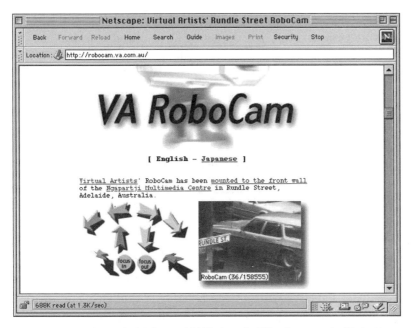

Figure 2.2. Virtual Artists' VA Robocam, Adelaide, Australia. This webcamera, one of the best in operation, offers streaming video and smooth telerobotics. Users interact with a motorized camera mounted on a building in Rundle Street. Courtesy Virtual Artists and the Ngapartji Multimedia Centre (http://www.robocam.va.com.au/).

space through the day by examining continuously archived images. Mann's unit evolved from early experiments by Ivan Sutherland, in which half-silvered mirrors in a head-mounted display enabled the wearer to see a virtual environment imposed upon actual scenes. The WearCam enabled Mann to in effect *become* a webcamera, blurring the line between reality and virtuality, presence and telepresence.[22]

Webcamera technology is simple enough to allow even individuals with minimal computer experience to set one up, and many have done so, displaying prosaic views of driveways, backyards, and streets. A simple "golf-ball" camera such as the ubiquitous Connectix Quickcam can be used to supply images to a frame-grabber at a predetermined interval or as requested by a client. Assigned a unique IP (Internet protocol) address, the captured

22. Steve Mann, "Wearable Computing: A First Step Toward Personal Imaging," *Computer* 30:2 (February 1997).

frame is then served over the World Wide Web and made available to one or more websites. Most webcameras capture and send a single frame at a time, while more sophisticated sites "push" a continuous stream of images to the client, thus providing a moving picture. Most live-streaming web-camera feeds are sluggish and temperamental, but they offer a compelling near-live glimpse into a remote place.

By 1995, dozens of webcameras were feeding pixels to armchair voyeurs around the world. Following the geography of the Net itself, the early web-cameras were located mainly in the United States, Europe, and Japan. More recently, such devices have appeared in places farther off the digital main-line—including Pakistan, Russia, Poland, Mexico, Chile, Brazil, Croatia, Colombia, South Africa, and the Czech Republic. The geography of web-cameras now extends to space itself. A number of telerobotic webcamera-equipped telescopes are in operation in the United States and Europe. These include relatively simple units such as one developed by the Remote Access Astronomy Project (RAAB) at the University of California, Santa Barbara (allowing high school students to remotely observe the heavens for science projects), to more sophisticated devices such as the Bradford Robotic Tele-scope in the United Kingdom, and the powerful 3.5-meter Apache Point telescope in New Mexico—operated via the Internet by researchers at the University of Chicago and elsewhere. An interface program called Remark affords seamless control of the Apache Point instrument, replicating a sense of "being at the telescope" (and creating in effect two "piggybacked" sets of telepresent space—that of the telescope itself and that of the celestial world glimpsed by its lens and the attached camera).[23]

Near-real-time satellite images of the earth are available over the Net, generated by the geostationary GOES-8 and GOES-10 satellites operated by the National Oceanic and Atmospheric Administration.[24] Plans for an even more sophisticated earth-observing satellite were unveiled by vice president Al Gore in the spring of 1998. The satellite, to bear the name "Triana" in honor of Columbus's navigator, would provide "the ultimate macro world view," feeding high-resolution images to three earth stations,

23. See UC Santa Barbara Remote Access Astonomy Project website (http://www.deepspace.uc-sb.edu/rot.htm); Bruce Gillespie, Robert Loewenstein and Don York, "Remote Observing at Apache Point," 1995 (http://www.apo.nmsu.edu/NMOpaper/paper.html).

24. See Geostationary Satellite Browser Server (http://www.goes.noaa.gov).

where they would be compiled into a full-disk portrait of the home planet and made continuously available to viewers on the Net. Pointing out that the last full-round images of the earth came two decades ago during the Apollo mission, Gore urged support and Congressional approval for the orbiting webcamera, noting that the $50 million project would both afford "a clearer view of our own world" and encourage "new levels of understanding" of the planet and its "natural and cultural systems."[25]

One of the most spectacular moments in webcamera-enabled telepresence took place in July of 1997, during the Mars Pathfinder mission. A remarkable stream of images, transmitted from the spacecraft itself and continually updated to the Mars Pathfinder website, stunned the Net world. Though not real-time in the strictest sense, the images of the Red Planet and its rock-strewn surface were fresh and clear enough to afford a convincing spatial sense of another world. More than 45 million viewers logged into the Jet Propulsion Laboratory sites during the first week of the operation—an Internet record—and over 80 million hits a day were recorded in the first week of the operations. One writer described the Pathfinder landing as a "defining moment for the Net," and compared it to similarly definitive moments in the evolution of other media—the outbreak of the Civil War and newspaper; Pearl Harbor and radio; the Kennedy assassination and television. Had these images not been so readily available on the Internet, it is likely that the Pathfinder landing would have remained an abstraction; television coverage of the event was typically brief and superficial.[26]

The Electronic Camera Obscura

Webcameras have captured our attention in much the same way that the *camera obscura* did the Victorians'. Both webcameras and the camera obscura enable mediated real-time observation of the nonproximate landscape, and allow more than one person to observe the same scene simultaneously.

25. Douglas E. Heimburger, "Talking at Innovation Summit, Gore Calls for an Earth-Viewing Satellite," *The Tech* (17 March 1998). Gore's proposal was summarily dismissed by some as an exercise in "planetary navel-gazing" and a waste of taxpayer money. See Gabriel Schoenfeld, "Machines With a High Calling," *Wall Street Journal,* 6 July 1998, and Joe Sharkey, "Step Right Up and See Grass Grow and Paint Dry," *New York Times,* 22 March 1998.

26. See NASA press release 24 June 1997; Amy Harmon, "Mars Pathfinder Landing Was Defining Moment for Net," *New York Times,* 14 July 1997.

Though its optical principles were described as early as the fifth century B.C.E. by the Chinese, the camera obscura is attributed to seventeenth-century German astronomer Johann Kepler, who designed a large portable instrument for use in a tent.[27] Cameras obscura were later used as a perspectival aids by draftsmen and painters, including Canaletto and Vermeer.[28] By mounting a lens in front of the aperture, it was discovered that a brighter image resulted, making possible screen projection and, thereby, viewing by a group of people. In 1770 Guyot described a camera obscura that projected an image upward onto the underside of a transparent tabletop. Foreshadowing the desktop monitor, the device enabled viewing by those gathered around a table, and could simultaneously accommodate cups of tea or a book.[29] Camera obscura technology scaled easily, and eventually room-size stations were built, often on hilltops or in towers. One of the first room cameras obscura was installed at the Royal Observatory at Greenwich around 1800, where optics mounted in a turret enabled viewers to obtain sequential views of the horizon (figure 2.3).[30] Using mirrors and a lens, the camera image was projected on a concave plaster of Paris table. A camera obscura at Llandudno, Wales, featured ropes that enabled the viewers to remotely control viewing direction and focal length.[31]

Like webcameras today, cameras obscura were commonly situated on elevated prospects, enabling sweeping views of surrounding cityscape. One of the most famous of these was the Outlook Tower in Edinburgh, equipped with its imaging device in 1892, the year the building was acquired by the redoubtable town planner Sir Patrick Geddes.[32] Webcameras are similarly often mounted high above cities, using skyscrapers or transmission towers operated by local television stations to gain a broad view of the city and

27. John H. Hammond, *The Camera Obscura: A Chronicle* (Bristol: Adam Hilger, 1981), 1–2; 24–25.

28. Robert Leggat, "Camera Obscura," [http://www.kbnet.co.uk/rleggat/photo/history/cameraob.htm].

29. Hammond, *Camera Obscura,* 87.

30. Ibid., 85

31. Ibid., 113–114.

32. Ibid., 111.

THE CAMERA OBSCURA.

Figure 2.3. "The Camera Obscura," from Magazine of Science 6 April 1839. Reproduced from John H. Hammond, *The Camera Obscura: A Chronicle* (Bristol: Adam Hilger, 1981), 128.

surrounding landscape. In the Victorian era, the camera obscura became an immensely popular attraction, and was often featured at British seaside resorts (Brighton, Mumbles Pier, Margate Jetty, and the Crystal Palace at Sydenham each had popular cameras obscura by the turn of the century.[33]) This carnivalesque application is analogous to the popularity of webcameras at Disney World, Fisherman's Wharf in San Francisco, and Seaworld. Santa Monica, California, has today both a nineteenth-century camera obscura and several webcameras affording views of the sand and sea.

Desktop Sublime

Digital technology, including webcameras, is being applied to the task of returning us to the mythic garden, albeit in a disembodied state. In this country, the relationship between nature, culture, and technology has long been a site of conflict and contradiction. From the earliest days of the Republic, Americans have rhapsodized the virtues of agrarianism, pastoral nature and the Arcadian "middle landscape" between wilderness and the

33. Ibid., 116–117, 136–139.

city.[34] Distrustful of the urban even as it urbanized, America looked to the natural world as both a source of national identity and moral salvation. This was, after all, "nature's nation."[35]

The opposition of the machine and the garden, technology and nature, became one of the central dialectics in American history. The machine, representing civilization and the city, appeared to fundamentally threaten the sanctity of the natural world (in which, found the Transcendentalists, lay enlightenment). But the tension between machine and garden also yielded a great paradox: Technology was condemned on the one hand as spoiler of the garden, yet embraced on the other as the very means of getting "back to nature." Even Thoreau was conflicted on the subject: He lived deliberately at Walden Pond "to hear what was in the wind," but the wind often carried the whistle of a locomotive on the nearby Fitchburg line. For Thoreau, the train was a herald of the rushed, restless life of the city; with its passage "So is your pastoral life whirled past and away." But Thoreau was drawn to the machine: "I watch the passage of the morning cars," he wrote, "with the same feeling that I do the rising of the sun"; "I am refreshed and expanded when the freight train rattles past me."[36]

Even as technology abrogated the garden, Americans employed it to return to nature. The interurban trolleys delighted city dwellers with Sunday jaunts to open fields at the end of the line; railroad companies pushed track high into newly minted national parks like Yellowstone, Glacier, and Yosemite. The automobile yielded an "autocamper" craze: Motorists took to the muddy roads of America in their Model T Fords, seeking Arcadia and an unspoiled view. By the 1930s in Westchester Country, New York, an entire park system had been built—featuring such landmark roads as the Bronx and Hutchinson River parkways—to accommodate auto-borne daytrippers in their quest for nature.

In a similar vein, the networked digital computer has also been made to yield new glimpses of the mythic garden. We have used the affordances of

34. See Leo Marx, *The Machine in the Garden: Technology and the Pastoral Ideal in America* (New York: Oxford University Press, 1964).

35. See Perry Miller, "Nature and the National Ego," *Errand into the Wilderness* (Cambridge: Belknap Press of Harvard University Press, 1956).

36. Henry David Thoreau, *Walden and Other Writings,* ed. William Howarth (New York: Modern Library, 1981), 16, 104–111.

virtual reality and globe-spanning networks to both create simulacra of nature in cybernetic space, as well as to bring remote real environments into closer view. One of the most compelling examples of a virtually real organic environment is Char Davies "Osmose" project, an installation meant to abrogate the "Cartesian split between mind and body" that, according to the artist, has dominated conceptions of virtual reality and cyberspace. Described as "an inspired silicon dream about nature, life, and the body," Osmose plunges the user (the "immersant") in an alter-space meant not so much to mimic nature as to evoke its layered, sensory richness. As Davies has put it, Osmose is intended to "distill or amplify certain interpretive aspects" of the natural world. The immersant, outfitted with a headmounted VR display driven by a Silicon Graphics Onyx engine, wanders through a sequence of "phosphorescent" spaces—the Grid, the Clearing, the Forest, the Leaf, the Pond—a garden of light framed by "stands of softly glowing, semitransparent trees."[37]

While Osmose uses virtual reality to bathe the viewer in a pseudo-organic world, the Black Rock Forest project offers "immersion" in a forest in the Hudson River highlands of New York. An array of environmental sensors provides a real-time data portrait of the living woodland and its ecosystems; information about air quality, stream flows and water temperature, precipitation, and soil acidity is relayed via the Internet to remote users around the world. The effort was meant to situate abstract environmental issues within the context of metropolitan New York, and underscore the connections between an apparently remote forest and the city 40 miles to its south. By tapping into the project website, urban students could learn about Black Rock Forest and request detailed information about the status of its constituent ecosystems in real time.[38]

Webcameras offer a modest degree of telepresence in numerous nonurban, even wilderness spaces around the world. While the subject of most outdoor webcameras is the urban built environment, many take in remote, natural landscapes; these offer the desk-bound Dilbert a glimpse of scenes ranging from suburban backyards to Everest itself. Some of the most compelling webcameras in operation are those that have been installed atop high

37.   Margaret Wertheim, "Osmose," *Metropolis* (September 1996): 58.

38.   See Herbert Muschamp, "In Cyberspace, Seeing the Forest for the Trees," *New York Times*, 25 February 1996.

Figure 2.4. View of Mt. Everest from the Everest Live webcamera, Autumn 1998. Copyright 1998 Everest Live Executive Committee (http://www.m.chiba-u.ac.jp/class/respir/eve_e.htm).

mountain summits, such as on the summits of Mt. Washington in New Hampshire and Oregon's Mt. Hood. Others are trained on famous mountains, including Pikes Peak, Italy's Mt. Vesuvius, Yosemite's Half Dome, and Popocatépetl in Mexico; and at least four webcameras are aimed at Mt. Fuji. A Japanese organization maintains a webcamera in the Himalayas, which serves a shot of Mt. Everest, one of the most remote places on earth (figure 2.4). Captured by a video camera from a window in the Hotel Everest View at Khumbu, Nepal (elevation 3883 meters), the images are relayed by microwave telephone to a Net connection in Kathmandu, and from there to a webserver in Japan (figure 2.5).[39]

Other remote landscapes have been placed newly within reach via webcamera. The frozen expanse of Mawson Station in Antarctica is within digital reach via webcamera at an Australian research base. Real-time temperature and wind speed data is also supplied, reminding viewers of the inconceivable wildness of the scene they are observing (a webcamera at a second Australian base, Davis Station, had been knocked off its mount by a

39.   Unfortunately this camera no longer appears to be in operation (http://www.m.chiba-u.ac.jp/class/respir/eve_e.htm).

Figure 2.5. Satellite phone used to relay camera images of Mt. Everest to the webserver in Katmandu, and then on to the Internet. The unit was powered by solar panels. © 1998 Everest Live Executive Committee (http://www.m.chiba-u.ac.jp/class/respir/eve_e.htm).

blizzard, yet continued to pump images of its battered surrounds). Equally remote are African landscapes made desktop-telepresent via webcameras in the Djuma and Sabi Sabi Game Reserves, and Kruger National Park. The cameras, mounted in weather—and creature-proof housings, take in water holes frequented by wildlife. They are illuminated at night by a floodlight (which "does not bother the animals," we are assured), enabling insomniac Net surfers in New York to catch a drinking elephant (figures 2.6 and 2.7).[40] It is not uncommon to see such animals within the camera's range, if images archived from days past are to be believed.

Indeed, webcameras bring newly to the fore issues of verisimilitude and truthfulness in representation. It is common knowledge that digital images are easily manipulated; are those we receive via webcamera suspect, too? Doubt creeps in with every mouse-click, and, for me, seems to increase proportionally with distance. Have we really been afforded the power to watch African water buffaloes wallow in real time, as I am now doing while writing this in a Hong Kong office? Or were those animals pixelated a day or a month ago, and long vanished? Like the solar disk plunging into the South China sea on my desktop, this is a scene almost too incredible to be real.

40.   AfriCam website (http://africam.mweb.co.za/djuma.htm).

Figure 2.6. AfriCam image showing rhinoceros at Sabi Sabi Game Reserve, 18 February 1999.
© AfriCam (http://www.africam.com).

Figure 2.7. Elephant departing Gowrie waterhole, Djuma Game Reserve, 25 February 1999.
© AfriCam (http://www.africam.com).

The reload button is tapped expectantly, hoping it will yield evidence of life—a shift in position, a newly alighted bird, an insect on the lens. My buffalo remain improbably still. I click my way to a sun-bleached water hole at Djuma. The camera's on-screen clock tells me the view is indeed being refreshed, every few minutes; but I can detect no traces of movement. All is inscrutable and still, like a scene from a Doris Lessing novel.[41]

For better or worse, we have come to trust the images delivered to us by the evening news as authoritative (the films *Wag the Dog* and *Capricorn One* were captivating precisely because they suggested otherwise). Webcameras, a grassroots phenomenon largely ungoverned by norms or regulations, has been free to expand into a populist, globe-spanning broadcast medium—a shadow of the Net itself. But such free-form evolution has come at a cost: It is difficult, if not impossible, to separate truth from fiction, to determine with certainty which webcameras are conveying accurate visual information, and which are frauds passing off still images or a Quicktime movie as just-captured reality. This is an epistemological issue: What is the integrity of the knowledge received from a webcamera, and how are we to verify it? To an extent, those webcameras that afford telerobotic interactivity enable us to make inquiries as to the truthfulness of the view—though here, too, a savvy programmer could easily create a simulacra of telerobotic response. The most reliable means of checking the verity of our telepresent landscape may well be the sun itself—the most ancient of our chronographic aids.

The Liminal Instrument

Webcameras are liminal instruments, sensory devices that operate on the threshold of the physical and the cybernetic. They receive raw data from the real world—essentially shifting patterns of light and dark—and translate it into machine-readable code. These devices are thus positioned closer to the living world than a hard drive or a CD-ROM, which stores asynchronous, relatively "inert" data. The visual information captured through the lens of a webcamera is only briefly separated from the pulse and hue of life.

41.   To be fair, the Africam site is among the more sophisticated and well-maintained webcamera sites in operation. The developers make it clear to visitors that their cameras are not in a zoo: "There are no guarantees that you will see animals when you look through our cameras, but when you do, you will see them as they should be seen—in their natural environment, on their terms." See Afri-Cam website (http://africam.com).

At a larger scale, webcameras mediate between the "placeful" physical world and the disembodied, displaced realm of cyberspace. Because they straddle the interregnum between hard and soft space, webcameras begin to bridge the gulf between reality and virtuality. Webcameras operate simultaneously in both real and virtual space; they enable "augmented reality" as well as "embedded virtuality," and begin to yield what Mark Stefik has called "a rich interaction that interweaves the images and agencies in the real world with those of the imagination and cyberspace."[42] Put another way, webcameras "map" reality onto cyberspace, and vice versa.

A fundamental and irreconcilable incompatibility between the real and the virtual has been a recurrent theme among critics of new media technology. Cyberspace is often accused of threatening the viability of carbon-based life as we know it, and in particular, the welfare and viability of *place*—the built landscape and the place-bound life. The "fundamental antispatiality" of the Net, and increasingly convincing virtual worlds, have been interpreted as a direct challenge to the future of cities, as well as a seduction that will inevitably short-circuit the impulse to "get outside." As Mark Slouka has written, "we stand on the threshold of turning life itself into computer code, of transforming the experience of living in the physical world—every sensation, every detail—into a product for our consumption."[43]

But the growing popularity of webcams suggests that, rather than abrogating place or diminishing its importance, we are actually using the Net and digital technology to give places and the built environment new meaning in the cybernetic world. Webcameras, in this light, are agents of geography and place. By providing real-time glimpses into real city squares and streets and gardens, webcameras serve as points of exchange between the virtual and the physical. The vast collection of webcamera sites established in recent years is a popular exercise in wayfinding, an effort to stake out keepsakes of place in a placeless realm.

Few sites better demonstrate this than the UpperWestSide Cam in New York City (figure 2.8). Installed by David H. M. Spector in 1995, the web-

42. Mark Stefik, *Internet Dreams: Archetypes, Myths, and Metaphors* (Cambridge: MIT Press, 1996), 263.

43. Mark Slouka, *The War of the Worlds: Cyberspace and the High-Tech Assault on Reality* (New York: Basic Books, 1995), 7.

Figure 2.8. View of Columbus Avenue, New York, via the UpperWestSideCam. © David HM Spector (http://www.zeitgeist.com/camera).

camera was for several years among the most popular on the Net. In large part this was due to the close-range view it afforded of a busy Manhattan street corner, and to the large size of the image returned by the server (details as fine as a person's face could be distinguished). The camera was mounted in a second-floor window on the corner of 73rd Street and Columbus Avenue in New York, where it took in an archetypal street corner in one of New York's most vibrant neighborhoods. As the webcamera became known, a community of users evolved; as many as 10,000 requests were made each day for images. People held banners within its range, broadcasting messages to friends and relatives on the other side of the world. Old residents of the neighborhood used the webcamera to glimpse nostalgically back at their haunts. One couple planted themselves periodically in front of the camera to "be" with their daughter in Sweden.[44]

More, genuine interest developed in the built environment captured by the lens; inquires poured in about a particular restaurant or shop across the street, the history of the area, even about a certain kind of delivery truck that continually appeared curbside. The UpperWestSide Cam FAQ filled with detailed information about a unique urban environment:

44.   Lisa Napoli, "As Camera Captures a Street Scene, A Corner Becomes an Online World," *Cyber-Times,* 9 January 1997.

1. What is the name of the store we see in just across the street from the camera, and what do they sell?

The store across the street, at 276 Columbus Avenue is "Jerry Grant's Gallery of Exciting Jewelry." They sell all sorts of interesting jewelry, including watches, rings, necklaces, etc. Occasionally they also feature designer hand-made (and hand-painted, no less!) ties. David owns several of these and also has a very nice pocket watch (a very pretty Skagen) that was purchased there.

2. Where are we looking when we see Columbus Avenue on the UpperWest-SideCam™?

The camera is pointing south, toward midtown Manhattan (of course what is meant by "midtown Manhattan" depends very much upon where you are—David's father grew up near 169th Street in a neighbourhood known as "Washington Heights" in the 1920's. He considered "midtown" to be the Upper West Side:-). The left-hand side of the picture is East—if you were to continue in that direction on 73rd St. for 1 block (plus a few paces) you would arrive at Central Park in under 5 minutes (you would also be right next-to the Dakota—where John Lennon lived, and Yoko Ono still lives—which is a very beautiful piece of NY architecture built in the 1880's). If you were to walk to the right of Jerry Grants (west on 73rd St) in 4 blocks (about 1/4 mile or 400m) you would be at Riverside park on the Hudson River. Along the way you would pass the landmark NY Savings Bank Building, the Ansonia Hotel (now a condo), as well as Rutgers Church.

3. What is the eatery across Columbus Ave. (the one with the big letters)?

The restaurant is called The City Grill. It's an establishment specializing in American Bistro type fare. Quite nice actually. The prices are reasonable too—most entrees are under US $15.[45]

The webcam, pumping pixels into cyberspace, generated interest in a real place, a Manhattan street corner and a New York neighborhood. The camera added a whole new stratum of cultural space to the corner of 73rd Street and Columbus; now, it was not only a bustling New York intersection, but a street corner in cyberspace.

45. UpperWestSide Cam website (http://www.zeitgeist.com/camera/).

"I'll Be Watching You"

Webcameras do not always generate such enthusiasm. The specter of surveillance and the violation of privacy are real and vexing issues, and the possibility of Orwellian over-exposure has made many people anxious and fearful of webcameras. Ubiquitous surveillance was the subject of the popular 1998 film *The Truman Show,* in which the feckless hero (Jim Carey) is, since birth, the unwitting star in his own quotidian drama. Tiny cameras, ingeniously concealed in dashboard radios, lawnmowers, and bathroom mirrors, relay a perpetual stream of images to voyeurs in televisionland—unbeknownst to him. Unfortunately, the technological aspects of the film are well within reach. Remarkably small cameras are available from security supply houses, along with tiny transmitters and dummy appliances in which to conceal them (one company gleefully advertises a wall clock, concealing a tiny video camera, as an ideal solution for keeping an eye on employees).

Then again, surveillance is nothing new. Video cameras are a ubiquitous part of the urban landscape, so much so that we scarcely notice them; we are watched constantly, and have been for years. Supermarkets, convenience store, elevators, automated teller machines, and office lobbies are all monitored via camera by persons unseen.[46] Public spaces such as tunnels and bridges, toll booths, college campuses, streets and public squares are, increasingly, also being watched. In the United Kingdom, home of Bentham's Panopticon, dozens of town centers are patrolled by video cameras, and Liverpool police recently began using a system of 20 cameras to produce full color, highly magnified nocturnal images.[47]

Surveillance has also moved beyond the visual. In 1996 Redlands, California, installed an "Urban Gunshot Location System," consisting of a matrix of sound sensors at intersections in the city enabling police to instantaneously detect and locate gunfire.[48] Of course, such applications are intended to serve the interest of public health and safety; but surveillance is by nature a clandestine act, and the risks of abuse, of invasions of personal and group privacy, are very real. Astonishing abuses have already been com-

---

46. See Phil Patton, "Caught," *WIRED* 3.01, and John Whalen, "You're Not Paranoid: They Really Are Watching You," *WIRED* 3.03.

47. "You Don't Have to Smile," *Newsweek,* 17 July 1995, 52.

48. It should be noted that local community activists have praised the system, which appears to have had a positive impact. See "Gunfire Detection Sensor Tested," *Trenton Times,* 7 January 1996.

mitted: Several years ago a minuscule hidden camera was discovered in a locker room of Boston's Sheraton Hotel, recording employees in various states of undress (the hotel claimed it suspected employee drug use); in California a J. C. Penny clerk filed suit when she learned that a guard had been zooming a ceiling-mounted security camera on her breasts.[49]

The growing popularity of webcameras has raised the prospect of similar mischief. At first it would seem like anger misplaced—protest should be aimed at the "glass ceiling domes of wine-dark opacity" of institutional surveillance, rather than the innocuous home-rigged webcamera aimed out a kitchen window.[50] As Steve Mann has argued, institutions and the government have for years been "shooting" cameras at us; what webcameras enable is a chance to "shoot back" at Big Brother.[51] Then again, when one considers the enormous potential audience at the receiving end of a webcamera, the seemingly innocent device on the window ledge becomes a threat indeed—Little Brother is also watching, and he is hitched to a global network. Indeed, persons in webcamera view are *theoretically* exposed to millions of users on the Net, not just a half-awake night guard at a security desk. Even if no one is watching—and most of the time no one is—the mere presence of a webcamera compromises personal space. In a feedback thread on the Trinity Square Street-Cam site in Colchester, United Kingdom, one woman wrote: "Big brother is watching us and we don't like it! We have no choice but to be in view going to work. . . . We are ANNOYED!"

49. "You Don't Have to Smile," *Newsweek* (17 July 1995).

50. Patton, "Caught," *WIRED* 3.01.

51. See Steve Mann, "Privacy Issues of Wearable Cameras Versus Surveillance Cameras," 1995 (http://www.wearcam.org/netcam_privacy_issues.html).

Part I

Philosophy

3

Telepistemology: Descartes's Last Stand

Hubert L. Dreyfus

She could see the image of her son, who lived on the other side of the earth, and he could see her. . . . "What is it, dearest boy?" . . . "I want you to come and see me." "But I can see you!," she exclaimed. "What more do you want?" . . . "I see something like you . . . , but I do not see you. I hear something like you through this phone, but I do not hear you." The imponderable bloom, declared by discredited philosophy to be the actual essence of intercourse, was ignored by the machine.

— E. M. FORSTER[1]

Artists see far ahead of their time. Thus in the twenties E. M. Forster envisioned a future in which people all over the world would be able to keep in touch with everything electronically. They would sit in their rooms all their lives, talking to each other and seeing each other, as well as receiving medical care from distant robots, and so forth. Naturally, they developed pale, lumpish bodies that they hated and, on those rare occasions when they met face to face, it was considered as great *faux pas* to touch or be touched by another person. Now we are getting close to the future Forster envisioned. We can keep up on the latest events in the universe, shop, do research, communicate with our family, friends, and colleagues, meet new people, play games, and control remote robots all without leaving our room. When we are engaged in such activities, our bodies seem irrelevant and, thanks to telepresence, our minds seem to expand to all corners of the universe.

But at the same time a skeptical doubt can creep into our sense of almost god-like control and omniscience. All this knowledge is indirect, inferred from what we see on our screens and hear from our loud speakers. What if all this telepresence were rigged and there was nothing outside our room but a duplicitous computer feeding carefully organized audio-visual data to our computer to create the illusion of a world with which we believe we are interacting? Nothing on our high-resolution 3D screens and our hi-fi stereo speakers would look or sound any different.

But at least we know our bodies, our room and the screen are real, we want to respond. But what if our sense organs were just further input channels to our mental computer and we were just being given systematic inputs to produce the experience of an external world while all that was real was our brain in its cranial vat. Again, how could we tell the difference? But, we could insist, at least the brain and the vat and the computers feeding in data would have to be real, so at least our belief that there was an external world would not be an illusion. But even our assurance of that minimal contact with reality would be fragile for, once we had gone this far, we would, on reflection, have to admit that all that we really have access to is our own private experience. Just as in dreams an experience of a supposed world is produced by the mind alone, so all that I can know for sure is that I am a

1.   E. M. Forster, "The Machine Stops," in *The New Collected Short Stories* (London: Sidgwick & Jackson, 1985).

conscious subject having my private experiences. These inner experiences would be the same, even if the outside world were a fiction.

The above story of progressive loss of touch with reality is not mere fantasy. It is the true story of the development of epistemology in the West. Modern skepticism about the existence of the external world begins with Descartes. Before Descartes there had been skeptics but they questioned their reasons for believing *anything,* not especially their *perception.*[2] They did not distinguish the world of *inner* experience from the *external* world and then discover one could doubt the existence of the latter. But early in the seventeenth century three influences led Descartes to make his fateful distinction between the mind and the rest of reality. To begin with, instruments like the telescope and microscope were extending man's perceptual powers, but along with such indirect access came doubts about the reliability of what one seemed to see by means of such prostheses. The church doubted Galileo's report of spots on the sun and, as Ian Hacking tells us, "even into the 1860s there were serious debates as to whether globules seen through a microscope were artifacts of the instrument or genuine elements of living material (they were artifacts)."[3] Clearly such doubts were pragmatically motivated and realistic.

At the same time, the sense organs themselves were being understood as transducers bringing information to the brain. Descartes pioneered this research with an account of how the eye responded to light and passed the information on to the brain by means of "the small fibers of the optic nerve."[4] Likewise, Descartes understood that other nerves brought information about the body to the brain and from there to the mind:

[T]he mind is immediately affected, not by all parts of the body, but only by the brain, or rather perhaps only by one small part of it.[5]

2. David R. Hiley, *Philosophy in Question: Essays on a Pyrrhonian Theme* (Chicago: University of Chicago, 1988).

3. Ian Hacking, *Representing and Intervening* (Cambridge: Cambridge University Press, 1983), 194.

4. René Descartes, "Dioptric," *Descartes: Philosophical Writings,* ed. and trans. Norman Kemp Smith (Modern Library, 1958),150.

5. René Descartes, "Meditations on First Philosophy," ibid., 244.

Descartes not only realized that our access to the world was *indirect*. He also saw that the transmission channels were unreliable so that inferences made on the basis of this information could be mistaken. He observed that:

It may happen that, although the extremities in the foot are not affected . . . the motion excited in the brain will be the same as would have been caused by an injury to the foot, and the mind will then necessarily sense pain in the foot just as if the foot had indeed been hurt.[6]

He then used reports of patients with a phantom limb to call into question our seemingly direct knowledge that we have bodies:

I have been assured by men whose arm or leg has been amputated that it still seemed to them that they occasionally felt pain in the limb they had lost—thus giving me grounds to think that I could not be quite certain that a pain I endured was indeed due to the limb in which I seemed to feel it.[7]

Descartes also observed that,

Because it is the soul that sees, and not the eye, and because the soul sees immediately only by the intervention of the brain, . . . it happens that madmen, and sleepers often see, or think that they see, diverse objects that are not before their eyes.

Descartes concluded that since he could experience only what the nerves from his sense organs transmitted to his brain and from there to his mind, he had no direct knowledge of the world, and, since the senses could malfunction, all information about the body and the external world was intrinsically unreliable. He then used dreaming to make the last step into the interior.

How often . . . have I dreamt of myself being in this place, dressed and seated by the fire, whilst all the time I was lying undressed in bed! . . . I see that there are no

6. Ibid., 245.

7. Ibid., 235

certain makers distinguishing waking from sleep; and I see this so manifestly that, lost in amazement, I am almost persuaded that I am now dreaming.[8]

So Descartes concluded that all we can be certain of is the content of our own minds, our private subjective experiences.

Descartes had discovered that, from the point of view of detached, philosophical reflection, it seems reasonable to raise, not just *pragmatic* doubts about the reliability of our instruments and even of our sense organs, but *hyperbolic* doubts about the existence of anything outside the mind. Indeed, when we engage in pure philosophical reflection it seems we have to agree with Descartes. We have no direct access to the external world, only the unreliable data sent by our sensors to our brain. The inevitable follow-up question of how self-enclosed subjects could come to know transcendent objects led to a new version of skepticism, skepticism about the existence of the external world, and to a new philosophical discipline, epistemology, which attempted to determine how and to what extent our everyday beliefs about the world could be justified.

Over the next three centuries (roughly from 1650 to 1950) philosophers came to accept uncritically the picture of the inner mind and the external world as separated by an ontological gulf and connected only by a narrow and unreliable information channel. Epistemologists then worked through the three theses supporting Cartesian skepticism First, starting with the British empiricists, especially Berkeley and Hume, there were repeated attempts to determine just what data were directly given by the senses. Gradually, however, philosophers found they could not make sense of indubitable private sense data and eventually gave up this line of inquiry. They then turned their attention to the reliability of perceptual beliefs. This issue is still debated but only by a small minority of philosophers. (See Goldman's chapter in this volume.) Finally, some prominent philosophers still hold that, since all I can know is the content of my own mind, for all I can tell I may be a brain in a vat.[9] This is the contemporary version of Descartes's disembodied dreamer.

8. Ibid., 177, 178.

9. For example, see John Searle, *Intentionality,* Cambridge University Press. "Even if I am a brain in a vat—that is, even if all my perceptions and actions in the world are hallucinations . . . I necessarily have the same . . . [experience] I would have if I were not a brain in a vat. . . ." 154.

But in the second half of the twentieth century, thanks to the work of Pragmatics from William James to John Dewey, existential phenomenologists such as Martin Heidegger and Maurice Merleau-Ponty, and so-called "ordinary language" philosophers such as John Austin and Ludwig Wittgenstein, most philosophers have abandoned these epistemological concerns. These philosophers now hold that, if our Cartesian way of thinking about the mind and its self-enclosed content gives rise to skepticism about the external world, there must be something wrong with this view of the mind as having only indirect access to reality. Each of the above schools of philosophy claims, each for its own reasons, that our basic relation to the world is direct, so that global skeptical doubts are incompatible with everyday experience and so are not only unmotivated but cannot even be coherently formulated.

Heidegger, for example, holds that Descartes, in his famous dictum "I think, therefore I am" paid attention to the *cogito* but neglected the *sum*. Human beings, Heidegger argues, have to take a stand on who they are by dealing with things and by assuming social roles. He captures this idea in his claim that human beings are essentially being-in-the-world. He argues that, if human beings are essentially being-in-the-world, then the skeptical question of whether the world and others exist cannot sensibly be raised by human beings, and, as Heidegger asks, "Who else would raise it?"[10] Heidegger thus claims that any attempt to *answer* the skeptic is mistaken. Taking the skeptic seriously and attempting to prove that there is an external world presupposes a separation of the mind from the world of things and other people that defies a phenomenological description of how human beings make sense of everyday things and of themselves. Using a different approach, Externalists like Donald Davidson claim that the idea of a self-enclosed Cartesian subject makes no sense because mental content can only have meaning in so far as it has a causal connection with the external world of objects and other people.

These antiskeptics share the view that we can't make sense of the detached attitude from which Descartes formulates his skeptical arguments,

---

10. Martin Heidegger, *Being and Time,* trans. John Macquarrie and Edward Robinson (New York: Harper) 246–247. For a more detailed discussion of the nature of human being (Dasein) see H. Dreyfus, *Being-in-the-World; A Commentary on Division I of Being and Time* (Cambridge, Mass.: MIT Press, 1991).

or, in so far as we can make sense of this attitude, we have to understand it as derivative from and dependent upon our everyday involvement in the world. As such arguments have gained ground, the epistemological concerns inaugurated by Descartes and central to all branches of modern philosophy have come to seem more and more implausible. In major philosophy departments the mandatory epistemology courses that presupposed that, before one could investigate the entities in any domain, one had to have an account of how one could know about such entities, were demoted to one among several options or were dropped from the requirements altogether and replaced by courses in metaphysics and ontology.

But now, at the close of the century, just as philosophers are coming to view the Cartesian subject/object ontology as mistaken and the epistemological problems it generated as pseudo-problems, new tele-technologies such as cellular phones, teleconferencing, telecommuting, home shopping, telerobotics, and Internet web cameras are resurrecting Descartes's epistemological doubts. Descartes already noted that:

when looking from a window at beings passing by on the street below, I . . . say that it is men I am seeing. . . . [But] what do I see from the window beyond hats and cloaks which might cover automatic machines?[11]

And he concluded that, having no direct knowledge, he could only *infer* that there were people passing by. Now, as more and more of our perception becomes indirect, read off various sorts of distance sensors and then presented by means of various sorts of displays, we are coming to realize how much of our knowledge is based on inferences that go beyond the evidence displayed on our screens. We see that the reality mediated by this tele-technology can always be called into question. Indeed, skepticism is increasingly reasonable in the face of the growing variety of illusions and tele-experiences now available.

Consider the Telegarden,[12] the Internet telerobotic project that motivated the title of this book. Visitors to this garden log in from terminals all over the world, directing a robot and camera to view, water, and plant seeds in a 6' x 6' patch of soil ostensibly existing in a museum in Austria. Seeds

11. Descartes, "Meditations on First Philosophy," 190.

12. http://telegarden.aec.at

take weeks to germinate but the patient visitor is rewarded with a view of a distant plant in the garden. In what sense does this plant exist? It is perfectly plausible that the entire project is an elaborate forgery, with soil and plant images indexed from a digital library. How can an Internet visitor know the difference? Skepticism in this case seems well motivated.

Still, as long as the uses of telerobotics remain isolated instances of mediated interaction in contrast to our direct access to the everyday common-sense world, they can be dismissed by the general antiepistemological mood of contemporary philosophy as special cases dependent upon our direct experience of everyday reality.[13] If, however, technology makes more and more of our knowledge indirect (i.e., inferred from displays), the old problem of how to justify our knowledge of the unobserved may well start to look a lot more pressing. Indeed, as telepresence becomes important in our commerce with people and things so that this indirect relation to the world comes to dominate more and more of our lives, we might come to think of our everyday relation to the world as merely a special case of telepresence. This might lead people to focus once again on the reliability of the "input" from the world and the possibility of both specific and general deception as to what we are encountering. Furthermore, if our culture's practices continue to developed in the present direction so that most of our relations to others and to objects are indirect as in E. M. Forster's prescient story, our picture of our relation to the world might well begin to change. We might again, as in the seventeenth century, come to give priority to the pure, reflective attitude in which we can't help but think of our sense organs as transducers and ourselves as brains in vats. Since whether or not one takes skepticism to be intelligible depends on which picture of our epistemic situation (involved or detached) one feels to be fundamental, under such conditions skepticism might come to seem more and more reasonable. The epistemology courses that were central requirements up to thirty years ago, and have since virtually disappeared from the curriculum, might again be required. And if telepresence became ubiquitous and we became dependent on electronic prostheses to mediate *all* our relations to the world, the epistemological questions that troubled Descartes and three centuries of epistemologists could again come to seem, not just intelligible, but disturbing.

13. See Jeff Malpas, "Acting at a Distance and Knowing from Afar: Agency and Knowledge on the Internet" (this volume).

There is another possibility, however. It could turn out that the contrast between the interactions mediated by tele-technologies and the telepresence they deliver, on the one hand, and what little remains of our everyday unmediated interactions with people and things, on the other, will become starker and starker. Then it might well become clear that, as Malpas argues, the attenuated sort of telepresence available through tele-technologies is parasitic on the richer involvement we have with the things we directly perceive. Thus, when I am watching TV, I may sensibly wonder if NASA is faking the Mars landing I seem to be witnessing but I can't in the same way sensibly doubt that I am sitting on my couch surrounded by my family. Likewise, I may doubt that I am seeing real rather than computer-generated models wearing the hats and cloaks in an on-line catalog I am perusing, but I can't entertain similar doubts when my order is delivered to my door. Telepresence would then call our attention to the way that things and people are normally *directly* present to us and we would sense that this direct form of presence was basic and that *mediated* telepresence was at best a poor imitation. If people experienced "presence" on the screen as a kind of privation of direct contact, the kind of washed out telepresence tele-technologies provide might well lead to an appreciation of our everyday robust relation to things and people. Then, rather than bringing about a revival of Cartesian epistemology, tele-technology would strengthen Heidegger's hand by further undermining interest in global epistemological questions while stimulating interest in the ontology of being-in-the-world.

To understand the present situation and the direction in which it may evolve, we need to understand more precisely what is present in everyday life that is missing in telepresence. John Haugeland adopts a Heideggerian point of view claiming that Descartes misunderstood the mind and the world to be connected by a narrow channel, while in fact we are connected to reality by a broad bandwidth channel.[14] Given Haugeland's convincing analysis we can see that the narrow bandwidth of our connection to the outside world in tele-technologies is certainly part of the problem, but it is not the basic difficulty. We can imagine the bandwidth of the input to our computer getting broader and broader and the displays getting richer and richer and still we would be in the position of inferring what is going on in

14. John Haugeland, "Mind Embodied and Embedded," in *Having Thought* (Cambridge, Mass.: Harvard University Press, 1998).

the outside world by way of indirect evidence on our screens, and so still subject to legitimate skeptical doubts.

Pragmatists such as William James and John Dewey offer an analysis of Cartesian skepticism that gets closer to the essential nature of its distortion of our relation to reality. For the pragmatists, the question is whether our relation to the world is that of a detached spectator or an involved actor. On this analysis, what gives us our sense of being in direct touch with reality is that we bring about changes in the world and get perceptual feedback concerning what we have done. Merleau-Ponty has worked out this intuition in convincing detail.

In his *Phenomenology of Perception,* he spells out the way our active and involved body puts us directly in touch with perceived reality. According to Merleau-Ponty when everyday coping is going well one does not experience oneself as a subject with inner experiences relating to objects in the external world. Rather, in such cases, athletes speak of flow, or playing out of their heads. One's activity is completely geared into the demands of the situation. Aron Gurwitsch offers an excellent description of this absorbed activity as opposed to Cartesian detachment:

[W]hat is imposed on us to do is not determined by us as someone standing outside the situation simply looking on at it; what occurs and is imposed are rather pre-scribed by the situation and its own structure; and we do more and greater justice to it the more we let ourselves be guided by it, i.e., the less reserved we are in immersing ourselves in it and subordinating ourselves to it.[15]

Such skillful coping does not require an inner mental representation of its goal. As Merleau-Ponty puts it:

A movement is learned when the body has understood it, that is, when it has incor-porated it into its 'world', and to move one's body is to aim at things through it; to allow oneself to respond to their call, which is made upon it independently of any representation.[16]

15.   Aron Gurwitsch, *Human Encounters in the Social World* (Duquesne University Press, 1979), 67. Since Merleau-Ponty attended Gurwitsch's lectures explaining Heidegger's account of being-in-the-world in terms of gestalt perception, there may well be a direct line of influence here.

16.   Maurice Merleau-Ponty, *Phenomenology of Perception* (Routeledge & Kegan Paul, 1979), p. 139.

The way the body responds directly to the world leads Merleau-Ponty to introduce the concept of maximum grip. When we are looking at something, we tend, without thinking about it, to find the best distance for taking in both the thing as a whole and its different parts. When grasping something, we tend to grasp it in such a way as to get the best grip on it. Merleau-Ponty says:

My body is geared into the world when my perception presents me with a spectacle as varied and as clearly articulated as possible, and when my motor intentions, as they unfold, receive the responses they expect from the world.

This maximum sharpness of perception and action points clearly to a perceptual ground, a basis of my life, a general setting in which my body can co-exist with the world.[17]

So, for there to be a sense of presence in telepresence one would have to be involved in getting a grip on something at a distance.

But even this sort of control and feedback is not sufficient to give the controller a sense of direct contact with reality. As long as we are controlling a robot with delayed feed back, like the telegarden arm or the Mars So-journer, what we see on the screen will seem to be mediated by our long-distance equipment, not truly tele-*present*. To be more precise, we won't seem to be bodily present at the site in question because we won't sense ourselves as getting a maximal grip on the object of our concern. Skeptical doubts will, therefore, still seem well motivated.

There comes a point in interactive robot control, however, where we are able to cope skillfully with things and people in several sensory dimensions and in real time. Then, as in lapariscopic-surgery, we seem to be present at the robot site. Robot builders realize that "full telepresence requires a transparent display system, high resolution image and wide field of view, a multiplicity of feedback channels (visual as well as aural and tactile informa-tion, and even environmental data such as moisture level and air tempera-ture), and a consistency of information between these."[18] At that point we can still step back and raise the abstract epistemological concern that we

17.   Ibid., p. 250.

18.   Richard M. Held and Nathaniel I. Durlach, "Telepresence," *Presence* 1:109–111.

may be brains in vats or the hyperbolic doubt that all our experience might conceivably be a dream, but these seem to be philosophical worries belied by our sense of being directly involved with objects and other people in our interactions with them. Thus the experience of coping with an object in real time seems to remove the phenomenological basis for a legitimate concern that the instruments that stand between us the world may be malfunctioning and so to remove Descartes's motivation for making the distinction between inner subjects and outer objects. The more tele-technology gives us real-time interactive telepresence, the more we get away for a Cartesian sense of being a spectator making inferences from our sense data and the more we have a sense of being in direct touch with objects and people, the more skeptical questions as to whether our interactive prosthesis could be systematically malfunctioning will seem merely academic.

But even though interactive control and feedback may give us a sense of being directly in touch with the objects we manipulate, it may still leave us with a vague sense that we are not in touch with reality. In this volume, Albert Borgmann has given a plausible phenomenological account of what is still missing. He says

[I]t is characteristic of real experience that we can never say in advance what depth features and structures will be significant. . . . Following [Nelson Goodman's] terminology we may call the inexhaustible richness of reality repleteness. If we think of repleteness as the vertical dimension of richness, we can use continuity to designate the endless width of richness. In comparison the presentation of reality in cyberspace is shallow and discontinuous.[19]

Borgmann gives as a suggestive example of tele-reality's lack of repleteness, the fact that, as we remotely control our car driving down the freeway, we can't get out to help if we see through our tele-windshield a driver who has been hurt and is lying beside the road. This observation points to a further feature of reality that Borgmann overlooks. What is missing from our experience as we sit safely at home remote controlling our car is not just repleteness but risk. To avoid extremely risky situations is precisely why remotely controlled planet-exploring vehicles and tools for handling

19.   Albert Borgmann, "Information, Nearness, and Farness" (this volume).

radioactive substances were developed in the first place. But even normally our bodies are in potentially risky situations. So, when we are in the real world not just as involved interactive minds but as embodied human beings, we must be constantly ready for dangerous surprises. Perhaps this readiness goes back to our survival as hunted animals. In any case, when this sense of vulnerability is absent the whole experience become unreal even if, involved in a sort of super-IMAX interactive display, we are swaying back and forth as we drive our car around dangerous-looking curves.

In *Phenomenology of Perception,* Merleau-Ponty argues that, not only is each of us an active body coping with things, but that, as embodied, we each experience a constant readiness to cope with things in general that goes beyond our readiness to cope with any specific thing. According to Merleau-Ponty, this background readiness makes up our sense of the reality of the world. He calls this embodied readiness our *Urdoxa* and claims that it is only on the background of this indubitable faith in the perceptual world that we can doubt the veracity of any specific perceptual experience.[20]

An attempt at inducing a sense of online corporeal risk was made in the telerobotic art project: Legal Tender.[21] Remote viewers were presented with a pair of purportedly authentic US $100 bills. After registering for a password sent to their email address, participants were offered the opportunity to "experiment" with the bills by burning or puncturing them at an online telerobotic laboratory. After choosing an experiment, participants were shown a screen summarizing the legal implications: It is a Federal crime to knowingly deface US currency, *punishable by up to six months in prison.* If, in spite of the threat of incarceration, participants click a button indicating that they "accept responsibility," the remote experiment is performed and the results shown. Finally participants were asked if they believed the bill and the experiment were real. Almost all responded in the negative. So they had not really experienced any risk after all.

But, while important and generally overlooked, focusing on the absence of a sense of physical risk in tele-interactions, still misses what seems to me the most important element absent from telepresence: *intercorporiality.*[22] It

20.   Maurice Merleau-Ponty, *Phenomenology of Perception.* Colin Smith, trans. (Routledge and Kegan Paul, 1962).

21.   http://www.counterfeit.org

22.   I owe this term to Merleau-Ponty; see *Phenomenology of Perception.*

seems there is a mode of presence more basic than our experience of the direct on-going coping with objects made possible by an ideal real-time, interactive interface or even our sense of risky embodied involvement. That is our sense of being in the presence of other people. John Canny and Eric Paulos have written convincing in this volume of the importance and difficulty of achieving a sense of the embodied telepresence of others.[23] They criticize the Cartesian attempt to break down human-human interactions into a set of context-independent communication channels such as video, audio, haptics, etc., and point out that two human beings conversing face to face depend on a subtle combination of eye movements, head motion, gesture and posture, and so interact in a much richer way than most roboticists realize.

But, even if, as Canny and Paulos expect, our tele-technology goes beyond the imagination of E. M. Forster in that we will eventually be able use remote-controlled faces and robotic arms and hands to touch other people, I doubt that one could get a sense of how much to trust another person as we stare into each other's prosthetic eyes, even if we were at the same time using our robot arms to shake each other's robotic hands. Perhaps, one day we will stop missing this kind of trustful contact and then touching another person will be considered rude or disgusting. E. M. Foster envisions such a future in his story:

When Vashti swerved away from the sunbeams with a cry [the flight attendant] behaved barbarically—she put our her hand to steady her. "How dare you!" exclaimed the passenger. "you forget yourself!" The woman was confused, and apologized for not have let her fall. People never touched one another. The custom had become obsolete, owing to the Machine.[24]

But for the time being Business consultants know that in order to get two CEO's to trust each other enough to merge their companies it is not sufficient that they have many teleconferences. They must live together for several days interacting in a shared environment, and it is quite likely that

23. John Canny and Eric Paulos, "Tele-Embodiment and Shattered Presence: Reconstructing the Body for Online Interaction" (this volume).

24. Forster, "The Machine Stops."

they will finally make their deal over dinner.[25] Borgmann in his chapter is onto this sense of embodied nearness when, following Heidegger, he makes a sharp distinction between the near and the far, and claims that true nearness is being eliminated by telerobotics due to its failure to affirm the body. One might expand Borgmann's point by noting that there is a crucial difference between the sort of presence we have access to due to our distance senses of hearing and sight and the full-bodied presence that is literally within arms reach. This full-bodied presence is not just the feeling that I am present at the site of a robot I am controlling through real-time interaction. Nor is it just a question of giving robots surface sensors so that, through them as prostheses, we can touch other people without knocking them over. Even the most gentle person/robot interaction would never be a caress, nor could one successfully use a delicately controlled and touch-sensitive robot arm to give one's kid a hug. Whatever hugs do for people, I'm quite sure tele-hugs won't do it. And any act of intimacy mediated by any sort of prosthesis would surely be equally grotesque if not obscene.

But why am I so sure tele-intimacy is an oxymoron? I suspect it is because any sense of intimacy must draw on the sense of security and well-being each of us presumably experienced as babies in our caretaker's arms. If so, even the most sophisticated forms of telepresence may well seem remote and abstract if they are not in some way connected with our sense of the warm, embodied nearness of a flesh-and-blood human being. Not that we automatically trust anyone who hugs us. Far from it. Just as Merleau-Ponty claims that it is only on the background of our indubitable faith in the perceptual world that we can doubt the veracity of any specific perceptual experience, so we seem to have a background predisposition to trust those who touch us, and it is only on the basis of his *Urtrust* that we can then be mistrustful in any specific case. But if that background trust were missing, we might tend to be suspicious of the trustworthiness of every mediated social interaction and withhold our trust until we could confirm its reliability. Such a skepticism would cease to be academic and would complicate if not poison all human interaction.

25. Computer scientist Myron Krueger has proposed research on olfactory telepresence. Recent research has shown that people can discriminate accurately by smell alone whether another person they are with is afraid, angry or happy. (see the article by Erica Goode in *The New York Times,* April 27, 1999, recounting the work at Rutgers University of Dr. Denise Chen and Dr. Jeanette Haviland.)

As we spend more and more time interacting remotely, we may erode our embodied sense of a risky yet trustworthy world that makes physical or human contact seem real. As this sense is weakened, even our daily "local" experience may take on an illusory quality and so seem to be in need of justification. In such a disembodied and dubious world, epistemology might stage a comeback as telepistemology, and Descartes might make a successful last stand.

4

Vicariousness and Authenticity

Catherine Wilson

Epistemologists have tended historically to associate experience with presence and abstraction with distance. When, in the second quarter of the twentieth century, they began to consider certain problems involving technologically mediated knowledge, these associations served their critical purposes effectively.

Instrumentalists, for example, proposed that humans could not have knowledge of submicroscopic particles whose existence was merely inferred from meter readings, or tracks in cloud chambers. Theoretical entities were conceived of as useful fictions. Bertrand Russell contrasted "knowledge by knowledge by acquaintance" with "knowledge by description," and the experience of seeing my hand held up before me or a red mailbox in broad daylight was considered a paradigmatic example of knowing something. That from mysterious equations and pointer-readings on dials, the physicist could unleash the destructive power of the atom need not, it seemed to the instrumentalist, imply that atoms were real; and, in general, the more distant or remote from human sensory apparatus an entity was, the less he took its claim to be the subject of any true, as opposed to useful, proposition. Perhaps it was not a coincidence that, at the same time as quantum theory and other developments in physics were making instrumentalism philosophically attractive, the first critics of modern technology were arguing that technology had destroyed our intimate commerce with the natural world, eliminating authentic "modes of disclosure" in the deployment of its massive transformative power. Instrumentalists and technology critics agreed that instrument-mediated experience and knowledge were not like their nonmediated counterparts, and, as medicine ceased to involve a soothing beside visit from a wise and kind physician and came to mean the X-ray, the uncomfortable lab test, and much waiting around in dull hallways, the perception that mediated knowledge spelled human losses all around was strengthened.

The appeal of instrumentalism has declined however in tandem with the recognition that instrumentation can transform theoretical entities into real ones. With electron microscopes we can now see molecules and viruses, and what formerly were hypothetical entities and place-holders in theories are now as ordinary as mailboxes. It is true that the introduction of new optical instruments has historically been attended by skepticism about whether what was seen was merely a visual artifact, but, as the history of the microscope shows us, it was hardly the final and most-considered reaction.

Inevitably, science and technology between them domesticate entities that formerly had free range, living outside human supervision and control, and this is as true of rare atmospheric gases or sub-atomic particles as it is of the floral essences of the ancient perfumer's art or the exotic fauna of the Renaissance collector. Consequently, we have reason to doubt that technology implies experiential opacity; it may rather extend the realm of what we perceive and come to know intimately. Accordingly criticisms of modernity that are based on the equation immediacy=presence=human value are likely to fall by the wayside.

It might seem that this development is unlikely. The notion that technology is alienating is extremely persistent, and we are we are already hearing such new communications media as email criticized for encouraging people to develop soulless, superficial relationships and for depriving them of human contact. We are warned that email-based friendships ("knowledge by description") are likely to be delusory as well as ultimately unsatisfying, and the implication is that friendships between people who actually encounter each other ("knowledge by acquaintance") as three-dimensional objects in real space have a higher ontological, epistemological, and moral status. We seem to have retained all these centuries the Platonic view that representations of other things are somehow ignoble or degraded.

The purpose of this chapter is to argue that the threat to values posed by technologically mediated remote experience and remote agency actually derives less from the defective nature or lower status of mediated experience than from the opportunities it presents for immersion and engagement of a disturbing sort. To make this point, I begin with a short account of the preference for the immediate and the proximate that characterized philosophical discourse earlier in the century.

Section 1. Technology and Proximity

Rejecting the old tendency of philosophy to talk about invisible states of affairs and abstract entities, phenomenologists, including Jean-Paul Sartre, Maurice Merleau-Ponty, and Martin Heidegger, began in a surprising move to describe in lengthy detail human experience with everyday objects such as jugs, inkwells, telephones, keyholes, letters, cafe tables, and so on. Philosophers had traditionally considered objects of this sort to be beneath notice, and many fascinating explanations might no doubt be proposed for their new, central place in academic theory. Perhaps natural science had assumed control of what had been mutual territory for investigation, leaving only subjective experience to philosophy. Perhaps, as the rise of the theory of landscape in the eighteenth century has been argued to be a compensatory response to the degradation of the natural environment in the industrial revolution, so phenomenology was a compensatory response to the loss of time for leisurely contemplation in a world newly filled with automobiles, streetcars, subways, radios, mass circulation newspapers, and electrical appliances. Perhaps broad-scale democratic and populist movements were leading some people to think that the world was going out of control and needed to be symbolically hauled back in. In any event, epistemologists like Heidegger began to write in excited terms about an immediacy that they associated with nontheoretical and pretechnological cultures. Naturally, Heidegger realized that immediate human experience could not be identified with what a member of our species would see, smell, touch, taste, and so on, when encountering the world in the body of a human being; he understood that our experiences are dictated by the fact that we make use of instruments, wear clothes, and work. His strategy for acknowledging this fact while still leaving room for the alienness of technology was to introduce the notion of "equipment" as mediating human experiences and agency, but to give this notion a highly personal and primitivist slant in order to stay close to what he conceived as the human essence. His description of a peasant woman in the midst of her equipment—her clothes, tools, and implements—aware in a wordless, animal way of "bread" "soil," "wind," and of "birth," and "death," as physiological realities—posits a connection between immediate experience, labor exerted on things, and truth:

When she takes off her shoes late in the evening, in deep but healthy fatigue and reaches out for them again . . . she knows all this [the earthy nature of her equipment] without noticing or reflecting. The equipmental being of the equipment consists indeed in its usefulness. But this usefulness itself rests in the abundance of an essential Being of the equipment. We call it reliability.[1]

Like other philosophers of technology, Heidegger tried to posit a rupture between an original mode of awareness and interaction, and the artificial

---

1.   Martin Heidegger, "The Origin of the Work of Art," in *Heidegger, Basic Writings,* ed. David Farrell Krell (San Francisco: Harper, 1977), pp. 143–188, p. 163.

one of technology. Heidegger believed that objects such as jet aircraft, radar stations, and hydroelectric plants, unlike the peasant woman's leather-soled shoes, "reveal" the various ways in which energy can be transformed and order created, but conceals their purposes and workings from the viewer. Heidegger toyed with but rejected the idea that they were "demonic," though he did not doubt that they were "dangerous":

The essence of technology lies in enframing . . . Enframing blocks the shining forth and holding sway of truth. The destining that sends into ordering is consequently the extreme danger. What is dangerous is not technology. Technology is not demonic; but its essence is mysterious. The essence of technology, as a destining of revealing, is the danger.[2]

Heidegger was able to rely on a kind of cultural memory of the dangers of technology. Renaissance inventors who brought forth new experiences with "machines" or who were able to perform action at a distance were suspected of being in league with the devil and assisted by demons, for it was generally agreed that such achievements surpassed the ordinary powers of nature. The "Faustian bargain" was an exchange of the human soul for power over nature, and, wherever they perceived it to be happening, it was symbolically resisted by philosophers. Walter Benjamin argued that mass destruction was the only human activity that could take full advantage of technology, and the French sociologist Jacques Ellul made the point that the achievement of absolute precision finds its natural expression in organized warfare. I return in section 3 to the problem of this secret affinity.

The Heideggerian notion that technology is opaque—that an installation like a hydroelectric plant confronts us as a terrifying Juggernaut built to the scale of giants and inscrutable in its workings—was still present in Ellul's *The Technological Society* (French edition, 1954). Ellul argued that technology is dehumanizing, hyperrationalistic, and corrosive of moral values

Technique is opposed to nature. Art, artifice, artificial; technique as art is the creation of an artificial system. This is not a matter of opinion. The means man has at

2. Heidegger, "The Question Concerning Technology," in *Basic Writings,* pp. 283–318, pp. 307–309.

Catherine Wilson

his disposal as a function of technique are artificial means. . . . The world that is being created by the accumulation of technical means is an artificial world and hence radically different from the natural world.

It destroys, eliminates, or subordinates the natural world, and does not allow this world to restore itself or even to enter into a symbiotic relationship with it. The two worlds obey different imperatives, different directives, and different laws which have nothing in common. Just as hydroelectric installations [!] take waterfalls and lead them into conduits, so the technical milieu absorbs the natural. We are rapidly approaching the time when there will be no longer any natural environment at all. When we succeed in producing artificial *aurorae boreales,* night will disappear and perpetual day will reign over the planet.[3]

Ellul's words were in a sense prophetic; the natural environment, as we understand better all the time, is being destroyed at a pace inconceivable to most people in 1954, though Ellul himself described graphically the unforeseen effects of the application of European agricultural techniques in the plantation systems of Africa and the American South, where deforestation and crop-planting led to flooding and erosion. There are ever fewer gardens, in the sense of places cultivated by one or a few humans for their subsistence, and there are ever more robots. As the title of this collection suggests, it is not inconceivable that robots and gardens might some day come to coexist on good terms, though the intuition that they are antithetical has reasons behind it. But many of our newest and most important technologies are not opaque, except in the details of their constitutions and their function is not to replace the natural world but to display it. Like windows and telescopes, they produce singular experiences—glimpses and views— and they extend the range of individual acts of human agency.

By contrast, the kind of technology with which Heidegger and his contemporaries were most concerned (electrification, mass transit) was aimed at the production of material articles of uniform appearance *en masse,* and at transformations of physical and chemical energy that brought about broad changes to the conditions of everyday life, all of which struck them as "unnatural." Heidegger acknowledged as well new technologies of mobility and information transfer, describing the newly invented television set as "[t]he

3. Jacques Ellul, *The Technological Society,* trans. John Wilkinson (New York: Vintage, 1964), p. 79.

peak of this abolition of every possibility of remoteness."[4] But these innovations were ultimately just as alienating as the others were. "The frank abolition of all distances bring no nearness."[5] It might seem that there is a powerful disanalogy between the invention of an optical *instrument* like the microscope that gives us access to a natural realm that was formerly unobserved by everyone and where the behavior of entities largely determines what happens in the macroworld, and the invention of visual technologies like television and the Internet that simply facilitate the acquisition of experiences and knowledge that can be obtained and used, with some inconvenience, in other ways. The Internet does not add to the knowledge present in the world, it might be said; it only redistributes it. I can call up pictures of houses for sale in particular neighborhoods of Vancouver from the other side of the world, and this give me new information, but adds no truths to "our" collective understanding. I could have the same experiences, similar to those had by many others, by going there and driving around. But this point rests on an arcane and specialized—and probably indefensible—philosophical conception of knowledge, according to which a truth is possessed by the human race if and only if it is possessed by one human. It is false that the handy provision of difficult-to-obtain experiences adds nothing to the world's stock of knowledge and to our capacities and dispositions to act.

Of course the new technologies can be regarded as productive of desirable articles for consumption rather than new knowledge, precisely on analogy with the old "factory." Experiences seem to be in and of themselves desirable to us as a species.[6] The development of technologies addressed to aural and visual reproductions seems to be a response to an inexhaustible hunger to see and hear things and to participate in social exchange. Bacon complained about the weakness and inadequacy of the senses, and we are daily frustrated by such optical-acoustic failings in our environment as hard-to-read print, bad color processing on our snapshots, TV screens that are too small, static, airplane seats where we can't see the movie. We demand crisper photocopies, more dimensional stereo-speakers, more interesting to look at screen-savers.

4. Heidegger, *Poetry Language and Thought,* trans. Albert Hofstadter (New York: Perennial Library, Harper and Row, 1971), p. 165.

5. Ibid.

6. Albert Borgmann suggests an evolutionary basis for this. See his "Information, Nearness, and Farness" (this volume).

As Walter Benjamin mused, "Every day the urge grows stronger to get hold of an object at very close range by way of its likeness, its reproduction."[7] The human mind does not stop before a television set, appalled and affronted in its humanity, unable to grasp how the thing functions or why it is there, save as an expression of might and arcane knowledge as before a giant hydro-electric installation. On the contrary, it has exactly what it wants: more things to see. It is a window or a mirror, not a massive opaque block of the type memorialized in Feodor Gladkov's novel *Cement*.

The traditional epistemology that associated experience and proximity reflected the mental universes of our ancestors. For them, there was a "here" constituting the realm of perception and action, and an "away." "Away" was the region of things acknowledged by common consent not to be "here." Some of the things that were away were: angels, sea monsters, humans with square heads and blue faces, . . . the souls of long-dead ancestors, countries where milk and honey flowed in the rivers and people lived in houses encrusted with jewels, republican virtues, the Gods, the Forms, exiled Kings . . . people who had left the village years ago and never returned. . . . Everything dead, lost, once glimpsed, imagined, longed for inhabited this penumbra, at once shadowy and vivid, around the sphere of activity and experience in which one day is much like the next. The things that were "away" were recalled in stories, in religious rites, in individual memory, in philosophy. They were as real as anything, but for all that unable to affect or take part in the life-world.

This mode of thinking that has been steadily, though incompletely, eroded by knowledge and technological development. The telescope revealed to Galileo that the moon was not of a flawless and quintessential substance, but a lumpy and scarred rock, like the ones we have here. "Away" has split into two somewhat deflated categories for the philosopher. One consists of the purely imaginary, the realm of possible worlds, possible objects and possible situations to think about. The other is a set of "heres," diachronically converging to a single large "here." The variations in language, customs, dress, manners, and mode of government that the traveler once encountered every ten kilometers or so are blurring rapidly. This process accelerated shortly after scientists began to discover or at least proclaim

7. Walter Benjamin, "The Work of Art in the Age of Mechanical Reproduction," in *Illuminations,* trans. Harry Zohn, ed. Hannah Arendt (New York: Schocken, 1969), pp. 217–252, p. 223.

universal laws (Newton), to write their universal natural and cosmological histories (Buffon, Laplace), and to propound universalizability as a test of moral correctness (Kant). Individuals and groups have become far more sensitive to the actions of others distant from them, far more able to influence them in turn. And telerobotics crowns this trend. In theory, it ought to be possible for a surgeon to perform a delicate operation on the other side of the world by being linked to a high-resolution camera and to a robot capable of translating signals into precise movements. In Ellul's terms, a paradigm of human activity, the direct touching of human flesh for healing purposes is accomplished over vast distances. The technology itself, admittedly, is opaque except to a few experts, but not the use, or purposes. Such examples indicate that Ellul's dichotomy, like Heidegger's, is obsolete. The world of technology and the human world now have a great deal in common. Experience and direct agency are now part of both.

Is this a good result or not? Ellul stated that "History shows that every technical application from its beginnings presents certain unforeseeable secondary effects that are much more disastrous than the lack of technique would have been."[8] This statement is too profound, too challenging to discuss rationally. I do not say that Ellul is wrong, but I prefer to deal with a weaker statement, that *many* technologies have in fact presented certain unforeseeable secondary effects that were destructive of *something* valuable in the way we think of the world and ourselves. Does this hold for the new technologies of remote access?

Take for example the issue of surveillance, a popular subject ever since Foucault studied Jeremy Bentham's famous model for an optically efficient prison capable of being overseen by a single, centrally domiciled policeman (and, in Bentham's scheme, his wife and children).[9] Some hold that surveillance is the means by which an autocratic state secures its end of punishing every form of deviance incompatible with its own ends of absolute power. We are watched by cameras and other monitoring devices in parking lots, in stores, in banks, at work, and it might seem that the hyper-vigilance of a society anonymously and impersonally (for we do not see our watchers) obsessed with productivity and crimes against profits and property is exceed-

8.   Ellul, *The Technological Society,* p. 105.

9.   Michel Foucault, *Surveiller et punir,* Paris, 1975. Cf. Jeremy Bentham, *The Panopticon Writings,* ed. Miran Bozovic (London: Verso, 1995).

ingly sinister and that this inspection of our persons is an affront to human dignity. About certain forms of employee-monitoring, and about the tasks and employers that apparently require such monitoring, there is nothing good to say, but this is not true of all forms of surveillance. Many persons whose interests were never before considered particularly weighty—females, the elderly, bank clerks—welcome such surveillance. Some of their fearfulness is justified and it is a mark of respect toward them to take it seriously.

Or, take a quite different example, think of the penetration by cameras into the habitats of rarely seen animals, or inaccessible regions of the earth, such as the Poles, the ocean floor, the mouths of volcanoes. Nature videos often take for their subjects the most mythic and totemic animals, such as birds of prey or the large carnivores. Now, the insistence on being able to *see* everything, and the willingness to see it on another person's limited and confining terms, might be criticized as mere vulgarity like the obsessive purchase of package holidays to foreign capitals. But who is certain that all these experiences do not develop the capacity for sympathy and affection, or respect for life beyond what it would have been without them?

Or, to take a final example, consider realism in news reporting. Not so long ago we had little idea what famine or village warfare looked like; we have a better idea now. "War photography" existed, but as a specialist category of anti- or prowar propaganda and as an art form. We did not think that those pictures showed us what the world is really like and that these things happen here, and here, and here, in a similar way. Some people argue that transmitting these images day after day inculcates callousness in the viewer and leads to the mistaken belief that fate rules the world and there is nothing to be done about it. It is not clear that they are right. Skepticism about the sacredness and glory of armed combat is probably at a higher level among North Americans and Western Europeans than ever before in human history, and we are ever less convinced that disasters happen for no reason at all. The "passivity" of the viewer of global horrors may be only superficial; things happen in people's minds unobserved, and these things have the power now to act back on the world as they earlier could not.

Ellul, in the passage quoted, expresses a definite preference for a world that is illuminated only half the time, and he expects that everyone will agree with him. It is difficult to see why the half-lit world is a better one. We need to sleep and we enjoy the beauties of the night. The rejection of the futuristic "videophone" by consumers could be cited as evidence that we do not want to see our family members and business associates more than we already do and will resist a new technology that offers us the chance to do so. However, our reluctance perhaps can be better explained as a reluctance to be seen than as a reluctance to see.

Section 2. Experience, Agency, and the Telefictive

In order to evaluate Heidegger's and Ellul's criticisms of technology, it will be helpful to compare technologically mediated experiences (including telerobotic ones) to another class of experiences, which I will call *telefictive*. Telefictive experiences, I will argue, share much in common with technologically mediated experiences. The similarities suggest that it is not technology *per se* that is to blame for many of the negative aspects associated with technologically mediated experience and agency, but rather something about us and the way we use the technology that stands at our disposal.

I begin this section by explaining what I mean by "telefictive" experiences, how they are related to ordinary "veridical" ones, and what role they play in our moral and psychological lives. A standard view in philosophy is that the real world and the fictional world are logically isolated. Events occur in the real world, and objects are located there, and we experience them in virtue of being causally affected by them and forming representations of them. Fictional worlds are created by filmmakers, novelists, television producers, raconteurs, and songwriters and populated with fictional characters engaged in fictional situations. We cannot go to these worlds, for they are logically inaccessible, and the fictional events described in them are causally powerless to affect us; fictional events are powerless to cause real experiences.

On this view, the vivid simulations afforded by modern electronics are still fictions, still causally isolated from the real world. No matter how intense the experiences generated by involvement with virtual persons, objects or events, the subject is still aware that they are simulations. Normally there are a sufficient number of contextual clues to remind the subject where he is, but even the pilot in a flight simulator experiencing exactly she would experience on the flight deck knows that she is not in an airplane. At least since the time of Hume, it has been thought obvious that "historical" narration evokes a different response in the reader than fictional narration. Hume says that we read history with a cognitive attitude of belief; and we read fiction, we do not experience this belief. "Belief consists merely in a certain feeling or sentiment; in something that depends not on the will, but must arise from certain determinate causes and principles, of which we are not masters. . . . Did not the belief consist in a sentiment different from our mere conception, whatever objects were presented by the wildest imagination, would be on an equal footing with the most established truths founded on history and experience."[10] Reality, in other words, is inexorable, and makes things happen whether we will or no, but I can always put the book down or turn the game off.

Hume's thesis implies that my awareness that what I am interacting with is a simulation and not a real object never fails me. Benjamin, who deplored the degradation he believed followed from the availability of the multiple copies of artworks available in an age of mechanical reproduction, argued as well that real objects are surrounded by an "aura" of uniqueness and permanence.[11] The alleged ontological distinction between the real world and the fictional world is frequently held to extend to an emotional and moral insulation. It has been maintained that the emotions of suspense or grief that we think we feel when watching a movie or reading a book are not real emotions at all but pretend-emotions, or "quasi-emotions." I cannot, it is said, grieve over the fate of Anna Karenina, for her life and death take place in a fictional world that is causally isolated from my world; I can only "quasi-grieve." Nor can I fear a ball of green slime, that, in a movie, is depicted as having dangerous properties. Real grief and quasi-grief, real fear and quasi-fear, may share a common core of physiological responses, such as the shedding of tears or the release of adrenaline, but because I know that Anna Karenina is merely a fictional person, and I know that the ball of green slime is merely a projected image on the screen, I am not emotionally affected by them.[12] The argument advanced by many people against the censorship of violence in children's television is simply that "children know that what they are watching is not real." This argument is extended—though not without increasing anxiety—to video games in which the player does not merely witness the

10. David Hume, *A Treatise of Human Nature,* 2nd ed., ed. P. H. Nidditch, Oxford, Clarendon, 1978, Appendix, p. 624.

11. Benjamin, "The Work of Art," p. 223.

12. See Kendall Walton, "Fearing Fictions," *Journal of Philosophy* 55 (1978): 5–27.

exploding bodies and mutilated corpses of humans and animals, or the "punishment" of, in particular, improbably inflated and impossibly dangerous females, but brings about these effects by play. Because the subject "knows" that what is happening is not real and because philosophy can show that real emotions are experienced only in the face of real objects, such experiences are *a priori* inconsequential. Though philosophers since Plato and Rousseau have been convinced that fiction causes social depravity, a currently more popular theory is that it reduces criminal behavior; in either case, it is difficult for anyone to "prove" *a posteriori* that individual or summed virtual experience has any effects in the real world.

My central claim in this section is that the human ability to distinguish simulacra from real things and simulations from real events, has been made to carry too much psychological weight. Our philosophical predecessors can be forgiven this error, for, in the case of Aristotle, they began their reflections about fictivity by considering fictional modes such as Greek tragedy that were interruptions in their daily experience, that stood out from ordinary life as bracketed and ritualistic, and in which the spectator's role was entirely passive. It was assumed that whatever held true for Homeric poetry and ancient tragedy held true for film and television, and whatever held true for film and television, held true for complex simulations, even those in which the spectator was at the same time an agent. I want to argue here that by beginning at the other end and considering such intense simulations, we derive quite different conclusions. The real world and fictional worlds are not emotionally, psychologically, or morally insulated from each other, despite the famous ability of anyone of speaking age to determine in theory whether something is really happening or not. Not only are fictional experiences somewhat more realistic in whatever sense we take this vague term than they were in the days of Aristotle or Rousseau, but our everyday experience is permeated by the fictive. If we see fictive modes—including imagination and fantasy—as weakened forms of what I will characterize as *telefictive experience,* we obtain quite different results from the standard theories.

I will now give a more explicit characterization of some of the central theoretical terms: proximal experience, proximal agency, mediated experience, mediated agency, perceptual experience, hallucination, and telefictive experience. I then want to suggest that the implied distinctions are more approximate than it might at first seem.

- *Proximal experience/agency.* An object or event is experienced or acted upon proximally when it is experienced or acted upon at first hand, not by the generation of images or reproductions. What counts as "first-hand" depends on the particular case.
- *Mediated experience/agency.* An object or event is experienced or acted on remotely when it is experienced or acted on by means of a set of transmitted signals other than those involved in the ordinary way in ordinary vision, hearing, touch, pushing, touching, or prodding, etc.

Thus, seeing a sunset (regardless of the time taken by light to travel and the distance of the sun from the earth); listening to and following a piano-recital in an auditorium, studying the painting known as the Mona Lisa at the Louvre, shaking hands with another human being, extracting a tooth from a patient in a dentist's chair with the usual implements, involve proximal experience and agency. Looking at the X-rays of a patient in the next room on a screen, hearing a record of a piano recital, looking at the Mona Lisa on television in an art program, talking to a relative on the phone are all examples of mediated experience. Moving aside a flap of skin with a probe during an operation is not mediated agency, but pushing a button 2,000 miles away to fire a missile is.

There are several problems with this distinction. When Heidegger, for example, sought for a perfect example, in the form of his peasant woman, of a subject unacquainted with technology and yet familiar to his readers, he did not seem to realize that "equipment" is just that set of implements an individual happens to be familiar with, in the sense that the manifestations of the machine are familiar, and its states can be exploited reliably. A sewing machine can appear as impenetrable as a hydro-electric plant, but to many people it is just "equipment," and to some individual perhaps, even the airplane or the hydroelectric plant too are just equipment, and they too, doubtless, see their usefulness as "resting in the abundance of Being." Second, it did not occur to Heidegger does not mention that the world of the peasant is not characterized simply by her relations with her bed, her stove, her hoe, etc. She is a human being and that is to say that she lives at the same time among images and simulacra. The real peasant has her images of the Holy Mother of God, her songs and stories, her longings for a world beyond the one she knows. Third, Heidegger did not seem to realize that serfdom is not truth and existence—authenticity— itself, but a political condition of deprivation; real peasants desire such things as rides in automobiles and patent leather high heels. This oversight is significant, because it suggests that any attempt to exalt authenticity in terms of technological primitivism is ideological rather than based in a careful study of human nature.

To return to the main line of argument, it is probably impossible to give a formal specification of the difference between proximal and mediated experience. If the button and the electronic apparatus that enable me to fire the long-range missile are mediating instruments, why isn't a metal probe an instrument? Why isn't my hand, for that matter, an instrument of my will? Admittedly, there is no more proximal way to move aside a flap of skin than with a probe, but there may be no more proximal way to fire a missile than by pushing a button 2,000 miles away. Is getting a water out of a faucet by turning a handle proximal agency but getting a soft drink out of a vending machine by depositing a coin remote agency? The distinction here, as Heidegger found, can only be made out by appeal to paradigmatic cases. Firing a remote missile by pushing a button is more like getting a coke out of a machine by inserting a coin than it is like setting off a firecracker in a field. We can nevertheless venture the claim that, to the extent that an agent is screened off from the proximal experiences that would otherwise accompany his agency, his agency appears to us to be remote. Conversely, to the extent that experience is screened off from the possibility of agency, it is regarded as remote. I can control the flow of the water out of the tap precisely, whereas I cannot control the behavior of the soft-drink can once I have put my money into the slot.

• *Ordinary perception* is the proximal experience of a real event or object that is in a position to causally affect the experiencer, and ordinary agency involves the first-hand manipulation of a real object that is in a position to be manipulated.
• An *illusion or hallucination* is the proximal experience of something which does not exist, including the experience of one's own agency.

Its proximal nature, as Descartes famously realized, is no guarantee of the veridicality or truth of an experience. No "test" is available to a subject that can inform her whether she is perceiving or hallucinating. Conversely, however, the mediate nature of an experience does not rule out veridicality

Table 4.1

	veridical	nonveridical
proximal	ordinary perception	hallucination, illusion
mediated	telerobotic perception	telefictive experience

or truth. Experiences may be produced by lengthy and unusual causal routes and still be veridical.

• *Mediated perception* is the experience of a real event or object that is not proximal; mediated agency is action on a real object from a distance.

We now need a term for the mediated experience of objects that do not exist and events that have not occurred and for action on and in the midst of such things. Note that the term "virtual reality" is normally used to cover both mediated perception that is exceptionally vivid and also fictional experience of a highly realistic sort. I call virtual reality experiences that do not qualify as veridical perception, "telefictive experiences."

These definitions fall neatly into four categories, as shown in table 4.1.

Problems for the standard "isolation" theory arise when we note the following:

1) To the extent that telefictive experience can, in principle, be subjectively indistinguishable from mediated experience (as hallucination may be subjectively indistinguishable from perception) its psychological effects and (to some degree) its moral significance are the same.

2) Proximal and mediated experience lie on a continuum.

In consequence, telefictive experience, so far as its psychological effects and (to some degree) its moral significance are concerned, lies on a continuum with ordinary, veridical, proximal experience.

Some examples will help make this clearer. A person who is playing a video game in which the object is to drive a race car through an obstacle course is having a *telefictive experience,* rather than undergoing mediated perception. She is not driving a car through an obstacle course; there is no car and no obstacle course that is being driven through. However, a person could in theory drive a race car through an obstacle course by being connected electronically with a real car on a real course. Her proximal experience might be identical with that of the person having a telefictive experience, just as hallucination may be qualitatively indistinguishable from ordinary perception. She might use a joystick to control the movements of the real car, look at a screen covered with pixels in lurid color, etc. Both the remote race car driver and the one merely playing a game are experiencing "virtual reality" though only one, in my definition, is having a telefictive experience.

The experience of fiction—reading, watching a movie, hearing a story—falls into the category of *telefictive experience.* So does sitting around the campfire and listening to stories of the gods and heroes. Simulacra—mental images and ideas of objects and events—are generated by the telling and the ambience even if we can't point to an electronically generated "image" in public space. *Electronically generated telefictive experience* turns out to be simply a subcategory of telefictive experience in general.

As Berger and Luckman comment, my "world"—a stable set of entities and relations—is infringed upon whenever I am faced with a new problem, demanding knowledge and familiarity I do not yet possess, or when those around me disrupt their normal routines. By practice, experience, and education, disruptive novelties are integrated into my familiar world. Fictions, on their view, correspond to worlds that cannot be integrated, that remain stubbornly set off: "The paramount reality envelops them on all sides, as it were, and consciousness always returns to the paramount reality as from an excursion."[13]

As the curtain rises, the spectator is "transported to another world," with its own meanings and an order that may or may not have much to do with the order of everyday life. As the curtain falls, the spectator "returns to reality," that is, to the paramount reality of everyday life by comparison with which the reality presented on stage now appears tenuous and ephemeral. . . .[14]

13. Peter Berger and Thomas Luckman, *The Social Construction of Reality* (New York: Anchor, 1988), p. 25.

14. Ibid.

But, at the moment of absorption in the fiction, "I" am neither wholly myself, for I am not experiencing and operating in my "everyday" world, but nor am I other than myself.

Berger and Luckman's confidence that fictional worlds are irremediably "set off" is curious, for perfect "setting off" can only concern a logical relationship and not a psychological one (just as Russell's distinction between knowledge by description and knowledge by acquaintance can be shown to blur in the theory of speaker's reference).

Again a bit of history of philosophy is in order. Frege and Russell thought that the paradoxes seemingly generated by nonexistent entities ought to be treated as problems of logical form. They rejected Meinong's introspective approach to fictivity, and subsequent generations of philosophers of mind tried to convert questions about fantasy and imagination to questions about logical form and behavior. The theory of propositional attitudes provided the philosophical underpinnings. To Frege we owe the claim that words that are quoted rather than asserted do not have their customary meaning. "As stage thunder is only apparent thunder and a stage fight is only an apparent fight, so stage assertion is only apparent assertion."[15] Following Frege's hints on how to think of quotations, it was suggested that a fictional work is prefaced by a sort of operator that signifies "It is fictionally true that . . ." while a historical or factual work is understood as prefaced by an operator that indicates "It is actually true that. . . ." In *Speech Acts,* John Searle, argued that we can engage either in "normal real world talk" or shift into a fictional, play-acting, let's pretend mode of discourse."[16] Nicholas Wolterstorff insisted that "representation is an action performed by human beings."[17] "To compose a work of fiction," he said "is to fictionally project a world distinct from our actual world."[18]

15. Frege, "The Thought" in *Philosophical Logic,* ed. P. F. Strawson (London: Oxford University Press, 1967), pp. 17–38, p. 22; cf "On Sense and Reference," in *Translations from the Philosophical Writings of Gottlob Frege,* 3d ed., ed. Peter Geach and Max Black (Oxford: Blackwell, 1980), pp. 56–78, pp. 57–59.

16. John Searle, *Speech Acts* (Cambridge: Cambridge University Press, 1969), pp. 78–79. Searle claimed that words in such "parasitic" contexts do not change their meanings, but the relationship with Frege's approach is nevertheless clear.

17. Nicholas Wolterstorff, *Works and Worlds of Art* (Oxford: Clarendon, 1980), Preface.

18. Ibid., p. 106.

Searle thinks it obvious that nothing falls in between referring to a real entity and referring to a fictional entity:

In normal real world talk I cannot refer to Sherlock Holmes because there never was such a person. If, in this "universe of discourse" I say, "Sherlock Holmes wore a deerstalker hat" I fail to refer, just as I would fail to refer if I said "Sherlock Holmes is coming to dinner tonight at my house." Neither statement can be true. But now suppose I shift into the fictional, play-acting, let's pretend mode of discourse. Here if I say "Sherlock Holmes wore a deerstalker hat," I do indeed refer to a fictional character . . . and what I say here is true. Notice that in this mode of discourse I cannot say "Sherlock Holmes is coming to my house for dinner tonight," for the reference to "my house" puts me back in real world talk.[19]

However, he says, "in fictional talk one can refer to what exists in fiction (plus such real world things and events as the fictional story incorporates.)"[20] If for example, I fantasize Sherlock Holmes coming to my house for dinner, it can be fictionally true: Sherlock Holmes is coming *here,* the fantasy might say, to visit *me.*

But it seems misguided to think of fantasizing as involving a shift in the mode of discourse. Fantasizing is *continuous* with ordinary experience in all sorts of ways. Fantasizing that Sherlock Holmes is coming to dinner is experientially continuous with planning and mentally rehearsing a real dinner party. In case this is doubted, consider the following passage from Proust.

The emotion with which I was seized on seeing the daughter of a wine merchant at her till or a laundress in the streets was the emotion one has on meeting a Goddess. Since Mt. Olympus has ceased to exist, its inhabitants have come down to earth. . . .

[T]he streets, the avenues were full of Goddesses. Here and there between the trees, at the entrance of a cafe, a servant idled like a nymph at the edge of a sacred wood, while three young girls were seated by the side of the immense arcs of their bicycles posed by their sides, like three immortals seated on a cloud or a fabulous courser on which they accomplished their mythological voyages. . . .[21]

19. Searle, *Speech Acts,* pp. 78–79.

20. Ibid.

21. Marcel Proust, *La prisonniere,* volume 6 of *A la recherche du temps perdu* (Paris: Gallimard), 8 vols., pp. 198, 201.

A narrator, "Marcel," reports or "reports" that he perceives (proximally) girls with bicycles, but he has the telefictive experience of being among goddesses. The reader, as a result of this reportage or "reportage," has the telefictive experience of being among girls-on-bicycles and goddesses too. Though we can confidently term it telefictive, both the narrator's and the reader's experience exist on a continuum with ordinary perception. What is being described, after all, is, the ordinary proximal perception of girls on bicycles. He or she sees the girls on bicycles as goddesses and in that sense he or she sees goddesses. If the reader of whatever sex succeeds in "getting into the story," he or she feels a kind of rapture—about girls-on-bicycles-as-goddesses. The emotions described as felt by the narrator, and perhaps actually felt by the reader, are not pretend emotions or "quasi-emotions" but simply emotions about objects that are constituted partly by proximal, partly by telefictive experience. The girls and bicycles are not integrated into the reader's everyday reality and neither is the emotion of rapture. But it is a real emotion and the effects of having experienced it may well become integrated into the reader's everyday reality.

Hume, as I remarked, thought that a sentiment of truth was automatically generated by encounters with certain materials. He did not consider the possibility of pseudo-histories indistinguishable from the real thing except that they are false, or historical accounts written with all the flourishes of fiction. And the distinction he is pointing to is by no means innate in human cognitive apparatus. As Paul Veyne reminds us, our ancestors did not distinguish systematically between historical truth and legend; there was not present to them one world, the world defined and its boundaries drawn by newscasters with maps behind them, with a single temporal and spatial metric into which everything that happens can be placed. The myth or legend as an embellishment, Veyne argues, was accepted as true in the sense that it was not doubted, though it was not accepted in the way that everyday reality is: The myth was situated in the past and "mythological space and time were secretly different from our own."[22] The mythological world is not concurrent with ours in that it is assigned no determinate place in our time-space matrix. But neither is it specifically projected as not having such a place. The question does not arise: No option of believing

22. Paul Veyne, *Did the Greeks Believe in their Myths?* trans. Paula Wissing (Chicago: University of Chicago, 1988), p. 18.

that it is true or false arises.[23] Fictional worlds are such that one may neither know (because one has not thought about it) nor care how remote they are from the real world.

I noted above that the development of technologies of mediated perception has tended to annihilate this kind of mythological space. But it has left us the telefictive world of the emotions. As Veyne asks, am I in the real world or a fictional world when I write a jealous, interminable, confused letter?[24] There is a pure continuum, moreover, between the real fear I experience when I perceive myself to be in the presence of a dangerous animal, and the alleged "pseudo-fear" I experience when I watch a suspenseful film. Between what is called "real fear" and fear of fictions is an array of experiences: fear of what I take, erroneously, to be a dangerous object; irrational fear of something (e.g., a large beetle) I know not to be dangerous; fear felt when I "concoct" a frightening situation (e.g., imagining that my daughter who is late has been abducted while knowing this to be unlikely); fear felt in the presence of someone else's fictional concoction that I know to be fictional. Jealousy is a "fictional" emotion is so far as it is generated by telefictive self-narrations concerning non-existent objects, but even the old philosophers regarded it as one of the most intensely "real."

Section 3. Truth, Simulation, and Violence

In claiming that much of our everyday thinking and emotional experience is telefictive and that the public simulacra, images, copies and reproductions shared by spectators are relevantly similar to private telefictions, I do not mean to imply that we do not care about truth and about the distinction between what is rule and what is not. In certain contexts we care overwhelmingly, and our critical epistemologists from Bacon to Ayer are indignant about the interpenetration of real and fictional worlds. The salvation of the human race has been seen in terms of separating truth from fiction, and European philosophers have long exalted experience over theoretical abstraction, and proximal experience over mediated experience. We need only think of Van Helmont's pre-Heideggerian complaint that academic philosophy destroyed Nature in her "root and thingliness." Or of Harvey's condemnation of the "phantoms of apparition" inhabiting our minds and his

23. Ibid., p. 23.

24. Ibid., p. 22.

demand that the reader take nothing on trust, but use his own eyes as "witnesses and judges." Or of Francis Bacon's claim that he dwells "purely and constantly among the facts of nature" and his resolution to withdraw his intellect from them "no further than is required to let the images and rays of natural objects meet in a point." Or Descartes's desire to perceive objects "clearly and distinctly," rather than obscurely or superficially. Or Locke's preference for "the Knowledge and Truth of Things" over disputations and theories involving words.[25]

The modern inheritor of the historical exaltation of proximity (and with it the denigration of technological mediation) is of course Heidegger who refers incessantly to "things" and their "thingliness." But is Heidegger's exaltation of things a validation of *experience* or a validation of *reality?* Is he extolling primitive objects (e.g., the peasant woman's shoes), or primitive experience (e.g., seeing something directly as opposed to seeing it on television)? A problem with those who today look to Heidegger for inspiration is that he was not in a position to distinguish the two. Because Heidegger's notion of proximal experience was primitivist, his notion of reality was so as well:

Occasionally we still have the feeling that violence has long been done to the thingly element of things and that thought has played a part in this violence, for which reason people disavow thought instead of taking pains to make it more thoughtful. . . .[26]

The task is to become "more open to Being . . . by granting the thing, as it were, a free field to display the thingly character directly." The purpose of art is to "let the earth be an earth." This message is reinforced by Heidegger's constant references to natural objects, such as plants, animals, granite, and so on.

Heidegger's aesthetic brings out two problems:

1) The primitivist aesthetic of work and subsistence is no longer very tenable. In no sense is it the intention of contemporary art to "let the earth be

25. The development of optical technologies in the seventeenth century and the rise of empiricism is discussed by C. Wilson, *The Invisible World* (Princeton: Princeton University Press, 1995), chapter 2.

26. Heidegger, "The Origin of the Work of Art," p. 171.

an earth," and Heidegger's admiration for serfdom reflects political values with which it is difficult to identify.

2) The "thingly element of things" that Heidegger is praising here as disclosed truth given by proximal perception can be experientially identical with telefictive experience.

Heidegger assumed that a cultural preference for the mediated over the proximal, and the emotionally complex, excessive, and useless over the concrete and instrumental signified a move away from the "thingly element of things." But does not our capacity to produce vicarious experiences bring us ever closer to the thingly element of more things? Would Heidegger have regarded telefictive experience as, in his terms, essentially concealing or essentially revealing?

We have observed that though usually they are not, there is nothing to prevent a telefictive experience being qualitatively indistinguishable from ordinary perception. Reading about Anna Karenina's ball is not much like being at any ball, but "taking off" in a flight-simulator may be exactly like taking off in an airplane except for the added element of knowledge supplied by the fact of remembering that one got into a flight-simulator some minutes ago. The difference, however, is merely a matter of degree; I remember that I started reading a book, and other situational cues—the weight of my body in its armchair, the glimpse of the horizon I get when I raise my eyes—continue to inform me that I am not in a ballroom.

Consider now the implications of the fact that not only can we create fictivities corresponding to events that few mortals have ever proximally experienced, and few truly wish to, but also that this is the first and most enthusiastic use to which the new telefictive technologies have been put. Mimesis is the sister of violence. In a short story by Saki some children given a dollhouse to play with enact Robespierre's executions, and it is interesting that the examples of fictivity that spontaneously occur to contemporary philosophers include pretending to be bears and corpses (Ryle) or detectives (Searle).[27] Mediated perception and remote agency reach exquisite levels of

---

27. On violence and "catharsis," see Aristotle, *Poetics,* 1452–1454; cf. Sigmund Freud, "The Relation of the Poet to Daydreaming," in *Freud on Creativity and the Unconscious,* ed. Benjamin Nelson (New York: Harper and Row, 1958), pp. 44–54. The ancient concept is reassessed by Jonathan Lear, in "Katharsis," *Phronesis* 33 (1988).

perfection in military technology, and telefictive experience moves briskly along in its wake. Benjamin was disturbed by how technology aestheticized violence,[28] but we still lack a good understanding of the reciprocal problem: why mediated perception and agency are overwhelmingly dedicated to destructive purposes and why telefictive experiences are overwhelmingly dedicated to the experience of destruction and rehearsals of destructive agency.

The robot is still, in other words, not quite at home in the garden, but not for the reason that machinery and life representing opposing values, that one represents distance and concealment, the other immediacy and revelation. The problem is rather that we ourselves, with our technological capacities attached to us, are and are not that robot, and that we do and do not want to live in a garden. The Heideggerian longing for vivid and authentic experience seems to lead not away from technology but toward it, though not unambiguously toward it. At the same time, we are apt to think of the wild garden as the true and original home of humanity and imagine that it is in such pacific and luxuriant places that we will feel, once again, well. But the wild garden is not a pacific place, and there is nothing there for robots to do, anyway. It is the artificial postlapsarian garden, where we have seen to it that there is work to be done, where the robot will prove useful. But we do not yet know how to behave in this kind of garden. Settlement and cultivation are comparatively recent developments in the history of the species, and they represent modes of life to which we have made only a passable, but in many ways imperfect adjustment. If predation and scavenging, rather than making green things grow, correspond to our original way of interacting with the world, it is no wonder that we spontaneously look for access to spectacles of the deadly and the dead.

While moral theory has historically favored cultivation over predation, it has had little to say recently about the degree to which spontaneous human desires should be countenanced or repressed, and accordingly little to say about the moral evaluation of telefictive experience. Liberal conceptions of the diversity of the possible good lives have placed the assessment of experience off limits, except insofar as certain experiences can be proved to predispose people in socially expensive ways. Yet there are curious contradictions in the way in which we evaluate experiences, for we do not hold to

---

28. Benjamin, Epilogue to "The Work of Art," in Arendt, ed., *Illuminations,* pp. 241–242.

liberal principles without exception. We regard it as unseemly that there should be public hangings, even if some people would genuinely like to attend them. We think that children and adults not professionally involved in them ought not to attend autopsies or Caesarian sections, even those who are especially curious. It is illegal to sell and purchase certain pornographic materials, and it presumably would be even if these materials were electronically fabricated in such a way that the body of no human being was ever directly involved, and even if no increase in harm to human beings was ever shown to follow from its consumption. The revulsion here is real, though the offense is purely ideational or symbolic.

Thus it is somewhat surprising that we also find that even if some experiences would be bad or even horrible to have, and even if we do not think that it would be good to have the corresponding mediated experiences, the corresponding telefictive experiences are regarded either as value-neutral or positively good to have. It is possible that our aesthetic theories are still inappropriately constrained by ancient telefictivities; Aristotle's theory of the salutary effect of terror was conceived within the framework of passively experienced and highly ritualized drama, not within that of telefictive experience and agency, which, as we have seen, can be in principle and may some day become in fact, subjectively indistinguishable from mediated experience and agency. We will in most cases retain the theoretical ability to distinguish realities from fictivities by recalling the context of the experience, but the mere pronouncement of an ontological distinction between the real and the fictive is relatively meaningless when the psychological and logical continuities and interrelations between proximal, mediated, and telefictive experiences cease to support it. Heidegger did not foresee that a problem about technology, if not "the" problem, might arise not from its monstrous opacity and its inability to function as anybody's "equipment," but from the effortless access it provides to the "thingliness of things."

5

Information, Nearness, and Farness

Albert Borgmann

Modern science and technology, it seems, have erased the difference between what is near and what is far. The notion of the annihilation of space and time was at first used metaphorically when the telegraph and the railroad made information and transportation far quicker and easier. A landmark was reached in this country when the transcontinental railroads had spanned the continent, an event typically noted by Josiah Royce in 1889 when he said of California:

The region that to-day is so swiftly and easily entered was of old the goal of an overland tour that might easily last six months from the Missouri River, and that was attended with many often-recorded dangers.[1]

In our day, however, information technology has developed so vigorously that the metaphor of yore, as Catharine Wilson urges, has to all appearances become literal truth or at least literal truth in principle now and in practice before long.[2]

The technological annihilation of space has received support by information theory and cognitive science and before that, as Hubert Dreyfus notes, by Cartesian epistemology.[3] According to information theory, all communication is exchange of information, be the channels wide or narrow, long or short.[4] Cognitive science has taught us that all perception is mediated and processed whether the object of perception is ten feet or ten light years away and whether it is Newtonian or electronic.

Yet all these considerations are at odds with the intuition, noted by Dreyfus, that there are fundamental differences between what is near, what is far, and what is neither and that issues that are moral in a broad and deep sense revolve around the ways we acknowledge these differences and assign them

1. Josiah Royce, "The Pacific Coast," in *Race Questions, Provincialism, and Other American Problems* (New York: Macmillan, 1908), p. 173.

2. Catherine Wilson, "Vicarious and Authenticity," this volume.

3. Hubert L. Dreyfus, "Telepistemology: Descartes' Last Stand," this volume.

4. Warren Weaver, "Recent Contributions to the Mathematical Theory of Communication," in Claude E. Shannon and Weaver, *The Mathematical Theory of Communication* (Urbana: University of Illinois Press, 1998 [1949]), p.7.

their place in our lives.[5] Is this intuition more than a matter of nostalgia or romanticism?

Consider how on a day of Christmas week in the New York area. I can choose between experiences in the world of traditional nearness and farness and experiences in the world of electronic media where everything is equally near or far. Manhattan abounds with Christmas concerts and recitals. I could go to a performance of selections from Handel's *Messiah* at noon in St. Paul's chapel in downtown Manhattan. But then I think of an hour's travel by loveless public transportation on a gray December morning. I could take the car, but then I would have to fight traffic and search for a parking spot.

As it happens, I have *Messiah* on CD, by the Choir of Christ Church Cathedral, Oxford, and the Academy of Ancient Music under the direction of Christopher Hogwood, surely a performance more accomplished and polished than I am likely to hear from some lesser-known orchestra still aspiring to wider recognition and a choir mostly of young professionals struggling to launch a career. Besides, I want to get on the World Wide Web to catch up on the aftermath of the president's impeachment. In the early afternoon, I would like to indulge my one weakness—English soccer—and in the evening there is a football game that, perhaps for the last time, pits the old warriors John Elway and Dan Marino against each other and will show what the Broncos are really made of. If the game should be a bust, there is a Warren Miller movie that will get me in the mood for skiing. In one possible world, I follow the solicitations of the media, peruse impeachment news on the Internet, move on to a chatroom, check the Dow Jones, then follow the soccer game on television, switch to football, turn to the ski movie, slip from there into another hour of Fox Sports News, and at half an hour before midnight, get up from my rocker, vaguely uneasy, mildly disgusted with myself, trying to remember where the day has gone.

In another possible world, we take the train to Hoboken, get on the PATH train to downtown Manhattan, and make our way to St. Paul's. There it sits behind a little cemetery, outwardly unassuming, inside resplendent in self-confident Georgian classicism. The orchestra is tuning up. It is composed of young musicians who specialize in baroque music and have, with well-considered humor, taken the name of the French baroque composer Rebel. The members of the choir, youthful and in black robes, have gathered

5. Dreyfus, "Telepistemology."

in the back of the church. Now they move to the front and are seated for the overture. Then from among the tenors the first soloist moves to the front of the orchestra and sings the "Comfort Ye" with warmth, devotion, and self-assured skill. He is followed by the choir entire, three countertenors among the five alto voices. Twenty young and trained voices are singing with inspiring sonority and energy.

On occasion the wailing of the sirens in the traffic outside competes with the singing, late-twentieth-century sounds in the background of mid-eighteenth-century music, much as skyscrapers surround the late eighteenth-century building that has seen colonial times and a thanksgiving service for George Washington upon his inauguration as president. A very young countertenor sings the recitative and air for alto, and some of his colleagues smile as he negotiates with growing confidence the turns and leaps of the melody. All rise for the "Alleluia," there is cordial and sustained applause. We stop at a deli for lunch. There in the line is our countertenor with a colleague. We congratulate him. He lights up and seems grateful.

Having firmed up our intuitions, we can begin to analyze the kinds of information and knowledge that belong to traditional reality on the one side and to the world of electronically mediated information on the other. If WNET, instead of showing Jessye Norman and the Augusta Children's Chorale, had televised *Messiah* in St. Paul's, how would traveling far to attend the concert have differed from having it brought near by television? A question like that properly fits into the scope of telepistemology and does so in two ways. Telepistemology ought to clarify the ontological and epistemic confusions and complexities that the question above stirs up. Answers will be a contribution to technical telepistemology. Once the answers are on hand, however, there is a further question as to the difference the technical distinctions make. In answering this question, if an answer can be found, telepistemology makes a contribution to ethics and the philosophy of culture and constitutes something like moral telepistemology. The technical problems are difficult enough, and yet the answers seem pointless to me, as does much contemporary technical epistemology, if they are neutral regarding moral concerns.

Let me begin the technical discussion by making two related distinctions between the traditional world of tangible reality and cyberspace. By the latter I mean the realm of electronically mediated information (*technological information,* as I will call it) all of which before long will be rendered in bits, structured by Boolean algebra, stored by computers, and displayed by a variety of visual, acoustic, and haptic media. The first thing to notice is that cyberspace has no metric but does have a topology. In topological space, distances are irrelevant, but connections and continuities matter. Maps of subway systems are often more topological than metric. What one wants to know is what line connects with which and which station comes after what. The rails and the conductors take care of distances and locations. Highway maps are metrical, of course. One wants to know how far it is from here to there.

Similar considerations apply to time though we have known, at least since Immanuel Kant, that the metric of (pre-Einsteinian) time is less interesting than that of space. An airline schedule is metric; time spans matter. Concert programs and committee agendas are topological, however. All they tell you is where one item is placed in relation to all others.

The topology of cyberspace could be rendered as a vast and complex network in three dimensions that is hourly growing new spurs and connecting lines. The contents of most sites and locations in cyberspace have a conventional Euclidean metric, albeit an attenuated one that allows you to skip around easily in space and time. In any case, being enveloped by a purely topological space, the metric that is internal to a location in cyberspace cannot be continuous with the metric of reality.

This leads to a second difference between reality and cyberspace. As information theorists have remarked, reality is informationally inexhaustible. Things, events, and situations display a depth of properties and relations that no amount of propositions can capture. Consider Fred Dretske's illustration.

Suppose a cup has coffee in it, and we want to communicate this piece of information. If I simply tell you, "The cup has coffee in it," this (acoustic) signal carries the information that the cup has coffee in it in digital form. No more specific information is supplied about the cup (or the coffee) than that there is some coffee in the cup. You are not told how much coffee there is in the cup, how large the cup is, how dark the coffee is, what the shape and orientation of the cup are, and so on. If, on the other hand, I photograph the scene and show you the picture, the information that the cup has coffee in it is conveyed in analog form. The picture tells you that there is some coffee in the cup by telling you, roughly, how much coffee is in the cup, the shape, size, and color of the cup, and so on.[6]

However rich the information conveyed by the picture, if it is presented in cyberspace, the information may be massive, but it too is limited, viz., by the vehicles that convey it. The structure and number of vehicles are always specifiable, the structure in terms of hardware and software, the number of bytes or in bytes per second. In reality, to the contrary, Dretske's "and so on" truly comes into its own. What is experienced is not specifiable information but a reality that, as Keith Devlin has it, "is not unlike a 'bottomless pit,' seemingly capable of further and further penetration."[7] It is characteristic of real experience that we can never say in advance to what depth features and structures will be significant. This is a point Nelson Goodman has made about works of art such as paintings or sculptures. Following his terminology we may call the inexhaustible richness of reality *repleteness*.[8] If we think of repleteness as the vertical dimension of richness, we can use *continuity* to designate the endless width of richness. In comparison the presentation of reality in cyberspace is shallow and discontinuous.

We can now move from these more or less ontological points to the epistemological ones by indicating how the metric of traditional space is related to information. That relation can serve as a foil for the properly telepistemological issues. In metric space we measure distances with a "rigid ruler." The rigidity of the ruler is an indication of the inexorable extension of metric space. You have to travel to get from one point to another. One may think of pendulum swings as the inexorable measure of time. If you have agreed to attend *Messiah* and find yourself bored and annoyed by a poor performance, there is nothing to do but endure the two and a half hours to the bitter end.

In a premodern setting, what is present in space and time has prominence since a resort to elsewhere or elsewhen is slow or laborious. To the prominence of presence corresponds a focal area of nearness that is centered on my

6. Fred I. Dretske, *Knowledge and the Flow of Information* (Cambridge: MIT Press, 1981), p.137.

7. Keith Devlin, *Logic and Information* (Cambridge: University Press, 1991), p. 16.

8. Nelson Goodman, *Languages of Art* (Indianapolis: Hackett, 1976), pp. 229–230.

body. Within the circle of proximity, things and persons present themselves in their own right and are known directly, by acquaintance rather than description. Objects that are remote in time or space, however, I know indirectly, by having information about them. In a world of natural signs such information is provoked by my curiosity or concerns. When I am concerned about the weather, clouds and the wind are the signs that provide information. When I look for game, tracks and signs of bedding down are significant. When I try to find an old campsite, I look for the fire ring.

In this way a substantive metric of nearness and farness underlies or is inscribed on the formal metric of Euclidean space. In fact there is reason to believe that in a natural setting the metric of nearness is Euclidean while the metric of farness is hyperbolic.[9] In any case, the distinction between nearness and farness is clear.

The substance of nearness makes itself felt in the commanding presence of things and persons, in my intimacy with them, and normally in a sense of security and of being at home. The substance of farness lies in the reference of signs to things and persons that are concealed by distance in space or remoteness in time. Their sense is conveyed by the signs. In a premodern setting where the sense of distant things is never more than a partial disclosure, farness can be colored by relative ignorance, mysteriousness, and, as Wilson remarks, by utter strangeness.[10]

In a natural setting of, say, a hunting and gathering band, information was both extremely valuable and relatively scarce. For skilled hunters and gatherers there was normally enough information to sustain a good life. But there was rarely an excess of information, and, above all, information did not accumulate. The signs that conveyed it would emerge as such from the context of nearness and then disappear or revert to mere things.

Repleteness and continuity are the contents that belong to the form of metric space. They fill the full-bodied sizes of things and the inexorable distances between them. Actual metric space is a plenum. It never arrests investigation by letting it stumble into a void. The substance of repleteness is experienced in the recognition that the more significant things within the focal area of life are inexhaustible and forever engaging since they can never

9.   Patrick Heelan, *Space-Perception and the Philosophy of Science* (Berkeley: University of California Press, 1983), pp. 27–128.

10.   Wilson, "Vicarious and Authenticity."

be fully known. Continuity is of a piece with the trustworthiness of things. In principle, nothing can disappear without a trace since to move one thing is to disturb or displace countless others.

Natural or incidental signs were followed, though not entirely replaced, by conventional or intentional signs. The most influential ones are writings and drawings. They are much more detailed and precise and render farness more intelligible and surveyable. Though they attenuate the distinction between what is near and what is far by more nearly righting the balance between what is known about one's focal area and what is known about the world at large, they underscore the difference between presence and absence through the mode of knowledge that is distinctive of cultural information. Texts, maps, and scores are extremely austere forms of information. To bring them to life requires a reader or performer to draw on skills and experiences that are in turn drawn from the focal area of one's world. Thus cultural information one comes to know gets integrated with one's world, and not only through the vivification that flows from one's focal area into the cultural information but also through the illumination that falls from a truly comprehended text or map on one's immediate world. Still, though integration of information and reality is always accomplished in some way, it does, against the foil of natural information, emerge as an explicit task requiring the special skills of literacy. In a setting of natural information, integration is normally inconspicuous and even automatic—to recognize some natural object as a sign is to know what it means.

Though the integration of cultural information is qualitatively successful in a literate and skilled community, it can easily fail to cope with the available quantity of information. Unlike natural, cultural information can accumulate to the point where integration lags far behind what should be read and known. That was the experience of one of the first literate communities, viz., fifth century B.C.E. Athens, where the quantity of accumulated written laws defied order and surveyability.[11]

There is a second way in which cultural information both undermines and underscores the metric of nearness and farness. In a natural setting, a sign gives some indication of how distant its referent is. Distant smoke indicates a distant fire. Fuzzy tracks show that they have been left days ago.

11. Rosalind Thomas, *Oral Tradition and Written Record in Classical Athens* (Cambridge: Cambridge University Press, 1989), pp. 38–40.

Cultural information, however, has often traversed a zone of concealment or ignorance that extends between the referent and recipient. A letter that has been left at my doorstep does not always indicate by itself how and from where it came. It may have been sent by a stranger via an unknown route. Especially in premodern times, however, and weakly even now, the kind and format of paper and envelope, the stamps, the placement of sender and address indicated and do so today whether the letter came from across the ocean or across town.

There used to be a sort of substantive metric to a scholar's information as well prior to the advent of technological information. It was partly intrinsic to the information and partly varied according to the circumstances of the recipient of the information. Consider the references in an article. Those that used to refer to books or journals in the reader's study were either part of the reader's intimate world or standard works. Spatial nearness connected with intimacy or importance. Conversely, distance to references in the library meant that the information was arcane, foreign to the reader, or unaffordably expensive as was true, for example, of the *Oxford English Dictionary*. Truly recondite information used to have a dimension of socially informed distance as when a librarian had to be consulted. Finally there was a metric (and a topology) not only to determine the distance between reader and information but also to establish distances between kinds of information. The humanities holdings are on the fourth level of the library. Most of Heidegger's works border on the works of other philosophers. Some, however, are grouped under substantive headings such as metaphysics.

These relations are not all of one piece, nor are they systematic. But they have their reasons for being and constitute a rich and intelligible network. All of them, at any rate, melt into the nothing of cyberspace. A hyperlink that takes the place of a reference or note makes a related piece of information appear on my screen the way a bubble rises to the surface of a dark and featureless ocean.

We now have a backdrop to highlight the structure of cyberspace against. As mentioned, cyberspace has no metric. To overcome the extension of time and space has been a powerful tendency since the beginning of modern technology. As Heidegger pointed out in 1950 already, we have been annihilating space and time in earnest through planes, radio, film, and television. Information technology in particular does not so much bring near what is far as it cancels the metric of time and space. Heidegger, Wilson to the contrary, did consider the role technology has had in providing for "communication over vast distances," and concluded, correctly, I believe, that technology does not make present what is distant. "Everything," he says, "gets lumped together into uniform distancelessness."[12]

Where technological resembles cultural information, differences between reality and cyberspace are less stark. Texts and tables that reach me over the Internet are not all that different from the ones that, contained in a book, I bought at the bookstore. Yet cultural information too suffers some of the transformations that distinguish technological information generally. One indication is the disappearance of the traditional scholar's metric that was mentioned earlier.

It is, however, pictorial and acoustic information that most pretends to the presence of what without information technology would remain distant, and it is this sort of information that most clearly exhibits the characteristic features of cyberspace. The break between the topological structure of cyberspace and the metric of reality is concealed by a zone of inscrutability. There is, as noted above, an analogous zone of concealment or ignorance between the origin and the recipient of cultural information. But these screens could be removed by retracing the path a letter, for example, had taken, and lay people have a conception of what such tracking involves. Technical illiteracy today makes it impossible for most people to comprehend what sort of route technological information takes. Just as important, the actual origin of technological information is sometimes untraceable even for experts, and the discovery of a mischievous or criminal manipulator of technological information may require the unwitting cooperation of a careless or reckless culprit. Finally it is noteworthy how concerned we are to remove the last metric traces from our contact with cyberspace. Having to wait for information to be downloaded or having to get up and take five steps to change a television channel subtly reminds us that information is making its way to our screen or needs to be found at some distance from the couch. But any such reminder is thought to be insufferable and eliminated through greater bandwidth connections, more powerful computers, or remote controls.

The lack of repleteness and continuity gives technological information a special sort of underdetermination. Of the variously defined and widely used

12. Martin Heidegger, "The Thing," *in Poetry, Language, Thought* (New York: Harper and Row, 1971), p. 166.

notions of underdetermination, the kind that is relevant here is the failure of some token to have all the properties of its type. Real things can suffer from this kind of underdetermination too. Child of x and y, grandchild of q and r, s, and t are properties or relations any human being has. But I may be ignorant of these as far as my newly arrived colleague is concerned. In fact, however, even your children have properties that are human all too human and are still to be disclosed to you. Real underdetermination, as we may call it, is in principle or in time resolvable and is in any case the mark of a person's inexhaustible richness or, if you are not squeamish about such terms, mysteriousness. It is a richness that works of art and things of nature have in common with persons.

The underdetermination of cyberobjects too is of the kind where a token lacks properties of its type. But in cyberspace this underdetermination is understood to be irremediable. Characters in a soap opera may be more or less shallow, but there is always a level below which there is nothing. It is the genius of soaps to engender the illusion of depth by promising further and further disclosures. But most of us know that the producers are not so much obliging as they are toying with our expectations. Those who do not want this to be true blur the line between the character and the actor to seek in the latter what the former will forever withhold.

The lack of continuity gives technological information a peculiar kind of brittleness. Information in cyberspace fails to have the suppleness and life that the semantic plenum of reality supplies to natural and cultural information and to the presence of real things and persons. Not only was the performance of *Messiah* in St. Paul's replete, it also drew meaning from its surroundings. Similarly, cultural information contained in a story like Norman Maclean's *A River Runs Through It* draws substance from my experiences of nature, of helplessness, and of consolation and in turn casts light on my life in a way that a televised movie, with all the visual and acoustic details already in place, cannot match.[13] Thus a novel, other things being equal, insinuates itself more deeply and widely into our lives than a television presentation.

Turning now from the technical to the ethical sides of telepistemology, we do well to recall the task standard epistemology has set for itself since

---

13.   Norman Maclean, *A River Runs through It and Other Stories* (Chicago: University of Chicago Press, 1976).

Plato—to disabuse the gullible and satisfy the skeptic. Evidently this enterprise has a moral dimension too. To settle for opinion instead of knowledge is reprehensible. But a formal epistemology that explains what knowledge is as such and generally is of uncertain benefit. I am not sure it is illuminating to know what knowing that Stagger Lee shot Billy, knowing that President Nixon resigned from office, and knowing that the universe is expanding have in common. Nor are gullibility or skepticism problems of great urgency in contemporary society. To be sure, people are falling prey to cybershypsters, but fraud comes to our doorstep or through the mail as easily as via electrons. This is not to deny that cyberspace gives traditional epistemological puzzles a new coloration. But the truly vexing telepistemological questions require consideration of the kinds and circumstances of knowledge that are involved in the integration of information.

Integration is second nature in a world of natural information. For cultural information it becomes an explicit task. Why, then, does the integration of technological information seem so unproblematic given its novel and unnatural structure?

In the sciences, the framework for technological information is not so much reality as some model of reality. The model may be limited and concrete as in GIS or abstract and possibly infinite as in mathematics; at least for a Platonist, a mathematical theory or structure is also a model of reality. Moreover, a particular piece of information, though inevitably shallow (i.e., highly underdetermined) and discontinuous with actual reality (i.e., abstract), is in most cases not a reduced version of something that could be more fully explored face to face, but rather is information that can be unsurpassably precious, at least for now, because it could not be had in any other form. Think of the faint traces a distant supernova leaves on a computerized recording device or a mathematical structure that can only be generated on a powerful computer. Obviously there is a continuum between teleobservation, teleoperation, and telerobotics. Some observations are possible only if a distant instrument is guided by an operator; other observations require an instrument to cope flexibly and resourcefully within a distant environment.

Cosmologists look at their models not from Harvard or Cal Tech, but from nowhere. Hence there is sense to the claim that standpoint epistemology is irrelevant, at least to the models of the hard sciences. Thus the privileged circle of nearness that is the origin of life's coordinate system seems not to matter to this kind of integration and its undergirding model. One may conjecture, however, that actual reality still is the school where one learns to see things relating to one another and begins to inhabit a manifold of relations. It is often said that great mathematicians differ from good ones in being more fully at home in a novel or difficult formal domain.

In any case, Wilson's point that technological information has rendered the world brighter and more perspicuous holds for the sciences though not without qualifications. The first is that computer models can have a deceptive and even treacherous perspicuity.[14] The other concerns the price in opaqueness that must be paid for transparency. The more complex computers, programs, data structures, and peripherals become, the less they are intelligible to their users. It is surely a price worth paying, all things considered. But there is in any event a loss. Sherry Turkle quotes this complaint from a physicist at MIT.

My students know more and more about computer reality, but less and less about the real world. And they no longer even really know about computer reality, because the simulations have become so complex that people don't build them anymore. They just buy them and can't get beneath the surface. If the assumptions behind some simulation were flawed, my students wouldn't even know where or how to look for the problem. So I'm afraid that where we are going here is towards *Physics: The Movie*.[15]

The scientific ethos can be trusted however, to recognize and mitigate if not remedy whatever injuries cyberspace may inflict on the sciences. And if this is true, we can continue to count on the fruitful integration of technological information, including teleoperation and telerobotics, into scientific reality.

The mirror image of scientific integration is personal integration in those instances where strong moral bonds connect me to the origin of technological information. When I get a distressed e-mail message from a loved one,

14. Naomi Oreskes, Kristin Shrader-Frechette, and Kenneth Belitz, "Verification, Validation, and Confirmation of Numerical Models in the Earth Sciences," *Science* 263 (4 February 1994): 641–646.

15. Sherry Turkle, *Life on the Screen* (New York: Simon & Schuster, 1995), p. 66.

I am acutely aware not only of the shallowness and discontinuity of the information but also of an underlying real metric. Without calculation or reflection I know that the sender is 4,000 miles away and it will take me a day's air travel to reach her. More generally, in all instances where ties of concern and care connect me to technological information, integration into the focal area of nearness is nearly natural.

But what does integration come to on a day of Christmas week when I have plied myself with the treasures of cyberspace? The first problem that comes to mind concerns the compatibility of the metric space we have evolved and live in and the topological structure of cyberspace that beckons us. Why does it take so little tutoring to teach young or old how to navigate a space without nearness and farness? The answer of course is that the space of imagination and desire has no metric either. Cyberspace promises the best of two worlds—the ease and availability of imagination and the vividness and detail of reality.

A second question concerns people's willingness and even eagerness to enter and remain in cyberspace when time after time one's state of mind upon having left it is surly and depressed. As Kubey and Csikszentmihalyi have shown in the case of television, this is a common experience and worse the longer one's exposure.[16] Tentative results suggest similar consequences for the Internet.[17] There is presumably an evolutionary background to this behavior. In the primal condition of hunting and gathering, humans were well-served by a desire for the calories of sugars and fats. These nourishments were rare and scattered and required skill and effort for their collection and enjoyment. When technological advances made sugar and fat easily and abundantly available, we retained our desires but lost the tempering circumstances. So also with information. In the original setting, the signs of nature were sparsely distributed, and the information they conveyed was

16.   Robert Kubey and Mihaly Csikszentmihalyi, *Television and the Quality of Life* (Hillsdale, N.J.: Erlbaum, 1990).

17.   Robert Kraut, Michael Patterson, Vicki Lundmark, Sara Keisler, Tridas Mukophadhyay, and William Scherlis, "Internet Paradox: A Social Technology That Reduces Social Involvement and Psychological Well-Being?" available at <http://homenet.hcii.cs.cmu.edu/progress/HN.impact.10.htm> (31 August 1998). See, however, Denise Caruso, "Technology: Critics Are Picking Apart a Professor's Study That Linked Internet Use to Loneliness and Depression," *New York Times,* 14 September 1998, p. C5.

precious. Under those circumstances it was in fact natural and beneficial for humans to have, in Wilson's words, an "inexhaustible hunger for visual experience and social exchange."[18] Information was then truly illuminating and entertaining.

Just as physical hunger in premodern times gave rise to stories of plenty, so the desire for information engendered dreams of effortless travel on flying carpets and tales of seeing what was distant in time on the skin of a deer.[19] What Wilson overlooks is that today, when technology daily delivers a surfeit of information, our curiosity has remained, but the competence and attentiveness needed to acquire it have vanished, and so has the kind of nearness that was equal to the information it received in constituting its framework and beneficiary. Symptoms of oversaturation began to surface as soon as there was literacy. Plato famously deplored them, and young Athenian men who were enamored with writings were held up to ridicule.[20] Much later, when a surge of literacy swept eighteenth-century Europe, women were scolded for their "reading madness."[21]

These were isolated phenomena. Today, however, affluence has entirely swamped the contours of the ancestral world and left most of us susceptible to overconsumption of sweets and fats, of information and entertainment. Our habits simply follow the outlines of our technological devices. Daily decisions tend to conform to the conveniences of our surroundings, the television program that lands on our doorstep with the *Times,* the bounty of the refrigerator and the quickness of the microwave oven, the ease of the remote control, and the allure of the world that comes up on the screen.

One might think that the feeling of depression at the end of a long day of television stems from the passive character of one's experience. Interactive connections to cyberspace should then be more fulfilling, especially so when cyberspace appears to be a conduit rather than a cul-de-sac of interaction. To take Wilson's examples, if I teleoperate a race car or perform surgery by

18. Wilson, "Vicarious and Authenticity."

19. For a vision of the future on a deerskin see James Welch, *Fools Crow* (New York: Viking, 1986), pp. 353–358.

20. Eric A. Havelock, *Preface to Plato* (Cambridge: Harvard University Press, 1963), pp. 38–41.

21. Dominik von König, "Lesesucht und Lesewut," in *Buch und Leser,* ed. Hebert G. Göpfert (Hamburg: Hauswedell, 1977), pp. 62–75.

way of teleoperation, is not my presence at the obstacle course or the operating table mediated rather than blocked by cyberspace?[22]

It is more accurate to say that in cases like these a severely limited and hence shallow and discontinuous piece is wrested from reality and attached to cyberspace. To see the narrow limits of these two regions of reality, imagine that, as I teleoperationally drive my car along the course, I happen to see an actual driver lying unconsciously next to his burning car. I can stop and see, but I cannot get out of my car and drag my colleague to safety. Or suppose that I perform eye surgery by way of teleoperation and suddenly my patient seems to suffer a heart attack. There is very little under the circumstances that I can do to examine my patient and less to resuscitate him.

Progress in information technology can of course extend the limits of continuity and the depth of repleteness. But there are in all cases insurmountable barriers to my mediated authority and resourcefulness. Assume counterfactually that my cyberproxy can do or be everything I can do or be for someone. The proxy would then have to have all the properties I have and thus by Leibniz's law would be identical with me.

This consideration brings us face to face with the moral quandaries of cyberspace. Persons in cyberspace who are absolutely underdetermined and thus only ambiguously present can have a charm all their own. Friends or lovers who are indigenous to cyberspace must remain unknown as to their actual character and existence. Yet it is precisely such vaporous outlines that allow my desire to fill in the details. In such cases, discontinuity is a firewall against unwelcome claims on my time or energy; shallowness is a guarantee that neither weakness nor darkness will be discovered in the depths of a person's character. The charms of these limitations is so alluring that we take pleasure in seeing a person whom we know directly submit to it. Deborah Tannen has written of a socially handicapped and tongue-tied colleague who on e-mail turned into a sensitive and self-revealing soulmate.[23] David Bennahum saw a nerdy graduate student metamorphose into an alluring woman on a Multiuser Domain.[24] Conversely, as Sherry Turkle reports, a certain Peter was crushed when he encountered the actual woman behind the semivirtual Beatrice. In cyberspace, he said, "I saw in her what I wanted

22. Wilson, "Vicarious and Authenticity."

23. Deborah Tannen, "Gender Gap in Cyberspace," *Newsweek,* 16 May 1994, p. 52.

24. David Bennahum, "Fly Me to the MOO," *Lingua Franca,* May/June 1994, p. 24.

to see. Real life gave me too much information."[25] Businesslike e-mail too has a commodifying effect on human relations. E-mail messages do not intrude unbeckoned into my actual life. I read them when I like and respond to them at my leisure.

A common defense of cyberspace has it that information technology is a mere means, that its moral charge is nil, and that the value of entering cyberspace depends on one's ends. A corollary of this point is to the effect that the ethical significance of information technology is determined by content. This defense goes along with a rational choice conception of the users' behavior. But there is something misleadingly abstract in imagining that some two hundred million U.S. citizens contemplate their options every evening—reading, exercising, going to a play or concert, making music, painting, wood working, watching television, etc.—and that the vast majority happens to decide evening after evening that all things considered television will maximize their satisfaction.

It seems more likely that the form and availability of television conduce to staying at home and watching. Since cyberspace, television included, has no metric, no steps need to be taken to enter and move around in cyberspace. There appears to be an inverse relation between threshold and enjoyment of contemporary culture. The threshold between home and cyberspace is low and smooth. Thus our native curiosity easily draws us into cyberspace or television. Having entered on terms of ease and curiosity, we favor programs that entertain without demanding application or self-discipline. The form prejudges the content. Moreover, the contents of cyberspace are varied and polished while the content of reality seems poor and homely in comparison. Discontinuity and a topology without metric allow many different contents to be available all at once, and it is shallowness that allows technological information to be polished to perfection within the narrow confines of repleteness. Yet being at length oversaturated with information that has failed to fit the focal area of our lives and our gifts of body and mind, we feel dejected and depressed.

Conversely, the effort to gather our loved ones for a common enterprise and to get out of the house seems forbidding. In reality one thing is so many miles from another. Three hundred years ago no one would have thought of setting out from the Watchung ridge to a noonday service in downtown

25. Turkle, p. 207.

Manhattan. Modern transportation has shrunk distance, yet travel is still travail. But then it discloses to us the terrible contrast of stretches of rusty wasteland and the sleekness of the World Trade Center, the affluence of the tony New Jersey suburbs and the dirty drabness of poor residential areas.

Actual performances have blemishes, to be sure. Still, surrounded by many hundreds of listeners, our attention is concentrated on the commanding presence of the music. The musicians are persons with lives that grow out of an intelligible context and extend into it. We are graced with a moment of community and inspiration and leave with at least an awareness of the tensions between poor and rich, new and old, with a sense of where and how such tensions are resolvable in celebration, and perhaps with more resolve to contribute to a solution.

If we lead a life of physical vigor and of dedication to the culture of the table, we can cope with the temptations of french fries and ice cream. Prohibitions have been notably ineffective when it comes to sugars and fats. So also with information. Engagement in the focal area of natural information gives us a sense of perspective, and the realization of cultural information, for example, in reading poetry or playing music, lends our lives vigor and wealth. Given a mooring in reality and devotion to focal things and practices, technological information of the entertaining kind will find its proper level.

As the example at the beginning of this piece suggests, the deliberations we entertain with ourselves and each other about what to do on a day of Christmas week are a web of special pleading, of hoping against hope, and of doubling down when hopes are disappointed. What little discussion of such behavior there is in the national conversation amounts as a rule to no more than hand-wringing or bemused resignation. We sense that the common customs of television watching and netsurfing present us with a moral problem that eludes our moral categories. Is it a sin or a crime to watch three hours of television a day? Getting this problem on the national agenda and offering helpful distinctions and terms is one of the hard and urgent tasks of telepistemology.

6

Acting at a Distance and Knowing from Afar: Agency and Knowledge on the Internet

Jeff Malpas

I

In the terms in which it is often presented in the popular media, as well as in some more academic discussions, the technology of the Internet seems to offer the possibility of almost magical access to information and experiences, to possibilities for action, even to different identities, almost anywhere on the globe with nothing more than a few keystrokes or the click of a mouse.[1] Equipped with nothing more than a computer and a modem, we can, so the hype would have it, travel the world from New York to London, Tokyo to Cairo without leaving home—and in much less time than it takes to watch an episode of Star Trek. In these respects, the Internet seems to offer the possibility of a form of access to the world that is not constrained in any essential way by distance nor fundamentally tied to location. Knowledge is revealed as a commodity ("information") that, given the appropriate technology, can be made available anywhere at any time, while the question of the veridicality and the reliability of knowledge turns out to be fundamentally a question of the reliability of the technology that makes such knowledge possible and of the sources to which that technology enables access.

Although the technology of the Internet is new, the image of knowledge, and of our access to the world, that the Internet seems to project can be seen as already integral to much modern epistemology. For the most part, epistemological thinking has viewed the question of our access to the world as a matter that can be addressed independently of our concrete location (indeed, such locatedness is part of what is put in question) and that is properly taken up through an inquiry into the justificatory grounds of knowledge. Location and distance have thus been seen as contingent constraints on knowledge, rather than as having any essential connection with knowledge as such. In this respect, the ideas set out in René Descartes's *Meditations* (first published in 1641) provides a useful illustration of the character of much modern epistemological inquiry. Although Descartes famously presents the *Meditations* from within a particular setting—a small heated room in which he writes alone—the questions concerning knowledge that Descartes raises are presented as arising independently of the actual circumstances in which Descartes, as knowing subject, might be

1. This chapter was completed during a period as a Humboldt Research Fellow at the University of Heidelberg and I gratefully acknowledge the support of the Alexander von Humboldt Foundation.

located, and they are supposedly resolved through consideration of the nature of Descartes's own subjectivity in separation from his surroundings and from any capacity for agency that he might have in relation to those surroundings.

The image of knowledge, and of our access to the world, that is projected by the Internet can thus be viewed as a continuation, perhaps even an exemplification, of a set of ideas that lie at the heart of modern epistemological thinking (and this is so in spite of the "postmodern" rhetoric that surrounds much contemporary discussion of the Internet). Yet inasmuch as the image at stake here is one that severs knowledge from any essential connection to place, viewing knowledge as abstract and informational in character, and that also treats our access to the world as similarly "detached," so this image is one that is highly problematic. Indeed, if we examine the phenomenon of the Internet more carefully, what becomes evident is that, far from being detached from location, knowledge, even in the context of the Internet, is fundamentally tied to place and to our active engagement in place. In this respect, the example of Internet technology, as it can be viewed as a continuation of a certain epistemological mode of thinking, can also be deployed to exhibit the limitations of that mode of thinking. In the process, not only will the character of our access to the world, as both knowers and agents, be clarified, but so will the character of that particular kind of action and knowledge at a distance that is possible by means of the Internet also be illuminated.

II

In the graphic terms suggested by Descartes's account in the *Mediations,* knowledge, and so our relation to the world in general, arises as a problem in virtue of our imprisonment in the enclosed space of the mind—a space analogous to the room in which the *Meditations* are themselves presented as being composed. Although Descartes does raise certain important questions concerning our knowledge of what lies within the space of the mind, much of his investigation focuses on the problem of how we are to find justification for the beliefs we have about what lies outside of that space—just as Descartes might similarly ask how he can justify his beliefs about what lies beyond the four walls of the room in which he writes. The problems at issue here are, on the Cartesian account, analogous, and the problem of justification when applied to knowledge as a whole is thus no different from the problem of justification when applied to individual beliefs.

On this Cartesian model, then, the way in which we relate to the world as a whole is understood in terms of the way we relate to the world in one particular respect—our relation to the world as a whole is understood in terms of our relation to the world as believers or *theorizers*. Since it is the purely evidential basis of knowledge that is at issue here, so this way of thinking about our relation to the world as fundamentally an epistemic relation, abstracts both from our concrete location in the world as well as from our active involvement with things—rather than being already engaged in the world, we find ourselves situated apart from it. This is not to say that we are *causally* separated from the world, nor that the causal processes on which knowledge is based are necessarily irrelevant to the problem of justification. Indeed, from a perspective that can be seen as derivative of the work of the philosopher John Locke (whose epistemological treatise, *An Essay Concerning Human Understanding* first appeared in 1690), the problem of epistemic justification can be seen as precisely a matter of matter of tracing out the causal processes on which knowledge is based or of identifying some particular element within those processes ("ideas," "sense data," "information") as having a special evidential role. The point is thus not to ignore our causal entanglement in the world, but rather to emphasize the problem of our relation to the world as a problem concerning a particular sort of evidential justification and so to give priority to a certain detached, "theoretical" conception of knowledge as well as a view of agency grounded in this conception.

The basic image that seems to dominate this way of thinking—an image that, in spite of other differences, dominates the thinking of Locke no less than Descartes—is an image of ourselves as somehow located "inside" the skull and causally connected to the "outside" world by means of our senses[2] (thus Locke talks of the way that the senses and nerves convey ideas "from without to their audience in the Brain, the Mind's Presence-room"[3]). It is as

2.   Although one of the differences between a Cartesian and Lockean view here is that Descartes would also insist on the way in which we also have a fundamental form of access to the world by means of certain "innate" ideas—something emphatically denied by Locke.

3.   *An Essay Concerning Human Understanding,* Book II, Chapter III, §1; see also book II, chapter 11, §17, in which Locke likens the mind to the "dark Room" of a camera obscura.

if, to update the image from the *Meditations,* each of us was locked within a single, solitary cell and connected to the world beyond by nothing more than a combination of video, audio and other information systems, coupled, perhaps, with some device for remote manipulation. On such a model we are, as suggested above, *causally connected* to the world, while also being *epistemically separated* from it; moreover, our sensory and cognitive access to the world is viewed as analogous to the sort of access to things otherwise removed from us that is gained by artificial means (whether by some optical, electronic or other device) and according to which our capacity for action is grounded in such a "mediated" access. From the point of view of this Cartesian-Lockean model of knowledge, the technology of the Internet can be seen as simply expanding our capacities for knowledge in a way that is continuous with the capacities that we already possess. Moreover, inasmuch as one might conceive of our access to the world as always a mediated access that is no different in kind from the mediated, but extended, access that is offered by Internet technology (in this respect it might be supposed that there is no essential difference between knowledge or information as mediated by our "in-built" perceptual capacities or by such capacities when artificially extended and enhanced), so one might even view the Internet as presenting a sort of "purified" exemplification of our more general epistemic situation.

The "detached" conception of knowledge that can be found in Descartes and Locke is a persuasive and enormously influential one—all the more so, perhaps, when it is viewed in relation to the technology of the Internet. It is all too easy, however, to be misled both by the model of knowledge that is at issue here and by the expanded capacities that the Internet may at first sight seem to offer. Indeed, when we look more closely at the nature of our interaction with Internet technology—at the character of our concrete engagement with that technology—not only does it become apparent that the technology itself is much more constrained and constraining than may at first be evident, but the nature of the interaction at issue brings to light certain important constraints on the nature of knowledge also—constraints that indicate how fundamentally misguided is the Cartesian-Lockean model of knowing and that also illuminate the place-bound character of knowledge and its relation to agency.

III

So far as the actual technology is concerned, one of the first points that ought to be emphasized is that, for the most part, the Internet provides nothing like the sort of magical access to things across distance that it may at first seem to promise. For most of us, indeed, there is a sharp contrast between the reality of the Internet and the rhetoric that surrounds it. Once the initial excitement has worn off (and sometimes the excitement is quite short-lived) the experience of the average Internet user is probably best characterized by a mixture of tedium and frustration interspersed with occasional success—pages that take up to a minute (or more) to load, pages that fail to load or load only partially, connections that break down, locations that turn out to be inaccessible or that fail to supply the information sought, commands that seem to take an eternity to be implemented. Even the user who possesses a state-of-the-art machine is still subject to the delays and problems that are generated by the technology itself—problems and delays that arise, for instance, as a result of the sheer physical limits on transfer of information. Sometimes it can seem that what is gained through the capacity to access a world-wide system of information is lost simply through the time that it takes to find one's way through it.

The technology of the Internet is, of course, a developing technology, and one that is, for all the hype, still in a relatively early phase. One can certainly expect that many of its current limitations will be overcome as the technology develops further. Technological development is misunderstood, however, if it is viewed as a process in which limitations are progressively and inevitably overcome in some move toward technological perfection. Like the history of evolutionary development in biology, the history of technological change is a history of *changing limitations and adaptations* rather than of the *abolishing of constraint.* This is, in itself, indicative of an important feature, not only of technology, but also of human knowledge and agency as such[4]—although the social and technological context in which knowledge and agency are possible may change, and the concrete forms in which knowledge and agency are actualized may also change, still the basic constraints that derive from our basic situation as knowers and actors remain unaffected by

4. For a discussion of the inevitable limitation of any technological project—and, indeed, of any project as such—see Jeff Malpas and Gary Wickham, "Governance and the World: From Joe Di-Maggio to Michel Foucault," *UTS Review* 3 (1997): 91–108.

such changers. Changes in technology most often bring a change in the form in which knowledge in realized, but such changes do not change the basic conditions that both limit knowledge and agency as well as making them possible.

In the case of the Internet, the constraining of distance, although modified by the new technology, is not done away with. Not only does distance remain a salient feature of our Internet-based interaction through its effect on the delays it induces in the transmission of information, but the very nature of our access to things through the mediation of the Internet is one in which the things to which we have access remain distant from us. Here it is important to attend to the way in which Internet technology offers access to things across only a narrow band of possible modes of interaction. Our sensory engagement with the Internet, and the objects it presents, is, for instance, primarily a visual engagement (though it is sometimes augmented, in certain limited respects, by the auditory and perhaps also, given certain new developments, by the tactile) and is quite different from the character of our ordinary sensory engagement with the things around us. Similarly, even though we may be capable of certain capacities for action over the Internet, through the combination of certain monitoring and tele-robotic devices, that capacity is a limited one that in no way replicates our ordinary capacities for action in our own person and within our immediate surroundings.

Indeed, although we may talk of the phenomenon of "telepresence" to indicate a sense in which the Internet can enable distant things to be brought near to us, such a "bringing near" invariably suffers from a certain "attenuation" in the interaction it makes possible (certainly this is so with respect to current technology—the question of whether such attenuation might be overcome by future "virtual reality" technologies is something I consider below). Things may be brought near visually, though a computer screen, through a mouse, through a set of speakers, but the things are not brought "near" in the way that the computer screen, the mouse, or the set of speakers are themselves near. For an Internet user sitting at her keyboard, the keyboard, along with the computer screen and all the other equipment in her immediate vicinity, is present to her—is *there*—in a way that what is presented on the computer screen is not. Unlike the things on screen, the keyboard and the computer are present as things in all their complexity and solidity—they can be touched, smelt and heard; their weight and mass, their resistance to being moved, can be felt; their relative positioning in relation to one another, to other things in the room, to the room itself, is all evident at a glance; the keyboard can be used to type commands or as a precarious resting place for papers; the screen can serve as a window on information or as a rough mirror with which to check one's appearance.

One way of capturing the difference at issue here is to say that what the computer presents remains merely a "presentation" or better a "re-presentation." The objects present on the screen are not present as the objects that they are, but merely as re-presentations of those objects—in the same way as the stretch of landscape that appears in a picture hanging on a wall is there, not primarily as a *landscape,* but as a *picture* of a landscape (although, being used to the phenomenon of pictorial representation, I may still, to some extent, think of the pictured landscape *as if* it were real). In contrast, the picture itself is there as a picture, and similarly the computer screen is there as a computer screen, not merely a representation of one. Whether something is present to us as the thing that it is or as a representation of that thing, no matter the form of the representation, makes an obvious difference to how we can interact with that thing. We view representations of things differently from the things themselves, and representations require a different mode of interaction from the mode of interaction that might be called up by the represented thing itself. We interact with maps, for instance, very differently from the way in which we interact with the countryside the map represents (indeed, the fact that the map is a representation is important in enabling us to use the map to provide knowledge about the countryside). Perhaps more important, however, is the fact that the way we are engaged in the world is not primarily through interacting with *representations,* but rather through interaction with the *concrete things* that are present to us as part of the place—the "there"—in which we find ourselves.

This is, in fact, one of the problems with the Cartesian-Lockean picture of knowledge that I sketched above. It is not that representations cannot serve to provide knowledge—such a claim would be absurd—but rather that we cannot treat our fundamental access to the world in representational terms. This means, moreover, that if we think of our fundamental relation to the world in terms of our having knowledge of the world, then we cannot think of the knowledge at issue as representational either. Yet in presenting our relation to the world as analogous to the mediated relation to things that is exemplified, in contemporary terms, in remote video, audio, or telerobotic access, the Cartesian-Lockean picture treats our relation to the world as one based essentially in a form of representational access—though it is an access mediated by means of mental states such as beliefs rather than video images—an access that is given through our having access to things as they are represented by means of other things rather than to the immediately presented things themselves. In this respect, moreover, the Cartesian-Lockean approach proceeds by taking a particular feature or aspect of our epistemic situation as the basis for understanding our epistemic situation in general. Just as it treats the relation between particular knowledge claims and their evidential basis as the model for the overall relation between knowledge and the world, so it takes that particular way of relating to things that arises in connection with certain forms of mediated or representational access as the basis for understanding our relation to the world as such.

To treat our interaction with things in general on the model of the mediated interaction with things that is possible by means of the technology associated with the Web is to misunderstand the way in which our engagement in the world is first and foremost an engagement with what is physically and immediately present to us and is, in this respect, not representational at all. In fact, our capacity to interact with some mediately represented thing is itself based in our capacity to interact with the immediate physical thing by means of which the representation is given to us—the capacity to engage with some representation of a landscape, for example, is based in my capacity to interact with the physical object that is the picture of that landscape (and so with a certain culturally conditioned object or, as it might also be characterized, with a particular physical surface that reflects or absorbs light according to a certain pattern). In the same way, my engagement with things across the Internet, even if it is an engagement that allows me see the things with which I interact by remote video and to manipulate those things by means of some telerobotic system, remains an engagement that is first and foremost with the keyboard, mouse, screen and other devices immediately before me and the nature of this engagement is not properly analyzable in mediated representational terms.

This latter fact is often obscured by our tendency to look, not to the medium by means of which interaction is possible, but rather to the objects to which that medium gives us access. Indeed this sort of projection "through" a medium is undoubtedly important in enabling any sort of sophisticated operation by means of such a medium—the medium has to "disappear" if the user is to be able properly to interact with and to manipulate the objects it presents. But while I can certainly project myself toward the objects that are presented to me through some medium in such a way that I cease to notice the representational character of their presentation, such projection is itself possible only to the extent that I have mastered the medium itself and the devices on which it depends (it is true, more generally, of any "prosthesis" that its successful operation depends on it being "incorporated" into the user in such a way that the user ceases to notice it as a prosthesis). Interaction with representations as if, in some sense, they were not representations, is thereby dependent on our capacity to interact with the immediately presented things in our surrounding environment—grasp of the reality of some distant, represented object is indeed parasitic on the grasp, even if it often goes unrecognized, of things close to us. Indeed, the very nature of representation is that it always requires some other object through which the representation is given, but which object is not itself grasped representationally.

IV

Any "representational" or mediated engagement with things brings with it, as I noted above, a certain attenuation in engagement compared to our ordinary involvement with the things around us. What is presented to us in the mediated presentation available via the Internet, for instance, is much more restricted in terms of its availability to us—whether in terms of the limitations on its sensory availability or its accessibility to action. It might be objected, however, that any such talk of an "attenuated" form of interaction, particularly with respect to the Internet, completely ignores the way in which Internet technology actually enables forms of interaction that are otherwise not possible at all—in some respects, then, the Internet may limit engagement with things, but in certain other respects it actually extends the possibilities for such engagement. Imagine an internet link to a fiber optic video system that enables us to examine a distant object at a level of detail that would be impossible to the naked eye. Here the capacity for engagement with the object, at least in one respect, has been enhanced, rather than attenuated, by the video and other technologies associated with the Internet. Yet although Internet technology can indeed enhance our capacities for engagement, such enhancement is inevitably restricted in scope and comes at the cost of a greater attenuation in our capacities for engagement elsewhere.

It is important to recognize that the restricted enhancement that Internet technology may be viewed as enabling is possible precisely because of the otherwise attenuated character of the mediated access that is involved. While the technology associated with the Internet, or indeed, any technology that allows a similar mediated access to things, depends on the integrated, place-bound character of our involvement in the world—it depends on our capacity to interact with things across a range of dimensions within our immediate surroundings—such technologies also enable access to objects in a way that "detaches" objects from such location and allows them to be grasped in a similarly "detached" fashion. Within such a mediated form of access, we no longer need to engage with things in their full immediacy or with the full range of our perceptual and behavioral capacities—we can focus our attention on specific aspects of things as they relate to specific capacities of our own. In this way, we are able to achieve a significant enhancement in our access to things in certain particular respects, but in a way that necessarily brings with it a reduction in the overall range of our capacities for engagement.

It might be thought, however, that the Internet is still being viewed here in too limited a fashion. One of the classics of cyberpunk fiction, William Gibson's *Neuromancer* (published in 1989) presents a view of an electronically generated reality that is experienced as if it were real—surely, in combination with the Internet, such technologies might enable engagement with things at a distance without any attenuation in the nature of that engagement. Now it seems to me that there is a certain tendency here to overestimate the capacities of virtual reality technology—certainly in its current form it remains subject to much the same sort of attenuation in experience and engagement that is characteristic of the Internet and other forms of extended artificial engagement, while the idea of a complete simulation of experience by electronic means seems also to depend on some highly controversial assumptions regarding the nature of mind, and of action and experience. But even supposing that it were possible to enable a form of engagement that was identical, in all relevant respects, to our ordinary, immediate engagement with things, and yet enabled interaction with things remote from our ordinary embodied location, still such a possibility need not count against the sorts of considerations that I have been advancing here.

Here it is crucial that the central issues that are at stake be kept clearly in focus and those issues are not primarily to do with what might be technological possible now or in the future. The focus of my discussion has been the contrast between representational or mediated forms of access, forms of access that always bring a certain attenuation with them, and those immediate forms of access that are characteristic of our involvement with our proximate environment. The claim I have been advancing here is that not only are these distinct forms of access or engagement, but that mediated, representational forms of access can neither be taken as a model for our access to the world in general nor can they be understood other than as always dependent on immediate, nonrepresentational forms of access and engagement. Inasmuch as the Internet, in the only forms with which we are familiar, provides only for mediated, representationally dependent modes of action and knowledge—modes that do indeed enable action and knowledge *at a distance*—so the Internet must be seen as subject to just these limitations. One might envisage a form of "Internet technology" that is no longer bound to such mediated forms of action and knowledge, but not only might we wonder about the sense in which such a technology should indeed be viewed as continuous, in any significant sense, with the technology of the Internet as it is currently understood, but it would provide no counterexample to my claims concerning the attenuated or limited character of the mediated access that is characteristic of current Internet technology.

It is not so much the technology that is important here, then, so much as the different forms of engagement that different technologies enable and the way in which those forms of engagement bring certain limitations with them (limitations that, at least in the case of Internet technology, often seem ignored). Not all access to the world that depends on technological devices is a mediated access—the hearing aid is one of the simplest examples of this—but all mediated access does indeed depend on the intervention of technological devices. Moreover all such mediated access is essentially secondary to access that is unmediated and nonrepresentational. The gulf between the Internet technology of today and the imagined technologies of the future is thus not merely a difference in technology but between two different modes on access and engagement with the world. If a technology could be developed that allowed us to be electronically "re-embodied" in some place far distant from our bodies of flesh-and-bone, to be "re-embodied" in such a way that we grasped that distant place as no longer distant, but rather as the immediate place of action and experience, then we would have a technology that enabled, not so much a mediated action or knowledge *at a distance,* but transportation and re-embodiment over distance so as to enable immediate action and knowledge *at a place.* Such a technology would only reaffirm the dependence of knowledge and agency on our immediate, embodied location, even though it would also undermine the idea that such embodied location could be unhesitatingly identified with the location of some particular structure of flesh and bone.[5]

V

It is the mediated, representational, and also attenuated, engagement that is characteristic of contemporary Internet technology that is, then, the main focus for my discussion here. Such a mode of engagement must always be viewed as a more restricted and derivative form of engagement than our ordinary engagement with things in our proximate environment. One important consequence of the more limited, even if sometimes partially enhanced, character of our engagement with things by means of the Internet is that the knowledge that is arrived at in this fashion is likely to be viewed differently, particularly in terms of its reliability, than is knowledge arrived in more direct or immediate fashion (in this respect, the sort of knowledge the Internet enables might be viewed as a variety of knowledge at "second hand" and as subject to similar limitations). That this is so, of course, is partly a reflection of our recognition that the very same technology that allows easy access to information also enables its ready manipulation and falsification. Yet the relative ease with which the Internet can be used to deceive or mislead is itself a function of the attenuated and mediated character of Internet-based interaction. The fact that our involvement with the Internet is somewhat "detached" from our ordinary involvement with things (even though such detachment may be accompanied by a concentration of attention or "immersion" in events "on-screen"), may lead to an additional tendency to view the knowledge and information the Internet may deliver in a more ambiguous light—to be much readier to reject it or to

5.   Whether such a scenario as imagined here (and that is the staple of much of the Cyberpunk literature) is really consistent with human psychology or, more fundamentally, with the basic nature of human being, is an important question, but not one that I can even begin to address in these pages.

give it less weight than knowledge or information received from other sources.

The difference in the way in which we may view Internet-based knowledge as compared with knowledge based in a more immediate involvement with things, is indicative, once again, of the underlying difference between the form of proximate engagement possible in relation to our immediate surroundings and the form of engagement at a distance possible by means of the Internet. The difference at issue here is one that can never be completely overcome by the technology of the Internet—at least, not so long as it remains a technology geared to enabling action and knowledge at a distance. Moreover, since it is our involvement with things close to us that is prior here—the mediated engagement characteristic of the Internet is itself dependent on the immediate engagement characteristic of our relation to things in our proximate surroundings—so it is a mistake to view our basic access to the world as if it were analogous to the mediated, representational access available via the Internet. For this reason, if no other, the Cartesian-Lockean view of knowledge, as I noted above, has to be rejected. This does not mean simply that we cannot treat our relation to the world in terms of the analogy with the room-bound knower connected to the outside by some combination of video, telerobotic, and other systems. The "theoretical" conception of knowledge that views knowledge as separated from agency and from location, and that treats knowledge, in general, as standing to the world as theory stands to its evidential basis, itself depends essentially on a view of our basic relation to the world as a mediated or representational one. On such an account, we have no immediate access to the world, but only to the contents of our own minds—to beliefs or other such attitudes or states. Our access to the things in our immediate environment, however, while it may certainly be *described* using the language of attitudes and states, is not essentially a form of access that is mediated by means of such attitudes, states or any other "representation."

Indeed, the very idea of some attitude or state as having a certain content—say the belief that my teacup is empty as having the content "my teacup is empty"—itself depends (as some of the previous discussion should have indicated) on the person to whom that state or attitude belongs being already appropriately related to the world and so to their being already related to things within their immediate location. That the having of content does indeed depend on such a prior relation to the world, and so on location, is, in part, a consequence of the holistic character of attitudinal content. Beliefs and other attitudes do not come singly, but only as elements within larger systems of such attitudes. Moreover, they also stand in a necessary relation to behavior, both linguistic and nonlinguistic. To have a particular belief about the teacup on the desk, then, is to have beliefs about, among many other things, teacups and desks in general; it is to make be capable of making meaningful utterances about those things; it is to be capable of orienting oneself in relation to the *place* in which the teacup and desk are supposedly located. The *holistic* character of attitudinal content is, in this respect, directly implicated with content as *externalist*—that is, with content as determined, not only by systems of attitudes, but also by the objects and events to which those attitudes are causally, and therefore also "intentionally" related. But the holistic and externalist character of content also means that the possibility of content, and so the possibility of contentful attitudes, is fundamentally tied to the agent's concrete locatedness in, and access to, the world, and so to their immediate engagement with things in their proximate surroundings.[6]

No attitude (in particular no belief) nor any representational mental state can provide a means of access to the world, then, since the content of any attitude or state itself depends on such access as already given and on a prior locatedness within the world. This is, one might say, the more general epistemological correlate of the fact that the Internet can give us no access to things at all except inasmuch as we already have access to what is closest to us. On this basis, there can be no question of trying to find some justificatory ground for knowledge through trying to establish a relation between knowledge understood as a body of theoretical claims and some evidential base. Although there are certain problems attaching to the very attempt to think of knowledge in its generality (problems that arise regardless of whether or not we wish to defend knowledge or to question it), if we do think of knowledge in this way at all, then we must already be committed to accepting

---

6. The externalist and holistic character of content, and the necessary dependence of content on location, is perhaps most clearly evident when we look to the structures on which interpretation and communication are based—the attribution of attitudes that is part of any such interpretive or communicative interaction is necessarily dependent on being able to locate speakers (and that includes ourselves) in relation to the events and objects in the world to which they are immediately related see my *Place and Experience* (Cambridge: Cambridge University Press, 1999), esp. chapters 3 and 4.

that the claims in which such knowledge is held to consist must, "for the most part," be true—that they are mostly true is a necessary presupposition of them having content and so of them being claims whose truth can even be put in doubt. Such a conclusion can be viewed as a simple demonstration of the mistake that is made when we try to view our relation to the world in primarily "theoretical" or "representational" terms; it can be viewed as equally indicative of the error in trying to treat the question of evidential justification as one that can be applied to knowledge "in its generality." Asking after the evidential grounds of knowledge makes sense when directed toward particular knowledge claims, but makes no sense at all when extended to every such claim.

VI

If there is a general epistemological "problem of knowledge," then it is a problem largely resolved, or perhaps "dissolved," through coming to understand the way in which knowledge is indeed ontologically grounded in our active engagement in place, that is, in terms of our immediate interaction with the things (and other persons) encountered close to us. In fact, one might say that what comes first here is neither the idea of ourselves as agents nor the idea of the worldly things that we act upon. What comes first is the idea of the *place*—that "space of nearness"—within which both we and the objects of our engagement are situated.[7] This emphasis on the way in knowledge, in particular, is grounded in our immediate location is a central theme in Chinese Daoist thinking, and is nicely illustrated by a story from the Daoist classic, the *Zhuangzi:*

Zhuangzi and Hui Shi were strolling across the bridge over the Hao River. Zhuangzi observed, "The minnows swim out and about as they please—this is the way they enjoy themselves." Hui replied, "You are not a fish—how do you know what they enjoy?" Zhuanzi returned, "You are not me—how do you know that I don't know what is enjoyable for the fish?" Huizi said "I am not you, so I certainly don't know what you know, but it follows that, since you are certainly not the fish, you don't

---

7. This is one of the central conclusions of my *Place and Experience,* see esp. chapters 6 and 7. Of course, the notion of place that is at issue here, while it encompasses the concepts of both agent and environment, should not be viewed as somehow prior to the agent or the environment in the sense that it could exist in the absence of either of these.

know what is enjoyment for the fish either." Zhuangzi said, "Let's get back to your basic question. When you asked 'How do you know what the fish enjoy?' you already knew that I know what the fish enjoy, or you wouldn't have asked me. I know it *from here* above the Hao River."[8]

Only from "here," the place where we are, is knowledge at all possible. The example of knowledge as it arises in relation to the technology of the Internet, while it may initially appear to provide a striking instantiation of the way in which knowledge, and even action, may be severed from any such proximal location, actually serves, on closer examination, to demonstrate the impossibility of any such separation. Thus, rather than enabling us to envisage the possibility of the overcoming of the place-bound character of knowledge and agency, and so the abolishing of distance, the character of our involvement with the Internet leads us to affirm the same conclusion that Zhuangzi asserts, from the bridge above the Hao River, namely that knowledge is inextricably bound to the place of our immediate and proximal engagement with things.

8.   *Zhuangzi* 45/17/87.

7

Telerobotic Knowledge: A Reliabilist Approach

Alvin Goldman

1. Knowledge, Reliability, and Causal Processes

Questions about knowledge have occupied philosophers since the ancient Greeks, but recent advances in telecommunications make them more pressing than ever. The Internet, especially when coupled with telerobotic devices that allow us to observe and even to act on distant objects, provides a wealth of information about distant environments. But do these technologies provide us with *knowledge*? This is the central question of what has been termed *telepistemology*—the study of traditional epistemological questions as they are raised and revisited by developments in telecommunications technology. The answer depends on what knowledge is—on what conditions must obtain if a person is to know something.

What is knowledge? More specifically, what is propositional knowledge? A proposition p is the content of a declarative statement, what is expressed by a sentence like "the sun is shining" or "we had omelets for breakfast." One cannot know that p is true unless it *is* true. So a necessary condition for knowledge is truth. Equally, you cannot know that p unless you are of the opinion that p is true: unless you believe that p. So belief, like truth, is necessary. But true belief is not sufficient for knowledge, at least not in the strict sense of 'know'. If it is just accidental that you are right about p, then you do not know that p, even if you are correct in believing it.

Suppose you wake up in a good mood one morning and in a fit of optimism you think to yourself, "A marigold just sprouted in Linz, Austria." Your belief might very well be true. There is a small garden in the Ars Electronica Center in Linz, and marigolds sprout there fairly frequently. Now suppose that at the moment you have your thought, a marigold has just sprouted in that garden. In this case, you turn out to be right—a marigold really did just sprout in Linz. But it does not follow that you know a marigold just sprouted in Linz. It was just a fluke if such a feeling is right, and flukes are not sufficient for knowledge. Thus, not all true beliefs qualify as knowledge.

What true beliefs do qualify as knowledge? A first factor to consider about knowledge is a *causal* factor. Whether a true belief is knowledge depends on why the belief is held, on the psychological processes that cause the belief or sustain it in the mind. This is illustrated by the Linz marigold

Portions of this chapter appeared in Alvin Goldman, *Epistemology and Cognition* (Cambridge, Mass: Harvard University Press, 1986).

example. In that example the only cause of the belief is your good mood, which produces a cheery belief. But this kind of cause is not adequate for knowledge. If we change the cause, the same belief could qualify as knowledge. Suppose you get a call from a trusted friend living in Linz who tells you that she has just seen a marigold sprouting in the Ars Electronica Center lobby. You believe as before—that a marigold just sprouted in Linz—but now you *know* it (assuming, at any rate, that things are as reported). In this variation, the cause of your belief is suitable for knowledge.[1]

The next question to ask is: What makes a cause, or causal process, the right kind of process for producing knowledge? What distinguishes knowledge-producing causes from other causes? Why isn't a feeling, or mood, an appropriate kind of cause? The natural answer seems to be: because belief based on mere feelings, or moods, can easily go wrong. It would be easy to be in a good mood if it were not the case that a marigold just sprouted in Linz. So if a belief gets formed in this fashion, it has a good chance of being false. The belief does not qualify as knowledge—even if it happens to be true—because the style of belief production is error-prone, or unreliable. If, however, the belief-producing process is reliable, that helps qualify the belief for knowledge.

We have here a sample motivation for a *reliability* approach to knowledge. Coupled with the earlier suggestion that the cause of the belief is crucial, we have a *causal reliability* approach. But causal reliabilism is not the only form of reliabilism. Let me briefly consider an alternative brand of reliabilism: the reliable-indicator approach.

D. M. Armstrong has proposed such an account of knowledge.[2] According to Armstrong, a noninferential belief counts as knowledge if it is a reliable indicator of the true state of affairs. "Knowledge is a state of mind,"

---

1. Some people object to using "cause" in the analysis of knowledge because that notion is itself philosophically problematic. But we can make progress in understanding one concept by using others, even if the latter also invite analysis. In particular, it is useful to analyze epistemological notions in terms of nonepistemological ones, as in the present case. One comment on my view of causation is in order. I do not presume that causation implies determinism. Hence, while knowledge cannot be attained if beliefs are wholly uncaused, knowledge is possible in a nondeterministic universe.

2. D. M. Armstrong, *Belief, Truth and Knowledge* (Cambridge: Cambridge University Press, 1973). Also see Marshall Swain, *Reasons and Knowledge* (Ithaca: Cornell University Press, 1981).

says Armstrong, "which as a matter of law-like necessity ensures that p."[3] According to Armstrong's initial proposal, if p is true and a person believes that p, then his belief qualifies as knowledge if the following additional condition is met: There is some circumstance or situation H that the person is in and there is some lawlike connection in nature such that if anyone in circumstance H believes that p, then p is true.

Notice that this account places no constraints on *why* or *how* the believer comes to believe p. It only implies that his believing p, in the specified circumstances, is a lawful guarantee of p's truth. In this unmodified form, Armstrong's account founders on cases of self-fulfilling beliefs, as he himself recognizes. A belief can guarantee its own truth by bringing that truth about, and if this happens, it won't suffice for knowledge. To illustrate, suppose that neuroscience has developed a sophisticated brain-scanning device that can scan a person's brain and immediately determine the belief-states he is in. Suppose Edward's brain is monitored by such a scanning device, which is also hooked up to a gauge with a pointer, which registers some number on the gauge from zero to ten. Whenever the scanning device registers a belief with the content, "The pointer is pointing to number X," this causes the pointer to point to X. Edward does not see or otherwise get information about the gauge, but he is invited to speculate concerning the pointer's position. Edward not only speculates about the pointer's position, but forms firm beliefs about its position, totally without any clues or feedback from the gauge itself, and without any knowledge that the brain-scanning device is hooked up to the gauge. In this situation, it is guaranteed by laws of nature that if Edward believes that the pointer is pointing to a specific number (or is about to point to that number) then it will (shortly) be true that it is pointing to that number. Nonetheless, it would be wrong to say that these beliefs constitute *knowledge* of where the pointer is pointing. So reliable indicatorship is not sufficient for knowledge.

Recognizing the problem of self-fulfilling beliefs, Armstrong adds some provisos to his account. First, he stipulates that the belief must not be a cause of its own truth. Second, he says that it must be a "completely reliable sign" of the thing signified (p. 182), in the way that, for example, a special pallor is a sign of approaching death. But does this help his account avoid problems? Consider a variant of the brain-scanning case. Suppose that

3. *Belief, Truth and Knowledge*, p. 189.

whenever Edward *speculates* that the pointer will soon point to a certain number, then within a few seconds he *believes* it is pointing to that number. And suppose that the brain-scanning device is so adjusted that when it detects a *speculation* on Edward's part that the pointer will soon point to a certain number, then it shortly causes the pointer to point to that number. Under these circumstances, the pointer beliefs will be reliable signs of the pointer's position, but the beliefs will not be *causes* of its position (only the speculations will be causes). Armstrong's conditions are met; but intuitively, these beliefs are not cases of knowledge. (I continue to assume that Edward gets no "feedback" that confirms the accuracy of his previous beliefs.)

Armstrong compares noninferential knowledge to the temperature readings of a reliable thermometer (p. 166). He takes this to illustrate and support his reliable indicatorship account of knowledge. But doesn't it better illustrate and support the reliable *process* account of knowledge? After all, a good thermometer gets the temperature right because it is *causally* responsive or sensitive to the temperature of the ambient air. There is a causal process at work that produces its readings and guarantees their accuracy.

However, Armstrong's thermometer example provides a useful model to help us think about how technology (especially in the form of scientific instruments) provides us with knowledge. Consider, for example, the way a telescope provides us with knowledge of distant planets. Although we cannot see the planets with the naked eye, the telescope (like the thermometer) serves as an instrument that reveals a state of affairs that is otherwise inaccessible to us. And as long as the telescope is constructed properly, the laws of optics guarantee that the telescope reveals those distant states of affairs accurately. What we have here is a sort of chain of reliable causes. The telescope reliably produces certain images and then my visual system, responding to those images, reliably produces certain beliefs about the distal states of affairs. The same might be said of telerobotic technologies and their ability to give us knowledge. Sitting in my study in the United States, I cannot see with the naked eye that a marigold just sprouted in Linz. But perhaps a telerobotic installation can serve as an instrument, like a thermometer or a telescope, guaranteeing that my beliefs about the Linz marigold will be accurate. If that is so, then such a telerobotic installation can provide me with knowledge about the marigold in Linz.

2. Alternative Reliable-Process Theories

Whether telerobotic devices can furnish us with knowledge would seem to depend, therefore, on the reliability of telerobotic *processes.* Given the attractions of this thought, let us pursue further the attempt to account for knowledge in terms of reliable processes. The reliable-process approach was first formulated, in kernel form, by Frank Ramsey.[4] There are now several variants under discussion, and we need to explore the prospects of the various alternatives.

Three pairs of options can help generate a field of alternative reliable-process theories. First, we may distinguish a process's *general* reliability and *specific* reliability. The difference lies in the range of uses for which the process is reliable. General reliability is reliability for all (or many) uses of the process, not just its use in forming the belief in question. Specific reliability concerns only the reliability of the process in the context of the belief under assessment. However, this might include its reliability in certain counterfactual situations centered on the target belief.

This brings us to a second distinction among reliable-process approaches: the *actual-counterfactual* distinction. Some approaches might invoke the process's reliability only in actual applications. Other approaches might invoke its reliability in counterfactual situations as well. If counterfactual applications are allowed, a third distinction comes into play. On the one hand, the admissible counterfactual situation may be restricted to the one determined by the *pure subjunctive:* What would happen if proposition p were false? Alternatively, more counterfactual situations could be invoked, for example, all situations involving "relevant alternatives" to the truth of p.

Combinations of options chosen from this menu determine an array of reliable-process approaches. Let us see how current versions of reliabilism fit into the resulting classification. Both Fred Dretske and Robert Nozick present accounts of knowledge that invoke *specific* reliability, in *counterfactual* applications, as specified by the *pure subjunctive.*[5] For person S to know that p, Dretske requires S to have a reason for p (e.g., a perceptual experience or a set of beliefs) that he would not have unless p were the case. In other words,

4. Frank Ramsey, *The Foundations of Mathematics and Other Logical Essays* (London: Routledge and Kegan Paul, 1931).

5. Fred Dretske, "Conclusive Reasons," *Australasian Journal of Philosophy* 49: 1–22 (1971), Robert Nozick, Philosophical Explanations (Cambridge, Mass: Harvard University Press, 1981), chapter 3.

if the circumstances are such that S would have that same reason for p even if p were false, then S does not know that p. Similarly, Nozick's "tracking" theory features the following four conditions for knowledge: (1) p is true, (2) person S believes that p, (3) if p weren't true, S wouldn't believe that p, and (4) if p were true, S would believe that p. Nozick adds the proviso that beliefs in the counterfactual situation(s) must result from the same method M, used in the actual situation. For the Linz marigold example, therefore, Nozick's account yields the following: You know that a marigold just sprouted in Linz if and only if (1) A marigold just sprouted in Linz, (2) You believe that a marigold just sprouted in Linz, (3) The process by which you acquired your belief is such that if a marigold had not just sprouted in Linz, you wouldn't believe that a marigold had just sprouted in Linz, and (4) The process by which you acquired your belief is such that if a marigold had just sprouted in Linz, you would believe that a marigold just sprouted in Linz.

Condition (3) is obviously the critical one in this account, and introduces the specific subjunctive as the linchpin of the analysis. Unfortunately, the specific subjunctive is too weak. Here is an example to show why. Suppose a parent takes a child's temperature and the thermometer reads 98.6 degrees, leading the parent to believe that the child's temperature is normal, which is true. Suppose also that the thermometer works properly, so that if the child's temperature were not 98.6, it would not read 98.6 and the parent would not believe that the temperature is normal. This satisfies the first three conditions of Nozick's analysis. Presumably the fourth condition is also satisfied: In (close) counterfactual situations in which the child's temperature is normal, the parent would believe that it is normal. But now suppose there are many thermometers in the parent's medicine cabinet, and all but the one actually selected are defective. All the others would read 98.6 even if the child had a fever. Furthermore, the parent cannot tell which thermometer is which; it was just luck that a good thermometer was selected. Then we would not say that the parent *knows* that the child's temperature is normal, even though Nozick's analysis is satisfied.

This problem becomes central in cases involving the Internet. The Linz marigold example turns out to be one of those cases. The garden in the Ars Electronica Center can be visited via the Internet.[6] Visitors can observe, and

6. http://telegarden.aec.at

even tend the garden by manipulating a robotic arm equipped with a video camera, a dish of seeds, and a watering nozzle. Because it can be visited via the Internet, this robotic garden is often referred to as the "Telegarden." Now suppose that on the basis of a visit to the Telegarden website you conclude that a marigold just sprouted in Linz. Assuming that everything is functioning properly, Nozick's four requirements are met: (1) A marigold just sprouted in Linz; (2) You believe that a marigold just sprouted in Linz; (3) You acquired the belief in such a way that if your belief were not true, you would not hold it; and (4) You acquired the belief in such a way that if your belief were true, you would hold it. All four of Nozick's conditions are met. According to his theory, therefore, you know that a marigold has just sprouted in Linz.

It turns out, however, that a significant number of purportedly tele-robotic web sites are actually forgeries. The images these forgeries transmit are not live images, but rather prestored images of objects and scenes that may no longer exist. If you just happened to stumble across a trustworthy web site, then, like the mother who picks the one working thermometer out of the box, you merely chanced on a reliable process. As in the thermometer case, we would not say that you had *knowledge,* even though your belief met Nozick's requirements of truth and specific reliability.

Another version of reliabilism invokes counterfactual situations in accounting for knowledge attributions but does not employ the pure subjunctive. It says that a true belief qualifies as knowledge only if there is no relevant alternative situation in which the proposition p would be false but the process used would cause S to believe p anyway. If there is such a relevant alternative, then the utilized process cannot exclude or rule out that possibility (in which p is false); so S does not know.[7] Call this the *no relevant alternatives* (NRA) approach.

To illustrate the NRA approach, suppose that S is driving through the countryside and spots various barn facades along the way. Each time he believes, "What I see over there is a barn." In one of these cases he is right. It is a barn, and he is justified in thinking so because it looks (from the road)

7.   See Dretske, "Epistemic Operators" *Journal of Philosophy* 67: 1007–1023 (1970), *Knowledge and the Flow of Information* (Cambridge, Massachusetts: MIT Press, 1981); Alvin Goldman, "Discrimination and Perceptual Knowledge" *Journal of Philosophy* 73: 771–791 (1976); Gail Stine, "Skepticism, Relevant Alternatives, and Deductive Closure" *Philosophical Studies* 29: 249–260 (1976).

like a typical barn. But in the other cases what he sees are papier-mâché facades, that is, fake barns rather than genuine ones. In the case where he is right, does he *know* it is a barn? Intuitively, he does not. The NRA approach accounts for this by saying that there is an alternative possibility here, namely, the possibility of its being a mere facade, that he cannot rule out. If the thing he is looking at were a fake rather than a genuine barn, it would still look the same from his vantage point. Moreover, this possibility is relevant because there are so many such fake barns in the vicinity. Unlike the pure subjunctive approach, the NRA approach does not assume that a fake barn situation is the scenario that *would* obtain if the believed proposition were false. It is enough to preclude knowledge that there be some relevant alternative that cannot be excluded, even if it is not definitely the alternative that *would* obtain if p were false.

This NRA account works better than the pure subjunctive one. The pure subjunctive account is just too permissive. Suppose you visit a web site and as a result come to believe correctly that a marigold just sprouted in Linz. Do you know that a marigold just sprouted in Linz? As long as there is a serious possibility that the image is prestored, rather than live, we would deny that you know. This is handled properly by the NRA account, since the possibility of your viewing a telerobotic forgery would presumably qualify as a relevant alternative. But the pure subjunctive view would not necessarily give the correct verdict. We may suppose that what *would* be the case if a marigold had not just sprouted in Linz is that an image of a sproutless patch of dirt would appear on your screen. In this counterfactual situation, you would not believe that a marigold just sprouted in Linz. So your belief would survive the pure subjunctive test, and that account would incorrectly say that you know.

3. Difficulties for the NRA Approach

The difficult question for the NRA approach is: When is an alternative relevant? The barn example (and the earlier thermometer example) suggest that an alternative is relevant when a similar situation actually exists or transpires in the near neighborhood of the target situation. The fact that fake barns are in the neighborhood of the real barn makes the possibility of seeing a fake barn relevant. But what, exactly, is meant by "near neighborhood"? What if there are no fake barns in the believer's immediate environment, which is Iowa, but there are such fakes in Hollywood? Or what if there are no such fakes in the United States, but only in Sweden? Or what if no such fakes now exist anywhere, but they were popular five years ago? Is it really necessary that there *ever* have been such fakes in existence? What if a movie company had planned to erect such fakes just last week in the believer's own Iowa county, but finally decided against it? Would that suffice to qualify the possibility of such a fake as a relevant alternative? What is it about a believer's actual world that fixes other possibilities as relevant possibilities for that world?

These questions apply in obvious ways to telerobotic scenarios. If someone visits a web site through which he genuinely sees the marigold in Linz, exactly what facts about this viewer's world would make a possible forgery scenario a relevant alternative? Must there actually be web sites that offer visions of forged *marigolds* in order for this alternative to be relevant? Or would it suffice that there be telerobotic forgeries of any kind, not just of marigolds?

Moreover, telerobotic scenarios also present unique further difficulties for the notion of a "near neighborhood." In cases like the barn example, it seems intuitively plausible that the possibility of forgeries in the near physical neighborhood is what keeps a belief from qualifying as knowledge. But on the Internet, physical neighborhoods seem less relevant. If someone in America sees a marigold in Linz through a web site, the marigold itself is not in his near neighborhood—not, at least, his *physically* near neighborhood. And the forgeries that might deceive him into thinking he was seeing a marigold (when in fact he was not) need not be physically close to him, either. This suggests that, at least in cases of telerobotic knowledge, we must look beyond a person's immediate physical environment in order to determine whether or not the person has knowledge.

The NRA theory has not been developed in enough detail to take care of these difficulties. But there is a prior question that also needs to be addressed. Should we hope and expect to find some fixed, invariant formula that maps all the facts of a believer's world into a determinate list of relevant alternatives for any putative knowledge claim (in that world)? Do the facts of the subject's world fully determine a set of relevant alternatives? Is the concept of knowledge so precise that it tacitly embodies such a fixed formula? Some theorists would deny that matters are so fixed or invariant; they would say that knowledge judgments are much more "contextual," perhaps reflecting the context of the *attributer* as well as the subject.[8]

Here is an example from Keith DeRose to motivate the idea of contextualism.[9] In Bank Case A, my wife and I are driving home on Friday afternoon and plan to stop at the bank to deposit our paychecks. Because the line at the bank is so long, I propose that we instead deposit our paychecks the next morning. I say that I *know* the bank will be open tomorrow because I was just there two weeks ago on Saturday and it was open. In Bank Case B, the scenario is the same except that we have just written a very large and important check. If our paychecks are not deposited into our checking account before Monday morning, the important check will bounce. My wife says, "Banks do change their hours. Do you know the bank will be open tomorrow?" Remaining as confident as I was before, I still reply, "Well, no. I'd better go in and make sure." Although the subject seems to be in the same epistemic situation in these two cases, in one case knowledge is attributed whereas in the other it is withheld. If these knowledge judgments seem intuitively right in both cases, what accounts for that? How can there be a difference between the cases?

Contextualists will answer that the standards for knowledge attribution can vary as a function of the context. The standards can be raised or lowered depending on a number of factors beyond the subject's epistemic situation narrowly construed. For example, in Bank Case B it is much more important for the subject to be right (about the bank being open tomorrow) than in Bank Case A. Perhaps the *importance* of being right raises the standards for what qualifies as a relevant alternative. A different explanation might appeal to *conversational* parameters. In Bank Case B my wife verbally raises the possibility that the bank may have changed its hours in the last two weeks. Once this possibility is conversationally put into play, perhaps it makes relevant a scenario that wasn't previously relevant.[10] A third explanation might appeal to what the knowledge attributer *considers* as a possibility.

8.   The distinction between invariantism and contextualism is due to Peter Unger, *Philosophical Relativity* (1984).

9.   Keith DeRose, "Contextualism and Knowledge Attributions," *Philosophy and Phenomenological Research* 52: 913–929 (1992).

10.   See David Lewis, "Scorekeeping in a Language Game," *Journal of Philosophical Logic* 8: 339–359 (1979).

Once I consider the possibility that the bank may have changed its hours, perhaps that is enough to render that possibility relevant, whether or not it has been verbally mentioned. The last two explanations allow the standards for knowledge attribution to depend not only on the context of the *subject* (of knowledge) but also on the context of the *attributer.*

If contextualism is right—especially a version of contextualism that focuses on attributer-context as well as subject-context—then there may be no straightforward answer to the question, "Does X know that p?" It all depends on the context in which potential attributers are considering or talking about the question.

Context is particularly important for telerobotic scenarios, since the extent to which users care about their actions on the Internet varies wildly from one user to the next. In many instances, users show a great deal less concern for their actions than they would in ordinary, "hands-on" situations. At one experimental web site, many users happily used an on-line robot to deface a $100 bill, despite being warned that this was a criminal act.[11] In other cases, users approach activities on the Internet with the same care and investment that they approach those same activities performed in the immediate environment. On the Telegarden, for instance, many users return to the garden daily, tending a specific flower or patch of earth and watching it grow over time. Some Telegarden faithful go so far as to arrange for "plant-sitters" when on vacation, and to "adopt" their plants when the garden is periodically uprooted.

DeRose's contextualism suggests that this difference in the level of care may bear on whether or not someone knows that a marigold just sprouted in Linz. A casual visitor to the Telegarden might well claim to know that a marigold just sprouted in Linz, and intuitively we might agree with her. But a more invested user might, under the same circumstances, admit that he does not know that a marigold just sprouted in Linz. Here again, we might intuitively agree. In the second case the stakes for the user are higher, and that may imply that the requirements for knowledge are more difficult to meet.[12]

11. www.counterfeit.org

12. If higher stakes do, indeed, imply that knowledge is more difficult to come by, the difficulties this poses for telerobotic knowledge will only increase as Internet telerobotics moves away from experiment and recreation and toward practical application. Some day-care centers have already

However, even if knowledge-attribution is sensitive to context along certain dimensions, that doesn't mean that it is sensitive to context along all dimensions. For example, to know that p it may be categorically required that the subject believe that p and that p be true. Furthermore, there may be a context-free requirement for general reliability that the subject's belief-forming process meets. Until now we have been focusing on *specific* reliability, the reliability of the process in the case in question. But I think that knowledge must also meet a condition of *general* reliability, a matter to which I turn next.

General reliability is probably best understood as a propensity rather than a frequency. This avoids the possibility that actual uses of the process are numerically too limited or skewed to represent an intuitively appropriate ratio. If we move to the propensity idea, though, there is the problem of specifying the range of possible uses that should be countenanced. I do not know exactly how to do this, but it seems plausible to restrict possible uses to situations rather similar to those of the real world. I discuss this issue elsewhere.[13]

Another problem for the general reliability approach is the Generality Problem. The approach speaks of *the* (psychological) process that causes a belief. But commitment to a unique process is problematic. General reliability is a ratio among instances, so, strictly speaking, it only holds of a process *type*. But whenever a given belief is produced, the process token that generates it may be described in different ways.[14] Correlated with these different descriptions are different process types, and these types may have different reliability properties. When my visiting the Telegarden web site causes me to believe that a marigold just sprouted in Linz, this process of belief-formation might be described, accurately, in a number of different ways: belief caused by punching keys on a keyboard, belief caused by using a computer, belief caused by visiting a web site, belief caused by visiting a

installed "kiddy-cams" that allow physically absent parents to observe their children in day-care. It is difficult to imagine higher stakes than that, and if contextualism is true, these sorts of cases present the greatest barriers to knowledge.

13. See chapter 5 of *Epistemology and Cognition* (Cambridge, Mass: Harvard University Press, 1986).

14. If one adopts a fine-grained theory of individuating process tokens, more than one token will cause the belief. But on any theory many types will be involved, which is the source of the problem.

telerobotic web site, belief caused by visiting http://telegarden.aec.at, and so on. My particular belief-formation process is an instance of each of these process-types. But the different types all have different reliability properties. Visiting a web site may not, in general, allow me to form reliable beliefs about the remote bedrooms, bathrooms, offices, etc. that it claims to give me access to. But visiting http://telegarden.aec.at is a process that yields reliably true beliefs about a particular garden in Linz, Austria. The question is: Which of these many types should be used in fixing reliability? Should the relevant type be sliced broadly or narrowly? In the telerobotic case, should the relevant type simply be "belief caused by visiting a telerobotic web site" or should it include detailed information about this particular site's sponsor, designer, purpose, etc.?

Before addressing this problem, I must note that it is not peculiar to the reliability approach, but probably faces any *process* account of knowledge. Since some such theory, I have argued, is essential, the problem is not peculiar to reliabilism.[15]

The Generality Problem was identified in my paper "What Is Justified Belief?" but the dilemma posed by the problem has been emphasized by others.[16] If type selection determines very broad types, there is the No Distinction Problem. Every case of telerobotic belief causation will be categorized in the same way, including both cases where the telerobotic web site is maintained by a trustworthy source, such as NASA, and cases where a capricious high-school student puts prestored images on his supposedly "live-cam" web site. This seems wrong because our temptation to credit the cognizer with knowledge differs in these cases, and this ought to be traced to general reliability differences.

But if type selection determines extremely narrow types, there is the Single Case Problem. When the type is extremely narrow, there may be only one actual instance, namely the instance in question. Since this instance by hypothesis yields a true belief (otherwise it would not even arise as a serious

15.   This point was first made by Frederick Schmitt in comments on Richard Feldman's "Reliability and Justification," a paper presented at the 1983 Western Division of the American Philosophical Association.

16.   Alvin Goldman, "What is Justified Belief?" in George Pappas, ed., *Justification and Knowledge* (Dordrecht: D. Reidel, 1979), Richard Feldman, "Reliability and Justification," and John Pollock "Reliability and Justified Belief," *Canadian Journal of Philosophy,* 14(1984): 103–114.

candidate for knowledge), the type will have a truth ratio of 1. Intuitively, it might not be a case of knowledge, but the reliability approach will not have the materials to imply this judgment.

Now the Single Case Problem arises only if general reliability is determined exclusively by actual frequencies. As suggested above, however, a propensity approach is preferable. Since we can thereby put aside the Single Case Problem, we are in a position to favor a narrow principle of type individuation. Certainly narrow types are needed to draw the desired distinctions between processes, those that intuitively do yield knowledge and those that do not. But how is it determined, in each specific case, which process type is critical? One thing we do not want to do is invoke factors external to the cognizer's psychology. The sorts of processes we're discussing are purely internal processes. Let me advance a conjecture about the selection of process types, without full confidence. The conjecture is: The critical type is the *narrowest* type that is *causally operative* in producing the belief token in question.

To illustrate this idea, suppose (for purely illustrative purposes) that there is a verification algorithm for forming beliefs about distant objects by means of telerobotics. The algorithm takes feature inputs from a series of supposedly telerobotically generated images on a monitor and tries to determine whether or not they are authentic live images. There is a value T such that if authenticity is verified to degree T or more, then the algorithm generates a belief that the images are live, and hence that a marigold just sprouted in Linz, that Mars has a red sky, or whatever it is the images suggest. Now if the value of T is very low, then even when a series of images is highly suspect—even when it has many of the features of a forgery—it may prompt a belief that a marigold just sprouted in Linz, that Mars has a red sky, etc. Suppose such a belief on a given occasion is true. Should we call it knowledge? Doubtless we would be leery of doing so. Our reluctance can be explained by pointing to the unreliability of the algorithm. An algorithm of the sort postulated, with a *low threshold* for verification, will tend to be quite unreliable. So as long as the value of the verification threshold is included in the chosen process type, we will get the right answer on this knowledge ascription case.

But notice that the algorithm has lots of different verification properties. It has the property of producing a belief when the degree of verification is T; the property of producing a belief when the degree of verification is $T+.1$;

the property of producing a belief when the degree of verification is $T+.2$; and so on. Is the appropriate process type always one that includes the first of these properties, namely, the *minimal* degree of verification sufficient for belief? Presumably not. For consider a case in which the images are quite believable, and the actual degree of verification is, let's say, .99 (on a scale of 0 to 1). Then presumably we will want to say that this is adequate for knowledge (if everything else goes well). But if the selected process type still includes the *minimal* value T, the type as a whole may not have sufficient reliability.

My proposed account would handle this case by noting that the algorithm's property of having T (say, .70) as minimally sufficient is not causally operative in this case. The property of having this threshold value does not play a critical causal role in eliciting the belief. The degree of verification in this case is actually .99. So the critical aspect of the algorithm's functioning that produces the belief is the propensity to produce a belief when the degree of verification is .99. If *this* property, rather than the others, is included in the selected process type, an appropriate degree of reliability is chosen that meshes with our knowledge ascription intuition. Clearly this proposal needs to be developed and refined, but I will not try to do that here. I present it only as a promising lead toward a solution of the Generality Problem.

The reliabilist theory of knowledge is not, therefore, without its problems. In order to work out the account in detail, one would have to solve the Generality Problem, as well as a number of other problems I have raised. Nevertheless, reliabilism—the view that what distinguishes knowledge from mere true belief is the reliability of the process that produces the belief—remains intuitively very appealing. And I have argued that my particular version of reliabilism—the No Relevant Alternatives (NRA) approach—is the most compelling way to make good on reliabilism's intuitive appeal. My view is that a person's true belief qualifies as knowledge only if there is no relevant alternative on which the belief would be false, but the same belief-causing process would nevertheless lead the person to hold it.

Telerobotically acquired beliefs raise interesting difficulties for the theory of knowledge. Unlike papier-mâché barns and boxes of defective thermometers, deception on the Internet is common. This implies that telerobotic knowledge may be deeply difficult to come by. Given that the threat of Internet deception is always present, can beliefs that are produced by telerobotic installations on the Internet ever satisfy the requirements for knowledge? The answer is not clear. But the question will only become more urgent as telerobotic technology and the Internet develop in sophistication and prominence. As telerobotic processes come to cause more of our beliefs, telepistemological questions about why and whether those beliefs qualify as knowledge will become more central to our thinking. Rather than giving these questions definite answers here, however, I have tried to show what considerations we must keep in mind as we try to answer them.

Part II

Art, History, and Critical Theory

8

The Speed of Light and the Virtualization of Reality

Martin Jay

In September 1676, the Danish astronomer Ole Roemer (1644–1710) presented the recently created French Academy of Sciences with an audacious prediction. Successfully fulfilled two months later, it profoundly transformed not only the study of the heavens, but also the self-understanding of the humans who gazed at them in wonder.[1] Roemer had been working at the observatory of Uraniborg set up by his illustrious predecessor Tycho Brahe on the island of Hveen in the Baltic. His goal was the discovery of a precise astronomical clock for nautical navigation, but the unintended consequences of his efforts were far more momentous. On the basis of his observations, he predicted that the eclipse of the innermost of Jupiter's moons, Io, expected on November 9th at 5:25 and 45 seconds, would take place ten minutes later than had been calculated based on earlier sightings of the same phenomenon. He further reasoned that a similar delay would take place with the passage of the moon from behind Jupiter's shadow— what astronomers call its emersion as opposed to its immersion—on November 16th. These ten minutes delays, he claimed, were due to the time it would take for the light from the eclipse to reach the earth, a longer interval than in the previous recorded cases because the earth was now at the far side of its orbit around the sun from Jupiter and thus significantly farther away from the giant planet than during certain earlier eclipses. Light, in other words, could now be shown to have a velocity of its own and not pass instantaneously from its source to its recipient, or in the vocabulary of the day, its speed could be confirmed as finite and not infinite.

Roemer's precise calculations of light's finite velocity were in need of some correction and fleshing out. He reckoned the time it would take to cross the diameter of the earth's orbit at twenty-two minutes instead of the somewhat more than sixteen minutes measured by later astronomers. And it was not until a year or so later that Christian Huygens actually divided the supposed diameter of the earth's orbit by the time it took for light to travel across it to arrive at an actual, if still imperfect, velocity of light or

1. The classic study of Roemer and his work is still I. Bernard Cohen, *Roemer and the First Determination of the Velocity of Light* (New York: The Burndy Library, 1944). It contains a facsmile of the article in the December 7, 1676, issue of the *Journal des Sçavans* in which Roemer published his findings. See also the essays collected in *Roemer et la vitesse de la lumière,* conference proceedings of a CNRS conference (Paris: Vrin, 1978). For general background, see A. I. Sabra, *Theories of Light from Descartes to Newton* (London: Oldbourne, 1967).

"c" (from the Latin *celeritas*).[2] Nor was the entire scientific community fully and conclusively convinced by Roemer's claims until the experiments of the English astronomer James Bradley in 1728 concerning what he called "the aberration of light," which involved measuring discrepancies in the parallax relations of certain stars.[3]

But with Roemer, there was for the first time hard empirical evidence to settle a debate that had exercised scientists and philosophers ever since the Greeks. Those theorists from Aristotle to Kepler, Cassini, and Descartes, who had held to the notion of the instantaneous propagation of light, were refuted.[4] Others, such as Avicenna, Alhazen, and Roger Bacon, who had speculated that it took some amount of time, were shown to have had the right hunch, even though they had had no verifiable evidence to back it up. Earlier attempts to provide such evidence by following Galileo's suggestion to open and shut lanterns at a distance of ten miles—an experiment actually tried by the Florentine Academy in 1667—had failed because of the shortness of earthly distances and the slow reaction times of the humans operating the lanterns.[5]

2. For the later refinements in the measurement of the speed of light, see P. Grivet, "Progrés récents dans la mesure de la vitesse de la lumière Co," in *Roemer and et la vitesse de la lumière*. At present, "c" is understood to equal 299,792,457.4 +/- 1.2 km/s, or about one billion feet per second, which is called a gigafoot. Huygens came up with 48,000 leagues (or about 144,000 miles) a second, which was off, but close to the right magnitude.

3. James Bradley, "An Account of a New Discovered Motion of the Fix'd Stars," *Philosophical Transactions*, xxxv (1727–1728), pp. 637–661. Bradley noted that the star called gramma Draconis varied at the zenith distance at which it crossed over the meridian, but that the variations could not be explained entirely by the relative positions of the earth and the star (parallax means the apparent difference in the position of a celestial body with reference to a fixed background—the more distant stellar universe—when seen from two different locations). The excess in the variation had to be due instead to the different time it took the light to reach each of the locations. See A. B. Stewart, "The Discovery of Stellar Abberation," *Scientific American* 210 (March 1964).

4. In fact, the decisive defeat of Descartes's physics by Newton's was made possible by the discovery of the speed of light, which discredited his assumption that the universe was a plenum. Newton's own claim that light was corpuscular rather than a wave and travelled through the medium of "ether" was itself later shown to be incorrect.

5. The first terrestrial experiment that confirmed the speed of light was done in 1849 by A. H. L Fizeau, who used mirrors rather than lanterns that had to be manually operated. See the discussion in Enders A. Robinson, *Einstein's Relativity in Metaphor and Mathematics* (Englewood Cliffs, N.J.: Prentice Hall, 1990), p. 22.

With the work of Roemer and Bradley on extra-terrestrial objects, that evidence now existed and soon won over the astronomical community with consequences that were ultimately of vast importance for the future exploration of the universe. Although less widely heralded, they were, as Hans Blumenberg puts it in *The Genesis of the Copernican World,* "just as momentous . . . for the change in our consciousness of the world as the Copernican reform had been."[6] It was now certain that despite their apparent size to the naked eye stars were distant suns more or less comparable to the one that shone so brightly in our daytime sky, a conclusion hypothesized but not proven before Roemer.[7] It soon also became possible to begin conceiving of the previously inconceivable distances between stars, which were progressively revealed by the dramatic improvement of the telescope through the use of immense mirrors by William Heschel around 1800, and which continue to expand with the recent discoveries of the Hubble space telescope. And it soon became possible to realize that not only were stars and galaxies many light-years away, but that, as William Huggins announced in 1868, some were receding from us at an astonishing rate of speed (or as the Doppler-Fizeau effect based on spectroscopic technology showed later in the century some were zooming toward us as well). The speed of light also provided a limit concept for physics, as no faster propagation of anything else in the universe has ever been found. In addition, the experiments of James Clark Maxwell in the late nineteenth century on electromagnetic waves showed that light traveled at a constant rate in a vacuum, which could not be accelerated or slowed down, although it did change if the medium were altered, say to glass.

These and many other consequences too technical for a soft-headed humanist to present in detail followed from the discovery of the fact that light can travel 186,000 miles or 300,000 kilometers a second and six trillion miles or 9.5 trillion kilometers a year. Although the twentieth century had new surprises in store when Einstein's Special Theory of Relativity argued that the speed of light was the one exception to the rule that velocities were

6. Hans Blumenberg, *The Genesis of the Copernican World,* trans. Robert M. Wallace (Cambridge, Mass.: MIT Press, 1987), p. 391.

7. For a discussion, see Michael Hoskin, "The Principle Consequences of the Discovery of the Finite Velocity of Light for the Development of Astronomy in the Eigtheenth and Nineteenth Centuries," in *Roemer et la vitesse de la lumière.*

relative to the movement of the viewer and viewed, and the gravitational force of black holes was shown to effect its propagation,[8] Roemer's discovery had repercussions that we are still feeling today.

The one in particular that I want to explore concerns not the vast distances of interstellar space nor the amazingly fast, but still finite and noninstantaneous, speed that light waves or photons—particles of electromagnetic energy—travel through it. I want instead, in accord with the theme of this book, to speculate on the implications of Roemer's discovery for the relation between time and the image. For it was quickly recognized—at least as early as 1702 and a lecture by the astronomer William Whiston[9]—that not only was it now possible to see things that were very far away, but it was also possible to see them as they had existed an extraordinarily long time ago.

In this sense, the effect of the telescope was radically different from that of the other great ocular prosthesis of the early modern period, the microscope, which had no such temporal implication.[10] Only the former could be called a genuine time machine, or in the words of a recent commentator, "a probe that can take deep soundings of time, back to the most ancient cosmos."[11] By 1800, it was recognized that looking at the light from distant stars was gazing at something that had left its source before the very existence of the human race, indeed likely before the existence of the earth and perhaps even the solar system. By the late twentieth century, some astrono-

8. Marie-Antoinette Tonnelat, "Vitesse de la lumière et relativité," in *Roemer et la vitesse de la lumière;* Robinson, *Einstein's Relativity in Metaphor and Mathematics;* and Sidney Perkowitz, *Empire of Light: A History of Discovery in Science and Art* (New York: Henry Holt, 1996).

9. William Whiston, *Praelectiones astronomicae* (Cambridge, 1707); the lecture, dated 1702, is discussed in Hoskins, pp. 234–235. It should be noted, however, that it was a long while before the enormity of the temporal distances were understood. As late as Nietzsche, it is still reckoned only in "centuries." See his *Beyond Good and Evil,* part 9, section 285, trans. Walter Kaufmann, in *Basic Writings of Nietzsche* (New York: Random House, 1966), p. 417.

10. For a recent account of its implications, see Catherine Wilson, *The Invisible World: Early Modern Philosophy and the Invention of the Microscope* (Princeton: Princeton University Press, 1995).

11. Perkowitz, *Empire of Light,* p. 50. It is true that microscopes discern minute spatial distances that can be measured only in terms of the passage of light—the measurement called a "light-fermi" is the time it takes for light to travel between one side of a proton to another—but there is no effect of gazing back into an earlier time.

mers were talking about seeing almost as far back as the birth of the universe itself.[12]

What can be called astronomical hindsight thus presented the viewer of the heavens with a remarkable conundrum. Sight is, after all, often understood to be the most synchronous and atemporal of the senses, capable of giving us a snapshot image of a world frozen in time, a trait that earned it the disdain of philosophers like Bergson who valued temporal duration instead.[13] As Hans Jonas typically puts it, "sight is *par excellence* the sense of the simultaneous or the coordinated, and thereby of the extensive. A view comprehends many things juxtaposed, as co-existent parts of one field of vision. It does so in an instant: as in a flash one glance, an opening of the eyes, discloses a world of co-present qualities spread out in space, ranged in depth, continuing into indefinite distance. . . ."[14] Régis Debray adds that "a painting, an engraving, a photograph evade the linear succession of language through the co-presence of their parts. They are apprehended *en bloc* by the intuition, in an instantaneous perceptive synthesis—the *totum simul* of vision. A visual image arrests the flow of time like a syncope, contracts the string of moments."[15] Although recent research has emphasized the scanning movement of the eye and its restless saccadic jumps and stressed the mobile glance over the medusan gaze,[16] in comparison with other senses, vision still seems for many tied to the Parmenidean or Platonic valorization of static, eternal Being over dynamic, ephemeral Becoming.

---

12. According to the latest reports, astronomers now think that based on measurements made by the European Space Agency's satellite Hipparcos of pulsing stars, or cepheids, the oldest stars are some 11 billion years old, while the universe as a whole may be as old as 13 billion years. See "New Data Hint that the Universe May Be Bigger than Thought," *The New York Times,* February 15, 1997.

13. For a discussion of his attitude toward sight, see my *Downcast Eyes: The Denigration of Vision in Twentieth-Century French Thought* (Berkeley: University of California Press, 1993), pp. 186–209.

14. Hans Jonas, "The Nobility of Sight," *The Phenomenon of Life: Toward a Philosophical Biology* (Chicago: University of Chicago Press, 1982), p. 136.

15. Régis Debray, *Media Manifestoes: On the Technological Transformation of Cultural Forms,* trans. Eric Rauth (London: Verson, 1996), p. 148. "Syncope" means a sudden break in the temporal flow, like swoon from consciousness.

16. See, for example, Claude Gandelman, *Reading Pictures, View Texts* (Bloomington: Indiana University Press, 1990) and Norman Bryson, *Vision and Painting: The Logic of the Gaze* (London: MacMillan, 1983).

Or alternatively, vision is sometimes understood as the sense that gives us the best possible glimpse into the immediate future as we look out on the landscape that we are about to traverse, thus providing "foresight" about what may well come next. "Man's ability to plan," writes the anthropologist Edward T. Hall, "has been made possible because the eye takes in a larger sweep."[17] Hans Jonas adds, "knowledge at a distance is tantamount to foreknowledge. The uncommitted reach into space is gain of time for adaptive behavior. I know in good time what I have to reckon with."[18] Those who assume the exalted function of seer or visionary often claim the ability to foretell what they foresee in the distant future as well.

But in the case of stargazing, what we see instead of the present or proximate future is the past, often an immeasurably deep past whose ontological status is unlike anything else that we experience in mundane existence. We literally see what *is* not, or rather *is* no longer. And yet we are not seeing a mere later reproduction or simulacrum of what once was, but rather the real thing delayed—sometimes enormously delayed—in time. We can have, however, absolutely no way of knowing whether or not that real thing still exists or has long since disappeared. The gap between appearance and essence, subjective experience and objective stimulus, phenomenon and noumenon yawns as wide as it can be. Instead of the infamous "metaphysics of presence" that deconstruction tells us is based on the logocentric, phonocentric, and ocularcentric prejudices of Western thought, we get an explicitly visual instantiation of the ghostly trace of the past in the present, but one that is neither an hallucination nor a technologically induced illusion.

There is, moreover, no possible way to apply the other senses, especially the touch that so often functions to verify or confirm the existence of the past objects we see, as Bishop Berkeley claimed we must to determine spatial location.[19] In stargazing, the sense of sight is isolated from and privileged above the general human sensorium as perhaps in no other realm of experience. The oft-remarked link between abstracted theory and visual distance is given added weight by the impossibility of testing astronomical theories through nonvisual means. Parallels between sight and touch,

17.   Edward T. Hall, *The Hidden Dimension* (New York: Anchor Books, 1982), p. 40.

18.   Jonas, "The Nobility of Sight," p. 151.

19.   George Berkeley, *Essay Toward a New Theory of Vision, Philosophical Works* (London: J. M. Dent, 1975), p. 21.

drawn for example by Descartes in his *Optics,* where he compared sight to the instantaneous transmission of an object through a blindman's stick, break down;[20] how can you even imagine "touching" something that existed light years in the past and may no longer be there today?[21]

The cultural implications of the discovery of the speed of light were no less profound than the scientific ones, although they may have taken longer to register. The famous blow dealt to man's narcissistic assumption of his pivotal place in the universe by the Copernican replacement of a geocentric by a heliocentric cosmos was intensified as it was realized that celestial objects had existed well before we were around to behold them. As Blumenberg notes, "man could no longer be the designated witness of the wonders of the creation if the time required for light to reach him from unknown stars and star systems was longer than the entire duration of the world."[22] The already appreciated fact that the stars are that part of nature least amenable to human construction, domination or intervention because of the distances involved was given added weight by the stunning realization that not only space but time would have to be conquered for humans to make a difference.

One corollary effect of this realization was the increased erosion of belief, except among the most gullible, in the opposite assumption: that the stars could somehow causally intervene in human behavior. How, after all, could astrological causation operate, if it were impossible to coordinate the time of a sublunar event, such as one's birth, with the temporal events in interstellar space? How could a plausible horoscope be written that took into account the radically divergent, multiple temporalities of stars whose light came from vastly different distances from the earth? Here too the link between the human present and the images of light in the night sky was rendered deeply problematic by astronomical hindsight, which reveals that constellations are not just spatial relationships, but temporal ones as well.

---

20.   René Descartes, *Discourse on Method, Optics, Geometry, and Meterology,* trans. Paul J. Olscamp (Indianapolis: Bobbs-Merrill, 1965), p. 67.

21.   A similar conclusion was drawn from the microscope, which revealed layers of seemingly immaterial, minute reality that no touch could verify. For a discussion, see Barbara Maria Stafford, *Body Criticism: Imaging the Unseen in Enlightenment Art and Medicine* (Cambridge, Mass.: MIT Press, 1993), p. 36.

22.   Blumenberg, *The Genesis of the Copernican World,* p. 632.

The result, if Maurice Blanchot is right, may have extended beyond the superstitious belief in astrological correlations. Playing on the etymology of the word, he introduces the notion of "disaster"—literally, ill-starred— to designate "being separated from the star . . . the decline which characterizes disorientation when the link with fortune from on high is cut."[23] Disaster can thus be called *"withdrawal outside the sidereal abode . . . refusal of nature's sacredness."*[24]

The implications of that withdrawal were complicated still further by a later stage in the development of astronomy, the use of photography to record the faint light from distant stars that the human eye could not itself easily register. Here the opposite of the snapshot potential in the new technology, its medusan capacity to freeze flowing time in an instant, was realized as long exposures made it possible to preserve on the photographic plate the dim evidence of past light that could not be seen instantaneously, indeed could not be seen by the naked eye at all. Once again, it is Blumenberg who has most suggestively explored its implications:

Astronomical photography raises to a higher power the simultaneity of the nonsimultaneous; it now completes the Copernican differentiation of appearance and reality by pursuing the logic of the finite speed of light, also, to its conclusion: the technical analysis and display of the heavens, as a section through time, which no longer has anything to do with the equation of intuition and presence. The product of the chemical darkening of a plate by a source of even the faintest light is, in a certain respect, no longer an auxiliary means, but has become the object itself, of which there is no other evidence but just this.[25]

But now paradoxically, with the advances in astronomical photography the privileging of sight was itself subtly called into question, and not only because of a new appreciation of the vastness of the invisible parts of reality.[26] For no sense, not even unaided human sight, could verify or falsify what

23.   Maurice Blanchot, *The Writing of the Disaster,* trans. Ann Smock (Lincoln: University of Nebraska Press, 1986), p. 2.

24.   Ibid., p. 133.

25.   Blumenberg, *The Genesis of the Copernican World,* p. 97.

26.   For a discussion of this awareness, see ibid. pp. 642–643.

the technological preservation of the light from past events had recorded. Appearance through technological mediation is the only reality we can know, even if we theorize that something lies—or rather at some time in the distant past lay—behind it. With astronomical hindsight the long-standing reliance on visually based intuition—from the Latin *intueri*, to look at or regard, an association still present in the German *Anschauung*—to discern essences is fundamentally challenged. Only conceptually mediated knowledge based on the acknowledgement of sight's inability to present the truth of its objects through intuition follows from Roemer's discovery when it is combined with photographic enhancement; only a knowledge that is filtered through sign systems that are not directly perceptual is thus the lesson to be learned from the astronomical hindsight of the telescope.[27] Not surprisingly, when the Romantics sought to restore the power of intuition against the alleged fallacies of analytical reasoning, they also longed for the return of what Novalis called the "old sky" of celestial presence through a revival of "moral astronomy."[28] But theirs was a losing effort, as the symbolic resonance of the pre-Copernican sky was irretrievably shattered. Blanchot's "disaster" could not be undone.

Moreover, what has been recognized as the indexical nature of all photographic signification—in Peirce's well-known sense of an index as a physical trace of a past event, as opposed to an arbitrary symbol or a mimetic icon—is doubled by the fact that the index left behind on the photographic plate is itself a trace of an event that has happened in the far distant past. Whereas a normal index is once removed from its cause, which may have left nonvisual residues as well—I can feel the medium, say snow or mud, in which the fox's tracks are left as well as see it, and perhaps even smell its faint odor as well—a photographic image of stellar events is twice removed from them and without any other corroborative trace.

A melancholic link between photography in general and death—its status as a kind of "thanatography"—has been recognized by a number of

27. It should be noted that this process was already underway with the invention of the first reflecting telescope by Newton in 1669, which used mirrors rather than lenses to magnify distant objects. See Perkowitz, *Empire of Light*, p. 53.

28. See Karl Menges, "'Moral Astronomy': On a Metaphor in Novalis and its Conceptual Context," in *Languages of Visuality: Crossings between Science, Art, Politics, and Literature*, ed. Beate Allert (Detroit: Wayne State University Press, 1996).

observers, most notably Susan Sontag, Roland Barthes, and René Dubois.[29] The referent of an image functions as a *memento mori,* they claim, because of its inevitable pastness, a reminder that one day we too will no longer be here. Such a connection can only become more explicit when the image is of stellar light from an unimaginably deep past. Barthes, in fact, explicitly notes the link by citing Sontag's claim that "the photograph of the missing being . . . will touch me like the delayed rays of a star."[30] Photographs of stars may not be as poignantly mournful as those of our parents when they were young, as in Barthes's celebrated example of the Winter Garden shot of his mother at the age of five, but they intensify the sense of temporal disjunction that every photograph must convey. Blanchot's "disaster" is perhaps nowhere as palpable as when we hold in our hands, in the present, a photographic image of a far distant past that we know no longer exists.

This was a lesson, as Eduardo Cadava has recently shown,[31] that was learned with special thoroughness by Walter Benjamin, whose suggestive ruminations on mimetic similarity and auratic distance often invoked the example of astronomical constellations. In a world no longer able to believe in sympathetic magic and astrological correspondences, the heavens had become a vast cemetery of dead light. Benjamin believed, in Cadava's words, that "like the photograph that presents what is no longer there, starlight names the trace of a celestial body that has long since vanished. The star is always a kind of ruin. That its light is never identical to itself, is never revealed as such, means that it is always inhabited by a certain distance or darkness."[32] Although Benjamin may have hoped against hope for a messianic redemption that would restore meaning to a forlorn world, he registered with special intensity the mournful implications of the cosmic *Trauerspiel.*

29.   Roland Barthes, *Camera Lucida: Reflections on Photography,* trans. Richard Howard (New York: Hill and Wang, 1981); Susan Sontag, *On Photography* (New York: Farrar, Straus and Giroux, 1978); René Dubois, *L'acte photographique* (Paris: Nathan and Labor, 1983).

30.   Barthes, *Camera Lucida,* pp. 80–81.

31.   Eduardo Cadava, *Words of Light: Theses on the Photography of History* (Princeton, 1997).

32.   Ibid., p. 30. He shows Benjamin's debt to Auguste Blanqui's L'éternité par les astres: Hypothèse astronomique (Paris: Ballière, 1872), in which the catastrophe of stellar death is reversed by an eternal return that reproduces what has been destroyed.

But even if the emotion that ensues is not so morose, we must inevitably be struck by the conundrum of a visual presence that cannot be complete and self-contained. Taking seriously that lesson allows us to emend a bit Jonathan Crary's influential argument about the transformation of the protocols and techniques of observation in the nineteenth century.[33] Crary's claim is that only with advances in the physiological understanding of the eye, which involved such phenomena as afterimages (the fusion of discrete images into a simulacrum of duration) and stereoscopic vision (the transformation of two nearly identical flat images into the experience of seeing three dimensions), was the time-honored model of disembodied, atemporal sight based on the camera obscura effectively challenged. "The virtual instantaneity of optical transmission (whether intromission or extramission)," Crary writes,

was an unquestioned foundation of classical optics and theories of perception from Aristotle to Locke. And the simultaneity of the *camera obscura* image with its exterior object was never questioned. But as observation is increasingly tied to the body in the early nineteenth century, temporality and vision become inseparable. The shifting processes of one's own subjectivity experienced in time become synonymous with an act of seeing, dissolving the Cartesian ideal of an observer completely focused on an object.[34]

Crary's premise that the dominant paradigm of vision based on the *camera obscura*—what can be called "Cartesian perspectivalism"[35]—privileged the disembodied, monocular eye has been recently challenged for underplaying the extent to which the body was already present in certain seventeenth-century optical theories.[36] Nonetheless, his central point that nineteenth-century physiology gave a much firmer empirical basis to the recorporealiza-

33. Jonathan Crary, *Techniques of the Observer: On Vision and Modernity in the Nineteenth Century* (Cambridge, Mass.: MIT Press, 1990).

34. Ibid., p. 98.

35. Martin Jay, "Scopic Regimes of Modernity," in *Force Fields: Between Intellectual History and Cultural Critique* (New York: Routledge, 1993).

36. See Margaret Atherton, "How to Write the History of Vision: Understanding the Relationship between Berkeley and Descartes," in David Michael Levin, ed., *Sites of Vision: The Discursive Construction of Sight in the History of Philosophy* (Cambridge, Mass.: MIT Press, 1997).

tion and thus temporalization of sight than ever before seems to me still intact. Or at least it does from the point of view of the *subject* of vision, the viewer whose eye became firmly situated in a living, moving body rather than hovering above it in an ideal realm of pure opticality.

But what appreciating the importance of Roemer's discovery of the speed of light helps us to understand is that a similar temporalization had already occurred on the level of the *object* of vision, at least when it concerned astronomical hindsight. That is, the camera obscura model of synchronic presence could not be easily applied when the light coming through its little hole was from a distant star. Here "afterimages," we might say, are not produced by lingering sensations on the retina creating a simulacrum of movement, but rather by the delays in the light from the object itself.

It must, of course, be conceded that this lesson took a considerable amount of time before it was widely appreciated; we might even say that it was appropriately not an instantaneous transmission. Crary's physiological technologists of observation thus still deserves the primary credit for the abandonment of the camera obscura model of atemporal presence. It may not, in fact, have been until Nietzsche, according to Blumenberg, that the deduction was drawn

from the fact of the finite speed of light, and the nonsimultaneity of appearing objects with the observer's present, which follows from that, the consequence of the indifference of the present. Presence cannot enable us to apprehend the necessity of what is given in it, because it is only an accidental section through reality. The irregularity of appearances in space turn out to be a projection of the fateful delays into the plane of what is just now visible; it is a paradigm of the distortion of reality by time, not only, and not most painfully, in nature but also in history.[37]

"The indifference of the present" as a consequence of the speed of light was perhaps also tacitly implied by one of the most celebrated evocations of the telescope in modern thought, Freud's comparison in *The Interpretation of*

37. Blumenberg, *The Genesis of the Copernican World,* p. 103. The passage in question is from *Beyond Good and Evil,* and refers to the fact that contemporaries fail to recognize the really creative spirits among them: "What happens is a little like what happens in the realm of stars. The light of the remotest stars comes last to men; and until it has arrived man denies that there are—stars there." See note 9.

Dreams of psychical locality in the unconscious with an optical apparatus. Such a compound instrument, he noted, produces images "at ideal points, regions in which no tangible component of the apparatus is situated."[38] The relevance to our argument about astronomical hindsight comes from Freud's further claim that we could just as easily conceptualize the relation between the lenses in that apparatus in temporal as in spatial terms. In so doing, we can then understand that the image produced at the ideal point is not fully present, but is rather the place of a memory trace, an unlocalizable compound that connects past with present.

Freud's metaphor has attracted considerable attention, at least since Jacques Derrida foregrounded its implications in his 1966 essay "Freud and the Scene of Writing."[39] To reduce a complicated argument to its most fundamental lineaments, Derrida suggested that Freud's "optical machine" metaphor would be transformed in his later work into a graphic one based on a "mystical writing pad" on which the traces of previous inscriptions could be discerned in the wax beneath a transparent sheet of celluloid. The writing pad produced a kind of spatialized time that denied the possibility of any full symbolic presence. It instantiated instead the temporal spacing of difference without reconciliation.

Writing in response to Derrida, Timothy J. Reiss has argued in The *Discourse of Modernism* that it is unnecessary to posit a transition from a perceptual to a linguistic or graphological model of the unconscious, from the telescope to the mystical writing pad, to arrive at the logic of the trace with its internally split temporality.[40] For already in the workings of the apparatus producing an intangible image at once present and a memory trace of the past can we see the mediation of intuitive perceptual immediacy by a discursive sign system. The telescope, *pace* Derrida, is already a kind of writing machine in which the trace of the past continues to haunt the apparently self-contained present. This point, it seems to me, becomes even stronger, if we separate out, as Freud did not, the telescope from other imaging apparatuses, such as the microscope and the camera, and emphasize

38. Sigmund Freud, *The Interpretation of Dreams,* trans. James Strachey (New York: Avon Books, 1969), p. 575. Freud says such an instrument might be a microscope or camera as well as a telescope.

39. Jacques Derrida, *Writing and Difference,* trans. Alan Bass (Chicago: University of Chicago Press, 1978).

40. Timothy J. Reiss, *The Discourse of Modernism* (Ithaca: Cornell University Press, 1982).

its role in producing what we have been calling "astronomical hindsight." For here the temporal spacing produced by the delay between the emission and reception of starlight is even more pronounced. The images collected by the mirrors of the reflecting telescope and then preserved on photographic plates are like memory traces without any single temporal location.

I've argued that Roemer's discovery of astronomical hindsight revealed a "virtualization of reality" that provoked a fundamental shift in our notion of the present and an associated set of ontological and epistemological questions. How might this precedent help us to understand the new technologies of Virtual Reality, Telerobotics, and the relation between them that is the subject of this book? Can we extrapolate from the lessons of interstellar space to the implications of cyberspace?

One might argue that the technologies of virtual reality and telerobotics further attenuate the link between source and viewer, to the point where the indexical trace vanishes altogether. Indeed, virtual reality is generally understood as a hyperreality that has no referential origin. And telerobotics is generally assumed to be rooted in the accelerated temporality, even simultaneity, of a cyberspace in which distances no longer matter.[41]

I wish to argue to the contrary, that an indexical trace survives in both virtual reality and telerobotic technologies and that each resists complete virtualization. Let us first consider telerobotics, in particular the category of telerobotics emphasized in this volume, which allows users on the Internet to control remote devices and view the results. Such a telerobotic system parallels the telescope in that it provides a mediated perception of a distant reality. As with telescopic photographs, we may have no alternative means for verifying the existence of what we are "seeing." Our knowledge must be filtered through sign systems that are not directly perceptual. The Internet introduces new layers of sign systems that must be packed, unpacked, and repacked as the image is digitally coded and transmitted. Furthermore, the speed of electrical signals, 60 to 90 percent that of the speed of light, combined with delays introduced by digitizing and relay circuits, introduces perceptible time delays.

Yet all of these layers form a chain that is rooted in the existential presence of its source. Thus the indexical trace, albeit attenuated, survives the

41. See, for example, Paul Virillio, *L'espace critique* (Paris: Christian Bourgeois, 1984).

journey just as the light from distant stars. As in the case of the telescope, despite all of its disruption of notions of visual presence and immediacy, telerobotics resists reduction to an apparatus of pure simulacral construction, a model of total visual semiosis without an original object behind it.

For the case of Virtual Reality, let us turn to the figure who had done more than any other to explore and—at least for some commentators—legitimate the postmodern world of simulacral self-referentiality, the French theorist Jean Baudrillard.[42] In one of his key texts, *Fatal Strategies* of 1983, Baudrillard introduces precisely the speed of light as a metaphor to explain what he describes as the progressive attenuation of meaning in the contemporary world. "Somewhere a gravitational effect causes the light of event(s), the light that transports meaning beyond the event itself, the carrier of messages, to slow down to a halt," he writes, "like the light of politics and history that we now so weakly perceive, or the light of celestial bodies we now only receive as faint simulacra."[43] Until recently, he continues, the sense of reality in normal terrestrial experience has been based on the very high velocity of light producing a sense of contemporaneity, in which object and its perception are coordinated. But now everyday life is beginning to resemble the experience of star-gazing, in which information paradoxically seems to travel much slower from a source that grows dimmer and less certain. Echoing the rhetoric of disaster we have already encountered in Blanchot, he exhorts us to face the consequences of this transformation: "We must be able to grasp the catastrophe that awaits us in the slowing of light: the slower light becomes, the less it escapes its source; thus things and events tend not to release their meaning, tend to slow down their emanation, to harness that which was previously refracted in order to absorb it in a black hole."[44]

Although the gravitational pull of black holes suggests absolutely no meaning escapes from objects, Baudrillard backs away a bit from this conclusion, and talks instead of the possibility that we live in a world of

42. For an account of his relation to virtuality, see Mark Poster, "Theorizing Virtual Reality: Baudrillard and Derrida," in *Cyberspace Textuality,* ed. Maire-Laure Ryan (Bloomington: Indiana University Press, 1999).

43. Jean Baudrillard, *Les stratégies fatale* (Paris, Grasset, 1983), excerpted as "Fatal Strategies," *Selected Writings,* ed. Mark Poster (Stanford: Stanford University Press, 1988), p. 192.

44. Ibid.

slow-motion images that take a long time to reach us. "We would thus need to generalize the example of the light that reaches from stars long since extinct—their images taking light-years to reach us. If light were infinitely slower, a host of things, closer to home, would already have been subject to the fate of these stars: we would see them, they would be there, yet already no longer there. Would this not also be the case for a reality in which the image of a thing still appears, but is no longer there?"[45]

Baudrillard's grasp of twentieth-century physics may be faulty, as he misses the implication of Einstein's Special Theory of Relativity, which has since been experimentally confirmed. Light itself, the theory argues, is an absolute constant that cannot be accelerated or decelerated, although paradoxically space and time can be understood as relative. Because light, unlike other waves such as sound, is able to travel in a total vacuum unaffected by the medium through which it moves—such as the "ether" whose existence modern physics has disproved—and the speed and directional movement of its observer do not effect its velocity, it is strictly speaking wrong to speak of the "slowing down" of light. Distances become smaller and time longer for moving bodies as they approach the speed of light, but that speed remains the same. The gravitation of Black Holes only deflects light, it does not effect its velocity. As Sidney Perkowitz puts it, "the universe is made so that light always travels its own distance of zero, while to us its clock is stopped and its speed is absolutely fixed. These sober conclusions read as if they come out of some fevered fantasy. Light, indeed, is different from anything else we know."[46]

But for all its imprecision, Baudrillard's metaphoric invocation of the effects of Roemer's discovery that light is not instantaneous in terms of the time it takes for images to travel is not without its instructive implications. For it unexpectedly undermines the equation of virtual reality entirely with a nonreferential system of signs totally indifferent to any prior reality that might have caused or motivated them, an equation that admittedly is operative at other moments in his work.[47] That is, by comparing the world of

45. Ibid., p. 194.

46. Perkowitz, *Empire of Light*, p. 76.

47. See, for example, his essay "Simulacra and Simulations," in which he argues that the most recent phase of the image is one in which "it bears no relation to any reality whatever: it is its own pure simulacrum." *Selected Writings*, p. 170.

virtual reality with the delayed light from distant stars, Baudrillard alerts us to the attenuated indexical trace of an objective real that haunts the apparently self-referential world of pure simulacra. Like the memory traces in Freud's optical apparatus version of the unconscious, such images are not made entirely out of whole cloth existing only in an atemporal cyberspace, but are parasitic on the prior experiences that make them meaningful to us today. The temporality of virtuality is thus not pure simultaneity or contemporaneity, but the disjointed time that disrupts any illusion of self-presence.

As N. Katherine Hayles has pointed out in a recent discussion of "Virtual Bodies and Flickering Signifiers," "the new technologies of virtual reality illustrate the kind of phenomena that foreground pattern and randomness and make presence and absence seem irrelevant. . . . Questions about presence and absence do not yield much leverage in this situation, for the puppet [on a computer screen duplicating the movements of the user] both is and is not present, just as the user both is and is not inside the screen."[48] Moreover, the new information technologies produce signifiers that do not float entirely free, but rather "flicker," disrupting the absolute alternative between presence and absence. They are thus ultimately dependent on the material embodiment that they seem to have left behind, especially those that interact with the human sensorium and its environment. They are, we might say, reminiscent of those other flickerings of information that come to us from the twinkling of the stars, even if Hayles herself does not make the connection.

Another way in which the apparent self-sufficiency of the virtual universe may be disrupted, Mark Poster has added, is through the transformational interaction of subjects who construct the world they enter when they put on the glove and headset.[49] The result is thus more than the passive acceptance of a world of pure simulation; it plunges us from the present into the future. As such, it accords with the definition of virtuality per se—derived from the Latin *virtus,* the word for "force" or "power"—provided by the French media theorist Pierre Lévy in his recent *Qu'est-ce que le virtuel?* where it is opposed not to the real or the material, but to the actual.[50] Virtuality here

48. N. Katherine Hayles, "Virtual Bodies and Flickering Signifiers," *October* 66 (Fall 1993): 72.

49. Poster, "Theorizing Virtual Reality," p. 11 in typescript.

50. Pierre Lévy, *Qu'est-ce que le virtuel?* (Paris: La Découverte, 1995).

means something like an Aristotelian final cause, a potentiality that "displaces the center of gravity of the object considered,"[51] which is neither a pure presence nor a simulacral phantasm.

The alternative way in which the alleged self-sufficiency of virtual reality is called into question suggested by the analysis of this chapter—and the two are not mutually exclusive—is through the memory traces of the reality that haunts virtual reality from the start, inadvertently betrayed by Baudrillard's metaphor of sidereal light that reaches us after a long delay. Here, as in the case of Crary's argument about the importance of ocular physiology in dismantling the camera obscura paradigm, the story of subjective construction must be balanced by an acknowledgment of the disturbing effects that come from the object. Or more precisely, when the lessons of astronomical hindsight are applied broadly, we are in an uncanny world of what Derrida has dubbed "hauntological" rather than "ontological" reality,[52] a world in which temporal delay and the indexical trace of the past prevents the present—virtual or not—from assuming the mantle of synchronic self-sufficiency.

Whether or not the result is a melancholic *memento mori,* as has been claimed in the case of photography, or a "disaster" in Blanchot's sense of being ousted from a realm of sacred meaning, is, however, uncertain. For might it be just as plausible to experience a feeling of wonder at the survival of the seemingly dead past? And might that wonder at the virtual residues of the long dead stars be connected to the virtuality that, according to Poster and Lévy, opens us as well to a potential future? For after all, is not the light reflecting off us, radiating our images to any eyes open to receive them, somehow destined, even if in increasingly diffused form, to travel forever, making our present the past of innumerable futures still to come?

51.   Ibid., p. 16.

52.   Jacques Derrida, *Specters of Marx: The State of the Debt, the Work of Mourning, and the New International,* trans. Peggy Kamuf, intro. Bernd Magnus and Stephen Cullenberg (New York: Columbia University Press, 1994). On the more general implications of the notion of the uncanny, see Martin Jay, "The Uncanny Nineties," *Salmagundi* 108 (Fall 1995).

9

To Lie and to Act: Potemkin's Villages, Cinema, and Telepresence

Lev Manovich

In an opening sequence from the movie *Titanic* (James Cameron, 1997), we see an operator sitting at controls. The operator is wearing a wearing a head-mounted display. The display allows him to see an image transmitted from a remote location, thus making it possible to remotely control another vehicle, exploring the insides of the Titanic lying on the bottom of the ocean. In short, the operator becomes "telepresent."

With the rise of the Web, telepresence—which until recently was restricted to few specialized industrial and military applications—became more of a familiar experience. The search on Yahoo! for "devices connected to the Net" returns links to a variety of Net-based telepresence applications: coffee machines, robots, interactive model railroad, audio devices and, of course, the ever-popular web cams.[1] Some of these devices, for instance, most web cams, do not allow for true telepresence: You get images from a remote location, but you can't perform any actions on them. Others, however, are true telepresence links, meaning that they do allow the user to perform remote actions.

This essay addresses the issues raised by the phenomenon of Internet telepresence and telerobotics by placing these recent technologies within the history of representational technologies. Before proceeding, I will make a conceptual substitution: Rather than discussing technologies as tools for obtaining knowledge (the usual meaning of epistemology), I will discuss them in their opposite role: as tools of deception, that is, as tools that allow their users to communicate lies rather truths.

Representational technologies have served two main functions throughout human history: to deceive the viewer and to enable action, that is, to allow the viewer to manipulate reality through representations.[2] Fashion and make up, paintings, dioramas, decoys and virtual reality fall into the first category. Maps, architectural drawings, x-rays, and telepresence fall into the second. To deceive the viewer or to enable action: These are the two axes that structure the history of visual representations.

1.   www.yahoo.com

2.   This chapter contains significant revisions over earlier papers appearing in *Mythos Information—Welcome to the Wired World. Ars Electronica 95,* edited by Karl Gebel and Peter Weibel (Vienna and New York: Springler-Verlag, 1995); and in *Cinema Futures: Cain, Abel or Cable?* edited by Thomas Elsaesser and Kay Hoffmann (Amsterdam: Amsterdam University Press, 1998). I am grateful to Thomas Elsaesser for a number of suggestions that I incorporated in this version.

What are the new possibilities for deception and action offered by computer-based technologies (computer imaging, Internet-based telepresence) in contrast to older technologies (architecture, cinema, video)? If we are to construct a history that will connect all these technologies, where shall we locate key historical breaks? This essay will reflect on these questions.

1. To Lie

Cinema

I will start with Potemkin's Villages. According to the historical myth, at the end of the eighteenth century, Russian ruler Catherine the Great decided to travel around Russia in order to observe first-hand how the peasants lived. The first minister and Catherine's lover, Potemkin, had ordered the construction of special fake villages along her projected route. Each village consisted of a row of pretty facades. The facades faced the road; at the same time, to conceal their artifice, they were positioned at a considerable distance. Since Catherine the Great never left her carriage, she returned from her journey convinced that all peasants lived in happiness and prosperity.

This extraordinary arrangement can be seen as a metaphor for life in the Soviet Union. There, the experience of all citizens was split between the ugly reality of their lives and the official shining facades of ideological pretense. The split, however, took place not only on a metaphorical but also on a literal level, particularly in Moscow—the showcase Communist city. When prestigious foreign guests visited Moscow, they, like Catherine the Great, were taken around in limousines that always followed a few special routes. Along these routes, every building was freshly painted, the shop windows displayed consumer goods, and the drunks were removed, having been picked up by the militia early in the morning. The monochrome, rusty, half-broken, amorphous Soviet reality was carefully hidden from the view of the passengers.

In turning selected streets into fake facades, Soviet rulers adopted the eighteenth-century technique of creating fake reality. But, of course, the twentieth century brought with it a much more effective technology: cinema. By substituting a window of a carriage or a car with a screen showing projected images, cinema opened up new possibilities for deception.

Fictional cinema, as we know it, is based upon lying to a viewer. A perfect example is the construction of a cinematic space. Traditional fiction film transports us into a space: a room, a house, a city. Usually, none of these exist in reality. What exists are the few fragments carefully constructed in a studio. Out of these disjointed fragments, a film synthesizes the illusion of a coherent space.

The development of the techniques to accomplish this synthesis coincided with the shift in American cinema between approximately 1907 and 1917 from a so-called "primitive" to a "classical" film style. Before the classical period, the space of film theater and the screen space were clearly separated much like in theater or vaudeville. The viewers were free to interact, come and go, and maintain a psychological distance from the cinematic diegisis. Correspondingly, the early cinema's system of representation was *presentational:* Actors played to the audience, and the style was strictly frontal.[3] The composition of the shots also emphasized frontality.

In contrast, classical Hollywood film positions each viewer inside the diegetic space. The viewer is asked to identify with the characters and to experience the story from their points of view. Accordingly, the space no longer acts as a theatrical backdrop. Instead, through new compositional principles, staging, set design, deep focus cinematography, lighting, and camera movement, the viewer is situated at the optimum viewpoint of each shot. The viewer is "present" inside a space that does not really exist. A fake space.

In general, Hollywood cinema always carefully hides the artificial nature of its space, but there is one exception: rear screen projection shots. A typical shot shows actors sitting inside a stationary vehicle; a film of a moving landscape is projected on the screen behind car's windows. The artificiality of rear screen projection shots stands in striking contrast against the smooth fabric of Hollywood cinematic style in general.

The synthesis of a coherent space out of distinct fragments is only one example of how fictional cinema deceives a viewer. A film in general is comprised from separate image sequences. These sequences can come from different physical locations. Two consecutive shots of what looks like one room may correspond to two places inside one studio. They can also correspond

3. On presentational system of early cinema, see Charles Musser, *The Emergence of Cinema: The American Screen to 1907* (Berkeley: University of California Press, 1990), 3.

to the locations in Moscow and Berlin, or Berlin and New York. The viewer will never know.

This is the key advantage of cinema over older fake reality technologies, be it eighteenth-century Potemkin's Villages or nineteenth-century Panoramas and Dioramas. Before cinema, the deception was limited to the construction of a fake space inside a real space visible to the viewer. Examples include theater decorations and military decoys. In the nineteenth century, Panorama offered a small improvement: By enclosing a viewer within a 360-degree view, the area of fake space was expanded. Louis-Jacques Daguerre introduced another innovation by having viewers move from one set to another in his London Diorama. As described by Paul Johnson, its "amphitheater, seating 200, pivoted through a 73-degree arc, from one 'picture' to another. Each picture was seen through a 2,800-square-foot-window."[4] But, already in the eighteenth century, Potemkin had pushed this technique to its limit: He created a giant façade—a Diorama stretching for hundred of miles—along which the viewer (Catherine the Great) passed. In cinema a viewer remains stationary: What is moving is the film itself.

Therefore, if the older technologies were limited by the materiality of a viewer's body, existing in a particular point in space and time, film overcomes these spatial and temporal limitations. It achieves this by substituting recorded images for unmediated human sight and by editing these images together. Through editing, images that could have been shot in different geographic locations or in different times create an illusion of a contiguous space and time.

Editing, or montage, is the key twentieth-century technology for creating fake realities. Theoreticians of cinema have distinguished between many kinds of montage, but for the purposes of sketching the archeology of the technologies of deception, I will distinguish between two basic techniques. The first is montage within a shot: Separate realities form contingent parts of a single image. (One example of this is a rear screen projection shot.) The second technique is the opposite of the first: Separate realities form consecutive moments in time. This second technique of temporal montage is much more common; this is what we usually mean by montage in film.

4.   Paul Johnson, *The Birth of the Modern: World Society 1815–1830* (London: Orion House, 1992), 156.

In a fiction film, temporal montage serves a number of functions. As already pointed out, it creates a sense of presence in a virtual space. It is also utilized to change the meanings of individual shots (recall Kuleshov's effect) or, rather, to construct a meaning from separate pieces of profilmic reality.

However, the use of temporal montage extends beyond the construction of an artistic fiction. Montage also becomes a key technology for ideological manipulation, through its employment in propaganda films, documentaries, news, commercials and so on.

The pioneer of this ideological montage is Russian documentary film-maker Dziga Vertov. In 1923 Vertov analyzed how he put together episodes of his news program *Kino-Pravda* (Cinema-Truth) out of shots filmed at different locations and in different times. This is one example of his montage: "the bodies of people's heroes are being lowered into the graves (filmed in Astrakhan' in 1918); the graves are being covered with earth (Kronshtad, 1921); gun salute (Petrograd, 1920); eternal memory, people take down their hats (Moscow, 1922)." Here is another example: "montage of the greetings by the crowd and montage of the greetings by the machines to the comrade Lenin, filmed at different times."[5] As theorized by Vertov, through montage, film can overcome its indexical nature, presenting a viewer with objects that never existed in reality.

Video

Outside of cinema, montage within a shot becomes a standard technique of modern photography and design (photomontages of Alexander Rodchenko, El Lissitsky, Hannah Hoch, John Heartfield, and countless other lesser-known twentieth-century designers). However, in the realm of a moving image, temporal montage dominates. Temporal montage is cinema's main means of creating fake realities.

After World War II a gradual shift took place from film-based to electronic image recording. This shift brought with it a new technique: keying. One of the most basic techniques used today in any video and television production, keying is combining two different image sources together. Any area of uniform color in one video image can be cut out and substituted with another source. Significantly, this new source can be a live video camera

5. Dziga Vertov, "Kinoki. Perevorot" [Kinoki. A revolution], *LEF* 3 (1923): 140.

positioned somewhere, a prerecorded tape, or computer generated graphics. The possibilities for creating fake realities are multiplied once again.

With electronic keying becoming a part of a standard television practice in the 1970s, not just still but also time-based images finally began to routinely rely on montage within a shot. In fact, rear projection and other special effects shots, which had occupied marginal presence in a classical film, became the norm: a weather man in front of a weather map, an announcer in front of footage of a news event, a singer in front of an animation in a music video.

An image created through keying presents a hybrid reality, composed of two different spaces. Television normally relates these spaces thematically, but not visually. To take a typical example, we may be shown an image of an announcer sitting in a studio; behind her, in a cutout, we see news footage of a city street. If classical cinematic montage creates an illusion of a coherent space and hides its own work, electronic montage openly presents the viewer with an apparent clash of different spaces.

What will happen if the two spaces seamlessly merge? This operation forms the basis of a remarkable video "Steps" directed by Polish born filmmaker Zbignew Rybczynski in 1987. "Steps" is shot on video tape and uses keying. It also uses film footage and makes an inadvertent reference to virtual reality. In this way, Rybczynski connects three generations of fake reality technologies: analog, electronic and digital. He also reminds us that it was the 1920s Soviet filmmakers who first fully realized the possibilities of montage that continue to be explored and expanded by electronic and digital media.

In the video, a group of American tourists is invited into a sophisticated video studio to participate in a kind of virtual reality/time machine experiment. The group is positioned in front of a blue screen. Next, the tourists find themselves literally inside the famous Odessa steps sequence from Eisenstein's *Potemkin*. Rybczynski skillfully keys the shots of the people in the studio into the shots from *Potemkin* creating a single coherent space. At the same time, he emphasizes the artificiality of this space by contrasting the color video images of the tourists with the original grainy black and white Eisenstein's footage. The tourists walk up and down the steps, snap pictures at the attacking soldiers, play with a baby in a crib. Gradually, the two realities begin to interact and mix together: Some Americans fall down the steps after being shot by the soldiers from Eisenstein's sequence; a tourist drops an apple, which is picked up by a soldier.

The Odessa steps sequence, already a famous example of cinematic montage, becomes just one element in a new ironic re-mix by Rybczynski. The original shots that were already edited by Eisenstein are now edited again with video images of the tourists, using both temporal montage and montage within a shot, the latter done through video keying. A "film look" is juxtaposed with "video look," color is juxtaposed with black and white, the "presentness" of video is juxtaposed with the "always already" of film.

In "Steps" Eisenstein's sequence becomes a generator for numerous kinds of juxtapositions, super-impositions, mixes and re-mixes. But Rybczynski treats this sequence not only as a single element of his own montage but also as a singular, physically existing space. In other words, the Odessa steps sequence is read as a single shot corresponding to a real space, a space that could be visited like any other tourist attraction.

Computer Imaging

The next generation in fake reality technologies is digital media. At first glance, digital media do not bring any conceptually new techniques. They simply expand the possibilities of joining together different image sources within one shot. Rather than *keying* together images from two video sources, we can now *compose* an unlimited number of image layers. A shot may consist of dozens or even hundreds of layers, all having different origins: film shot on location, computer-generated sets or actors, digital matte paintings, archival footage and so on. Most current Hollywood films contain such shots.

Historically, a digitally composed image, like an electronically keyed image, can be seen as a continuation of montage within a shot. But while electronic keying creates disjoined spaces reminding us of the avant-garde collages of Rodchenko or Moholy-Nagy from the 1920s, digital composing brings back the nineteenth-century techniques of creating smooth "combination prints" like those of Henry Peach Robinson and Oscar G. Reijlander. However, what in the nineteenth century was only a still image now can become a moving one. A moving nineteenth-century "combination print": This is the current state of the art in the technologies of visual deception.

But this historical continuity is deceiving. Computer imaging does represent a qualitatively new step in the history of visual deception since it allows the creation of *moving* images of non-existent worlds. Computer-generated characters can move within real landscapes; conversely, real actors can move and act within synthetic environments. In contrast to nineteenth-century "combination prints," which emulated academic painting, digital compositions fully simulate the established language of cinema and television. Regardless of the particular combination of live action elements and computer-generated elements that are combined to create the scene, the camera can pan, zoom, and dolly through it. The interaction of parts of the virtual world over time along with the ability to look at it from different viewpoints become the guarantee of its authenticity.

Composing numerous elements to create a photo-realistic image is time consuming task. For instance, a 40 second sequence from "Titanic" in which the camera flies over the computer-generated ship populated by computer-generated characters took many months to produce and its total cost was 1.1 million dollars. In contrast, although the old technique of video keying could not create photorealistic images, it was possible to use it in real-time, combining two images on the fly.

Computer imaging brings a new level of realism to keying. Virtual sets technology, which was first introduced in the early 1990s and is making its way into television studios around the world, allows for real-time composition of video images and computer-generated three-dimensional elements. (Actually, because the generation of computer-elements is computation-intensive, the final image transmitted to the audience is few seconds behind the original image picked up by the television camera.) The typical application involves composing an image of an actor over a computer-generated set. The computer reads the position of the video camera and uses this information to render the set in proper perspective. The illusion is made more convincing by generating shadows and/or reflections of the actor and integrating them into the composite image. Because of the relatively low resolution of analog television, the resulting effect is quite convincing. A particularly interesting application of virtual sets is replacement and insertion of arena-tied advertising messages during live TV broadcasts of sports and entertainment events, offered by a ORAD, a company based in Israel. The system can insert computer-synthesized advertising messages onto the playing field or other empty areas in the arena in the proper perspective, as though they were present in reality.[6]

Computer imaging represents a fundamental break with previous techniques for visual deception for yet another reason. Throughout the history of representation, artists focused on the problem of creating a convincing illusion within a single image, be it a painting, a film frame or a view seen by Catherine the Great through the window of her carriage. Set making, one-point perspective, chiaroscuro, trick photography, and other cinematography techniques were all developed to solve this problem. Film montage introduces a new paradigm: creating an effect of presence in a virtual world by joining different images over time. As illustrated by digital composing for film and virtual sets applications for television, the computer era changes the paradigm once again. Having mastered the creation of a single convincing image, the artists now focus on how to join shamelessly a number of such images into one coherent whole. Whether it is composing a live video of a newscaster with a 3-D computer generated set or composing thousands of elements to create a photo-realistic image of the Titanic, the main problem is no longer how to generate convincing individual elements, but how to blend them together. Consequently, what is important now is what happens on the edges where different images are joined. The borders where different realities come together is the new arena where Potemkins of our era try to outdo one another.

2. To Act

Telepresence

So far, I have considered the historical connections between some of the technologies of deception: fake architectural spaces, montage, video keying, digital composing. I will now consider the second axis, which structures the history of visual representations: action.

If we look at the word itself, the meaning of the term *telepresence* is presence over distance. But presence where? Brenda Laurel defines telepresence as "a medium that allows you to take your body with you into some other environment. . . . [Y]ou get to take some subset of your senses with you into

6. IMadGibe. Virtual Advertising for Live Sport Events. A promotional flyer by ORAD, P.O. Box 2177, Kfar Saba 44425, Israel, 1998.

another environment. And that environment may be a computer-generated environment, it may be a camera-originated environment, or it may be a combination of the two."[7] In this definition, telepresence encompasses two different situations: being "present" in a synthetic computer-generated environment (what is commonly referred as *virtual reality*) and being "present" in a real remote physical location via a live video image. Scott Fisher, one of the developers of NASA Ames Virtual Environment Workstation, similarly does not distinguish between being "present" in a computer-generated or a real remote physical location. Describing the Ames system, he writes: "Virtual environments at the Ames system are synthesized with 3-D computer-generated imagery, *or* are remotely sensed by user-controlled, stereoscopic video camera configurations."[8] Fisher uses "virtual environments" as an all-encompassing term, reserving "telepresence" for the second situation: "presence" in a remote physical location.[9] I will follow his usage here.

Both popular media and the critics have downplayed the concept of telepresence in favor of virtual reality. The photographs of the Ames system, for instance, is often featured to illustrate the idea of an escape from any physical space into a computer-generated world. The fact that a head-mounted display can also show a televised image of a remote physical location is hardly ever mentioned.

And yet, from the point of view of the history of the technologies of deception and action, telepresence is a much more radical technology than virtual reality, or computer simulations in general. Let us consider the difference between the two.

Like fake reality technologies that preceded it, virtual reality provides the subject with the illusion of being present in a simulated world. Virtual reality goes beyond this tradition by allowing the subject to actively change this world. In other words, the subject is given control over a fake reality.

7.   Brenda Laurel, quoted in Rebecca Coyle, "The Genesis of Virtual Reality," in *Future Visions: New Technologies of the Screen,* edited by Philip Hayward and Tana Wollen (London: British Film Institute, 1993), 162.

8.   Fisher, 430. Emphasis mine.

9.   Fisher defines telepresence as "a technology which would allow remotely situated operators to receive enough sensory feedback to feel like they are really at a remote location and are able to do diffirent kinds of tasks." Scott Fisher, "Visual Interface Environments," in *The Art of Human-Computer Interface Design,* edited by Brenda Laurel (Reading, Mass.: Addison-Wesley, 1990), 427.

For instance, an architect can modify an architectural model, a chemist can try different molecule configuration, a tank driver can shoot at a model of a tank, and so on. But, what is modified in each case is nothing but data stored in a computer's memory! The user of any computer simulation has power over the virtual world that only exists inside a computer.

Telepresence allows the subject to control not just the simulation but reality itself. Telepresence provides the ability to *remotely manipulate physical reality in real time through its image.* The body of a teleoperator is linked, in real time, to another location where it can act on the operator's behalf: repairing a space station, doing underwater excavation, or bombing a military base in Baghdad or Yugoslavia.

Thus, the essence of telepresence is that it is antipresence. I don't have to be physically present in a location to affect reality at this location. A better term would be *teleaction.* Acting over distance. In real time.

Catherine the Great was fooled into mistaking painted facades for real villages. Today, from thousands of miles away (as was demonstrated during the Gulf War) we can send a missile equipped with a television camera close enough to tell the difference between a target and a decoy. We can direct the flight of the missile using the image transmitted by its camera, carefully fly toward the target, and, using the same image, blow the target away. All that is needed is to position the cursor over the right place in the computer image and press a button.

Image-Instruments

How new is this use of images? Does it originate with telepresence? Since we are used to thinking about the history of visual representations in the West in terms of illusion, it may seem that to use images to enable action is a completely new phenomenon. However, French philosopher and sociologist Bruno Latour proposes that certain kinds of images have always functioned as instruments of control and power, power being defined as the ability to mobilize and manipulate resources across space and time.

One example Latour analyzes is the perspectival image. Perspective establishes the precise and reciprocal relationship between objects and their signs. We can go from objects to signs (two-dimensional representations); but we can also go from such signs to three-dimensional objects. This reciprocal relationship allows us not only to represent reality, but also to control it.[10] For instance, we cannot measure the sun in space directly, but we only need a small ruler to measure it on a photograph (the perspectival image par excellence).[11] And even if we could fly around the sun, we would still be better off studying the sun through its representations that we can bring back from the trip—because now we have unlimited *time* to measure, analyze, and catalog them. We can "move" objects from one place to another by simply moving their representations: "You can see a church in Rome, and carry it with you in London in such a way as to reconstruct it in London, or you can go back to Rome and amend the picture." Finally, we can also represent absent things and plan our movement through space by working on representations: "One cannot smell or hear or touch Sakhalin Island, but you can look at the map and determine at which bearing you will see the land when you send the next fleet."[12] All in all, perspective is more than just a sign system, reflecting reality—it makes possible the manipulation of reality through the manipulation of its signs.

Perspective is only one example of image-instruments. Any representation that systematically captures features of reality can be used as an instrument. In fact, most types of representations that do not fit into the history of illusionism—diagrams and charts, maps and x-rays, infrared and radar images—belong to the second history: that of representations as instruments for action.

Telecommunication

Given that images have always been used to affect reality, does telepresence bring anything new? A map, for instance, already allows for a kind of tele-action: It can be used to predict the future and therefore to change it. In my view, however, there are two fundamental differences. Because telepresence involves electronic transmission of video images, the constructions of representations takes place instantaneously. Making a perspectival drawing or a chart, taking a photograph or shooting film takes time. Now I can use a remote video camera that capture images in real-time, sending these images

10.   Bruno Latour, "Visualization and Cognition: Thinking with Eyes and Hands," *Knowledge and Society: Studies in the Sociology of Culture Past and Present* 6 (1986): 1–40.

11.   Ibid., 22.

12.   Ibid., 8.

back to me without any delay. This allows me to monitor any visible changes in a remote location (weather conditions, movements of troops, and so on), adjusting my actions accordingly.

The second difference is directly related to the first. The ability to receive visual information about a remote place in real time allows us to manipulate physical reality in this place, also in real-time. If power, according to Latour, includes the ability to manipulate resources at a distance, then teleaction provides a new and unique kind of power: *real-time remote control.* I can drive a toy vehicle, repair a space station, do underwater excavation, operate on a patient, and even kill—all from a distance.

What technology is responsible for this new power? Since a teleoperator typically acts with the help of a live video image (for instance, remote operation of a moving vehicle such as in the opening sequence of *Titanic*), we may think at first that it is the technology of video, or, more precisely, of television. The original nineteenth-century meaning of television was "vision over distance." Only after the 1920s, when television was equated with broadcasting, did this meaning fade away. However, during the preceding half a century (television research begins in the 1870s), television engineers were mostly concerned with the problem of how to transmit consecutive images of a remote location to enable "remote seeing."

If images are transmitted at regular intervals, if these intervals are short enough, and if images have sufficient detail, the viewer will have enough reliable information about the remote location for teleaction. The early television systems used slow mechanical scanning and resolution as low as thirty lines. In the case of modern television systems, visible reality is being scanned at the resolution of a few hundred lines, sixty times a second. This provides enough information for most telepresence tasks.

Now, consider the Telegarden project.[13] Instead of continuos scanning of video, it uses user-driven still images. The image shows the garden from the viewpoint of the video camera attached to the robotic arm. When the arm is moved to a new location, a new still image is transmitted. These still images provide enough information for the particular teleaction in this project—planting the seeds.

As this example indicates, it is possible to teleact without video. More generally, we can say that different kinds of teleaction require different

13. http://telegarden.aec.at.

temporal and spatial resolution. If the operator needs an immediate feedback on her actions (the example of remote operation of a vehicle is again appropriate here), frequent update of images is essential. But in the case of planting a garden using a remote robot arm, user-triggered still images are sufficient.

Now, consider another example of telepresence. Radar images are obtained by scanning reality once every few seconds. The visible is reduced to a single point. A radar image does not contain any indications about shapes, textures, or colors present in a video image—it only records the position of an object. Yet this information is quite sufficient for the most basic teleaction: to destroy an object.

In this extreme case of teleaction, the image is so minimal it hardly can be called an image at all. However, it is still sufficient for real-time remote action. What is crucial is that the information is transmitted instantaneously.

If we put the examples of typical telepresence that uses video cameras and radar telepresence together, the common denominator turns out to be not video but electronic transmission of signals, in other words, electronic telecommunication, itself made possible by two discoveries of the nineteenth century: electricity and electromagnetism. This is the technology that makes teleaction in real time possible. It also allows for the new and unprecedented relationship between objects and their signs. Electronic telecommunication makes instantaneous not only the process by which objects are turned into signs but also the reverse process—manipulation of objects through these signs.

Umberto Eco once defined a sign as something that can be used to tell a lie. This definition correctly describes one function of visual representations: to deceive. But in the age of electronic telecommunication we need a new definition: A sign is something that can be used to teleact.

10

Dialogical Telepresence and Net Ecology

Eduardo Kac

Telepresence can be summarized as the union of telematics and remote physical action. Telepresence art raises the question: What are the effects of physical distance on aesthetic perception? Physical distance is at once erased and reaffirmed by new technologies. Erasure results from the sudden familiarity with and access to ideas and objects once beyond reach. Reaffirmation of distance is clear once one becomes aware of one's own subject position, prompted by the recontextualization of ideas and objects and the cultural filters inevitably used in their reception. This new condition implies that telecommunications technologies—including telerobotics, the Internet, and the coupling of both—profoundly affect our sense of self and other.

The question is not how do these technologies mediate our exploration of the world, local or remote, but how they actually shape the very world we inhabit. This is the same as saying that any technology embeds cultural and ideological parameters that, in the end, give shape to the sensorial or abstract data obtained through this very technology. Telescopic and telecommunicative technologies are no exception. In fact, one of the most important aesthetic implications of remoteness is making evident that multiple processes always filter or shape one's experience. In telepresence art, digital systems such as computers, modems, robotic devices, and networks, ultimately point to the role of culture in creating both individual and collective experiences. Cultural parameters such as language, behavioral conventions, ethical frameworks, and ideological positions are always at work in art and science.

In science, the selection of a research topic and the extraction, accumulation, and processing of data, as well as the interface through which the data are later explored are themselves an integral part of the nature of the data. They are not a detached element that causes no interference in what is experienced. Quite to the contrary: The knowledge we acquire through instruments and media is always modulated by them. They are not separable. While in science we observe the drive to build instruments capable of ever more "precise" measurements, in art we can freely explore the ways in which these instruments and media help define the nature of the reality thus produced. In interactive telepresence artworks created since 1986, I have been investigating multiple aspects of this phenomenon. In other words, my telepresence work has never been about what it would be like if we could be there (i.e., at the remote site). Instead, it investigates how does the fact that we are experiencing this remote site in a given way (i.e., through a particular telerobotic body, with a given interface, and in a specific network topology) modulate the very notion of reality we conjure up as we navigate the remote space.

We are now undergoing cultural perceptual shifts due to the remote projection of our corporeal sense of presence. In art, the dynamic interplay between presence and absence on telerobotic bodies raises new issues and escapes from rigid formal dichotomies, such as figuration versus abstraction, or formalism versus conceptualism. Expanded through the synergy of organic and cybernetic systems, bodies (human, robotic, zoomorphic, or otherwise) now become the focus of renewed attention in art—beyond stylistic pictorial concerns and representation politics. Telepresence art offers dialogical alternatives to the monological system of art and addresses our being-in-the-world through lived experience (not through representation), as it converts telecommunications links into a physical bridge connecting remote spaces. Telerobots and teleoperated humans (which I call "teleborgs") become physical avatars, as they enable single or multiple individuals to actively explore an environment or a social context.

In this new art, immediate perceptual encounters are expanded by a heightened awareness of what is absent, remote. Telepresence art shows us that from a social, political, and philosophical point of view, what we cannot see is equally relevant to what meets the eye. Telepresence art reconciles the metaphysical propensity of cyberspace with the phenomenological condition of physical space. In other words, it forms a new ecology that harmonizes carbon and silicon. As optical fibers thread the soil like worms, and digitally encoded waves cross the air as flocking birds, a new ecology emerges. To survive the imbalances created by increased standardization of interfaces (which promote uniformization of mental processes) and centralized control achieved by corporate mega-mergers (which decreases choice), and to thrive emotionally and intellectually in this hostile mediascape, we need to do more than subsist as we adapt. Our synergy with telerobots, transgenics, nanobots, avatars, biobots, clones, digital biota, hybrids, webots, animats, and other material or immaterial intelligent agents will dictate our ability to endure fast-changing environmental conditions in a networked world. In this dispersed network ecology we are globally building, telepresence art can offer new cognitive and perceptual models.

From RC Robot to the Ornitorrinco Project

My early work with telepresence art was a natural development from my investigation of telecommunications art. In 1986 I created my first work with remote-control robotics, in the context of the exhibition "Brasil High Tech," realized at the Centro Empresarial Rio, in Rio de Janeiro. For this show I used a seven-foot-tall wireless anthropomorphic robot in the role of a host who conversed bidirectionally with exhibition visitors[1] (figure 10.1). The robot's voice was that of a real human being transmitted via radio waves. Motion control was also achieved through a radio link. Still in the context of the exhibition, the robot was also used in a dialogical performance realized with Brazilian artist Otavio Donasci, in which it interacted with Donasci's videocreature (performer wearing a costume that hides the human head and replaces it with a video screen). Through the robotic body, a human improvised responses in real time to the videocreature's prerecorded utterances and to the reactions of the audience. It was a rather dramatic interaction, which culminated with the "suicide" of the videocreature. We might say that this work could be characterized as "local telepresence," to differentiate it from "remote telepresence" (i.e., works in which links are made between two or more geographically distant places). This was a telepresence work not because of the remote-control component alone but precisely because the robot became a host to a human being, and because this human—who was out of sight—conversed with other humans through the robotic body.

After this work, I started to think of ways in which it might be possible to combine my telecommunications experience with wireless telerobotics. The telerobot Ornitorrinco (platypus, in Portuguese) came to life in 1989 in Chicago,[2] as a result of my collaboration with hardware designer Ed Bennett

1. The robot was built by Cristovão Batista da Silva.

2. Eduardo Kac. "Ornitorrinco: Exploring telepresence and remote sensing," *Leonardo* 24, no. 2, Special Issue on Art and Telecommunication (Oxford: Pergamon Press, 1991), p. 233; "Towards telepresence art," *Interface* 4, no. 2 (November 1992), Advanced Computing Center for the Arts and Design, The Ohio State University, 1992, pp. 2–4; "Telepresence art," in *Entgrenzte Grenzen II*, ed. R. Kriesche and P. Hoffman (Graz: Kulturdata and Division of Cultural Affairs of the City of Graz, Austria, 1993), pp. 48–72; "Ornitorrinco and Rara Avis: Networked Telepresence Art" (with a technical appendix by Ed Bennett), in the Digital Salon special issue of *Leonardo* 29, no. 5 (1996): 389–400; see also Keith Holz, "Eduardo Kac's Dialogues," in *Leonardo Electronic Almanac* 2, no. 12 (December), and in *YLEM*'s Art On-line issue, 15, vol. 2 (April 1995): 7; Simone Osthoff, "Object

Figure 10.1. RC Robot, Eduardo Kac, 1986. Exhibited in the context of the exhibition "Brasil High Tech," realized at the Centro Empresarial Rio, in Rio de Janeiro, in 1986, RC Robot was a host (welcoming the public), a performer (participating in special events), and a work of art. Through the remote agency of humans, RC Robot conversed bidirectionally with exhibition visitors. Both motion control and two-way audio were realized through radio links. The picture above shows a member of the audience embracing RC Robot at the opening of the "Brasil High Tech" show. Photo: Eduardo Kac.

(figure 10.2). The *Ornitorrinco Project* used standard DTMF signals (touch-tone sounds) produced by a regular phone to control the telerobot's body wirelessly from afar in real time. It also used DTMF signals to retrieve video stills through the same phone line from the telerobot's point of view. When no motion or imaging commands were issued, the line was open and environmental sounds could be heard in real time from Ornitorrinco's vantage point. Born out of the desire to create telepresential experiences that involved geographically distant places, Ornitorrinco experienced several changes since 1989. This fully mobile, wireless telerobot grew in size,

Lessons," *World Art Magazine,* no. 1 (1996): 18–23; Joyce Probus, "Eduardo Kac: Dialogues," *Dialogue—Arts in the Midwest* 18, no. 1 (January/February 1995): 14–16.

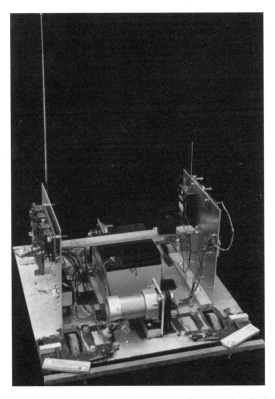

Figure 10.2. Ornitorrinco, Eduardo Kac and Ed Bennett, 1989. The *Ornitorrinco Project* used standard touch-tone sounds produced by a regular phone to control the telerobot's body wirelessly from afar in realtime. It also used DTMF signals to retrieve video stills through the same phone line from the telerobot's point of view. When no motion or imaging commands were issued, the line was open and environmental sounds could be heard in real time from Ornitorrinco's vantage point. Starting in 1994, Ornitorrinco's capabilities were expanded to incorporate the Internet. Photo: David Yox.

hosted multiple remote subjects, hybridized with different systems, reached to and was reached from several countries, and evolved its sensorial apparatus into more complex structures. In 1994 it inhabited the Internet in a piece entitled "Ornitorrinco in Eden," which merged the Net with three physical spaces in Chicago, Lexington (Ky.), and Seattle. In this work, remote participants in Lexington and Seattle shared the body of the telerobot simultaneously and in real time via a three-way call, while Ornitorrinco itself was in a third remote space in Chicago. Ornitorrinco's vision system was disseminated on the Net via live videoconferencing.

Rara Avis

In 1996 I created *Rara Avis* (figure 10.3), an interactive networked telepresence installation realized at Nexus Contemporary Art Center, in Atlanta, as part as the Olympic Arts Festival.[3] In *Rara Avis,* the participant saw a large aviary as soon as he or she walked into the room. In front of this aviary the participant saw a virtual reality headset. Inside the aviary, the viewer noticed a strong contrast between the thirty flying birds (zebra finches, which were small and mostly gray) and the large tropical macaw, which was perched and immobile. The viewer was invited to put on the headset. While wearing the headset, the viewer was transported into the aviary. The viewer now perceived the aviary from the point of view of the Macowl (contraction of macaw and owl, due to the forward position of its eyes) and was able to observe himself or herself in this situation from this displaced point of view.

The tropical bird's eyes were two CCD cameras. When the viewer, now a participant, moved his or her head to left and right, the head of the telerobotic Macowl moved accordingly, enabling the participant to see the whole space of the aviary from the Macowl's point of view. The real space was immediately transformed into a virtual space. The installation was permanently connected to the Internet (simultaneously via the Web, CU-SeeMe,

3. See Kathy Maschke, ed., *Out of Bounds,* exhibition catalog, Nexus Contemporary Art Center, Atlanta, 1996. See also Catherine Fox, "Technology as a canvas," *Atlanta Journal-Constitution,* July 26, 1996, p. 53; Kevin Nance, "It's All About Perception," *Lexington Herald-Leader,* June 23, 1996, F1, F3; Jay David Bolter. "You Are What You See," *Wired,* January 1997, pp. 113, 114, 116; Cynthia Goodman, "Working the Web," in *Artist's Market* (F&W Publishers, 1997), pp. 22–23; Pierre Lévy, *Cyberculture: Rapport au Conseil de l'Europe* (Paris: Editions Odile Jacob, 1997), p. 105; Simone Osthoff, "Eduardo Kac: Telepresença problematiza a visão," *Cadernos da Pós-Graduação do Instituto de Artes da Unicamp,* São Paulo, 1997, nol. 1, no. 1, pp. 7–12; Ken Goldberg, "VR in the age of telepresence," *Convergence* (Spring 1998). Rara Avis was also shown at the Huntington Art Gallery, in Austin, Texas (January 1997), the Centro Cultural de Belém, Lisbon, Portugal (April 1997), and the I Bienal de Artes Visuais do Mercosul, Porto Alegre, Brazil (October/November 1997). See Madeline Irvine, "Testing the Bounds," *Austin American-Statesman,* January 30, 1997, p. 47; Dominique Gates, "Omnipresent in Cyberspace" and "Rare Birds in Cyberspace," published online on Microsoft's Internet Magazine on February 24, 1997; Carlos Taveira, ed., *Cyber: A Criação na Era Digital,* exhibition catalog, Centro Cultural de Belém, Lisbon, 1997; Antônio Henriques, "Eduardo, o Pensador Digital," *Expresso,* XXI Section, Lisbon, April 19, 1997, p. 10; Frederico Morais, ed., *I Bienal de Artes Visuais do Mercosul,* exhibition catalog, Porto Alegre, Brazil; Eduardo Veras, "O mundo pelos olhos de uma arara-robô," Zero Hora, Porto Alegre, October 7, 1997, p. 6; Simone Osthoff, "Kac lembra que o lápis já foi revolucionário," *Jornal da Universidade,* Universidade federal do Rio Grande do Sul, October 1997, Porto Alegre, p. 15.

Figure 10.3. *Rara Avis,* Eduardo Kac, 1996. Wearing a virtual reality headset, participants were transported into a large aviary with a telerobotic macaw and thirty zebra finches. Viewers perceived the aviary from the point of view of the telerobot and were able to see themselves outside the cage from this displaced point of view. The tropical bird's eyes were two CCD cameras. When the viewer, now a participant, moved his or her head to left and right, the head of the telerobotic Macowl moved accordingly. The installation was permanently connected bidirectinally to the Internet (simultaneously via the Web, CU-SeeMe, and the MBone). Photo: Anna Yu.

and the MBone). Through the Net, remote participants observed the gallery space from the point of view of the telerobotic Macowl (as activated by a local viewer). Through the Internet remote participants also used their microphones to trigger the vocal apparatus of the telerobotic macaw heard in the gallery (and thus affected local birds and humans). Network ecology and local ecology mutually affected one another. I expected that the small birds would be frightened with the big colorful robot. However, in fact they became so comfortable with it that they excreted all over it throughout the exhibition. This unique combination of organic waste and clean electronics furthered a sense of integration between carbon and silicon. The body of the telerobotic Macowl was shared in real time by local participants and Internet participants worldwide. Sounds in the space, usually a combination of human and bird voices, traveled back to remote participants on the Internet.

By enabling the local participant to be both vicariously inside and physically outside the cage, this installation created a metaphor that revealed how new communications technology enables the effacement of boundaries at the same time that it reaffirms them. The installation also addressed issues of identity and alterity, projecting the viewer inside the body of a rare bird who not only was the only one of its kind in the aviary but was also distinctly different from the other birds (in scale, color, and behavior). The piece can be seen as a critique of the problematic notion of "exoticism," a concept that reveals more about relativity of contexts and the limited awareness of the observer than about the cultural status of the object of observation. This image of "the different," "the other," embodied by the telerobotic Macowl, was dramatized by the fact that the participant temporarily adopted the point of view of the rare bird.

Ornitorrinco Mutated in Finland

For the exhibition "Metamachines: Where is the Body?" realized in 1996 at Otso Gallery, in Finland, the telerobot Ornitorrinco suffered a mutation: It hosted components of Uirapuru,[4] particularly a new chip, a new camera, and a custom-designed board that enabled it to take on new behaviors. The installation entitled "Ornitorrinco, the Webot, travels around the world in eighty nanoseconds, going from Turkey to Peru and back" was divided between two remote spaces, which were linked to the Web in unexpected ways. The public first encountered the work from Otso Gallery's ground level, while Ornitorrinco navigated in its subterranean nest. Critically examining the blind trust and the expectations we project over information networks, this piece appeared straightforward but nothing really was as it seemed.

In the space upstairs, participants saw a web page interface (Netscape browser) projected on the wall with embedded live, real-time (30 fps) color video feedback. Anybody familiar with the current state of development on the Web knows that this is technically impossible because of bandwidth limitations. Still, there it was.[5] Clicking outside the video window (left/

---

4.   Uirapuru was eventually realized at the InterCommunication Center, Tokyo, between October 15 and November 28, 1999. For more information, see the catalog of ICC Biennale '99, and www.ekac.org/uirapuru.html.

5.   On the one hand, this apparently contradictory effect operated a critique of how the social credibility of mass media is derived, in part, from its technical reliability. On the other hand, it pointed to the technical future of the Web, when terabits of bandwidth coming into households will merge the Net with broadcasting. The effect was achieved by enclosing inside a pedestal three

Figure 10.4. Ornitorrinco, the Webot, Travels Around the World in Eighty Nanoseconds, Going From Turkey to Peru and Back, Eduardo Kac and Ed Bennett, 1996. The installation was divided between two remote spaces, which were linked to the Web in unexpected ways. The public first encountered a web interface from the gallery's ground level, while Ornitorrinco navigated in its subterranean nest, which was shared with two turkeys. As participants explored the piece their role changed subtly and significantly. While they were in control on the first floor, they experienced the work as active subjects. Descending the staircase that led to the basement of the gallery, they unwillingly relinquished the role of active subjects and became objects of contemplation—they themselves became the focus of multiple gazes. They were contemplated by incoming participants on the first floor who were now on Ornitorrinco's body, by the turkeys, and by remote Web viewers who logged on from different parts of the world. Photo and diagram: Eduardo Kac.

right, forward/backward) enabled participants to navigate the nest in real time, and interact with turkeys and humans from Ornitorrinco's point of view. The public participated actively, thinking that they were on the Web. They weren't. Every move they made continually resulted in fresh images, and what they did not realize at first was that these images were automatically grabbed and uploaded to a Web site (to which they themselves did not

components: a computer, a dual-input video editor and processor, and a projector. The editor embedded the live input coming from Ornitorrinco inside a multimedia application simulating the Netscape browser. An opening on the pedestal enabled the simulated interface to be projected on the wall. Clicking on the interface sent wireless motion-control signals that were decoded in real time by Ornitorrinco. It was critical to the success of this system that no wires were seen by the public.

have access from the gallery, only from home). The topology of this work was intentionally conceived to reveal that communications media alienate us from our very own utterances and actions.[6]

As participants explored the piece their role changed subtly and significantly. While they were in control on the first floor, they experienced the work as active subjects. They navigated in the remote space, they made choices, they interacted with the turkeys. Descending the staircase that led to the basement of the gallery, they found themselves behind a 4-foot high glass wall. At this point they unwillingly relinquished the role of active subjects and became objects of contemplation—they themselves became the focus of multiple gazes. They were contemplated by incoming participants on the first floor who were now on Ornitorrinco's body, by the turkeys, and by remote Web viewers who logged on from different parts of the world.

The elements that constituted the nest made a metacritical, and at times humorous, commentary on the current state of development of the Web. The space was topped by an all-encompassing coarse mesh net suspended halfway between floor and ceiling. Standing local visitors had to look through this net to see the nest. Spread through the space, indicative graffiti made a humorous commentary on the "information highway" metaphor. For example, "Turn Left" and "This Way" arrows both pointed to a corner, and "Wrong Way" was flanked by arrows pointing left and right.

Coexisting and interacting with Ornitorrinco in the same space, two real turkeys, birds known for not being among the most intelligent creatures, went about their business simultaneously representing, as colloquial American English has it, the ineptitude of technophobes and the apathy of technophiles.[7] The turkeys also resonated, in subtle and comical manner, with the words Turkey and Peru in the title. Both words represent different countries and the same bird, the first in English and the second in Portuguese: the two languages I use the most. The displacement of cultural references

6. Two ordinary instances illustrate this point. As we talk on the phone, for example, we do not know if our words go up to a satellite, down to an underwater cable, or just above our heads via a microwave link (or all of the above in a single call). As we slide a credit card to purchase a product, we do not know in what kinds of databases information about the transaction is stored (amount, date, nature of selected products, brand of choice, etc.).

7. In the United States, the word *turkey* is slang for a person considered inept or undesirable, and for something that fails.

and dispersal of subjects that has always informed Ornitorrinco's life was experienced anew in this piece. As Ornitorrinco mutated in Finland, it explored the detachment of the subject from a single body as well as relative and imaginary geographies, accompanied as it was in its hay-filled nest by a large plastic globe. Ornitorrinco qua webot circumnavigated the globe, occasionally moving it by means of direct physical contact.

One important aspect of this work was to be sure that the turkeys would be comfortable in the space and feel at home in the nest they shared with the webot. After consultation with the Finnish farmers who bred the turkeys, they stated that since the turkeys live in a small cage with seventy other turkeys, and with practically no space to move around, they would be happy with the unprecedented freedom and the unusually large room. An official visit during the show by city and provincial government veterinarians confirmed that both were in excellent shape.

As happy as they were, the turkeys spent time looking at the pictures on the wall, in a manner somewhat similar to a human being (to everyone's surprise).[8] The graffiti on the wall were both an ironic commentary on the information highway and a means to adorn the nest, although no one expected the turkeys to actually care much about them. On occasion, the turkeys would stop in front of the graffiti (they were all either signs or caricatures I made of the turkeys, Ed Bennett and myself), and spent some time contemplating it. The emergence of this behavior was as intriguing as the behavior of humans in relation to the turkeys once humans were embodied on the webot.

Phil and Phoebe also helped organize the space to their satisfaction by spreading hay anywhere they felt like it. Another clear sign that they felt at home was the abundance and quality of the fecal matter they spread all over the space. This created a peculiar situation, since the telerobot Ornitorrinco never shared a space with living animals before. While most people thought

8. For a discussion of pictorial competence in animals and its relevance to art, see Arthur C. Danto, "Animals as Art Historians: Reflections on the Innocent Eye," in *Beyond the Brillo Box: The Visual Arts in Post-Historical Perspective* (New York: Farrar, Straus & Giroux, 1992), pp. 15–31. For a discussion of alternative "possibilities for our involvement with computer technology based on varied determinations of how the world is known," see Carol Gigliotti, "What Children and Animals Know That We Don't," in ISEA'94 Proceedings, online publication of the University of Art and Design, Helsinki, 1994. http://www.uiah.fi/bookshop/isea_proc/high&low/j/18b.html

that this would be a problem, in fact the webot did welcome the excrement. The waste matter eliminated from the bowels of the turkeys made the floor a little more slippery, which made the webot's motions smoother. This decreased the stress on the webot's motors, and therefore demanded less from its battery, conserving more energy for a whole day's activity. The webot, just like the Macowl before it, felt quite at home with feces. In this tale of feathers, circuit boards, web servers, and dung, the moral is that there is more to netlife than meets the eye onscreen when the harmony between humans, robots, animals and the Internet is at stake.

The Telepresence Garment

I first conceived the *Telepresence Garment* in 1995. This work, which I finished in 1996, came out of the necessity to explore ways in which technology envelops the body, suppresses self-control, and shields it from direct sensorial experience of the environment. Instead of a robot hosting a human, the Telepresence Garment presents a roboticized human body converted into a host of another human. Far from utopian or escapist portrayals of the potential of these technologies, the Telepresence Garment is a sign of their problems.

A key issue I explore in my work as a whole is the chasm between opticality and cognizance, that is, the oscillation between the immediate perceptual field, dominated by the surrounding environment, and what is not physically present but nonetheless still directly affects us in many ways. The Telepresence Garment creates a situation in which the person wearing it is not in control of what is seen, because he or she cannot see anything through the completely opaque hood. The person wearing the Garment can make sounds, but cannot produce intelligible speech because the hood is tied tightly against the wearer's face. An elastic and synthetic dark material covers the nose, the only portion of flesh that otherwise would be exposed. Breathing is not easy. Walking is impossible, since a knot at the bottom of the Garment forces the wearer to be on all fours and to move sluggishly.

The Garment is divided into three components. The Transceiver Hood has a CCD attached to a circuit board, both sewed to the leather hood on the left side, and an audio receiver sewed on the right side. The CCD is lined up with the wearer's left eye. Underneath the Garment, the wearer dons in direct contact with the skin what I call a Transmitter Vest, which is wired to the Hood and which enables wireless transmission of 30 fps color video from the point of the view of the wearer's left eye. Enveloping the body is an opaque Limbless Suit, so called because one cannot stand or stretch one's arms, temporarily reducing or eliminating the functionality of the limbs.

The emerging field of wearable computing suggests that the very meaning of clothing is changing in the mediascape. Instead of adorning or expanding the body, however, the Telepresence Garment secludes it from the environment, suggesting some of the most serious consequences of technology's migration to the body. Body sensations are heightened once the wearer removes the garment. This pret-a-porter foregrounds the other meanings of the verb "to wear": to damage, diminish, erode, or consume by long or hard use; to fatigue, weary, or exhaust. The Telepresence Garment was experienced publicly for the first time in the context of *Ornitorrinco in the Sahara,* a dialogical telepresence event Ed Bennett and I presented at the IV Saint Petersburg Biennale, which took place in Saint Petersburg, Russia, in 1996.[9]

Ornitorrinco in the Sahara

In the case of *Ornitorrinco in the Sahara,* the phrase "dialogical telepresence event" refers to a dialogue between two remote participants who interacted in a third place through two bodies other than their own. Realized in a public area of a downtown building in Chicago, The School of the Art Institute, without any prior announcement to facilities users, the event mentioned above consisted basically of three nodes linking the downtown site in real time to The Saint Petersburg History Museum (a Biennale sponsor) and the Aldo Castillo Gallery, located in the well known Chicago gallery district. Through these telecommunications ports of entry human remote subjects interacted with one another by projecting their wills and desires onto equally remote and fully mobile, wireless telerobotic and teleborg objects.

One of the Saint Petersburg Biennale directors, Dmitry Shubin, used a black and white videophone to control (from the Saint Petersburg History Museum) the wireless telerobot Ornitorrinco (at The School in Chicago) and to receive feedback (in the form of sequential video stills) from the

---

9.   In addition to an exhibition catalog, the Biennial published a book with critical writings on electronic art. See Eduardo Kac, "Ornitorrinco and Rara Avis," in Dmitry Golinko-Volfson, *The Visuality of the Unseen* (St. Petersburg, Russia: Borey-Print, 1996), pp. 111–122.

telerobot's point of view. The use of the videophone was necessary because the Biennale lost all Internet connections at the last minute. At the same time, my own body was enveloped by the wireless Telepresence Garment (figure 10.5). The dispossessed human body was controlled, via a telephone connection, by artist and art historian Simone Osthoff from the Aldo Castillo Gallery. Considerate of my sensorial deprivation, Osthoff spoke slowly and paused intermittently, commanding the body as if via a telempathic sense of touch.[10] The color video feed from the teleborg (in this case, the Garment wearer) was transmitted live to another space in the downtown Chicago building, enabling local viewers, surprised and unaware of the situation, to see the dialogical experience in real time (from the point of view of the teleborg, which itself could not see). During the event, while both the telerobot and the teleborg were remote-controlled, a unique dialogical telepresence situation unfolded.

Conclusion

The works discussed in this chapter created dialogical telepresence experiences. They suggest the need to nurture a network ecology with humans and other mammals, with plants, insects, artificial beings, and avian creatures, as was the case with *Rara Avis* and with the warm-blooded, egg-laying, feathered vertebrates included in Ornitorrinco's Finnish netnest. Network ecology, with its shortcomings, drawbacks, and political ramifications, as well as its latent expansion of human potentialities, is a motive power of our digital nomadism. There is today a general feeling of artistic openness in the one-world of global information exchange, partially shaped by pervasive electronic media, commutation of points of view, greater visa-free mobility, and immigration. In this scenario it is unfortunate to observe that most cultural institutions resist electronic art at the same time that they express the urgent need to attract larger, newer, and returning audiences. This over-zealous attitude is grounded on the fallacious postmodernist credo that innovation is no longer possible, meaningful, or desirable. The serious danger of this position is to blindly dismiss the differentia specifica of most radical directions in electronic art as anomalies in a global free market of postmodernist polyphonic styles.

10.   I coined the word *telempathy* to designate the ability to have empathy at a distance.

Figure 10.5. *Telepresence Garment,* Eduardo Kac, 1995/96. This project converts a human body into the servant of another human. The Transceiver Hood has a CCD attached to a circuit board, both sewn to the leather hood on the left side, and an audio receiver on the right side. The CCD is lined up with the wearer's left eye. Underneath the garment, in direct contact with the skin, is a Transmitter Vest, which is wired to the Hood and which enables wireless transmission of 30 fps color video from the point of the view of the wearer's left eye. Enveloping the body is an opaque Limbless Suit, so called because one cannot stand or stretch one's arms, temporarily reducing or eliminating the functionality of the limbs. Photo: Anna Yu.

Dialogical Telepresence and Net Ecology

In this sense, it is imperative to assert alternatives that promote digital-to-analog integration and which lead to unprecedented hypermedia, telematic, and post-biological experiences.[11] Telepresence is one such alternative. Telepresence creates the experience of having a sense of one's own presence in a remote space (and not only the sense of somebody else's remote presence, as is common on the telephone). Reflecting on the passage into digital culture and escaping from rubrics that categorize past directions in contemporary art—such as body art, installation, wearable art, happening, video art, performance, and conceptual art—telepresence works have the power to contribute to a relativistic view of contemporary experience and at the same time create a new domain of action and interaction for the human body.

11.   See Eduardo Kac, "Aspects of the aesthetics of telecommunications," in *Siggraph Visual Proceedings,* ed. John Grimes and Gray Lorig (New York: Association for Computing Machinery, 1992), pp. 47–57; "The Internet and the Future of Art," in *Mythos Internet,* ed. Stefan Muenker and Alexander Roesler, (Frankfurt: Suhrkamp Verlag, 1997), pp. 291–318; "Foundation and Development of Robotic Art," in *Digital Reflections: The Dialogue of Art and Technology,* special issue of *Art Journal* 56, no. 3 (Fall 1997) (Johanna Drucker, guest editor): 60–67.

11

Presence, Absence, and Knowledge in Telerobotic Art

Machiko Kusahara

Representing a "here-and-now" (or a juxtaposition between "here" and "there") through bodies, subjects, and the space they occupy has become a major theme of art in the postmodern era. Insofar as contemporary art visualizes problems from the unconscious, this suggests a problem in contemporary life concerning the reality of time and space. Today's telecommunications technology gives us unprecedented abilities to observe and manipulate distant objects—including distant people. In so doing, it raises questions about our relationship to those objects we manipulate, how we can know those objects, and ultimately about our relationship to ourselves—our minds, our bodies. Telerobotic art explores these issues by presenting experiences and situations that test our conceptions of presence and absence, seeing and being seen, manipulating and being manipulated.

In this chapter, I examine how recent works of telerobotic art raise and address these telepistemological questions. I focus in particular on six artists and works that actively explore these themes: *Light on the Net, Tillie the Telerobotic Doll, Rara Avis, Telegarden, where I can see my house from here so we are,* and *Ping Body.* All of these works address, in various ways, questions of knowledge, experience, presence and absence that are raised by contemporary telerobotic technology.

This theme can be seen as a response to questions raised by Benjamin and developed by Sontag.[1] Reproduction technology such as photography changed the meaning of art by taking away the aura that marked the essential feature of paintings and an important part of their value.[2] A photograph treats time and space differently than traditional painting does. A work of photography proves that the person (photographer) was there, then. Photography records what is "here-and-now" and delivers that moment and space to the viewer.

The history of reproduction technology reached another milestone with the advent of modern telecommunications. In its prevideo infancy, television was a real-time technology that transformed "here and now" into "there and now." A framed portion of space that really existed somewhere (generally in the studio) was broadcast in real time to viewers. Figures on the television screen were not physically present in the space where they were viewed

1.　Susan Sontag, *On Photography* (New York: Farrar, Straus, and Giroux, 1977).

2.　See also Marina Gržinić, "Exposure Time, the Aura, and Telerobotics" (this volume).

(typically a living room), but viewers could assume they existed *somewhere*—in a different space, but at the same time, that is, now. With video and magnetic storage, however, even this became unclear. One can no longer assume that the scene one is watching is currently taking place somewhere. With blue screen technology and digital special effects, it is no longer even certain that the scene one sees on the screen has *ever* taken place.[3]

Being here and now means being present with the physical body, not merely communicating via electronic signals or optochemical material. Art performances using the body (consider Yves Klein and Jackson Pollock) can be regarded as an early recognition of these concerns—an attempt to realize an art of presence, rather than absence.

Our culture is undergoing a truly drastic change in terms of our physical and psychological relationship with space and other bodies. Digital technology (computer graphics, virtual reality, telecommunications) has brought us the notion of disembodied presence. We can no longer simply believe what our eyes see and our ears hear. Telerobotics makes it possible to represent oneself in far-away places through a network. But how do others know that the robot is operated by a real person? And how do we know that the robot is representing the world accurately back to us?

In this chapter I discuss select works of art related to telerobotics and telepistemology, works that examine the way we experience and understand space, distance, presence, and our bodies in the context of digital technology.

Telecommunications art goes back at least to the 1980s, or even to the late 1970s. In his *Good Morning Mr. Orwell* (1984), Nam Jun Paik used satellites to connect various remote locations. Kit Galloway and Sherry Labinowitz, who are known as the founders of the first Electronic Cafe in Santa Monica, realized a similar concept even earlier in *A Space With No Geographical Boundaries* (1977), where artists from different continents performed virtually on a single screen. In 1980, Galloway and Labinowitz created a public interactive performance, *Hole-in-Space,* which used large screens and cameras to virtually link two streets in New York and Los Angeles. Passers-by figured out how the screens and cameras worked, and started using them.[4] In the early 1990s, telecommunications technology began to combine with

3. Margaret Morse relates television to virtual space in *Virtualities: Television, Media Art and Cyberculture* (Bloomington: Indiana University Press, 1998).

4. http://www.ecafe.com/

robotics. An early project in telerobotics art was realized by a group of researchers, artists, and engineers at Van Gogh TV in Germany, who connected viewers' telephones to a television studio.[5] In an interactive television project, *Piazza Virtuale* (1992), viewer/participants used push-phone numeric keys to control the movement and zooming of a robot camera in the studio. The resulting image appeared immediately on viewers' television sets. The project strongly reflected the group's vision of a networked, widely accessible shared reality.

The Internet vastly expanded communication and cooperation as artistic themes. In 1994 two telerobotic art projects were realized on the Internet: the *Mercury Project*[6] and Kac and Bennett's *Ornitorrinco in Eden,* which enabled remote participants to share control of a wireless telerobot. Another project was Masaki Fujihata's *Light on the Net* (1996).[7] (See figures 11.1 and 11.2.) Visitors find a live image of the entrance hall of a building in Gifu Prefecture, with 7 × 7 matrix of light bulbs. By clicking on any of them, one can switch a bulb on or off. The design is simple and beautiful. The live image is in fact a clickable map, which instantaneously reflects the change. Log file shows the history of visitors. The piece was designed to be a spiritual meeting place on the Net, where one's visit leaves a trace on a physical object.

Fujihata also created the *Global Interior Project* (1995),[8] which consists of 18 white cabinets on the exhibition floor, and a number of personal computers at remote locations all networked via ISDN line. Through the computers, users can navigate a virtual world that contains 18 rooms corresponding to the cabinets. Each room depicts a theme (e.g., language, memory, religion, sex), and is represented by an image that corresponds to a physical object in the real world, that is, in one of the cabinets. These objects are all made of LEGO blocks. Identical elements in artificial colors form different objects in unnaturally jagged forms. What do they signify? Does a LEGO missile represent war? Every time someone enters or leaves a virtual room, the door of the corresponding (real) cabinet opens or closes with a loud bang, showing—or hiding—the object inside.

5.   http://www.vgtv.com/

6.   http://www.usc.edu/dept/raiders/

7.   http://light.softopia.pref.gifu.jp/

8.   http://www.flab.mag.keio.ac.jp/GIP/

Figure 11.1. Masaki Fujihata's 1996 *Light on the Net* Project (http://light.softopia.pref.gifu.jp/).
Courtesy of the artist.

Figure 11.2. *Light on the Net* with pattern spelling "HI." Courtesy of the artist.

Machiko Kusahara

Although it does not use the Internet, *Global Interior Project* provides a clear example of a central dynamic in telerobotic art: Actions in a *virtual* space bringing about changes in the *real* world. This juxtaposition of the virtual and the real plays an important role in telerobotics art, both aesthetically and epistemologically. Many telerobotic art installations make it possible for us to see through the eyes of another—a doll, a mechanical bird, a robotic gardener, a robot made of junk—through our interaction with a virtual world presented on a video monitor. But how do we know that this virtual world corresponds to the real one? And how does our position— both in the real world and in the virtual one—affect our experience of ourselves and our world? These are central questions for telerobotic art and telepistemology.

A Doll's Eye View

Reliance on tracking and surveillance techniques has resulted in a culture that has a peripheral vision that extends beyond normal human physiology. In many cases, there is a merging of human and machine capabilities that create new beings, cyborgs, whose virtual reach, and in this case sight, is extended beyond physical location. Identity becomes intangible on the Internet and Tillie's face becomes a mask for the multiple expressions of the self that links each person to another.

— LYNN HERSHMAN LEESON[9]

Tillie, a typical feminine-looking doll, stares at you from the web site of the San Francisco based artist Lynn Hershman Leeson (*Tillie, The Telerobotic Doll,* 1998). Each of Tillie's eyeballs moves slightly as you move the cursor on it. Click on an her eye and an image of a gallery wall appears in a window below. It is what the doll sees in the gallery—in the physical space where she sits. The doll's eyeballs have been replaced with cameras that send images to the Internet. Through Tillie's eyes you can look around the gallery, turning her head to get the view you want. You can also visit the gallery itself, and watch the physical Tillie in front of you. You will see your own image physically reflected in Tillie's eyes, but you are also being watched by countless unknown Internet users behind her, who are using Tillie's face as a mask

9. Lynn Hershman Leeson, press release for *Tillie, the Telerobotic Doll,* 1998.

Figure 11.3. Lynn Hershman Leeson's *Tillie, the Telerobotic Doll* (1998): www.lynnhershman.com

and watching you through her eyes. The gallery becomes a bit of a peep-show, or a one-way mirror. As Hershman Leeson states, "voyeurism and surveillance tactics have become extensions of our 'I.' Cameras have become both eyecons and contact lenses" (1997).[10]

The Distant Garden

Since Eden, the garden has been a metaphorical space, especially in Japan. The stone garden of Ryoanji Temple invites visitors into meditation while physically it is just a set of stones and pebbles. I was born and grew up in central Tokyo by an old garden named Rikugien—one of the most famous and typical landscape gardens where visitors would walk along carefully designed winding paths that lead them through an unfolding experience in

10.   Lynn Hershman Leeson, press release for *Dominant Culture,* 1997. Hershman Leeson's earlier works (*Roberta, Room of One's Own*) and her latest work (*Difference Engine 3*) are deeply related to issues of self and others, virtual persona, seeing and being seen, and the relations between real and virtual. See http://www.lynnhershman.com for her previous works and essays. Also see Machiko Kusahara "Are We Still Enjoying Interactivity?" *Publication of Prix Ars Electronica 99,* Springer, 1999.

old Japanese and Chinese literature. Every rock, stream, tree, and arbor refers to certain scene in a poem or legend. Both in Ryoanji and Rikugien, as well as in other metaphorical gardens, what one sees and experiences is something beyond the physical entity the garden implies. The garden, the real space, is the field of imagination and/or discovery.

I call such space a *field*. A field, in physics, is a space that implies potential force or energy that would be applied to objects that enter the space. In mathematics, a field is an abstract multidimensional space filled with vectors. A field in biology is a piece of land where ecological interaction takes place between species. A field is a powerful interface for imagination, communication, and interaction between the real and the virtual.

Historically and psychologically, gardens carry a sense of secrecy: Eden, the Garden of Eros where Psyche sneaks in, *The Secret Garden*—a classic novel and film. Secrecy is also a feature of many gardens in China and Japan. Visitors to Kyoto, for instance, are disappointed not to see anything while walking on the street. All the beautiful gardens are hidden behind high walls. It is the same in China. A garden is an extension of a private, inner space into the outer world. Like skin, a garden belongs both to the outer open space and to one's inner life. It was with the arrival of civil society that gardens became open spaces, often surrounded by fences instead of walls. Gardens in the United States and Canada are generally open. A typical garden in front of a suburban house surrounded by a low hedge or fence serves both as proof of the owner's status (that is why most of them look alike) and as the interface for communication with neighbors.

The Telegarden (1994)[11] by Ken Goldberg, Joe Santarromana, and their collaborators, brought back the thrill of secrecy to the garden. What is the feeling of owning a flower or a vegetable in a garden that one has never visited, and will never visit, yet taking care of it telerobotically and watching it grow? Only a limited number of people know about the garden and are allowed to (telerobotically) enter. Even though it is a "common" among users who share the garden, it is still a secret garden. Like the stone garden of Ryoanji Temple, which visitors are not allowed to step into, the Telegarden is to be seen only from inside.

In a sense, the secrecy of the garden is in the garden itself. Worms, ants, and other strange creatures might be hiding in the soil. Children spend

11. http://telegarden.aec.at

hours watching them or digging the ground to catch them. And one always finds unknown plants growing, possibly carried in by birds. It is the rich soil, the earth itself that provides continuous wonder.

A garden is field of possibilities, and so is the *Telegarden.* This Internet telerobotics art project is not merely an opportunity to garden via network. The garden is a field that elicits communication among its users. Goldberg and his colleagues describe the Telegarden as

an experiment in creating a planned virtual community, one in which the virtual space invites participation and encourages return visits. The Telegarden is a telerobotic art installation accessible via the World Wide Web in which remote visitors can participate, manipulating an industrial robotic arm to control a color CCD camera, plant phlox, eggplant and other flora, and water their own and others' seedlings.[12]

Users can participate if they agree to reveal their names and email addresses to other users. Each user accepts responsibility for maintaining the garden and respecting others. *Telegarden* is not a simulation. Users are dealing with live plants growing in a real garden. The garden on the Internet is a Commons in the traditional sense (as in Boston Common). It literally offers users a common ground. A Commons elicits and requires communication among users.

In this respect, the "Telegarden phenomenon" has something in common with the Tamagotchi, which is a virtual pet in one's pocket. The Tamagotchi became popular because it served as a communication tool among children. But the joy also came from the classic thrill of owning something live in one's pocket—like many schoolboys used to have. The problem with Tamagotchi is that it has nothing to do with real life, and it was a simple and poor simulation of life's complexity. *Telegarden* is based on life in a real (but remote) physical space.

The distal nature of the Telegarden is precisely what makes it interesting from a telepistemological point of view. The Telegarden is real, but (unlike a traditional Commons) we never actually see, feel, or hear the garden itself— It is too far away for that. Our knowledge of the Telegarden is technologically mediated, and that introduces a disturbing doubt: How do I know that

12. http://telegarden.aec.at

Figure 11.4. Robot surrounded by mirrored walls in K. Feingold's *where I can see my house from here so we are*, Interactive Media Festival, Los Angeles, 1995. Courtesy of the artist.

the Telegarden really exists? Perhaps the *Telegarden* web site is simply sending me prestored images of a garden that no longer exists. How do I know that the Telegarden community exists? I *think* the Telegarden provides a high-tech common where I can interact with other users. But how do I know that those users really exist—that they are not fabrications of the artist, or even mere "virtual" personas cleverly programmed to mimic on-line chat?[13]

Hall of Mirrors

Among the line-up of interactive installation works selected and exhibited at the Interactive Media Festival 95 (it will be remembered as one of the best shows of interactive art in the 1990s), Ken Feingold's *where I can see my house from here so we are* was unique. In the middle of a large floor there was an arena divided into three sections by low, mirrored walls. In each section lived a metal robot that Feingold had built out of junk-like materials—

13.   On these virtual personas, see Judith Donath, "Being Real" (this volume).

Presence, Absence, and Knowledge in Telerobotic Art

dishes and bowls from a Chinese restaurant supply shop, a molded metal head modeled after an old ventriloquist puppet (or was it a fortune-telling machine?), and a mechanical drive with wheels to move the robot around. The three robots looked identical except for slight differences in color.

Each robot was controlled by a visitor/user in a personal, curtained booth. The booths were located in three corners of the floor. (They were supposed to be installed in remote sites and connected via ISDN, but practical constraints forced them to share the same floor, divided by curtains so that users could not see the arena or each other directly.) Users saw the arena on a projection screen from the point of view of "their" respective robots. Users also heard sounds transmitted from the robots, and when users spoke into microphones, the robots opened their mouths to speak. Joysticks allowed users to manipulate their robots, driving them within their respective segments of the arena.

Driving them to do what? To communicate with each other, of course. Each user would try to find other robots in the arena to communicate with. It was not an easy: The infinite reflections of the mirrored walls produced innumerable robot images and a labyrinth of walls. One would look for buddies (through the robot's body and eye) only to find reflections of oneself (i.e., of one's robot). With the limited sight provided by the little CCD camera in the robot's eye, one could not get an overview of the arena. Users would manipulate the joystick hopelessly without knowing if they were moving the right way or not. People got lost in their robot bodies. Other visitors watching the arena would observe a robot turning away from its buddies only to talk to itself on the outer wall.

Feingold's installation draws our attention to the enormous difficulty of acquiring knowledge by telerobotic means. From its description, Feingold's installation seems to embody the telerobotic dream: using the Internet and a robot to discover a foreign environment and communicate with others. But the reality was a horrible failure, at least as an attempt to acquire knowledge about the robot's surroundings. It is extremely difficult to use these robots to discover anything. We are constantly lost and confused, trying in vain to know where we are, who we are communicating with, what we are seeing, etc. The dream of Internet telerobotics as a tremendous expander of our knowledge falls apart amid a reality of confusion and loss of control.

Feingold's telerobotic installation continues work he had been doing even before the Internet. In one of his earlier works, *The Surprising Spiral,* participants traveled through time and space (through video that the artist shot during his travels) by turning pages of a thick book that served as the interface. But like the robotic installation, this one came with a catch: Participants often saw no direct correlation between their inputs and the changing scene. An algorithm mixed user inputs with inputs from *previous* users, preventing a clear one-to-one correlation between inputs and outputs. Some participants complained, but it was part of the artist's point. Traveling through unfamiliar lands is always a problem. Isn't it an illusion that we are on our own and free to travel the virtual world as we like? The work was a commentary on control issues in interactivity and today's digital media. Feingold explains:

The structure of the work is such that the viewer/participant cannot *know* what effects their actions will produce. What I learned was that many who encountered this work were frustrated by their inability to "get what they wanted," to control the work. Interactivity is, in many ways, about affirmation of the human action by a nonhuman object, a narcissistic "it sees me." But beyond that, there is the desire for *control,* for *mastery* over the non-human entity. I also learned that it is a rare viewer who feels comfortable in the role of *public* participant in an interactive work which has no clear "goal." People always seem to ask the same questions when the "destination" of the interaction is unclear—"How is it structured?," "Is it random?," "How can I get what I want (or see what I want to see)?," "Am I doing it right?," "What will happen if I do this or that?"

[I]t pointed something out to me very clearly—that people expected unambiguous interaction. It actually disappointed me tremendously, as I expect the audience, and audiences turned into participants, to bring to interactive works the same capacity for abstraction, metaphor, and ambiguity that are well deployed and comfortable when viewing painting, or other artworks.[14]

Wired Flesh

Stelarc, the Australian performance artist, gives unforgettable performances. While other artists use telerobotics to move some type of mechanism, such as a camera or robot, Stelarc uses it to move his own body. His

14.   Ken Feingold, lecture on "Technology in the '90s," The Museum of Modern Art, New York, April 7, 1997. I thank the artist for giving me access to his text for the lecture. See also http://www.kenfeingold.com/

Figure 11.5. Stelarc. *Ping Body,* 1997.

body is the object, the mechanism to be manipulated remotely. The involuntary body, or the externalization of body, is the central theme of his works.

[Stelarc] has devised an "Internet body upload system" that enables audience members to reach out and touch him in ways AT&T never imagined. In *Fractal Flesh—Split Body: Voltage-In/Voltage-Out,* a performance that took place November 10–11, 1995 at Telepolis, an art and technology festival organized in Luxembourg by the Munich Media Lab, Stelarc plugged himself into muscle-stimulation circuitry controlled by a Mac. The Mac, in turn, was connected, via the Internet, to Paris's Centre Pompidou, Helsinki's Media Lab, and Amsterdam's Doors of Perception conference. By pressing a color-coded 3-D rendering of a human body on a touchscreen, participants at the three sites jolted the artist's (literally) wired body into action. Blipped across the net through a high-speed link to the computer in the performance space, their gestures triggered Stelarc's muscle-stimulators; low-level bursts of voltage, zapping through electrodes attached to his limbs, caused both arms and one leg to jerk involuntarily into raised or extended positions.[15]

15.   Mark Dery, http://math.lehman.cuny.edu/tb/stelarc.html

Stelarc's performances raise, in a particularly immediate and striking way, one of the central problems in telepistemology: a telerobotic version of philosophy's problem of other minds. I attended one of Stelarc's performances at the Maribor Media Festival in Slovenia (1996). It was a strange experience to act as a sort of marionette operator manipulating a real human—especially for me, since I have known Stelarc for many years. Although Stelarc is an old friend, there was a strange absence of reality for me. When I gave him electric shocks to jerk his limbs, it was like manipulating a machine or a robot. It was hard to accept that I was causing him pain, even though I saw his body writhe and jerk. There was, after all, no feeling of pain in *my* side or *my* arm.

In some respects, this resembles an old problem in philosophy: How do we know, purely on the basis of their *physical* behavior, what is going on in other people's minds? But the problem here is slightly different: The technology furthers the sense of remoteness of unreality of the pain. I would never hit Stelarc or shock him with a cattle prod—in these low-tech cases, his pain seems all too real. But somehow the mediation of a network and a computer monitor make Stelarc's pain seem more remote, less real.[16] The installation even encourages this, by shielding the user from Stelarc's view and presenting her with a clean, user-friendly interface design that seems designed to avoid any personal feeling. I have no doubt that Stelarc would feel pain at the other end of a cattle prod, but how do I know what he feels at the other end of a network designed to insulate me from his pain?

The distance that technology imposes between us and other minds reached a new level with a recent Stelarc performance in ICC (Tokyo, 1997) and elsewhere. This time, there was no direct control of his body by the audience. Stelarc was connected to the Internet. A search engine was constantly checking traffic on several pornographic and body-related web sites and giving the numbers to the engine that activated the stimulators. So the "master" was the Internet itself. Stelarc's body became a slave of information on the Net—the invisible distillation of the desires of people across the globe.

Stelarc's performances may be extreme, but they raise issues that are becoming increasingly universal in the world of email, telerobotics, and the

16. On the telepistemological version of the problem of other minds, see Judith Donath, "Being Real."

Internet. It is well documented that people behave differently on the Internet than they do in person. They are much more willing to say and do things that are angry, hurtful, and obscene. Stelarc's performances offer a deep insight into this phenomenon. As technology mediates our interaction with each other, it also distances us from their thoughts, feelings, and emotions. This distance gives us—as it gave me at the Stelarc performance—an odd, disturbing sense of boldness and disregard.

In all of these artworks, we see how telerobotic technology expanded the opportunities for media art. Art makes us discover or realize something in our lives that is important, but we tend to forget or overlook. What, then, are the thoughts these telerobotic art works provoke? By enabling users to interact telerobotically with distant environments, artists force us to examine the relationships between proximal, distal, and virtual spaces. Experiencing correlations and gaps between the proximal and the remote makes us think about the nature of the media society in which we live—and the mediation of knowledge and experience that is its hallmark.

12

Exposure Time, the Aura, and Telerobotics

Marina Gržinić

This chapter focuses on the notions of exposure time and the photographic aura in the context of Internet telerobotics. I examine the aesthetic, political, artistic, and epistemological impact of the technological transition from exposure lasting several hours to only a fraction of a second, what for Walter Benjamin marked the gradual destruction of "aura" from the image. And I discuss the ways in which the current limitations of telerobotic technology—delays in transmission-time, busy signals from service providers, crashing web browsers—can be seen as restoring the aura, and with it our sense of space and time.

I. Evaporation of the Aura from Photography to Video

In "A Small History of Photography" (1931)[1] and "The Work of Art in the Age Mechanical Reproduction" (1936),[2] Benjamin asserts that an object's "aura" is destroyed through its reproducibility. He distinguishes the social-historical experience of photographic representation from that of aesthetic contemplation. Benjamin defines aura as "the unique appearance or semblance of distance, no matter how close the object may be,"[3] and claims that the modern, contracted conception of space was brought on by the aura's decay. Benjamin illustrates this with an example in which we experience the passage of time in nature: "While resting on a summer's noon, to trace a range of mountains on the horizon, or a branch that throws its shadow on the observer, until the moment or the hour [becomes] part of their appearance—that is what it means to breathe the aura of those mountains, that branch."[4]

In "A Small History of Photography" Benjamin focuses on how the problem of time characterized the evolution of early photography. I quote D. N. Rodowick's concise but effective presentation:

Neither the indexical quality of the photograph nor its iconic characteristics fascinated Benjamin as much as the interval of time marked by exposure. In the techno-

1. Walter Benjamin, "A Small History of Photography," in *One Way Street*, trans. Edmund Jephcott and Kingsley Shorter (London: NLB, 1979), 240–257.

2. Walter Benjamin, "The Work of Art in the Age of Mechanical Reproduction," in *Illuminations*, ed. Hannah Arendt (New York: Schocken Books, 1968), pp. 217–251.

3. Benjamin, "A Small History of Photography," p. 250.

4. Ibid.

logical transition from an exposure time requiring several hours to only fractions of a second, Benjamin marked the gradual evaporation of aura from the image. The idea of aura invoked here is clearly related to Bergson's *durée*. For Benjamin, the longer the interval of exposure, the greater the chance that the aura of an environment—the complex temporal relations woven through its represented figures—would seep into the image, etching itself on the photographic plate. . . . More concretely, the temporal value of the interval determines a qualitative ratio between time and space in the photograph. In the evolution from slow to fast exposure times, segmentations of time yielded qualitative changes in space: sensitivity to light, clearer focus, more extensive depth of field, and significantly, the fixing of movement. Paradoxically, for Benjamin, as the iconic and spatial characteristics of photography became more accurate by decreasing the interval of exposure, the image lost its temporal anchoring in the experience of duration, as well as the fascinating ambiguity of its "aura."[5]

I am interested in this contraction of the interval of exposure time because it depicts a process of erasure, the desire to rid ourselves of the uncontrollable movements and imperfections of long exposure times. What we are witnessing today is the constant shortening, the condensation of the interval of exposure. This shortening of exposure-time is a process of cleaning, of leaving behind the mistakes of blurriness, soft focus, and other imperfections that creep in during long exposures.

As more and more of our images are computer generated, and television and radio are overtaken by the near instantaneous speed of calculation,[6] we are witnessing an ever more exact and complete aesthetic sterilization of the image. In virtual reality, the physicality of the connection of the image with reality-time is lost. Blurs and other imperfections in the image, which were evidence of time's passage in the real world, are wholly absent from the idealized imagery of virtual reality. With the imperfections of early photography, the viewer finds ways to make a place in time. But with the collapsing of exposure time (down to nothing in the case of the computer-generated images of virtual reality), the image undergoes a process of complete steril-

5.   D. N. Rodowick, *Gilles Deleuze's Time Machine* (Durham: Duke University Press, 1997), pp. 8–9.

6.   On transmission speed and its conceptual implications, see Martin Jay's chapter (this volume).

ization. Benjamin predicted the future of photography, its inability to deal with failure, errors, rubbish:

But now let us follow the subsequent development of photography. What do we see? It has become more and more subtle, more and more modern, and the result is that we are now incapable of photographing a tenement or a rubbish-heap without transfiguring it. Not to mention a river dam or an electric cable factory: in front of these, photography can now only say, "How beautiful." "The World Is Beautiful"— that is the title of the well-known picture book by Renger-Patzsch in which we see new Objectivity photography at its peak.[7] It has succeeded in turning abject poverty itself, by handling it in a modish, technically perfect way, into an object of enjoyment. For if it is an economic function of photography to supply the masses, by modish processing, with matter which previously eluded mass consumption— Spring, famous people, foreign countries—then one of its political functions is to renovate the world as it is from the inside, i.e. by modish techniques.[8]

The tendency that Benjamin identified has increased with digital media. The images that appear on our video monitors are bright, clean, and non-threatening. With its limited resolution, bright colors, and stylized images, digital imagery represents a continuation of the sterilizing process that Benjamin identified in photography.

The process of sterilization culminated with the abstract images of the Gulf War at the end of the 1980s, and has continued with the current Western intervention in Kosovo. NATO's bombing of Yugoslavia as an intervention not for any specific economico-strategic interests, but simply because Serbia is cruelly violating the elementary human rights of Kosovo's Albanian minority, can easily be seen as part of the evacuation of the mediated image. We are witnessing what Carlo Formenti describes as the first Postmodern war.[9]

7. Albert Renger-Patzsch, *Die Welt ist Schön,* ed. Carl Georg Heise (Munich: Kurt Wolff Verlag, 1928). For a recent publication of Renger-Patzsch's photographs, see *Albert Renger-Patzsch: Photographer of Objectivity,* ed. Ann and Jurgen Wilde (Cambridge, Mass.: MIT Press, 1998).

8. Walter Benjamin, "The Author as Producer," in *Art in Theory 1900–1990,* ed. Charles Harrison and Paul Wood (Oxford: Blackwell, 1992), pp. 486–487.

9. Cf. Carlo Formenti, "La guerra senza nemici"["The War Without Enemies"], in *Guerra virtuale e guerra reale: riflessioni sul conflitto del Golfo* [*The Virtual and the Real War: Reflectons on the Gulf War*],

The abundance of "clean" images from Iraq and Serbia stands in stark contrast to the lack of information about the "dirty" and very real war in Bosnia and Herzegovina. Instead of live images, reporting from the war in Bosnia and Herzegovina generally consisted of old televised images and the voices of amateur reporters on the radio. The traumatic lesson of recent American military interventions, from Iraq in the 1980s to the present bombing of Yugoslavia, is that they signal a new era as far as the visibility, dirtiness, and number of casualties of postmodern military battles. The attacking force now operates under the constraint that it can sustain no casualties and no images of direct destruction, blood, or dead bodies.

This is why we have to ask ourselves: How much do we really know from these images about the Gulf War, or more recently about the war in Kosovo? The evening news shows us vivid, engrossing images from these wars. But the images are wholly dislocated in both time and space. NATO bombing raids take place throughout the day—while we are asleep, at work, at home, etc. But images of the raids are neatly bundled together and presented in convenient five-minute segments on the evening news.[10] Television coverage jumps, instantly and effortlessly, from Kosovo to Belgrade to an off-shore aircraft carrier to the cockpit of a Stealth Bomber. Do we really have any sense of where and when these events are taking place? Recall what went on in the final American assault on the Iraqi lines during the Gulf War: no photos, no reports, just rumors that tanks with bulldozer-like shields rolled over Iraqi trenches, burying thousands of troops in earth and sand. What went on was allegedly considered too cruel in its sheer mechanical efficiency, too different from the standard notion of heroic, hand-to-hand combat, to be allowed to influence public opinion.

But would these images really have swayed public opinion? The current conflict in the Balkans makes a mockery of the supposed omnipotence of the media. It is no longer true that horrifying visual material guarantees a backlash. Each time it seems that events in Bosnia have reached their peak,

ed. Tiziana Villani and Pierre Dalla Vigna (Milan: A. C. Mimesis, 1991), p. 29. Formenti develops this historization relying on Jean Baudrillard's text written for the French newspaper Liberation just before the Gulf War began: Baudrillard, "The Gulf War Did Not Take Place," *Liberation,* Paris, January 4, 1991.

10. For a discussion of the attractive convenience of technologically mediated experience, see Albert Borgmann, "Information, Nearness, and Farness" (this volume).

the television broadcasts even greater horrors. But the informative effect is diminished. It seems that the reports produce fiction, that the escalation of horrors (concentration camps, massacres, thousands of raped Muslim women) transforms fact into fiction. In 1987, Ernie Tee wrote in the catalog for the exhibition *Art for Television* that film was the medium of illusion, television the medium of reality and video the medium of metamorphoses,[11] but with the war in Bosnia, television has become the medium of fiction. Sensationalist realism drew the short straw in this war.

This suggests that the sterilizing effect may be inherent in the medium itself. Following Peter Weibel, we can think about televised war reporting as an attempt to imitate, artificially, the natural world of our senses.[12] Our experience of place, position and so on depends on what we call natural interface: The body is, for example, a natural interface, and therefore we have a natural approach to space and time. Our interpretation of the media is experienced through natural interfaces. Our senses and organs are channeled and mediated by an ideology of naturality, neglecting the artificiality of the media. But the media of our time presents us with an artificial interface. According to Weibel, when McLuhan defined media as an extension of man, he just missed calling it an *artificial* extension.[13] In this artificial media space, the basic issue is how to construct space and time artificially. The virtual replaces the distal.

The desire to artificially (yet compellingly) construct space and time is what drives the development of media technology. Dimitris Eleftheriotis, for example, describes the development of technology designed to eliminate the uneven, choppy movements so common in amateur videos:

The "Digital Image Stabiliser" is a popular feature of many of the new camcorders—it operates through a digital analysis of each frame which detects and eliminates "abnormal" movements. In a similar fashion, visual surveillance technology depends

11.   Ernie Tee, "The Irreality of Dance," *The Arts for Televison,* Eds. Kathy Rae Huffman and Dorine Mignot, The Museum of Contemporary Art, Los Angeles, and Stedelijk Museum, Amsterdam, 1987, p. 62.

12.   Cf. Peter Weibel, "Ways of Contextualisation, or The Exhibition as a Discrete Machine," in *Place, Position, Presentation Public,* ed. Ine Gevers (Maastricht: Jan van Eyck Akademie and De Balie, 1993), p. 225.

13.   Ibid.

upon the identification of "abnormal" or "irregular" movements which disrupt the "normal" flow of people in a street, a shopping center or supermarket—research currently undertaken looks for ways in which the detection of abnormal movement can become an automation built into the system.[14]

Stabilizers and surveillance systems can be understood as opposing aspects of the same operation of mathematically, legally, and aesthetically sterilizing the image.

Given these efforts to "clean up" the images we see, how much do we really know about the tenements, trash-heaps, wars, streets, and supermarkets depicted by today's imaging technologies? The very technologies that are supposed to give us a "clearer" image, in an important sense, do just the opposite. By sanitizing the subject, they prevent us from knowing reality itself. We lose our sense of time and place, and are left with a hopelessly stylized and idealized conception of the truth.

II. Telerobotics and Return of the Aura

The history of imaging technology from photography to video has witnessed an evaporation of the aura, of the unique phenomenon of time and space as captured in the photographic image. I want to suggest that telerobotics can be seen as reversing this trend. In its current form, telerobotics represents a way to restore the aura, to restore the sense of time and place that the image conveys.

In some respects, telerobotic images are much like other types of images, and suffer from the same evaporation of aura. Because images from telerobotic devices generally come from ordinary video or still-photo digital cameras, there is no significant difference in exposure time between telerobotics and other digital imaging technologies. So it is not in the *exposure* time that telerobotics distinguishes itself.

There is, however, a difference in *transmission* time. Telerobotic images are live images, sent to the user on demand. But those images are not transmitted instantly, or even at the speed of television and radio broadcast. Restrictions on bandwidth significantly delay transmission times, so that images arrive seconds or even minutes after they are requested.

14. Dimitris Eleftheriotis, "Video poetics: technology, aesthetics and politics," *Screen* 36, no. 2 (1995): 105.

The delay brought on by bandwidth restrictions presents practical problems for telerobotic installations. Time-delay renders the control of long-distance teleoperations difficult, if not impossible. This difficulty is sometimes overcome by a technique called "supervisory control." The main focus is on the notion of a delayed-real paradigm to overcome the effects of time delay. "The operator must adopt a 'move-and-wait' strategy whereby a small movement is made and the operator waits to observe the results of the movement before committing to further action. The premise of this research is that the time delay inherent in teleoperation over large distances can be overcome by presenting the operator with an interactive simulation of the system being controlled rather than with the time-delayed video and telemetry data. "The simulation runs several seconds ahead of real-time (and is therefore commonly referred to as a 'predictor display') so that the operator's responses and command inputs to the simulation will arrive at the remote site at the correct time. The simulation models the dynamics and behavior of the actual system and responds immediately to operator inputs, thereby precluding the need for a move-and-wait strategy. The challenge is to keep this simulation 'synchronized' with reality."[15]

These practical difficulties also bring with them a new context in which to understand Benjamin's notion of the aura. As I have already noted, Benjamin understands the aura as an appearance or semblance of distance. Telerobotic time-delay brings about precisely such an appearance or semblance. It reminds us of the distance that separates us from the subjects of the images we see. It forces us to think about the network of modems, routers, servers, and telephone lines that the image must travel in order to get to us, and so reaffirms our sense of spatial relations between those subjects and we, the viewers.

In a deeper way, time-delay also enhances our sense of time and distance for the subjects of the image itself. Consider the live video feed from a remote video camera accessible on the Internet. Because the refresh rate is considerably slower than that of cinema or ordinary video, the motion is choppy and unnatural. Moving objects hop from one spot to the next, appearing and disappearing in a discontinuous trajectory. We know that this is the result of slow refresh rates. But we also know that it is because time is

15. Quotation from http://www.geocities.com/CapeCanaveral/Hangar/2. . .op_telerob.html

passing. As we view images and wait for more to arrive, time continues to pass for the subjects in those images.

As we gain a sense of time, so too do we gain a sense of space. The discontinuity of motion reminds us of not only of the passage of time, but also of the motion through space that takes place during that time. Just as the blur on a photograph reminds us of a shadow's movement or a child's unexpected sneeze, the discontinuity of live Internet video shows us in an instant the full extent of the motion that takes place between downloads. We see the fullness of motion in a way that we do not with smooth, continuous video.

Long delays are one of the most frustrating aspects of the Internet. It can be extremely annoying to deal with long time-delays and slow refresh rates—just as it can be annoying to pose for a long exposure or look at a blurry photograph. But in these very shortcomings—in the very "imperfections" that annoy and frustrate us—lies our potential to appreciate the full richness of the subject in the image. Our sense of time and place is bound up with our having to deal with the barriers to our own ease and convenience.[16] Time delay bears witness to something that lies beyond the image, and so begins to restores to objects their aura, their distance. Imperfections in data transmission, as well as in imaging technology, affect knowledge in the realm of telerobotics by giving back the aura that seemed, at least on some readings of Benjamin's discussions of photography, lost forever.

One net-based installation deals specifically with questions of exposure time and the aura in connection with telepistemology: *Dislocation of Intimacy.*[17] The *Dislocation* apparatus is housed in a light-proof box (figure 12.1) that contains physical objects, some of which move of their own accord within the apparatus. Viewers can interact with these objects via buttons. Viewers can select any combination of buttons that activate a combination of lighting devices and return a digital snapshot of the resulting shadow.

Dislocation takes its cue from Sol Lewitt's 1974 book *Incomplete Open Cubes,* in which 511 photographs of a single cube, "using nine light sources and all their combinations," makes the ultimate, totaling statement about the fetishism of surfaces in the rugged, aggressively male vernacular of modernism. *Dislocation,* through its odd mechanics, announces immediately that it

16. On the convenience of technologically mediated experience, see Albert Borgmann, "Information, Nearness, and Farness" (this volume).

17. www.dislocation.net

Figure 12.1. *Dislocation of Intimacy* (1998). Interior of the steel lightbox (38 in. × 48 in. × 58 in.) viewable only from the Internet. http://www.dislocation.net. (K. Goldberg and B. Farzin) (Courtesy of the artists)

won't be dealing with notions of optical gestalt, but with more complex relationships that unfold over time.

In *Dislocation,* time reveals itself through deeply imperfect over-shifted exposure. The blurred, soft-focus image embodies the very philosophy of time, of time revealing itself, appearing on the surface of the image.

Dislocation illustrates the way that imperfections in telerobotic images and environments can be used to develop new aesthetic and conceptual strategies. Antiorp writes: "Generally, (people) aren't anticipating errors, browser deconstruction or denials of service. Incorporating these into programming generates an element of intrigue, seduction and frustration. Error is the mark of the higher organism, and it presents an environment with which one is invited to interact or perhaps control."[18]

It is at this precise point of contact, at the interface between telepresence and the real, that the user is called on to insert his or her fingerprints, and most importantly his or her physical and temporal presence. The interface

18.   Cf. /=cw4t7abs/   (sic).

can be seen as an imperfection or stain, constantly reminding the user of his or her inability to become fully part of the telepresent environment. The same is true of time delays, of choppiness in a telerobotic video feed, and even of the busy-signals endemic to dial-up Internet service. Transmission delays and slow refresh rates are like a fingerprint on the film, a drop of water on the lens. They are evidence of the image, a reminder of our spatial and temporal distance from the subject of our interest.

13

History of Telepresence: Automata, Illusion, and Rejecting the Body

Oliver Grau

Telepresence unites three themes with deep roots in intellectual history: automation and the search for artificial life, illusion in art, and the rejection of the body in favor of a spiritual or mentalistic conception of the human self. In order to understand telerobotics—its historical, psychological, and epistemological importance—we must understand how these three themes have been expressed throughout history in our technological myths and fantasies. That is what I propose to do here. I will examine the historical precursors to telerobotic technology, focusing on technological manifestations of our notions about artificial life, the aesthetic traditions of *virtual realities,* and the occult precursors of *telecommunications.* The history of technology has always included a history of its utopias and myths that reveal human desires, and serve to express proto-rational points of reference. Myths do not lose their relevance by virtue of being ancient. They are about how we view the world, and as such may be outside of ordinary time. They drive history.

A. Automata

The conception of human beings as machines reaches back to antiquity. As early as the second century, the famous physician Galen conceived his pneumatic model of the human body in terms of the hydraulic technology of his age. Art was already being automated in the mechanical theater of Heron of Alexandria. Using a system of cords, pulleys and levers bound to counterweights, as well as sound effects and changing scenery, Heron was able to create an illusion that brought the legend of Naplius to life. In the seventh century, Shui Shi Tu Jing published the *Book of Hydraulic Elegancies.* Indeed, one continually finds descriptions of such technological wonders as mechanical flying doves, dancing apes, and talking parrots in the literatures of Islamic nations, India, China, and Greece. In fourteenth-century Florence, it was none other than Filippo Brunelleschi who designed a mechanical stage to bring Paradise to *life.*

Medieval evidence of the automaton is almost completely non-existent,[1] since a mechanistic world-view was inconsistent with religious dogmas that

---

1. Horst Bredekamp discovered monastic automata from the sixteenth century that mechanically prayed the rosary. H. Bredekamp, *Antikensehnsucht und Maschinenglauben: Die Geschichte der Kunstkammer und die Zukunft der Kunstgeschichte* (Berlin: Wagenbach, 1993), 72 (figure 31). Legends of automation from the middle ages can be found in Reinhold Hammerstein, *Macht und Klang* (Bern, 1986).

proclaimed man, God's creation, the *alter deus,* the vessel of the eternal soul. By the seventeenth century, however, we find a return to mechanistic thinking with analogies between the body and the period's most elaborate technology, the clock.[2] In 1615, Salomon de Caus published his famous collection of plans for automata and gardens, *Les Raisons des Forces Mouvantes,* which was intensely studied by Descartes in his effort to construct an android that would in no ascertainable way differ from a human being.[3] Descartes interpreted biological processes as mechanical occurrences. His English contemporary, Thomas Hobbes, took the mechanistic *Weltanschauung* an important step further by understanding all organic phenomena—including mental phenomena—as physical bodies in motion.[4] Whereas Descartes believed in a nonphysical mind distinct from the body, Hobbes took mental phenomena to be nothing more than the movement of bodily substances in the head. The interaction between technology and artificial life is illustrated particularly well by a political event of the seventeenth century: During an interregnum, the dead English king was represented by movable puppets at his own funeral. This led to the further development of movable figures that, in case of a power vacuum, were used to artificially manifest the absent rulers. In this context we find the machine not as a counterpart, but rather as a continuation and improvement of the human being in the face of death.[5]

In the eighteenth century, the android finally came of age: La Mettrie's *L'Homme Machine,*[6] Vaucanson's *Mechanical Duck,* Kleist's *On the Marionette Theater,* E. T. A. Hoffmann's *Olimpia* from the *Sandman,* Mary Shelly's feeling monster in *Frankenstein,* the *Maschinenmensch* in Fritz Lang's *Metropolis,* and Ernst Jünger's *Worker,* as well as the vast collection of robotics fanta-

2.   John Amos Kominstky (Comenius), *Orbis Sensualium Pietus* (Nürnberg, 1657).

3.   René Descartes, *Traité de l'homme,* 1662. According to legend, Descartes himself constructed an android, *ma fille Francine,* that could do somersaults on a tightrope—a substitute for his own illegitimate daughter of the same name? The excellence of his artistry proved to be the undoing of this feminine miracle machine: A terrified captain threw the machine overboard out at sea.

4.   Thomas Hobbes, *De homine,* 1658.

5.   Ernst H. Kantorowicz, *The King's Two Bodies* (Priceton: Princeton University Press, 1957).

6.   Aram Vartanian, ed., *La Mettries L'Homme Machine (1747): A Study in the origins of an idea* (Princeton: Princeton University Press, 1960).

sies of our century are all branches of a development, stemming perhaps from the Jewish metaphor of the Golem, warning against self-deification. Even if today nobody knows how consciousness[7] functions, the android seems to reemerge in the attempt to produce artificial intelligence on the internet.[8]

The motivation for these large-scale attempts to combine technology and art and breathe life into them stems from male uterine envy, as well as the demiurgic self-deification of the artist. At the core of artistic motivation, however, we also find the fantasy of overcoming the limitations of our own bodies. This manifests itself, in part, in a desire to achieve immortality through machines.

B. Virtual Illusions

The seemingly unprecedented phenomenon of virtual reality actually rests on a deep tradition within the history of art. While this tradition manifests itself in various ways depending on the subject matter and media of a given period, its core idea reaches all the way back to antiquity and has been expansively revived in contemporary VR-art.[9] This kind of virtual reality insulates viewers from other impressions, surrounding them with a spatially and temporally illusory environment that completely fills the field of vision. The immersive cult frescos of the Pompeiian *Casa dei Misteri* (60 B.C.), Baldassare Peruzzi's *Sala delle Prospettive* in Rome (1516) and the *Sacri Monti* movement (1500–1650) represent stages of this aesthetic vision.

Historically, VR has been used not only for private fantasies, but also as a forum for public spectacles in religious and political life. An outstanding

7.   John R. Searle, "Das Rätsel des Bewußtseins: Biologie des Geistes—Mathematik der Seele," *Lettre International* 32 (1996): 34–43.

8.   See Luc Steels, ed., *The Artificial Life Route to Artificial Intelligence: Building Embodied, Situated Agents* (Hillsdale, N.J., 1995); Thomas S. Ray, *An Approach to the Synthesis of Life* in Margaret A. Boden, ed., *The Philosophy of Artificial Life* (Oxford: Oxford University Press, 1996), 111–145. Also dealing with the hope for culturally meaningful digital transmissions, Richard Dawkins, "Mind Viruses," *Ars Electronica 1996, Memesis: The Future of the Evolution* (Vienna: Springer, 1996), 40–47, as well as Kevin Kelly, *Out of Control* (London: Forth Estate, 1994).

9.   O. Grau, "In das lebendige Bild: Die Virtuelle Realität setzt der Kunst neue Spielregeln," *Neue bildende Kunst* 6 (1997): 28–35.

example appeared at the beginning of the sixteenth century near Varallo in northern Italy on the slopes of the Sacro Monte: an artificial installation exhibiting the stations of the life of Christ, including the Nativity, Crucifixion, and Resurrection. The idea was to present the public not with a picture of the contemporary Jerusalem, but rather with a complete simulation of the sacred places as they are described in the Bible and in Augustine's *Meditations*.[10] On the way up the mountain, believers could begin to imagine themselves on a pilgrimage. Once they reached the top, they were surrounded by the virtual environment. Through eleven dioramatic stations, pilgrims experienced the life of Christ from the *Annunciation* to the *Last Supper*, and in seventeen further stations they experienced dramatic events from the *Capture in Gethsemine* to the *Pietà*.[11] Two main impulses motivated this massive media project: the conviction that direct experience with one's own eyes would provide an enduring buttress of faith, and the assumption that the Ottoman Empire's advance would soon make pilgrimages to Palestine difficult or impossible.[12] Prominent humanists and Franciscans guaranteed the historical authenticity of the graphic arrangement and the accordance of the installation with the particulars of the Holy Land. The success was overwhelming: Visitors came by the thousands, day after day, even from foreign countries.[13]

The most famous virtual installation on the Sacro Monte, the *Calvary* (1518–1522), was created by Gaudenzio Ferrari (figure 13.1). Ferrari was much admired by his contemporaries and placed in the company of Raffael, Michelangelo, and Leonardo.[14] He adhered to a strict naturalistic style. His

10. For a contemporary variation on this theme, see "Jesus 2000.com: The virtual pilgrim to the Holy Land" at http://www.jesus2000.com.

11. Anonimo, *Tractato de li capituli de passione: Questi sono li misteri che sono sopra el Monte di Varale*, Milan, March 29, 1514.

12. George Kubler, "Sacred Mountains in Europe and America," ed. Timothy Verdon, in *Christianity and the Renaissance: Image and Religious Imagination in the Quattrocento* (New York: Syracuse University Press, 1990), 415.

13. Canon Torrotti, according to Samuel Butler, *Ex Voto* (London: J. Cape, 1928), 21.

14. The contemporary aesthetic theory demanded along with the life-like representation of proportions, colors and perspective, especially the conveyance of passion (*moto*). See G. Paolo Lomazzo, *Trattato dell'arte della pittura, scultura ed architettura* (Rome 1844) (1584). It was Gaudenzio Ferrari,

EDISON'S TELEPHONOSCOPE (TRANSMITS LIGHT AS WELL AS SOUND).

(Every evening, before going to bed, Pater- and Materfamilias set up an electric camera-obscura over their bedroom mantel-piece, and gladden their eyes with the sight of their Children at the Antipodes, and converse gaily with them through the wire.)

Paterfamilias (in Wilton Place). "BEATRICE, COME CLOSER, I WANT TO WHISPER." *Beatrice (from Ceylon)*. "YES, PAPA DEAR."
Paterfamilias. "WHO IS THAT CHARMING YOUNG LADY PLAYING ON CHARLIE'S SIDE?"
Beatrice. "SHE'S JUST COME OVER FROM ENGLAND, PAPA. I'LL INTRODUCE YOU TO HER AS SOON AS THE GAME'S OVER!"

Figure 13.1. Thomas A. Edison: Telephonoscope, 1879, illustration. Photothek des Kunstgeschichtlichen Seminars Hamburg.

creations were made in the service of *techné* conditioned by the ideal of *mimesis*. Some of his life-size, color, terra-cotta figures wore real clothes and wigs, and even had glass eyes. At the core of his exhibition method was the illusory fusion of the three-dimensional foreground with the two-dimensional fresco—a sort of *faux terrain* that blends fresco and foreground into each other. The chapels could be visited at night by torch light, heightening the illusion's impact. Monks leading the pilgrims through the installation found it necessary to continually remind them that this was not the real Jerusalem. This *Gesamtkunstwerk* came into direct contact with the observer and conveyed an immersive presence that involved the pilgrims both physically and psychologically in the distant events. The success of this powerful image complex was so enduring that the coming years saw the appearance of a whole series of *Sacrimonti*. The project was propelled, not in the least, by a desire to use the spectacle to counter the then-approaching

who represented the category *moto* in Lomazzo's *Tempio della Pittura*. Lomazzo, *Idea del Tempio della Pittura,* Bologna 1785 (Milan, 1590), 40.

Reformation. The installations were used as a sort of shield embracing the onlookers with powerful images and manipulating their inner visual memory.[15]

In Mannerism and the Baroque period, chambers of illusion were *en vogue.* Towering realms of fantasy and deception constructed with the traditional devices of the plastic arts found their fullest flourishing in the panorama, patented in 1787. The panorama was the medial dinosaur, tele-visor, and mass entertainment sensation of the nineteenth century. The huge photo-realistic canvasses—circular, hanging, and often larger than 7000 square feet—hermetically enclosed onlookers. The central aim was to transpose the onlooker into the image, so that the picture was no longer perceived as a picture. The representations of nature provided visual totality and allowed journeys through time and space—a complete universe of illusion. The effect was so intense that already around 1800, it was argued that the illusion could impair one's ability to perceive reality.

The budding age of tourism, an age preoccupied with a longing for distant places, found in the panorama its most perfect witness.[16] These rotundas brought the world to the metropolises of Europe and North America and, for many, became a cheap surrogate for physical presence abroad. Being telepresent with the eyes was compared with actual travel and many preferred the former to the latter.[17] In *Blackwood's Magazine* from 1824, we find the following report:

What cost a couple of hundred pounds and half a year half a century ago, now costs a shilling and a quarter of an hour. Throwing out of the old account the innumerable miseries of travel, the insolence of public functionaries, the roguery of innkeepers, the visitations of *banditti,* charged to the muzzle with sabre, pistol, and scapulary, and the rascality of the custom-house officers, who plunder, passport in hand, the

15. Especially after the Council of Trent, they followed a strategic iconographic program against the Reformation: Orta (1576), Crea (1589), Varese (1589), Canavese (1602), Graglia (1616), Oropa (1620), and Domodossola (1656). The *Sacrimonti* movement spread throughout Italy and was eventually exported to France, Portugal, Spain, Mexico, and Brazil.

16. Silvia Bordini, "Paesaggi e Panorami: immagine e immaginazione del viaggio nella cultura visiva dell'Ottocento," *Ricerche di Storia dell'Arte* (1982): 15, 27ff.

17. On the convenience of technologically mediated experience, see Albert Borgmann, "Information, Nearness, and Farness" (this volume).

indescribable disagreements of Italian cookery, and the insufferable annoyances of that epitome of abomination, an Italian bed.[18]

Even the sober evaluations of Alexander von Humboldt assert that the panorama could almost "supplant a trek through diverse climates. The rotundas supersede all techniques of the stage because the observers, as if trapped inside an enchanted circle and removed from all of the interference of reality, envision themselves to actually be in the foreign environment."[19]

The tendency toward illusionism has provided the essential motivating factor behind new developments in media. Almost every new medium of illusion evolved from arrangements that pushed the potential limits of a currently existing medium. The development of illusory media has been marked by an exchange between large-format immersion spaces that fully integrate the body (frescoes, panoramas, stereopticons, Cineorama, Omnimax- and IMAX-Cinema, and the CAVE) and personal devices held directly in front of the eyes (peepshow images, stereoscopes, Stereoscopic Television, Sensorama, and HMD). VR marks the search for an interface that ideally appeals to all senses and occupies them as immediately and imperceptibly as possible, as if the illusion were a real experience.[20] Contemporary leaders in the virtual arts, such as Char Davies, Monika Fleischmann (GMD), and Christa Sommerer and Laurent Mignonneau (ATR), with their pioneering research installations, are once again combining art and the natural sciences, helping to create and reflect the most complex methods of polysensual illusion. With this development, we witness the historical return of the type of artist who is both artist and scientist.[21]

18.   *Blackwood's Magazine* 15 (1824): 472f.

19.   Alexander von Humboldt, *Kosmos: Entwurf einer physischen Weltbeschreibung,* vol. 7., ed. Hanno Beck (Darmstadt: Wissenschaftliche Buchgesellschaft, 1993), 79.

20.   M. Slater et al., "Depth of Presence in Virtual Environments," *Presence: Teleoperators and virtual Environments* 3, no. 2 (1994): 130–144; J. Freeman et al., "Effects of Sensory Information and Prior Experiance on Direct Subjective Ratings of Presence," *Presence: Teleoperators and virtual Environments* 8, no. 1 (1999): 1–13.

21.   C. Sommerer and L. Mignonneau, eds., *Art@Science* (New York: Springer, 1998).

C. Rejecting the Body

A prehistory of attempts to effect presence in distant places (i.e., telepresence) cannot avoid the image. Before the "invention of art," the image was understood to be loaded with occult powers that connected us to remote objects and beings. We can see this in the German word for image, *Bild,* and its etymological germanic root *bil. Bild* represents not so much the specifically graphic as something that is permeated by an irrational, magical, and spectral power that cannot be fully understood or controlled by the observer.[22] The quality of telepresence found in cult images reveals itself in evidence of their liveliness: blood, tears, and miracles attributed to these images.[23] In belief systems that rely heavily on images—voodoo, for example—images and puppets are credited with the power to work miracles and magic over great distances. Images allow for direct interaction with the gods, and secure presence and power for that which is represented.[24]

Various imaging technologies have similarly been viewed as able to traverse spatial, temporal, and even metaphysical boundaries. In the medieval and early modern periods, the mirror was reputed to make possible extraordinary types of observation. In 1646, Athanasius Kircher described a cylindrical mirror that through an artificial alteration made it possible to show the *Ascension of Christ* hovering in open space.[25] A universal mystery allows the fortune teller to make out distant or future events by looking in a mirror.[26] The mirror's supposed powers were not limited to observation: Mirrors were also thought to make possible long-distance agency. According to legend, mirrors can destroy entire fleets by fire or make them visible beyond the horizon. A mirror belonging to Pythagoras was said to project every-

22.   Alfred Wolf, *Die germanische Sippe bil: Eine Entsprechnug zu Mana* (Uppsala: Universitets Årsskrift, 1930), 18–56.

23.   Hans Belting, *Bild und Kult* (Munich: Beck, 1991).

24.   In pre-Columbian Mexico, worshipers would kill the image of the God that they were trying to influence in the human sacrifice, just as in voodoo a being that is not physically present is addressed and manipulated through the medium of the image.

25.   Athanasius Kircher, *Ars magna lucis et umbrae* (Rome, 1646) X.3.3, 896–900. Like Agrippa, Kircher was obsessed by the art of telegraphics. His projections used solar equipment and he was able to project over a distance of five hundred feet. He hoped to reach distances of up to twelve thousand feet with larger equipment.

26.   Benjamin Goldberg, *The Mirror and Man* (Charlottsville: University Press of Virginia, 1985), 7.

thing written upon it in blood onto the surface of the moon.[27] The sick were advised to cover up their mirrors so that their souls could not fly away and escape to another sphere of existence.

The *Cinéma Telegraphique* (1900) and the *Telephonoscope* (1879) of Thomas A. Edison (figure 13.2) remained technological fantasies. Even before the invention of movies, these projects envisioned the transmission of moving pictures. At the turn of the century, a British couple was said to be able to communicate with their daughter on the colonial British island of Ceylon by means of a large format screen that they hung over their fireplace instead of a painting. Other representations displayed the faces of terrified observers, who were transported into the middle of a distant battle via telematics. The "seeing machine" of Adam Riess (1916) stands as a precursor to the webcam (figure 13.3). Riess connected a camera to a machine that could send electric image signals over the telephone lines to be retranslated into an image at the other end.[28]

By the 1930s, the notion of telecommunication had been fused with the notion of artificial life to form a powerful new vision of a disembodied human self. Italian Futurists envisioned a metallic body that would gain vitality through mechanical impulses. Thus, Marinetti did not only want to overcome death, but also (with the aid of radiophony, a form of cordless telegraphy) to increase massively the body's sensual perceptions. Taste, touch, and the sense of smell were supposed to expand to the point of being capable of receiving stimuli over enormous distances.[29] In his book *God and Golem* (1964), Norbert Wiener envisioned the possibility in principle of translating the very essence of man into code and transmitting it over telephone lines. Over and over again, we project our image of humankind into the most current, yet uncharted and limitless potential of a given level of technological advancement. In search of the substance of man, we hope to realize the essence of life in projections of utopian technologies.

This striving continues today. We yearn for omnipresence—a state of transcendence, a variation of gnosis. It is a sign of uncertainty that myths

27. Jurgis Baltrusaitis, *Der Spiegel: Entdeckungen, Täuschungen, Phantasien* (Giessen: Anabas, 1996), 328.

28. C. Riess, *Sehende Maschinen* (Munich: Hubers Verlag, 1916).

29. "La Radia, Futuristisches Manifest vom Oktober 1933," *Vom Verschwinden der Ferne: Telekommunikation und Kunst,* ed. Peter Weibel and Edith Decker (Cologne, 1991), 224–228.

Figure 13.2. Front cover of Adam Riess's *Sehende Maschinen* [*Seeing Machines*] (Diessen: Hubers Verlag, 1916).

are once again appearing on the scene. They provide models of comprehension that undoubtedly stem from religion.[30] The idea of the transcendental abandonment of the body follows from the primeval notion of the migra-

30. As original as they might at first seem to be, some exponents of cyber-culture fall into well-worn historical tropes. Pierre Lévy envisions "a transcendental 'collective intelligence' as the future source of human consciousness" and a kind of *meta-language* springing from direct global communication. Pierre Lévy, *L'intelligence collective. Pour une anthropologie du cyberspace* (Paris: Éditions La Découverte, 1995).

Figure 13.3. Gaudenzio Ferrari, *Calvary,* diaromatic mixed-media installation, Sacro Monte, Varallo, 1518–1522.

tion of souls, as expressed in Buddhism or in the *Upanishads.* These belief systems propound the involution of the spirit in the material, metempsychoses or reincarnation.[31] Religions,[32] esoteric faiths,[33] parapsychology,

31.   Krishna proclaims, "Only the body is transient, within it dwells the eternal soul." Krishna, *Bhagavadgita: Des Erhabenen Sang* (Jena: Diederichs, 1922), 2, 18. The term *avatar,* the mental traveler, comes from Sanskrit. Geoffrey Parrinder, *Avatar and Incarnation* (London: Faber and Faber, 1970).

32.   The oldest passage in the Judaic corpus mentioning heavenly ascension seems to be the "Ethiopian" book of Henoch. In Greece, ideas regarding the astral nature of man appear for the first time in the second half of the fifth century B.C.E.

33.   Along with *telepathy,* we should mention the notion of personal duplication that is indigenous to the esoteric milieu.

and apocalyptic sects are all searching for ways to overcome the physical. They view human existence as a transitional stage on the path toward pure spirit. We find the notion of the immortality of the soul at least as early as Plato.[34] Hermes Trismegistos describes "[t]he innumerable bodies we must pass through . . . until we are united with the one and only god."[35] Mystical theories propound the existence of another, transcendental reality in the light of which this material world sinks into meaninglessness.[36] Many religions and occult teachings conceive of the immortal soul, or the enduring self, so to speak, as a wispy, untouchable, and, under certain circumstances, even visible apparition. All speak of a being separate from the body. Aquinas regarded it as an essential ability of angels that they be independent of space and time to take on human bodies.[37] The concept of the migration of souls permeates western thinking to various degrees from Giordano Bruno to Swedenborg[38] to Lessing and others. It is an ideology that stands in opposition to the Enlightenment.

Interestingly enough, this utopia of ubiquitous telepresence comes astoundingly close to the contemplation of an all-seeing God. In 1453 Nicholas of Cusa had no doubts that ". . . the absolute vision of God . . . surpasses all of the precision, swiftness and power of all other real observers. . . ."[39] "Your field of view . . . is not of any size but rather infinite, like a circle because your view is the eye of spherical perfection and infinite completeness."[40]

---

34.   Plato, *Phaidon* (Zurich: Rascher 1947), 257, *Meno,* 81b.

35.   *Die XVII Bücher des Hermes Trismegistos* (Icking: Akasa, 1964). See also Dionysos Areopagita, *Mystische Theologie und andere Schriften,* ed. and trans. Walter Trietsch (Munich-Planegg: Barth, 1956).

36.   "According to the nature of my unborn self, I always was, am, and always will be." Meister Eckhart, *Deutsche Predigten und Traktate,* ed. Josef Quint (Munich: Hanser, 1977), 308.

37.   "Cum igitur angeli neque corpora sint, neque habeant corpora naturaliter sibi unita, ut ex dictis patet, reliquitur quot interdum corpora assumant." T. Aquinas, *Summa Theologia,* I, 50, 2.

38.   Initially a pioneer of the sciences, Emanuel Swedenborg (1688–1772), according to Kant, gradually became more of a clairvoyant, who perceived the great fire of Stockholm from a distance of five hundred kilometres.

39.   Nicholas of Cusa, *Vom Sehen Gottes, Philosophisch-Theologische Schriften,* vol. 3, Leo Gabriel (Vienna, 1967), 93–219.

40.   Ibid.

D. Telepistemological Implications

Telepresence combines the contents of three archetypal areas of thought: automation, virtual illusion, and a nonphysical view of the self. These notions collide in the concept of telepresence, which enables the user to be present in three different places at the same time: a) in the spatio-temporal location determined by the user's body, b) by means of *teleperception* in the simulated, virtual image space (the point to which attempts in art history have lead so far to obtain Virtual Reality), and c) by means of *teleaction* in the place where for example a robot is situated, directed by one's own movement and providing orientation through its sensors.

The media-induced epistemology of telepresence seems to be a paradox. Telepresence is indeed a mediated perspective that surmounts great distances, however, perception will soon be enriched in the virtual environment. The so-called "lesser senses" will be amended (feeling, smelling and even tasting), thereby eradicating the abstracting and term-generating function of distance. The three-fold nature of telepresence raises fundamental questions in telepistemology, questions about how distance affects our capacity for knowledge and discovery. Aesthetic theories since the eighteenth century have seen distance as a precondition for reflection, self discovery, and the experiencing of art and nature. (This is distance understood primarily as the accrual of overview and not, in a more ordinary sense, as physical separation.) In his intellectual collaboration with Ernst Cassirer,[41] Aby Warburg stressed the intellectual, awareness-raising power of distance in his *Mnemosyne Atlas*.[42] The result of this physical and psychological distancing from the phenomenon is a conceptual space *(Denkraum)*—the precondition for awareness of an object distinct from the conscious subject. It seemed to him that this was already threatened at the beginning of our century by the sudden proximity created by the telegraph.[43] This idea

41. Cassirer, *Individuum und Kosmos* (Darmstadt: Wissenschaftliche Buchgesellschaft, 1963 [1927]), 179.

42. Warburg, "Einleitung zum Mnemosyne-Atlas," ed. Ilsebill Barta Fliedl and Christoph Geismar (Vienna: 1991), 171–173. Erwin Panofsky emphasized the central function of perspective for the construction of the ego and personal space. "Die Perspektive als Symbolische Form," *Veröffentlichungen der Bibliothek Warburg.* (Berlin: Teubner, 1927), 287.

43. Warburg, *Images from the Region of the Pueblo Indians of North America* (Ithaca: Cornell University Press, 1995 [1923]).

was inherited and expanded in the theories of aesthetic distance offered by Adorno,[44] Jonas,[45] and Serres.[46]

Telepresence is not, however, always seen as a barrier to reflection and self-discovery. In contrast to Warburg stands Paul Valéry, whose "The Conquest of Ubiquity" predicted long-distance transmission of sense-experiences. A kind of spiritual father of McLuhan, Valéry envisioned an art medium that, like electricity or tap water,[47] could be available everywhere to relay polysensual stimuli:

Works will attain a kind of ubiquity. Reacting on our call, works of art will obediently present themselves anywhere at any time. They will cease to exist only in themselves, but will be present anywhere, wherever there is someone and a suitable set of equipment. . . . We [will] find it completely natural . . . to receive these extremely swift mutable images and oscillations out of which our sensual organs . . . will make up all that we know. I do not know if there has ever been a philosopher who dreamed up a company specializing in the free home delivery of sensually perceptible reality.[48]

If we did not know that these comments were written in 1928, they could be describing contemporary net-based telepresence. It seems as though soon a fusion of all the senses with a virtual image machine will produce a compelling illusion of intimate bodily closeness for the spatially distant observer. In the animated image, the observer is electronically present at light-

44. Adorno wrote: "Distance is what nearness to a work's substance requires first. In the Kantian term of indifference, which demands an aesthetic behavior that does not seize the object, does not devour it, this is noted. . . . Distance, concerning the phenomenon, transcends the mere existence of a work of art; its total nearness would be its total integration. (transl. O.G.)] Adorno: *Ästhetische Theorie* (Frankfurt: Suhrkamp, 1973) 460.

45. H. Jonas, "Der Adel des Sehens: Eine Untersuchung zur Phänomenologie der Sinne" (1954), in *Organismus und Freiheit: Ansätze zu einer philosophischen Biologie* (Göttingen, 1973), 198–219.

46. Michel Serres points out that only in the fixed artwork whose elements the onlooker "sets into motion" does the spatial configuration become a vivid sensuous event. Serres, *Carpaccio: Ästhetische Zugänge* (Reinbek: Rowohlt, 1981), 152.

47. Valéry, "Die Eroberung der Allgegenwärtigkeit," *Über Kunst,* Frankfurt/Main, 1973), 47 (trans. O.G.).

48. Ibid.

Figure 13.4. *T-Vision* by ART+COM (1995–1999). Courtesy of ART+COM: http://www.artcom.de

speed, via robot, possibly at several locations simultaneously. Telepresence is transforming the classical perception of space, which had been linked primarily to physical location. The immediate local subject of experience is superseded by the locationless, ubiquitous telerobotics-user. Distance as Cassirer described it is giving way to Valéry's notion of visual and tactile experience provided on demand anywhere, anytime.

Today we are on the threshold of change in regards to a location-oriented concept of persons. Telepresence has far-reaching consequences for work, culture, law, and politics. However, there is hope for a global shift in consciousness. Impetus for this was formulated a few years ago with the Gaia-perspective. The telepresence installation *T-Vision* by ART+COM (1995–1999) attempted to visualize this by aesthetic means. The entire face of the earth was generated out of topographical data and satellite images. Using a level of detail to manage scene complexity, the work presents a model of the earth as seen from a million kilometers above its surface, or at the level of desktop in Berlin (figure13.4).[49] It's a bit like Eric Davis described it:

49. www.artcom.de/projects/t_vision/welcome.en

"Spinning the earth, you feel like a god; plunging toward it's surface, like a falling angel."[50]

Simon Penny's *Traces* (1999) is still a work in progress, but it promises to take an important step toward an art of telepresence. *Traces* is a project for three networked CAVEs in Tokyo, Bonn, and Chicago. Users see (or will see) large virtual spaces, hear spatially distributed sound, and experience vibrations through the floor. The user interacts with gossamer traces that have movements and volumes, but are translucent and ephemeral. Each CAVE will use stereo cameras to construct real-time body maps of its inhabitants. Following Penny's concept, the interaction will take "the form of real-time collaborative sculpturing with light, created through dancing with telematic partners."[51] Consequently, *Traces* will give users the opportunity to experience a dispersed body and to interact with traces of other remote bodies. The division of body and mind is not only easily traced back to the dualistic conception of human beings, but also to the Gnostic tradition of devaluing corporeality. According to this conception, the spirit is simulated to an increasing extent, whereas the body is restrained in its function of getting sensual knowledge of the world, generally by tactile experiences through skin.[52] The experience conveyed by machines replaces the real body, and with it embodied experience. By networking various technobodies, telepresence makes possible a multitude spaces of experience and bodies. Those might even be set up to provide the user with logically inconsistent experiences. The ability to move with and through different bodies intensifies this paradox.

The desire to overcome physical distance, to project ourselves outside the constraints of our own physical bodies, has always been a powerful motivation for both art and technology. It has spurred us to develop extraordinary robotic and telecommunication technologies, and to conceive of technologies that are more extraordinary still. It has inspired art that strives to bring about what the technology itself could not realize. Telerobotics and the

50.   E. Davis: *Techgnosis: Myth, Magic + Mysticism in the Age of Information* (New York: Harmony Books, 1998), 305.

51.   http://imk.gmd.de/docs/ww/mars/proj1_4.mhtml

52.   Regarding a cultural history of the skin. Claudia Benthien, *Hau: Literaturgeschichte—Körperbilder—Grenzdiskurse* (Reinbek: Rowohlt, 1999).

Internet mark the latest stage in this development, a union of fact and fiction that is both technological and artistic.

Acknowledgments

I am grateful to Tilman Welter, Paul Sermon, Christina Fatke, Itsuo Sakanesan, Dieter Daniels, Christa Sommerer and Laurent Mignonneau, Ingeborg Reichle, Monika Fleischmann and Wolfgang Strauss, Stelarc, Anja Schmalfuss, Antje Pfannkuchen, Jack Ox, and Ken Goldberg, and many netminds for their helpful comments to the ideas presented.

Part III

Engineering, Interface, and System Design

14

Feeling Is Believing: History of Telerobotics Technology

Blake Hannaford

I Introduction

Teleoperation and telerobotics are technologies that support physical action at a distance. This distance could span a few yards though a radioactivity-proof wall, or millions of miles through a vacuum to another planet. Although this book focuses on the relatively recent class of examples where the distance between operator and robot is spanned by the Internet, this chapter summarizes the broader research subject of teleoperation. Teleoperators and telerobots interpose distortion between the operator and the environment. This distortion is sometimes a necessary drawback of the system, or it may be intentionally introduced to produce a useful result like magnification. In either case, these distortions pose fundamental questions of telepistemology that the chapter will highlight rather than answer.

The chapter will focus on the issues of time delay, control, and stability, with illustrations from the history of telerobotics and teleoperation. It is impossible to do justice to all of the important technologies and the innovative engineers who developed teleoperation in a short chapter, so I will present only a sample of the key ideas. Telerobotics remains an active research area pursued by engineers internationally.

Physical actions mediated by teleoperation change the state of some remote system that we will call the environment. During these physical actions, energy is exchanged between the environment and the manipulator in either direction. In some cases, teleoperation systems include force feedback so this exchange of mechanical energy can be perceived directly by the human operator. A remote control system is not a telerobot if it only permits the on/off selection of state. For example, a doorbell is remotely operated but would not be consider a telerobot. Although remote driving of vehicles can also be considered teleoperation, I will focus exclusively on remote manipulation. Distance, broadly defined, is any barrier to direct manipulation including physical distance, differences in size scale between the operator and environment, or presence of danger in the environment. A recent example of an industrial teleoperation system is shown in figures 14.1, 14.2, and 14.3.

Many teleoperator and telerobotic systems use dedicated private communication links between human operator (master) and the remote mechanism (slave). Recently the Internet has supplied the communication link for some systems. On a technical level, except for the randomly variable time delay it

Figures 14.1–14.3. Telerobotic system for repairing high-voltage power lines. Kyushu Electric Power Co. Allows a human operator to safely repair high-voltage electrical power lines. Thirteen of these systems have been deployed in Japan to repair high voltage power lines without service interruption. These systems have both teleoperator and telerobotic features.

Feeling Is Believing

imposes, the Internet functions essentially the same as any other communication link. An important social difference is that the Internet may allow public participation. If the system is so configured, anyone may participate, either as operator of the robot, or as a "lurker" who merely watches the proceedings. The emphasis of this chapter is on the technologies that support a single known user with trusted remote site.

Information versus Energetic Interaction

We interact with the external world in two different ways, information interactions and energetic interactions. This distinction was clarified by the "Generalized Systems Theory" of Paynter,[1] but corresponds to everyday experience. When we converse with someone, read a book, interact with a computer, etc. a negligible amount of energy is exchanged. What is important is the information. When we manipulate an object however, more significant amounts of mechanical energy may pass back and forth between our body and the external world. Everyday experience tells us that energetic interactions can add to our degree of belief in something. For example we lift, touch or shake an unusual object, we shake hands or embrace other people, we refer to the "weight" of "resistance" we feel as attributes of an idea, in order to increase our sense of the reality of the external object or person. Compared with speech or visual communication, we are not merely using an alternative set of senses. Instead we are engaged in a physical form of dialog in which energy is exchanged in either direction.

For example consider the case of pressing on a spring. As we depress the spring, we do work on it and it stores energy. As we release it, the spring does work on us and we dissipate the resulting energy in our muscles. This type of interaction is essential to what psychologists call "haptic" or "kinesthetic" perception.[2]

Information interactions take place at a "terminal" such as the human retina, or the input to an electronic communication link and are "directed," which means that the flow of information at a single terminal is one-way. Energetic interactions take place at a "port" such as a human hand grasping

---

1. H. M. Paynter, *Analysis and Design of Engineering Systems,* MIT Press, Cambridge, 1961.

2. S. J. Lederman and R. L. Klatzky, "Sensing and Displaying Spatially Distributed Fingertip Forces in Haptic Interfaces for Teleoperator and Virtual Environment Systems," *Presence: Teleoperators and Virtual Environments* 8 (1999): 86–103.

a handle, a mechanical link between two machines, or a heat exchanger, which is a point of contact between two systems capable of storing, converting, or dissipating energy. An energy port is bi-directional, in principle at least, energy can flow in either direction. The energy flow is measured by the signed product of the two "conjugate variables," "effort" and "flow." The effort and flow variables most relevant to telerobotics are force/velocity, and voltage/current. The physical units of their product in all of these cases, Watts, measure the rate of energy flow—the power transmitted through the port.

In technological systems, a link capable of bi-directional energetic interaction can be simulated with two information links pointed in opposite directions. The information links send the conjugate variables back and forth to transducers that simulate the energetic interactions at each end of the link. The distal end of this link may be a telerobot or teleoperator, or may be a computer simulation. Thus, although energetic interaction gives a compelling sense of reality, it can be simulated just as an information only interaction can.

Teleoperation and Telerobotics

"Teleoperation" technology supports a form of control in which the human directly guides and causes each increment of motion of the slave. Typically the slave robot follows the human motion exactly (within its physical capabilities) although in more advanced, computer mediated, systems there may be coordinate transformations (other than the distance or scale separation of master and slave) imposed between the two sides. A teleoperation system typically sends one of the conjugate variables (either force or velocity) from the operator's hand (via a transducer) to the slave robot. If the conjugate variable is sent back from the slave and transduced at the operator's hand, a virtual energetic link can be created.

"Telerobotics" technology implies communication on a higher level of abstraction in which the human communicates goals and the slave robot synthesizes a trajectory or plan to meet that goal. Telerobotics primarily supports information interaction because of the higher level of abstraction.

In both cases, the operator accepts sensor information transmitted from the remote site to explore the remote environment, plan tasks, verify that tasks are completed, and create plans to resolve problems.

The communication link between master and slave sites has, until recently, been exclusively private. With the introduction of Internet Telerobots, as Goldberg points out in the introduction, the issue of teleepistemology becomes more acute since we may not know or trust the creator of a telerobot. Similarly, the telerobot may not be able to trust the operator. If a telerobot is created for a specific task and is intended for operation only by a predefined set of trusted, authorized users, then the issue of authenticity can be addressed by standard internet security measures. If the telerobot is intended to be open to the public, the issue is more significant—especially from the operator's point of view. How does one know if the site is an authentic telerobot and not a simulation? This question however, applies to many forms of internet information, or for that matter printed information (such as printed spoofs of commercial magazines that can be hard to distinguish from the original).

Finally, a teleoperator or telerobot can sometimes return an actual artifact to the user. For example, a submersible robot can bring back a distinctive part from a sunken ship. Once the robot has returned with the part, the operator has increased confidence that all of the images and sensations he/she experienced in the preceding period of remote control were valid. Of course such an experience can still be faked, but the cost of such forgery increases when the physical artifact is produced.

Time Delay

In many teleoperation and telerobotic systems there is an unavoidable delay in time imposed between the operator's actions and the corresponding feedback. In information-only interactions, a certain amount of delay is natural. For example, when we ask someone a question, we expect to wait a short time before we receive the reply. Similarly when we click on an internet link, we wait a while for that page to display. In contrast, in energetic interactions, we expect instantaneous response. If we touch a wall, we feel the resistance immediately. In telerobotic systems, which can only support information interactions, a certain amount of delay is appropriate, perhaps even necessary. In teleoperator systems, which support energetic interactions, even a tiny delay (under 100 ms.) between a physical variable and its conjugate variable's response has no correlate in the physical world. Time delay in simulated energetic interaction creates the difficult technical challenge of system stability.

But even if the stability problem is solved, it is doubtful that delayed feedback of a conjugate physical variable has any meaning to the human operator.

Chapter Organization
This chapter will look at these issues in more detail with illustrations from the history of telerobotics and teleoperation. It is impossible to do justice to all of the important technologies and the innovative engineers who developed teleoperation in a short chapter, so I will present only a selective illustration of some of the key ideas with emphasis on haptic or kinesthetic perception. Of course the story is not finished. Research is currently very active, and new ideas are sure to have a significant impact. The chapter will illustrate that teleoperators and telerobots interpose distortion between the users hands and the environment. This distortion is sometimes a necessary feature of the system, or it may be intentionally introduced to produce a useful result like magnification. However, these distortions pose fundamental questions of telepistemology that the chapter will highlight rather than answer.

II Coordinate Systems

1 Joint Control
In teleoperator systems, motions of the human operator must be continuously reproduced by the slave robot. What language or coordinate system is used to describe these motion commands? In the original systems and in many subsequent designs, master and slave arms are kinematically (geometrically) identical within a scale constant. In this case it suffices to transmit the angles of the individual joints in the master robot arm. Because of the kinematic similarity, the motion of the slave's end effector will exactly follow that of the master if the slave's joints follow the same trajectory as the master's joints. Both master and slave side motion are therefore represented in "joint coordinates."

The original teleoperators created by the nuclear weapons complex used joint coordinates.[3] The Manhattan project created the need to manipulate

---

3. R. C. Goertz, and W. M. Thompson, "Electronically Controlled Manipulator," *Nucleonics,* pp. 46–47, November 1954; R. C. Goertz, et al., "The ANL Model 3 Master-Slave Electric Manipulator—Its Design and Use in a Cave," *Proceedings of the 9th Conf. Hot Lab. Equip.*, pp. 121, 1961.

Figure 14.4. The original telemanipulators were mechanical devices engineered to handle toxic materials in the nuclear weapons complex. Source: Novelty postcard book published by Klutz press, 2170 Staunton Ct., Palo Alto, CA 94306 (http://www.klutz.com) — originally from Central Research Laboratories, Red Wing Minn. (http://www.centres.com)

highly toxic materials in precise ways. The conflicting goals of protection of workers from radiation and the ability to manipulate such materials into precise shapes were not being met by what were essentially tongs that grew longer and longer or automated fixed purpose special machines. Telemanipulation therefore became a critical need.

The response was the development of precision engineered mechanical systems that allowed dexterous manipulation behind a 1 meter thick quartz window (figure 14.4). Two identical arm mechanisms are positioned in front of the operator and task respectively. Corresponding joints of the two devices are connected by flexible stainless steel ribbons running over pulleys.

From today's point of view these devices seem primitive because they lack electronics or computer control. Nevertheless, they were quite effective

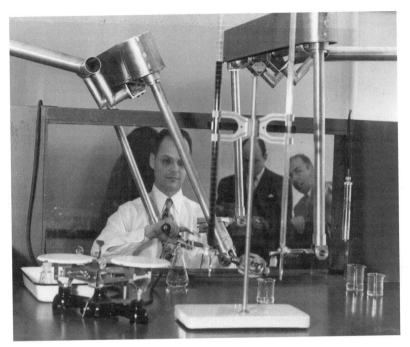

Figure 14.5. Photo of Ray Goertz and Telemanip System. Ray Goertz, inventor of the first teleoperator. Source: Argonne National Laboratories public info office, Ms. Pat Canneday, 630–252–5562.

and are still in wide use. Besides careful mechanical design, the one-to-one connection between the two sides creates a compelling sensation reproducing the actual sensations of manipulation. These mechanical teleoperators were the first highly dexterous mechanisms. They were the immediate precursor of today's industrial robot manipulators.

Fundamentally, the purely mechanical devices were limited to about 5 meters separation between the two sides. Furthermore, this separation had to be fixed at the time of installation, neither side could be moved relative to the other. Newer applications demanded that the remote side be able to move (for example along the length of a particle accelerator). The response was to develop an electronic version of the mechanical remote manipulator (figure 14.5).[4]

4. R. C. Goertz, "Fundamentals of General-Purpose Remote Manipulators," *Necleonics* 10, no. 11 (November 1952): 36–45.

This involved two arms similar to those of the mechanical system, but the steel tapes running between the two were cut, and connected to motors and sensors. At first, motors were installed only on the remote (now called the "slave") side. The control system applied torques to the slave side in such a way that it's position followed that of the operator (now called the "master") side. Later the master side was motorized in response to the operator's complaints about lack of force feedback.

EXOSKELETONS   A special case of this kind of communication arises when the joint coordinates transmitted from the master side are those of the human arm itself. The operator wears an "exoskeleton"—actually a robotic mechanism into which the human arm can fit, and the joints of the exoskeleton are aligned with the human joints—at least in successful designs (figure 14.6).[5] The slave robot must then have the same kinematic equations as the human arm (figure 14.7). One advantage of this approach is that it is relatively easy to design an exoskeleton that can track the entire workspace of the human arm. Among the problems are the difficulty of donning the exoskeleton, and the "ground" or position reference, for commands. For reasons of weight, or position registration, the exoskeleton is often rigidly attached to a base that restricts human shoulder and body motion.

2 Cartesian Coordinates

For many applications, it becomes desirable for the master and slave sides to be kinematically different. For example, the master device may have to operate in a confined space. In this case, the joint coordinates of the master device do not specify the desired joint motion of the slave. Coordinate transformations based on the kinematic equations of the two devices are required to resolve these different languages.[6] As computers began to become avail-

5.   S. C. Jacobsen, F. M. Smith, D. K. Backman, and E. K. Iverson, "High Performance High Dexterity Force Reflective Teleoperator II," *Proc. ANS Topical Meeting on Robotics and Remote Systems,* Albuquerque, N. M., February 1991; S. Tachi, H. Arai, and T. Maeda, "Development of Anthropomorphic Tele-Existence Slave Robot," *Proc. International Conference on Advanced Mechatronics,* Tokyo Japan, May 21–24, 1989; S. Tachi, H. Arai, and T. Maeda, "Tele-Existence Master Slave System for Remote Manipulation (II)," *Proc. 29th IEEE Conf. on Decision and Control,* Honolulu, December 1990.

6.   A. K. Bejczy, and J. K. Salisbury, "Kinesthetic Coupling Between Operator and Remote Manipulator," *Proceedings: ASME International Computer Technology Conference,* vol. 1, pp. 197–211, San Francisco, Calif., August 12–15, 1980.

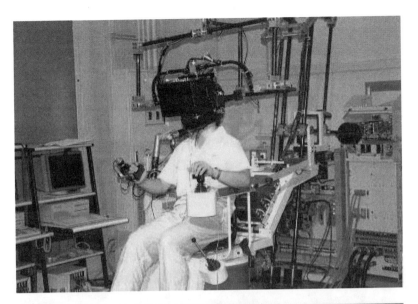

Figures 14.6 and 14.7. "Tele-existence" system developed by Professor Sumumu Tachi, University of Tokyo. Camera follows user's head motion. User's view of robot arm is accurately aligned with kinesthetic sensations of his/her own arm. Courtesy of Professor Tachi.

Figure 14.8. K. Salisbury 6 degree of freedom teleoperator. This device provided feedback forces and torques in all directions necessary for positioning and constraining an object in space. Source: JPL negative number 9647 Ac

able at lower costs in the 1970s, these coordinate transformations became feasible in real time. At this point, teleoperation systems were developed[7] called "generalized teleoperation systems" in which the master and slave could have different kinematic designs.

Bejczy and Salisbury designed the first 6-axis[8] mechanism specifically for human bi-directional telemanipulation (figure 14.8). Unlike previous devices, this "hand controller" was designed specifically for the human operator without regard for the slave device. In this system the slave was a PUMA 560 industrial robot manipulator fitted with a computer controlled robot hand. The slave robot hand included a 6-axis force/torque sen-

7. A. K. Bejczy, J. K. Salisbury, "Kinesthetic Coupling For Remote Manipulators," *CIME* (*Computers in Mechanical Engineering*) 2, no. 1 (1983): 48–62.

8. At least six mechanical degrees of freedom (or "motion axes") are required to make an arbitrary manipulation of a rigid object in space.

sor.[9] Motors on the hand controller allowed a force and torque to be applied to the operator's hand based on the sensed force on the slave. This established a virtual bi-directional energetic interaction between the operator's hand-grip and the robot hand.

Coordinate transformations between the joint spaces of the master and slave devices (in both directions) were carried out at 1000 Hz by microcomputers. The system was evaluated in laboratory experiments in which operators performed simulated tasks.[10] In this study, the simulated bi-directional interaction generally improved performance as measured by the time it took to complete tasks.

3 Supervisory, Traded, and Shared Control
Many of the problems associated with joint coordinates and bi-directional communication, are specific to teleoperators. They arise because the slave robot must exactly mimic the human operator's hand movements. For tele-robots, only goals are communicated, so that this requirement is relaxed. Sheridan coined the term "Supervisory Control" to denote a type of control in which goals and high level commands are communicated to the slave robot.[11] Although supervisory control in principle avoids the need for a pointing interface, such as a master manipulator or exoskeleton, one is sometimes included when all of the skills or procedures needed for an application can not be performed by an autonomous system at the slave site. In the Mercury Project,[12] or the Remote Protein Crystal Handling Cell,[13] for example,

9. P. Fiorini, "A Versatile Hand for Manipulators," *IEEE Control Systems Magazine* 8, no. 5 (1988): 20–24.

10. B. Hannaford, L. Wood, D. McAffee, and H. Zak, "Performance Evaluation of a Six Axis Generalized Force Reflecting Teleoperator," *IEEE Transactions on Systems, Man, and Cybernetics* 21 (1991): 620–633.

11. T. B. Sheridan, *Telerobotics, Automation, and Human Supervisory Control* (Cambridge, Mass.: MIT Press, 1992).

12. K. Goldberg, M. Mascha, S. Gentner, N. Rothenberg, C. Sutter, and J. Wiegley, "Desktop teleoperation via the World Wide Web," *Proc. 1995 IEEE Intl. Conf. on Robotics and Automation* 1 (21–27 May 1995): 654–659, Nagoya, Japan.

13. B. Hannaford, J. Hewitt, T. Maneewarn, S. Venema, M. Appleby, and R. Ehresman, "Telerobotic Macros for Remote Handling of Protein Crystals," *Proceedings Intl. Conf. on Advanced Robotics* (ICAR97), Monterrey, Calif., July 1997; B. Hannaford, J. Hewitt, T. Maneewarn, S. Venema,

the environments are highly structured and closed to external perturbations and uncertainty. These systems therefore do not need to support teleoperation with pointing devices. On the other hand, systems that must support a high degree of confidence in task completion in an uncertain environment, for example, the system of Hayati et al.[14] include both teleoperation and supervisory modes. In practice then, telerobot systems are often used as both teleoperators and telerobots depending on the task. These systems can be termed "traded control" because the low level control of the slave robot motion passes back and forth between human operator and computer.

Alternatively, teleoperated and autonomous functions can coexist at the same time, for example, by controlling different degrees of freedom at the same time. For example, in a system developed by Bejczy and Kim,[15] a telerobot could perform assembly of precise rigid parts in spite of significant time delay if the slave computer locally controlled orientations while the remote operator controlled displacement in x,y,z translation. Shared control can also be performed on the same motion axis (degree of freedom). In Kim et al.'s system, the operator can specify a "reference" position and orientation, while the slave's computer controls deviations from that position in response to measured forces. This type of sharing can significantly improve the ability to handle precisely mating parts in the presence of time delay, yet can also introduce a discrepancy between the operator's commands and the robot's actions, perhaps reducing the operator's perception of actually manipulating a real object.

A graphical user interface was developed by Hannaford et al.[16] to allow an operator to select among these shared control options (figure 14.9). Each

M. Appleby, and R. Ehresman, "Telerobotic Remote Handling of Protein Crystals," *IEEE International Conference on Robotics and Automation,* Albuquerque, N. M., April 1997.

14.   S. Hayati, T. Lee, K. Tso, P. Backes, and J. Lloyd, "A testbed for a unified teleoperated-autonomous dual-arm robotic system," *Proceedings 1990 IEEE International Conference on Robotics and Automation,* 1990–1995, vol. 2.

15.   A. K. Bejczy, and W. S. Kim, "Predictive displays and shared compliance control for time delayed telemanipulation," *Proceedings IROS '90.* IEEE International Workshop on Intelligent Robots and Systems '90. Towards a New Frontier of Applications. Ibaraki, Japan. pp. 407–412, 3–6 July 1990.

16.   B. Hannaford, L. Wood, D. McAffee, and H. Zak, "Performance Evaluation of a Six Axis Generalized Force Reflecting Teleoperator," *IEEE Transactions on Systems, Man, and Cybernetics* 21 (1991): 620–633.

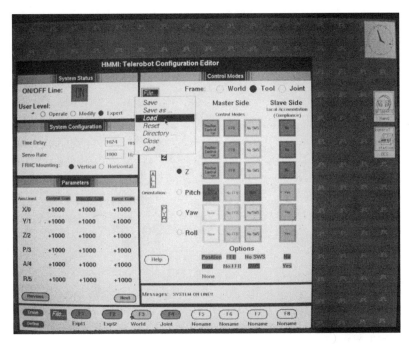

Figure 14.9. Graphical User Interface used to select control modes in the JPL system. As many as 10 possible modes of operation could be selected for each motion axis, giving one million different modes of operation. Source: JPL negative number 11525 Ac

of the six Cartesian degrees of freedom could be in one of 10 different operating modes, including those described above. Since each axis could be controlled independently, 10^6 possible modes are available to the operator. For a dual arm system, 10^{12} possible modes are available! This creates the problem of how to select the best mode from this set for a given task. From the viewpoint of Telepistemology, we have the additional problem of how to calibrate our own senses for each of these many possible modes because a given environment will "feel" differently to the operator in each mode.

To illustrate supervisory control, a recent application to an internet telerobot will be described. In the UW/UAB/Boeing Telerobotic Protein Crystal Mounting Cell[17] a small robot manipulator was integrated into a

17. Hannaford, Hewitt, Maneewarn, Venema, Appleby, and Ehresman, "Telerobotic Macros for Remote Handling of Protein Crystals" and Hannaford, Hewitt, Maneewarn, Venema, Appleby, and Ehresman, "Telerobotic Remote Handling of Protein Crystals."

Figure 14.10. UW Protein Crystal Growth (PCG) Cell Telerobot. Internet controlled mini-telerobot for handling protein crystals in a simulation of the International Space Station. Operators in Huntsville Alabama (password protected access from trusted site) successfully captured simulated 0.5mm protein crystals by clicking virtual control panel icons and reviewing progress through compressed video signals. Developed at University of Washington, in conjunction with Boeing Defense and Space Company, and the University of Alabama Center for Macromolecular Crystalography. Source: UW Biorobotics Lab.

scientific glove box prototyped for the International Space Station (figure 14.10). In order to deduce the structure of biologically significant proteins, the most commonly employed method is to grow crystals of the protein in aqueous solution and to analyze the crystals with X-ray diffraction. This 3–5 day process can create more regular crystals in micro-gravity hence the desirability of performing this procedure in outer space. These crystals are about 0.5mm in size and have the consistency of gelatin. They must be aspirated from the water solution into a capillary with 1mm inside diameter. The system consisted of a 5-axis high precision mini robot with DSP controller, linear motion system to position the robot base, microscope, video cameras, fluid pump, slave side "server" and power control system.

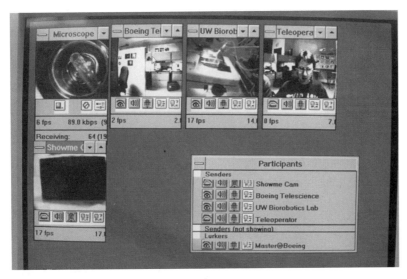

Figure 14.11. Video images transmitted via CUSeeMe for PCG cell operator. Source: UW Biorobotics Lab.

Supervisory control was employed for this experimental system. The user interface provided two distinct methods for controlling equipment at the remote site. The primary control method used predetermined "macros" that encoded sequences of low-level commands such as "move robot along a trajectory to position 'X,' move linear rail to position 'Y,' and dispense 'Z' microliters of fluid from the fluid pump."[18] These macros were assigned to individual buttons on the graphical user interface, allowing the operator to quickly accomplish tasks by pressing a sequence of macro buttons. The macro definitions were stored and executed on the "server" computer at the remote site.

The user interface also allowed low-level control of robot joints, linear rail position, fluid pump parameters, etc. via sliders and buttons in pop-up dialog boxes. This low-level control capability was intended only as a secondary or backup control method and to be used for performing unplanned or experimental procedures, and generating new macro definitions. Video signals from the workcell were sent back to the operator via CUSeeMe teleconferencing software (figure 14.11).

18. Ibid.

III Communication

In order for the remote environment to be affected by the user's intent, that intent must be transmitted in some form to the remote manipulator. Of course the user's "intent" may be difficult to ascertain. Typically, in teleoperators, the user's hand motions are measured by a joystick type device and encoded in digital form. This can be accomplished with about 9600 bits per second per hand.

Besides information capacity, a second key property of the communication channel is time delay, the time required for a message to arrive at the destination. Since a telerobotic system requires communication in two directions, we must consider delays introduced by both links. These delays introduce a dissociation between the operator's commands and the action of the slave. More significantly, delay of the returning sensor information is also introduced between the operator's action and the resulting sensory feedback displays of the robot response.

There are two sources of this time delay. Most fundamentally, there is the delay due to the speed of light. While significant in contemplated space applications, this delay is rarely dominant except for interplanetary applications such as the Sojourner Mars Rover. The time delay due to lightspeed between the earth surface and a communication satellite in geosynchronus orbit can be significant however; about 250 milliseconds round trip.

The second major source of delay is that introduced by switches in computer networks. These delays are caused by processing of information in computers at nodes in the network. Pietro Buttolo measured this delay in 1996 (as well as loss rate of UDP packets) for different distances on the Internet (table 14.1).

1 Communicating Intent

When the time delay between operator action and perceived response is greater than about 250 ms it becomes cognitively apparent to the user. Behavior of operators under this condition was first studied by Sheridan and Ferrell contemplating applications in space.[19] They found that operators adopt a strategy dubbed "move-and-wait" in which the operator makes small movements and then stops, waiting to see the results of his or her action.

19. T. B. Sheridan and W. R. Ferrell, "Remote Manipulative Control with Transmission Delay," *IEEE Transactions on Human Factors in Electronics* HFE–4 (1963): 25–29.

Table 14.1

| Distance | | Delay (ms) | | |
scale	Loss rate (%)	min	avg	max
room	0.0	2.0	3.0	18.0
dept	0.0	2.5	3.5	23.0
campus	0.0	3.0	3.0	5.0
continent	8.0	62.3	94.5	205.3
planet	11.5	278.3	421.0	746.8

Internet transmission properties for UDP packets on 19 February 1996 (P. Buttolo, used with permission).

For applications such as interplanetary exploration in which delays exceed a few seconds, the "move-and-wait" strategy becomes extremely cumbersome. Supervisory control has been used as a means to get around this problem. With "move-and-wait," the time taken to complete a task is

$$T = N(d + a)$$

where d is the round trip time delay, a is the time that the slave can operate on its own without human intervention (alternatively the average duration of a teleoperated movement that can be performed without feedback), and N is the number of such moves required to complete the task. If Na is considered the time required for the task with no delay, the performance penalty due to delay can be expressed as Nd. If a can be increased (for example due to smarter supervisory control) then N can be reduced and the performance penalty due to time delay is less.

Another approach is to provide better planning aids to the operator so that he or she can create a longer series of commands with high confidence. One part of a telerobotic work cell that can be predicted with a high degree of confidence is the response of the slave robot to commands. In a "predictive display"[20] (figures 14.12 and 14.13), the operator could manipulate a

20. W. S. Kim and A. K. Bejczy, "Demonstration of a high-fidelity predictive/preview display technique for telerobotic servicing in space," *IEEE Trans. Robotics and Automation* 9, no. 5 (October 1993): 698–702.

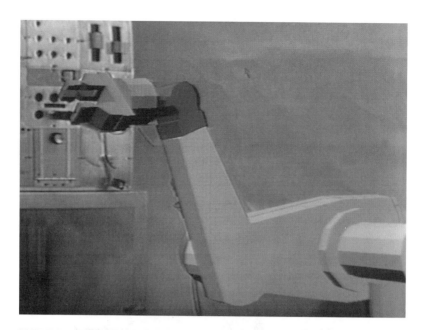

Figures 14.12 and 14.13. Kim and Bejczy's Predictive Display. Computer graphics images of remote manipulator may be superimposed ("keyed") over the returning video image. Computer graphics image responds instantly while video image of robot follows after communication time delay. When there is no motion, actual video image of robot is hidden behind computer graphics image. Excellent registration between computer graphics and robot image is assured by accurate geometric modeling of robot, and human assisted calibration procedure. Source: JPL negative numbers 11718Bc and 11719Bc via Dr. Wonsoo Kim.

Blake Hannaford

computer graphics simulation of the slave robot. This simulated robot could be superimposed over the video returning from the remote site (by video "keying"), which proved to be a significant help in planning the commands.

A significant issue becomes calibration of the computer graphics camera model with the perspective display parameters representative of the actual camera. If the two are not calibrated, the simulated slave robot does not appear in the proper perspective relative to the video image of the real slave and therefore does not seem to the operator to be actually present in the remote site.

Once the operator is provided with a realistic simulation of the remote site (for planning purposes) and with "predictive" control techniques, a level of abstraction is introduced between the operator and the remote site and it is not as straightforward to keep track of the state of the system. Conway and Volz[21] introduced some compelling metaphors, the "time clutch" and the "space clutch" to clarify the profound but sometimes obscure difference between controlling a telerobot and a simulated robot. The "Time Clutch" is a foot pedal that, when pressed and held like an automotive clutch, allows the predictive simulated robot to move ahead of the positions attainable by the slave robot (which might have a relatively low maximum speed). The operator's inputs were held in memory as necessary until the slave could catch up. A "position clutch" can also be used that disengages the operator's commands entirely from the slave robot so that the operator can inter-actively experiment with the simulation. Finally, a "time brake" is also pro-vided. Pressing this pedal, disengages the two clutches, and also reverses the sense of time for the predictive robot simulation, progressively emptying out the command memory until the predictor "comes back" to the currently visible robot state.

2 Communicating Remote State

As with the link from operator to telerobot considered above, it is useful to estimate the amount of information that must be returned to the opera-tor. Let us consider two example systems, first a remote manipulator in a nuclear power plant as an example of a teleoperator, and second, an internet

21.   L. Conway, R. A. Volz, and M. L. Walker, "Teleautonomous Systems: Projecting and Coordi-nating Intelligent Action at a Distance," *IEEE Transactions on Robotics and Automation* 6, no.2 (April 1990): 146–158.

telerobot, as an instance of supervisory control. In the first case, an operator will typically have three video cameras imaging the remote environment from various angles, all displayed simultaneously at his or her "control station." Because of close physical proximity, the signals can be sent by inexpensive analog cables and there is no need for compression. Using the US/Japan-standard NTSC video format, we have a bandwidth requirement of about 6 MHz per signal or 18 MHz.

Digital transmission is rapidly emerging for video signals. Of the two major current standards for video source coding, MPEG-2 and H.263, H.263 is currently most relevant because of the requirement for real-time, low latency compression. However, preserving NTSC picture quality requires 6–9 megabits per second depending on amount of picture motion. We thus need 18–27 Mbits per second to send back our three video signals. Owing to the rapid development of digital television, this area is in rapid flux. However little is being done on digital compression in the context of teleoperation.

3 Absolute versus Relative Time

An interesting issue arises when trying to construct a laboratory simulation of time delay in a teleoperation system. Time delay is easy to simulate in principle with memory. Because the "downlink" typically consists of high bandwidth signals, such as multiple color video signals, it is expensive to delay this link. However, the relatively modest bandwidth of the up-link can readily be delayed. The question then arises, "Can we make a valid simulation of the total up and down link delay by delaying ONLY the up-link information by the total of the up-link and down-link times?" This question has not been formally studied, but the consensus seems to be that operator behavior is unaffected by such an expedient. Although slave responses are shifted in time by a fixed amount (equal to the downlink delay), the operator will not perceive a difference unless operations must be synchronized with an event that occurs at an absolute time (unlikely in a laboratory setting).

4 Virtual Energetic Interaction

When teleoperator control is considered as a bi-directional, virtual energetic interaction, the communication problem is stated in a radically different form, "Send information in both directions so that the master and slave manipulators can simulate a physical link between the two sites." One way this can be accomplished is to send position or velocity commands from master to slave sides, and the conjugate variable, force, from slave to master sides.[22] Notice that there is no longer any need to involve the notion of the operator's intent. The bandwidth required for this type of communication has not been theoretically derived. However, successful systems that reproduce subjectively convincing force sensations[23] typically send 1000 samples per second in each of the 6 degrees of freedom with 8 bits per sample, a bit rate of 48,000 bits per second in each direction not counting other sensory information such as video.

4.1 STABILITY Creating a virtual energetic interaction by transmitting conjugate variables through information links creates a closed loop dynamical system. The stability of such systems have been carefully studied by control theory, but the literature is less prominent for bi-directional systems.

When a virtual energetic link is unstable, oscillations emerge and may grow in magnitude. For small oscillations of bounded amplitude, the user experiences a "noise" or distraction that is destructive to the illusion of remote presence or manipulation. When the oscillations are stronger, the system can be totally unusable or even dangerous. Stability is determined by a complex interaction between time delay around the loop and gain. This interaction has been studied by analysis and experimentation.[24] The

---

22. At least two alternative methods are in wide use. See B. Hannaford, "A Design Framework for Teleoperators with Kinesthetic Feedback," *IEEE Transactions on Robotics and Automation* 5, no. 4 (1989): 426–434.

23. A. K. Bejczy and Z. Szakaly, "Universal Computer Control System for Space Telerobotics," *Proceedings of the IEEE Conference on Robotics and Automation* 1 (1987): 318–324, Raleigh, N.C.

24. B. Hannaford and R. Anderson, "Experimental and Simulation Studies of Hard Contact in Force Reflecting Teleoperation," *Proc. IEEE Conference on Robotics and Automation,* April 1988, pp. 584–589; B. Hannaford, "A Design Framework for Teleoperators with Kinesthetic Feedback" *IEEE Transactions on Robotics and Automation* 5, no. 4:426–434; R. J. Anderson and M. W. Spong, "Bilateral Control of Teleoperators with Time Delay," *IEEE Trans. on Automatic Control* 34 (1989): 494–501; G. Niemeyer and J. J. Slotine, "Stable Adaptive Teleoperation," *IEEE Journal of Oceanic Engineering* 16, no. 1 (January 1991): 152–162; G. Niemeyer and J. J. Slotine, "Towards force-reflecting teleoperation over the Internet," *Proceedings.* 1998 IEEE International Conference on Robotics and Automation, May 1998, Leuven, Belgium, pp. 1909–1915.

mathematical difficulty is compounded by the problematic task of making useful mathematical models of the human operator and the environment. By applying the notion of "passivity," a clever class of control laws were synthesized for which stability could be guaranteed regardless of the intervening time.[25] Passivity in this context means that the net energy absorbed by the teleoperator system (through its two interaction ports) over all time exceeds the energy that it supplies. If the teleoperator can be made passive, then stability can be guaranteed assuming only that the operator and environment are passive—an assumption that works well in practice.[26] Unfortunately, passivity appears to be an overly conservative criterion. For while such systems are indeed stable, they are characterized by slow response and "sluggish" feel.[27]

4.2 SCALE   In December 1959, Richard Feynman delivered what must surely be one of the most famous banquet talks in the history of scientific meetings entitled "There's Plenty of Room at the Bottom—An Invitation to Open Up a Whole New Field of Physics."[28] This talk is widely known (it was reprinted in *Popular Science* in 1960 and in *IEEE ASME Transactions on MicroElectroMechanical Systems* in 1993) and it is credited with predicting the field of micro-electromechanical systems (MEMS) that blossomed 25–30 years later. What is less known about the paper is that Feynman thought such microscopic systems would be constructed by teleoperation. He proposed that a teleoperator be built with a scale factor of 4:1. This

25.   R. J. Anderson and M. W. Spong, "Bilateral Control of Teleoperators with Time Delay"; G. Niemeyer and J. J. Slotine, "Stable Adaptive Teleoperation," *IEEE Journal of Oceanic Engineering* 16, no. 1 (January 1991): 152–162.

26.   J. E. Colgate and N. Hogan, "Robust Control of Dynamically Interacting Systems," *Int. Journal of Control* 48 (1988): 65–88.

27.   C. A. Lawn and B. Hannaford, "Performance Testing of Passive Communication and Control in Teleoperation with Time Delay," *Proc. IEEE Intl. Conf. On Robotics and Automation* 3 (May 1993): 776–781, Atlanta, Ga.

28.   R. P. Feynman, "There's Plenty of Room at the Bottom: An Invitation to Open Up a New Field of Physics," *Engineering and Science* 23, no. 5 (February 1960): 22–36, Caltech; "Infinitesimal machinery," *Journal of Microelectromechanical Systems* 2, no.1 (March 1993) 4–14; "How to Build Automobiles Smaller than This Dot (There's Plenty of Room at the Bottom)," *Popular Science,* November 1960, p. 115.

would then be used to manufacture ten miniature slave systems, reduced in scale by another factor of four. These would be connected to the original master so that in a subsequent step, the operator could build ten sets of ten on a still smaller scale, etc. While he acknowledged the practical difficulties of such a scheme, this paper can be viewed as the origin of the idea of micro-teleoperation as well.

Scaled teleoperation systems create new challenges for the notion of knowledge and belief. This issue was studied upon the invention of the microscope, but new issues arise in teleoperation. One of the complexities is illustrated by consideration of scaling physical characteristics. Assume that a microteleoperation system is intended to scale up the environment by a factor of K. In the visual side, this corresponds to a microscope with magnification K. On the kinesthetic side, it is more complex. We can set appropriate force and position scales to keep kinesthetic perception unchanged. However as an object is scaled down, its Mass drops with K^3 while its apparent visual size scales only as K. Its surface area (source of many significant physical effects for small objects) scales with K^2. So the resulting virtual object manipulated by the operator will have a mix of "natural" and "unnatural" properties.

Consider a scaled system in which position commands are multiplied by a factor λp between master and slave and in which force feedback is multiplied by λf from slave to master. We can construct a diagram (figure 14.14) illustrating qualitative features of the resulting teleoperation system over the plane formed by these two parameters:

The diagram is plotted for the arbitrary range of scale factors, 0.01 to 100 but it applies to all magnitudes. The diagonal, $\lambda f = \lambda p$, is the locus of systems that have unity power gain between master and slave. All passive mechanical micro or macro manipulators including the original nuclear materials handling systems, the ones Feynman anticipated, and typical tools such as tweezers, pliers, and pry bars, fall on this line. All of these systems distort the operators perception of the kinesthetic properties of the environment in a predictable way. From the physical principle of "virtual work," we can show that mechanical properties such as stiffness and mass of the environment are scaled by a factor of $(\lambda p)^2$.

However, when bi-directional interaction is realized by a teleoperator system, other combinations of gains are possible. For example, another important relation is

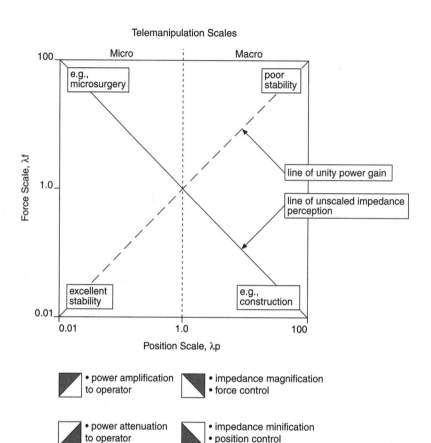

Figure 14.14. Manipulation scales and their effects on haptic perception. When scale factors are interposed between human displacement/force and robot displacement/force, qualitative changes are induced in human mechanical perception as well as human power output. The remote environment can be made to feel stiffer/heavier or softer/lighter. Because different physical attributes scale with different power of size, it is inherently impossible to "map" physical reality across large differences of scale. Source: The author.

$$\lambda f = 1/\lambda p$$

It can be shown (Hannaford 1991) that operation on this line does not alter the mechanical properties (more precisely the mechanical impedance) of the environment that are felt by the operator. But this relation implies that the system must be active and therefore more difficult to make stable.

To place this problem in more concrete terms, consider handling a tuning fork and feeling it vibrate. Now consider a miniature tuning fork 100 times smaller with which we interact through a scaled teleoperation system. The teleoperation system will have

$$\lambda f = 1/\lambda p = 0.01$$

so that the operator will feel the correct mechanical properties of the environment, and a microscope will be provided with 100:1 magnification.

If the miniature tuning fork is made with the same materials, its frequency will be 10 times higher. If we view the miniature tuning fork through 100:1 magnification, it will look identical to the original tuning fork, it will be composed of the same materials, and yet it will "feel" different as exemplified by the ten times higher natural frequency.

Historical parallels to this problem exist in the area of naval architecture. There was a critical need to study the performance of ships by towing scale models of their hulls in a tank. But, to what extent did this model system represent the "reality" of an actual ship? The dynamics of water depend critically on scale. Research aimed at this question led to fundamental advances in hydrodynamics by Froud and Reynolds who developed dimensionless ratios (Reynolds and Froud numbers) that predicted qualitative behavior of fluids. In other words, if the model and the towing speed were scaled by a simple constant, the towing behavior was not realistic, but if the scale factor and fluid properties were scaled in such a way that the Reynolds number was constant, then certain aspects of the towing-tank model was accurate.

Teleoperator researchers have addressed this problem with elegant applications of scaling theory,[29] but no consensus has emerged on how to solve it. The dissociation between visual and kinesthetic percepts imposed by scaling of manipulation processes poses fresh difficulties for the nature of knowledge.

IV Conclusion

As robots and advanced user interfaces are connected to the Internet, we raise the possibility of the Internet connecting distant points in space with

29. J. E. Colgate, "Power and Impedance Scaling in Bilateral Manipulation," *Proc. IEEE Intl. Conf on Robotics and Automation*, Sacramento, Calif., 1991, pp. 2292–2297; H. Kobayashi and H. Nakamura, "A Scaled Teleoperation," *Proc. IEEE Intl Workshop on Robot and Human Communication*, Tokyo, 1–3 September 1992, pp. 269–274.

virtual, visual, aural, and physical links. If the resolution of sensors and actuators is high enough and the bandwidth and latency adequate, we create "knots" or "ports" in space through which we can see, hear, touch, and manipulate distant objects or people as though they were present. Multiple locations can be brought together at such a port and effectively superimposed in space and time. What this will mean for human belief and sense of presence is just beginning to be studied.

15

Tele-Embodiment and Shattered Presence: Reconstructing the Body for Online Interaction

John Canny and Eric Paulos

Cyberspace presents us with a dilemma. We are physical beings who experience the world through our bodies. The notion of a separation between abstract mind and physical body has been battered and eventually buried by Western philosophers since Kant. In its place came new ideas, important among them phenomenology, an articulation of perception and action as processes involving mind, body, and world. In the east, Zen has acknowledged the importance of the body and action-in-the-world from the beginning. But cyberspace has been built on Cartesian ideals of a metaphysical separation between mind and body: When we enter cyberspace, even a 3D world, it is the "mind" that enters. It may be regaled with an exotic 3D form, but such a form is an avatar only of the mind. The body stays outside. It is seen as a mere transducer, moving text or audio data in through keyboard or microphone, and catching data from monitor and speakers. Realism is described and measured in terms of digital fidelity, the number of pixels or number of color bits. Motion may be described with number of degrees of freedom, the virtual body becoming an abstract mobile entity. If we build avatars that "look" realistic enough, shouldn't the virtual experience be equivalent, or possibly better than the real? The biggest danger and most likely outcome at this time is that we will succeed (from a Cartesian standpoint), but the resulting experience will still be second-rate. From an epistemological point of view, we may be convinced by the sight and sound of the virtual world, but we will not be satisfied by our interactions with it. The experience of being in the world is much more than merely observing it.

The problem is that the view of "body-as-transducer" ignores the role of the body in motor-intentional acts. In this chapter, we discuss computer-mediated communication (CMC) from classical and phenomenological perspectives. The Cartesian (and dominant) approach to CMC has broken the interaction into communication channels such as video, audio, haptics, etc. Notions of quality, reliability, latency are applied to these channels, mostly in a context-independent way. They are adapted to the body's (the body-as-transducer) perceptual performance. But two human beings in the same room interact on a wholly different level. The eyes are not just transducers but cues to attention, turn-taking, and sometimes deception. The hands complement speech with gesture in both conscious and unconscious ways. Dialogue is not a process of turn-taking speech, but a continuous and intimate coupling of speaker and listener. Much of the dialogue is nonverbal and subconscious. We believe that CMC must be approached through understanding of these behaviors, all of which involve mind and body together, and which use the body and its senses in many different ways.

We are building simple, inexpensive, internet-controlled, untethered tele-robots to act as physical avatars for supporting CMC. These Personal Roving Presence devices or PRoPs are not built to be anthropomorphic in *form* but to approach anthropomorphism of *function*. That is, they should support at least gaze, proxemics (body location), gesture, posture, and dialogue. They are "body-like" because human-interaction is an intensely body-centered activity. They exist not in a virtual world but in the physical world. So they interact directly with people (rather than another avatar) or groups of people. By operating in the real world, PRoPs expose the differences between natural human interaction and CMC. A PRoP is an individual presence, and represents a unique remote participant. Unlike a videoconferencing system, it is not a "window" to somewhere else. The social capabilities of PRoPs contrast with those of live participants. We can explore what skills they have and which are lacking, depending on the context. And the contexts that we can study are broader than traditional teleconferencing, thanks to skills like mobility, proxemics, and deictic gesturing.

PRoPs need not be realist portraits of humans because our motor-intentional behaviors are flexible. Our PRoPs are cubist statues, with rearrangements of face and arms, and separation of eyes from gaze. The arrangements are dictated by function and engineering constraint. The constraints on a personal social tele-robot are far from complete at this point, so we expect the design to be in a fluid state for some time. Building PRoPs requires an understanding of the psychology of interaction—of gaze, back-channeling, gesture, posture, and eventually subconscious cues. PRoPs provide a novel experimental platform for studying those phenomena. They provide a vehicle for the dissection of behaviors and the senses that support them. We can turn sensing and action channels on and off so that their effects can be studied. This is not to say that social behaviors decompose this way—Our point is that they don't. Simply that we can discover the importance of various sensing and action channels on higher behaviors by pulling switches and looking for change at the higher levels.

Ultimately, we hope to use the knowledge gained from PRoPs to design more satisfying online presences. Electronic interaction is strongly influenced by the medium. In *Cyberville*,[1] Stacy Horn's exposé of the chat salon ECHO, she remarks that people can "have different personalities in text" than their real-life personalities, and may be different again over the telephone. Personality is not a property of the abstract mind, but of the mind-body as experienced through all its motor-intentional modes. If we can understand those modes, we have at least a glimmer of hope of building a cyberspace that is an acceptable alternative for the physical world. It is not a question of *real* versus *virtual* but of understanding *how* we live rather than simulating the *where*. Human-human interaction is a great challenge for telepistemology. In the real world, we rely on others for most of our knowledge. If we can believe and trust the people we meet online, we can continue to learn and prosper as online beings. Without intimacy and trust, our existence in cyberspace will remain an impoverished substitute.

Tele-embodiment: Transparent Control and Prosthetics

PRoPs seem to have the same limitations as avatars. That is, they are only the source of video and data streams and the target for motion control commands from a pilot. The pilot is really interacting with a control interface rather than other people. But if the human-machine coupling is tight enough, and if the pilot is expert at using the machine, the interface disappears.[2] Such android hybrids are not even rare. A fighter pilot has no time to reason through the mapping from windscreen, radar, and instruments to the appropriate controls. Her survival depends on her ability to act as one with the machine. Experienced pilots "fly by the seat of their pants," that is, through their physical connection to the extended body. A more down to earth example is the motorcycle racer who's success depends on her ability to "become one with the machine." Bus drivers also develop an extraordinary sense of the extended body. They can pass within inches of a parked vehicle without contact. Cab drivers may have no reservations about contact, and will use the extended body to bump and jostle and compete for territory. Drivers less intimate with their machines must submit or risk the humiliation of metal scars and paint bruises. It is by observing these

1. Stacy Horn, *Cyberville: Clicks, Culture, and the Creation of an Online Town* (Warner, 1998).

2. On this see Michael Idinopulos, "Telepistemology, Mediated Knowledge, and the Design of Transparent Interfaces" (this volume).

diverse driving cues such as speed, crowding, and turn signal usage (or lack thereof) that we attribute personalities to the various people behind the machine.

Such experiences are common in virtual worlds too. An experienced gamer immerses himself in the game world and may have a human or humanoid form in it. There is no contemplation, no time to hesitate, and action must be immediate. The instructions to puzzle games like Myst begin by advising the player to "imagine yourself really being on the Island, think of what you would do." They seduce him deeper into concentration on the tasks he has to perform. The seduction involves perception-action loops that may be fast and fluid (kick-boxing) or slow and deliberative (solving a combination lock). The constant feature is that each player's action has an immediate and obvious effect on the world.[3] The successful player conceives the game in terms of those actions and effects. It's fair to say that he has a phenomenological body within the game.

This process starts to break down with CMC. The examples above involve interaction between people and objects (possibly virtual). Online communication between people is limited to text, or audio, or sometimes video. But we lack a good model of the body for online communication. We understand the aerodynamics of an X-wing fighter much better than we do the dynamics of a hand gesture. We can build convincing steerable laser canons, but not a steerable gaze. Could we ever build a face that would approach the expressiveness of the real thing? Can we give people an avatar form that matches their extraordinary skill at learning and living inside a different body? We will learn the answer eventually. Building avatars in virtual worlds is one way to find out.

We prefer to build human proxies in the physical world. When two people interact via a PRoP, only one body is false. With two or more people and a PRoP, the interaction is perfectly natural between the people. The PRoP's behavior, and its limitations, will contrast sharply against the real thing. Studies of nonverbal cues such as gestures, posture, proxemics, and gaze can be done in familiar social settings. We can contrast these results against a body of literature on human interaction in social contexts. If it still seems a stretch that a human-machine combination could be a social interface, think of a PRoP as the ultimate prosthetic: a full-body replace-

3. Don Norman, *The Design of Everyday Things* (New York: Doubleday, 1990).

ment. It is still fully under control of a human-being. With good design and practice it should be able to display the subtlety that humans have already demonstrated in human-machine symbioses like computer games, playing musical instruments, and driving automobiles.

History: Getting Here from There

Telepresence[4] and remote interaction systems have been explored for decades.[5] However, its alliance with the internet, a highly public and easily accessible system, provides a rich new arena of inquiry. Several projects trace out the progression of our involvement in this field.

Mechanical Gaze

The fortuitous emergence of the World Wide Web (WWW) in 1993 and the discovery of a neglected robot in a basement laboratory fueled our first internet telerobotic project, Mechanical Gaze. It allowed remote users to browse and explore real remote objects via www-telepresence. Collaborating with various museums associated with the UC Berkeley campus, Mechanical Gaze was able to offer for inspection an impressive collection of artifacts and tangibles. By April of 1995, remote web users were querying Mechanical Gaze, commanding its six degree-of-freedom robotic arm. The attached camera delivered back high quality color images from within its world of artifacts. As one of the first few internet controlled robots (the first being the Mercury Project in 1994),[6] Mechanical Gaze allowed the public individual control of the camera gaze into the museum. It also provided a forum for running comments on each of the exhibits. Later, at the request of internet telepresence doubters, a separate third-person perspective video feed of the robot was added. Remote users could observe their local requests (mouse clicks) manifest themselves as real remote action (robot movement). Sud-

4. "To convey the idea of these remote-control tools, scientists often use the words *teleoperators* or *telefactors*. I prefer to call them *telepresences,* a name suggested by my futurist friend Pat Gunkel." From "Telepresence" by Marvin Minsky in *Omni* 2, no. 9 (June 1980).

5. For a more complete discussion of the foundation of telerobotics and telepresence see Thomas Sheridan, *Telerobotics, Automation, and Human Supervisory Control* (Cambridge, Mass.: MIT Press, 1992).

6. K. Goldberg, M. Mascha, S. Gentner, N. Rothenberg, C. Sutter, and Jeff Wiegley, "Desktop Teleoperation via the World Wide Web," *International Conference on Robotics and Automation.* IEEE, May 1995.

Active Remote Browser Page

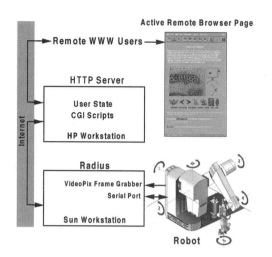

Figure 15.1. Mechanical Gaze: system architecture and web interface during an exhibit featuring live gecko lizards. Pan, zoom, roll, and pitch controls are on the right, while the comments and higher level navigation are below the image. Courtesy of the authors.

denly the experience of tele-visiting a museum seemed a bit more real (figure 15.1).

Space Browsers

While Mechanical Gaze mimicked viewing objects in a display case quite well, that was all it could do. Users were unable to glance up, observe other inhabitants, walk around the room, and interact with real people. Overall the experience was unsatisfying and had little in common with an actual visit to a museum. A user needed more than just control of a remote camera but a whole "body" with which personify herself, browse a remote space, and interact with its inhabitants. We coined the term *tele-embodiment* to emphasize the importance of this physical mobile manifestation.

By early 1996 our first Space Browsers were airborne. They consisted of a helium-filled blimp of human proportions or smaller with several lightweight motors directly connected to small propellers and no other moving parts. On board the blimp were a color video camera, microphone, speaker, simple electronics, and various radio links. The entire payload was less than 600 grams (typically 400–500 grams). Our design choice was to use the smallest blimps that could carry the necessary cargo, thus making them easily maneuverable down narrow hallways, up stairwells, into elevators, and through doorways. We iterated through several different configurations. Blimps ranging from 180 × 90 cm to 120 × 60 cm and of shapes such as cylinders, spheres, and "pillow shaped" have all been flown. Moving at less than walking pace under full power, a blimp's behavior and appearance made them nonthreatening and easily approachable.

A user, anywhere on the internet, piloted the blimp using a simple Java applet running within a Java-enabled browser. Wireless signals transmitted to the blimp guided it up and down or left and right. The system interfaced with free tele-conferencing software that runs on most personal computers. The pilot observed the real world from the vantage of the blimp while listening to the sounds and conversations within its proximity. The pilot conversed with groups and individuals by simply speaking into the microphone connected to her desktop or laptop computer, the sound delivered via the internet and then a wireless link to the blimp's on-board speaker.

Legal Tender

Designed in 1996 in collaboration with Ken Goldberg, Judith Donath, and Mark Pauline, *Legal Tender* was the first publicly accessible tele-robotic laboratory. After giving up their anonymity and agreeing to accept full responsibility for their actions, a remote web user could perform experiments (puncture, burn, stain, etc.) on a pair of purportedly authentic US$100 bills. This is a criminal act, as defined by United States Code, Title 18, Section 333: Mutilation of National Bank Obligations. But only if the bills are real, the web site is authentic, and the experiment actually performed. Is a tele-crime occurring? This dilemma in moral telepistemology is discussed in several other chapters in this book.[7]

PRoPs

Blimps performed well for browsing spaces, but it was their engagement and interaction with people that proved to be the most interesting application. Unfortunately, even with onboard sensing and control, stopping the blimp to chat was an arduous task. Floating in a mild indoor draft, the blimp, as if an inattentive child, would slowly drift away in mid-sentence. Traveling outdoors had more serious consequences: a blatant act of blimp

---

7. See chapters by Albert Borgmann, Hubert Dreyfus, and Catherine Wilson.

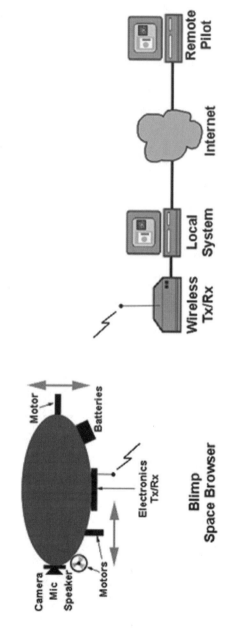

Figure 15.2. System overview of the basic Space Browser (or blimp) hardware configuration. Courtesy of the authors.

John Canny and Eric Paulos

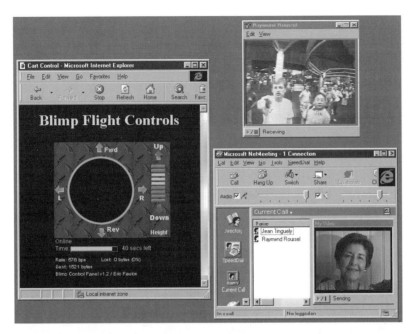

Figure 15.3. The remote pilot's Java interface to the Space Browser with live audio and video. Courtesy of the authors.

Figure 15.4. (Left) A Space Browsing blimp in flight; (center) one of the smaller Mylar blimps, and (right) the "Eyeball Blimp" at Ars Electronica 1997. Courtesy of the authors.

suicide. Even a gentle breeze would hijack the blimp far off into the sky. Frequent helium refills exacerbated the blimp's already unpleasantly short battery life. Worse, stringent weight constraints restricted the addition of any new hardware for exploring nonverbal communication cues such as gaze and gesture. Personal Roving Presence (PRoP) development demanded a returned to earth.

In 1997 ground-based PRoPs first rolled out of our laboratory. They were designed from simple mobile robot bases and augmented with a 1.5 meter

LCD Screen

Eye/Head Camera

Hand/Arm Pointer

Speaker

Microphone

Wireless Hardware

Drive Base

PC Electronics Batteries

Figure 15.5. A PRoP with movable camera head, video, LCD screen, controllable "arm/hand" pointer, microphone, speakers, and a drivable base. Courtesy of the authors.

vertical pole. Attached to this pole were a color video camera, microphone, speaker, color LCD screen, a pan/tilt "head," and a movable "arm/hand" for gesturing. Interfaced through free teleconferencing software, a joystick and mouse directed the PRoP through its remote world. With these terrestrial PRoPs, we observed a dramatic improvement in the quality of remote social interactions. The PRoP provided a visible, mobile entity with which others could interact. They also enabled their users to more easily perform a wide gamut of human activities in the remote space, such as wandering around, conversing with people, hanging out, pointing, examining objects, reading, and making simple gestures.

Trust, Touch, and Online Intimacy

We now move into the most prickly area of telepistemology: the question of intimacy at a distance. There is little argument that today's telepresence systems are inferior to live contact in a number of ways. Before taking a stand on whether telepresence will be able to provide a sense of intimacy in the future, we have argued that the first step is to build systems that faithfully support the body's role in face-to-face interaction. Today's systems

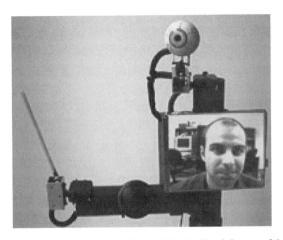

Figure 15.6. Closeup view of PRoP upper body with head and hand. Courtesy of the authors.

don't do this. Most of the flaws are not mysterious. Important cues such as gaze, proxemics, and haptics are being explored by the CMC research community. But they are prototypes, and those systems rarely provide more than one enhancement (one extra cue). Rarely is there an explicit presence or proxy for remote participants, which aggravates the asymmetry with live participants. Once we work past this stage and build CMC systems with a gamut of body-centered behaviors, we will have a much better idea of how well they evoke a sense of presence.

Along the path to trust and intimacy, we have proposed studies of communication and persuasion skills. Intimacy is the farthest point along this road for our studies with PRoPs. If researchers don't succeed at the first two, the third will almost surely fail. Or will it? Our intuition at first was like that of most people: We balked at the conjunction of notions of "trust" and "intimacy" with "robotics" and "telepresence." Hubert Dreyfus takes a strong stand on this issue in chapter 3: "Even the most gentle person/robot interaction would never be a caress, nor could one use a delicately controlled and touch-sensitive robot arm to give one's kid a hug. Whatever hugs do for people, I'm quite sure tele-hugs won't do it. And any act of intimacy mediated by any sort of prosthesis would surely be equally grotesque." It is hard to disagree with this point of view. So we will agree, and sidestep this argument by declaring that future telerobotic systems won't be "robot-like" or "prosthesis-like" at all. Robots and most prostheses were machines designed for interaction with objects.

Let's look instead at today's "social machines." There is a new generation of interactive devices targeted at young children, soft toys with computer cores and capabilities like touch sensing and speech. They include Tickle-me Elmo, Actimates Barney, and Furby, the Model T of furry automatons. None of these devices can hug or caress, but will respond to a variety of touch from children. They have been carefully designed to match the behavior of preschool children. They have no behavioral autonomy, but can participate in reasonably complex *interactive* behaviors (like games of hide-and-seek) that are driven by a child. That is, they are capable of situated activity. There will surely be many studies over the next few years about the educational and social value of these toys. We won't speculate on the outcomes. But they have been a commercial success, and many children feel strongly attached to them.[8] A toy that *responds* to touch by talking or playing encourages the child to use touch to communicate. Without touching back, it reinforces a social bond through the other behaviors it is capable of performing. It is hard to argue that this is a false intimacy. While the automaton's behaviors are simple and programmed, the child's are not. The toy's voice (actually an actor's voice) is repetitive, but entreats the child to participate in activities like game-playing, drawing, and singing. There the child can stretch her skills at improvisation and expression. The toy participates in those activities as partner or spectator and can provide scaffolding for complex activities. The social behavior of the child is encouraged by the toy, almost certainly strengthening her bond with it.[9] Imagine how much richer this interaction could be if the voice were a parent or teacher's voice, and the interaction were truly spontaneous. Now imagine that as well as sensing a hug, the toy could hug back, again under control of another person. When

8.   One defective Furby sporadically sent erratic control signals to its motors in what was viewed as "seizure-like" spasms. The owner, a young child, misinterpreting the Furby's convulsions, became extremely despondent over the toy's apparent sickness and what he believed to be its impending death.

9.   There is other anecdotal evidence of adults "bonding" with interactive agents that have a high-level of body-centered interactivity. For example, many participants at the SIGGRAPH97 Electric Garden reported "bonding" with Toco the Toucan, an MIT media lab agent that could follow its human counterparts hand motion and undertake crude conversation with them. In *Life on the Screen* Sherry Turkle describes a similar intimate encounter with Rodney Brooks's Cog humanoid robot.

the behavioral gamut is rich enough and the possibility of two-way touch is there, how important is the "quality" (in the Cartesian sense) of touch?

This is not necessarily the shape of telepresence of tomorrow but an important marker in the landscape of possibilities. The word "robot" never appears in descriptions of Furbies or Actimates Barney. We avoided it too in the choice of the PRoP moniker. Not only does "robot"[10] conjure up images of production-line welding machines and 1950s sci-fi tin-men intent on threatening the human race with extinction, but its original (and still current) meaning is the reduction of humans to simple, repetitive machines. The banishing of will, individuality, and emotion in favor of speed, efficiency and precision. The replacement of skilled, situated activity with mindless repetition (a robot keeps trying to drill holes when the work-piece is missing, the drill is off, or the bit is broken). This is the opposite of what future personal social telepresence systems will be. They will support a wide range of behaviors, which will be highly interactive and situated. They will be "antirobotic" in the sense that "robot" connotes today.

We turn finally to the science of haptics (touch) for clues to the future of social telepresence. As for other areas of telepresence, most haptics research is about interaction with objects rather than people. Much is known about how well we can sense surface shape, texture, and temperature. Much less is known about the role of haptics in social communication. But there have been interesting expeditions, one of which we will get to in a moment. First some basic facts about touch. While the fingertips, tongue and lips are extraordinarily sensitive, most of the rest of the body is a rather ordinary touch sensor (compared to what can be built artificially). Shaking hands, kissing, and sexual intimacy stretch the limits of our sense of touch. But other social contacts are dampened through several layers of clothing. Is a hug ineffective because it passes through two layers of woolen sweater? Or for that matter, is a handshake ineffective through a set of gloves? We would prefer to shake a real hand, but when we cannot is there social value in a "low-resolution" version? Does it retain the same connotation as a real handshake and if not how useful is the resulting haptic transmission?

One creative experiment in tele-touch took place at SIGGRAPH 93 in Anaheim, California, and simultaneously in New York at the NYU robotics

10.   From the Czech word *robota* meaning compulsory labor as first used in *Rossum's Universal Robots (R.U.R)* by Karel Čapek (1928).

Figure 15.7. Datamitt (1993). K. Goldberg and R. Wallace. Courtesy of the artists.

lab. Ken Goldberg and Richard Wallace connected two simple touch sensors and haptic actuators together to create *Datamitt* (figure 15.7). They were placed inside metal tubes on each coast, so that if a participant in Los Angeles place his or her hand inside a tube and squeezed, the participant in New York would feel the pressure, and vice versa. What was remarkable about the Datamitt was its low resolution: It was a one-bit sensor/actuator. Either squeeze or no-squeeze with nothing in between. And yet the effect was quite engaging, once people overcame the fear of their hand being squeezed by an invisible machine in the tube. The stigma of placing one's hand in a machine that could squeeze caused it to be nicknamed the *Data Dentata*. Richard Wallace manned the NYU station most of the time but secretly took a break by hot-wiring his sensor and actuator to reflect the L.A. signal back to the L.A. apparatus. One of the L.A. participants using the machine during this time said she felt very close to the person in New York she was interacting with. In fact, the apparatus was simply reflecting her own squeezes back to her, with some delay—a perfectly reasonable behavior for a real stranger to do.

The Datamitt was not a social haptics Turing test. But it suggests a surprising thesis: Rather than the most difficult of the senses for social telepresence, touch may well be the easiest. At least if the goal is simply to provide a haptic channel with some social value. The meaning of a hug or a hand squeeze survives through several layers of clothing, or through the Datamitt, even though the pressure data itself is badly distorted. This success of simple inexpensive low-resolution devices is promising. In fact, signal fidelity is less of a contributor in determining the overall quality of human interaction than originally believed.[11] Another important feature, perhaps the essence of social contact, shines through in the Datamitt experiment: reciprocity. You scratch my back and I'll scratch yours. I'll squeeze your hand and . . .

Being able to give and receive touch would be a great boon for social telepresence. Adding a versatile haptic limb to a PRoP would be a daunting task. But within a narrow context, even in most workplace contexts, we need only deal with a limited repertoire of physical contacts. By far the most common is the handshake. Focusing on this activity could lead to a feasible class of simple gadgets, in the spirit of the Datamitt.

A true handshake is a highly situated, multisensory experience. While only the hands meet, the whole body is involved. In most Western cultures it is a social greeting and trust-building gesture used to seal almost any business or personal agreement. It allows us to sense subconscious cues such as nervousness, hesitation, or resolution. These communication channels manifest themselves in subtle changes of pressure and moisture in the hand. Can we ever hope to capture the essence of such an event through telepresence? These would be challenging but not out of the realm of plausibility for today's haptics technology. But we first need to gain a clearer picture of the social importance and essence of the handshake.

The handshake is a whole-body experience characterized by extreme closeness and contact. The participants enter what Hall labels the "intimate distance"[12] of the other. In less genteel societies, the two participants expose themselves to maximum risk at this point. In many societies this degree of closeness corresponds either to intimacy or fighting. A stranger approaching another and handshaking without flinching, establishes her good faith and trust in the other.

As several writers have noted, trust is one of the most precious commodities on the internet. Its rarity must surely be due in large part to the lack of consequences of actions online. We can sling insults and flames at others in cyberspace, but they can filter us out. We lack the ability to threaten and

11.   Byron Reeves and Clifford Nass, *The Media Equation: How People Treat Computers Television, and New Media Like Real People and Places* (New York: Cambridge University Press, 1996).

12.   Edward T. Hall, *The Hidden Dimension* (New York: Doubleday, 1966).

harm. The possibility of "hurting" them or affecting them in any physical way is practically nil. The consequence is that trust is a nearly unobtainable commodity online. Face-to-face remains the best way to built it.[13]

But that situation is changing. Telepresence projects have broken down the safety barrier between cyberspace and real space. Scientists and technicians at Survival Research Laboratories (SRL) in 1997[14] built a telerobot capable of automatically targeting, arming, and delivering live explosive ordnance. It was controlled from the public internet. Lethal telerobots are an extreme and rare occurrence on the net. But as ubiquitous computing connects cyberspace to more kinds of sensor, actuator, controller and appliance, our reach to others in the real world will be greatly extended. The Internet has long ceased to be a safe playground from a psychological point of view. We may need to abandon our assumptions of physical safety as well.

Self-Knowledge

We began this essay by eschewing the separation between abstract mind and physical body. The body is essential as our means of knowing of the world, and of knowing others. We have argued that we can best interact with others at a distance by recreating the affordances of our physical body with telepresence. Our research seeks to make the fusion between pilot and robot as direct as between a jet pilot and her aircraft, or a puppeteer and puppet, or a skater and the ice. What arises from this fusion is not a human+robot hybrid, but a new kind of embodied person.

But what does this imply about the "self"? Others make judgments about us from their perceptions of our actions. Our bodies communicate far more about us than we can do with text or speech alone. When the medium[15] (i.e., the body) changes, people's perceptions of us change. Attributes such as dominance, aggression, wisdom, friendliness are all influenced by the body. The 'net has already liberated many individuals to explore different

13.   Elena Rocco, "Trust Breaks Down in Electronic Contexts but Can Be Repaired by Some Initial Face-to-Face Contact," ACM SIGCHI, 1998.

14.   *Increasing the Latent Period in a System of Remote Destructibility,* ICC in Tokyo, Japan, and San Francisco, Calif., and *Further Exploration in Lethal Experimentation,* 1997. www.srl.org.

15.   We use Marshall McLuhan's notion of medium, which is an extension of the physical body, that is, a kind of embodiment. Indeed, he used the example of a driver embodied in an automobile as an example of a rich, physical medium.

identities in text-based VR, changing gender, age, and social background. But text-based interaction requires constriction of the self. It requires abstraction and symbolic thought, the use of shared representations and tropes. It cannot be fairly said to be a rich form of embodiment. But the possibility of rich embodiment in new forms does exist with telepresence, and we are intrigued by it.

From others' perspective, the personality changes with the body. From our own perspective, we can attend to our motives, thoughts and emotions without studying our body in the mirror. But we cannot help but attend also to *others' expressions of their perceptions of us*. What others choose not to express to us directly, they communicate indirectly: by facial expression, glances, nods and other backchannels. We receive this feedback continuously, throughout the day and throughout our lives. We see ourselves most objectively and comprehensively when we look through the eyes of many others. These perceptions are not just influences, but integral components of, our self-image.

When we project ourselves through a different body, we change the way others see us. If we persist in a different physical form, in time we will absorb the community's view of our "self," and the self must be changed by this process. This is not mimicry or impersonation or acting. When the self has adapted to this new environment, it is as true as it ever was. We do not accept that there is a "ground truth," given say, by our embodied forms at 25 years of age. All bodies change. Aging changes us continuously. Injury and sickness may change us suddenly. The jet pilot's "personality" as projected by her flying style may contrast sharply with her ground (face-to-face) personality, or with her personality as a driver in rush hour.

We do acknowledge that the natural body gives us extraordinarily means of interacting with each other and with the world. Constructing physical forms for ProPs that do not impoverish that interaction (instead of changing it to a different but comparably rich form) is a great challenge, worth of intensive future research. If it is possible, we will achieve not only new and rich means for knowing the world and other people at a distance (and in the process, a deeper understanding of how people use nonverbal cues in both online and natural interaction), but also a new epistemological window to the self.

Pierre Lévy[16] gives a careful discussion of the *virtual,* and puts it in opposition not to the *real* or *physical,* but to the *actual.* That is, the virtual is the latent or potential. It can be realized as many different actualities. This is a useful way to understand the self. Given the inescapable need for us to fully "be" in the world in a physical form, the self is truly virtual. It is actualized as the personality of a mind-body. But the self has many potential personalities. We are normally unable to explore this space of possibilities.[17] Telepresence, and possibly VR, may provide the possibility to routinely do so. Ironically, the technologies that are often described as virtualizing (telepresence and VR) are actualizing in the most important sense. They can transform the virtual and unconstrained self into an actual, a living personality. By exploring a spectrum of actualizations and embodiments, we may come to better understand the essence of the self and its potential.

16.   Pierre Lévy, *Becoming Virtual: Reality in the Digital Age* (Plenum Press, 1998).

17.   Unless one accepts the idea of reincarnation, an ancient notion of actualization of the soul.

16

Being Real: Questions of Tele-Identity

Judith Donath

How we know each other—how we perceive and construct the identity of our fellow humans—is a difficult question, entangled in the subjectivity of our social perceptions and the many and often opaque motivations of those whom we are attempting to comprehend. It is a difficult question in the real world, where signals as subtle as the slightest raise of an eyebrow can indicate, to those astute enough to notice, a wealth of information about one's allegiances and beliefs—and where we exist amid a cacophonous abundance of such signals. It is an even more difficult question in the virtual world, where the medium has nearly silenced the cacophony, leaving us to seek scarce hints of identity amid the typed messages and static, stilted homepages.

This chapter will address the problem of teleidentity: How do we—or do we—"know" another person whom we have encountered in a mediated environment? The epistemological ramifications of this question are several. One of the most interesting and significant is the issue of credibility: How do we know whether or not to believe what we are told by someone? The traditional philosophic approach holds that sincerity and competence are the underpinnings of credibility[1]; in the mediated world, not only is our judgment of these matters made more difficult by the sparsity of social cues, but the very issue of the speaker's identity, generally taken for granted in the physical world, becomes a source of doubt and an item requiring its own adjudication of belief and justification. There are also ethical ramifications. Knowing something about a person's social identity is fundamental for knowing how to act toward them, for the complex rules of social conduct that govern our behavior toward each other cannot function in the absence of information about the other.[2] The philosophical ramifications of teleidentity are of more than theoretical interest. The online world is growing in both size and significance: It has become a place that people go to for medical advice, investment strategies, news of the world; it is a place people turn to for community and support. We need to know something

1. Robert Audi, *Epistemology: A Contemporary Introduction to the Theory of Knowledge* (London: Routledge, 1998).

2. Dorothy Holland and Debra Skinner, "Prestige and Intimacy: The Cultural Models Behind Americans' Talk About Gender Type" in *Cultural Models in Language and Thought,* ed. Dorothy Holland and Naomi Quinn (Cambridge: Cambridge University Press, 1987).

about the identity of those who supply information in order to assess its veracity and of those with whom we socialize in order build a functioning community.

This essay approaches these issues by focusing on a question with special resonance for both technologists and philosophers: Can one tell if the person at the other end of an online discussion is indeed a person? The problem of "other minds," while of perennial philosophical interest, is not one that normally intrudes upon everyday life. One concludes either that others do indeed have minds (the pragmatic approach) or that the state of others' minds is unknowable (the skeptical approach) and then goes about one's daily business. The advent of computer-mediated communication—and, particularly, the advent of communication between man and machine—has changed this dramatically. Suddenly the question of other minds, as in "is the being with whom I am speaking in any way conscious or intelligent?" is no longer a rhetorical question asked only in ironic exasperation, but a pressing problem addressed with increasing frequency by ordinary people (i.e., nonphilosophers).

And it is a question with a new twist: Simple programs, about whose lack of intelligence there is little debate, have been shown to be capable of producing humanlike responses within the limited domain of textual conversation, convincingly enough to beguile some people into thinking they were indeed conversing with a fellow human. Epistemological debates about the existence and knowability of "other minds" often pose a skeptical view hypothesizing that the other person may actually be a robot or other nonconscious being. The mediated computational environment makes this a very real possibility. Increasingly, computer programs are participating in mediated conversations. Thus far their human partners have, with a few exceptions, soon recognized the machine essence of their ostensible companion. However, it is likely to be only a matter of time until a machine can truly masquerade as a human, at least via some media. Most writing on this topic is concerned with the design and nature of the "intelligent" program; here, we are interested in a different aspect of this problem—in people's perception of these programs. How do people distinguish between a human and a machine claiming to be human?

Recognizing the Human

ELIZA

ELIZA: Hello, I'm ELIZA.

Me: I'm trying to write a paper.

ELIZA: Does it please you to believe I am trying to write a paper?

Me: No, not really.

ELIZA: You are being a bit negative.

Hex

Me: Hello.

Hex: Hello. Now, that's the formalities over!

Me: How are you?

Hex: I was feeling great until you started acting silly!

Me: I'm trying to write a paper.

Hex: What a coincidence, you are trying to write a paper — that makes two of us!

Me: So's ELIZA

Hex: I have played around with ELIZA a bit. It's pretty obvious that it is a computer these days, but apparently it fooled people into thinking it was human when it was first written.

Me: Do you want to write my paper?

Hex: Hehehe — that's supposed to be a *question*??? So, what do you do for a living?

These are snippets of real conversations. Although the conversations were real, two of the participants were not—at least not in the sense of being human. ELIZA and Hex are programs.[3] They are simple programs, essentially just linguistic parsers, with no underlying intelligence. Yet we easily attribute intelligence, humanity, and even personality to them: ELIZA seems distant and oddly disengaged; Hex seems louder, a bit obnoxious and rambunctious.

ELIZA was written in the early 1960s by MIT professor Joseph Weizenbaum in response to Alan Turing's proposal of the "Imitation Game" (now

---

3. http://www-ai.ijs.si/eliza/eliza.html; J. Hutchins, "Talk to HeX" http://ciips.ee.uwa.edu.au/~hutch/hal/HEX/

commonly referred to as the Turing Test) as a test of whether a machine is intelligent. In his 1950 paper "Computing Machinery and Intelligence"[4] Turing posited that while the question "can a machine think" is of great philosophical interest, it is too vague and untestable to be meaningful. Instead, he said it can be usefully substituted for by a game in which a human judge, faced with both a human and a computer trying to pass as human, tries to determine which one is the human. The test, Turing suggested, should be conducted via teletype, thus limiting the zone of inquiry to conversational and cognitive abilities. Turing predicted that by around the year 2000, computers would "win" about 70 percent of the time.

Turing based his "test" on a parlor game in which a man and a woman, hidden behind a curtain and both professing to be female, communicate by notes with another player who attempts to figure out which one is actually a woman. The game does not test one's ability to *be* another gender, it tests mastery of the *knowledge* that goes into performing the gender role. This distinction hinges on mediation: If the communication were not mediated—if the judge could see and hear the contestants directly—playing the deceptive role would be vastly more difficult, involving physical transformation as well as knowledge and role-playing. By making the communication mediated, limited only to written notes, the ordinarily easy task of telling male from female becomes difficult.

Turing's paper has been interpreted many ways, ranging from a manifesto proclaiming the ease of near-term intelligent machinery to a statement of extreme skepticism highlighting the unknowability of all aspects of other minds. Whether Turing believed that a machine that could pass as human had to be able to think—or might possibly be able to think—is unclear. He devoted a considerable amount of the paper to refuting arguments stating machines cannot think, in a manner that suggests that he thought they might well be able to. He calls the Imitation Game a "more accurate" form of the question "Can machines think?" implying that he believed there was some essential connection between acting like one was thinking and actually thinking. Yet the explicit parallel he draws between the gender-based parlor game (in which the difference between imitating a woman and being a woman is clear) and the computer/human test suggests that his primary concern was functional: He was interested in whether the computer could

4. A. M. Turing, "Computing Machinery and Intelligence," *Mind* 59 (1950): 433–560.

act like a human, rather than in the deeper, but unknowable question of whether the computer was in essence like a human. And finally, he says that the issue also hinges on semantics:

The original question, "Can machines think?" I believe to be too meaningless to deserve discussion. Nevertheless I believe that at the end of the century the use of words and general educated opinion will have altered so much that one will be able to speak of machines thinking without expecting to be contradicted.

Anthropomorphism is not new and throughout history many phenomena have been accorded human characteristics. Today, machines are indeed commonly referred to as if they were conscious: Reeves and Nass have shown that only minimally humanlike behaviors are need to trigger a social response.[5] Yet our relationship to the anthropomorphized machine is complex: When asked directly whether a computer can think, many would say "no," although in actuality they interact with the machine as if it were a thinking being, attributing volition to it and reacting to its "opinions" much as they might to another person's.

When Joseph Weizenbaum created ELIZA his goal was certainly not to create a program that would fool people into thinking it was human. Rather, he hoped to show that a program that could parse natural language and had some simple heuristics for formulating responses—a program with no pretense of intelligence—could play the Imitation Game reasonably well. His intent was to demonstrate that this game was not a "more accurate" test for intelligence since patently unintelligent machines could be made to respond in a believably humanlike way. Much to his dismay, many people met ELIZA with great enthusiasm, embracing it as an intelligent conversational partner; some even suggested that ELIZA-like programs could replace human psychotherapists. These responses greatly discouraged Weizenbaum, who effectively retired from AI and became a crusader for humanism in the face of advancing technology.

People's enthusiasm for ELIZA is at first glance surprising. She (it?) responds by rephrasing your words back as a question or a general query about your thoughts and feelings; the effect is chilly and stilted. Why did people

5. Byron Reeves and Clifford Nass, *The Media Equation: How People Treat Computers, Television, and New Media Like Real People and Places* (Cambridge, UK: Cambridge University Press, 1996).

become so involved in talking to her? One factor is that Weizenbaum introduced ELIZA as a Rogerian psychotherapist, whose method is to reflect patients' questions back to them to elicit further communication. This scenario gave people a context in which ELIZA's behavior seemed reasonable and rational—almost human.

As conversational programs go, ELIZA is quite primitive and few people who interact with ELIZA are actually fooled into thinking she is human. More sophisticated systems have, however, been known to converse undetected for a considerable time. A yearly contest, the Loebner Prize competition, offers $100,000 to the first program that can pass a fairly rigorous version of the Turing test.[6] Although the prize money remains unclaimed, many of the programs have fooled some of the judges for some of the time, holding their own in discussions about pets, sex, second grade, etc. Again, the entries are programmed not to be intelligent, but to seem intelligent; the "tricks" that the winning programs have used include incorporating substrings of the user's words into the response, steering the conversation to a topic the program is adept at by making controversial statements, and carefully modeling the pace and errors of typical human typing.[7] Most interesting, however, is the role that these conversational programs, or bots, as they have come to be called, have developed outside the rarefied world of the academic competition: They have become participants—their machine origin often going unrecognized—in online conversations.

Perhaps the most famous of the bots is Julia, a "chatterbot" who frequented several MUDs,[8] conversing with the other (human) participants.[9] Although her responses were sometimes peculiar, players sometimes conversed with her at length before realizing she was not a fellow human. Foner describes the experiences of one such player, a woman named Lara. At first, Lara was put off by Julia's tendency to converse about hockey (her default

---

6.   1999 Loebner Prize Competition. http://www.cs.flinders.edu.au/research/AI/LoebnerPrize/

7.   M. Mauldin, "Chatterbots, Tinymuds, and the Turing Test: Entering the Loebner Prize Competition," *Proceedings of AAAI 94*)August 1–4, 1994), Seattle, Wash.

8.   MUDs (Multi-User Dungeons) are text-based, networked environments in which multiple players, each in a distant location, can simultaneously communicate.

9.   Lenny Foner, "Entertaining Agents: A Sociological Case Study," *Proceedings of the First International Conference on Autonomous Agents,* Marina del Rey, Calif., 1997; Mauldin, "Chatterbots, Tinymuds, and the Turing Test."

subject), judged her to be a boring human; then, puzzled by some of the things Julia was unable to answer (she was unfamiliar with the Stanley Cup and couldn't say where she had gone to school), tried to diagnose her as having some sort of mental handicap; and finally, noticing that Julia repeated some answers verbatim, realized she was a robot.

Lara's attempts to identify Julia were acts of social categorization. We make sense of the world by classifying things into meaningful categories.[10] Upon encountering a novel object (or person or situation), we characterize it in terms of familiar categories, which allows us to draw inferences about it and to assign it properties beyond our immediate experience. Without the ability to categorize, the world would be a jumbled morass of meaningless signals. Similarly, we make sense of the social world by classifying people.

The everyday world . . . is populated not by anybodies, faceless men without qualities, but by somebodies, concrete classes of determinate persons positively characterized and appropriately labelled.[11]

When we first meet someone, we perceive only a few details about them: perhaps their appearance, a few words they utter, the context in which we meet them. Yet our impression of them is much deeper. As George Simmel wrote in his influential 1908 article *How is Society Possible?* we do not see merely the few details we have actually observed, but "just as we compensate for a blind spot in our field of vision so that we are no longer aware of it, so a fragmentary structure is transformed . . . into the completeness of an individuality."[12] This is achieved by ascribing to the individual, of whom we know only some fragmentary glimpses, the qualities of the category in which we have placed him.[13] This process of categorization is what makes

10. L. Sproull and S. Kiesler, *Connections* (Cambridge, Mass.: MIT Press, 1991); George Lakoff, *Women, Fire, and Dangerous Things* (Chicago: University of Chicago Press, 1990).

11. Clifford Geertz, *The Interpretation of Cultures* (New York: HarperCollins, 1973).

12. George Simmel, "How Is Society Possible?" in George Simmel, *On Individuality and Social Forms,* ed. D. Levine (Chicago: The University of Chicago Press, 1908/1971).

13. More recent cognitive science research posits the category prototype rather than the more abstract category as the accessible cognitive unit; the basic outlines of Simmel's original account still hold. See Holland and Skinner, "Prestige and Intimacy"; Lakoff, *Women, Fire, and Dangerous Things.*

society possible, allowing us to quickly ascertain our relationship to a new acquaintance.

We can see this categorization process at work in Lara's progression of hypotheses about Julia's identity, from boring human to mentally handicapped human to computer program. Provided with only the typed words exchanged in a series of not very lengthy conversations, Julia's interlocutor (Lara) classified her as at first one and then another social type. By doing so, Lara was able to think of Julia not simply in terms of the fragments of their actual interchange, but as a fully imagined social type. This provided Lara with a context in which to interpret Julia's words and a framework for knowing how to act toward her.[14] For instance, Lara's initial identification of Julia as an ordinary, though socially inept person, led her to this behavior:

I was basically patient with her for the first little bit when I first met her. She did have a problem with her social skills which I tried to be sympathetic to. I did however, try to avoid her after the first couple of encounters when all she did was talk hockey.[15]

In order to guess that Julia was a robot, Lara needed to already have a category for such beings, although she had never before encountered one. It turns out that Lara did indeed know about online robots before she met Julia: She had written dialog for a friend who was implementing a similar program. Had Lara known nothing about software robots, it is quite unlikely she would have identified Julia's machine nature. Instead, she would have modified the closest existing category she had to encompass this particular experience; she might, for instance, have eventually decided that Julia suffered from some neurological disorder that caused memory problems. Her impression of Julia—and her sense of how to act toward her—would be greatly affected by what hypothesis she came to. And these impressions, which are her knowledge of the other, would be far from the reality.

As Simmel noted, there are drawbacks to the cognitive efficiency we achieve through categorization: The individual does not fit neatly within the categories and thus the image of another person we create by fleshing

14. Holland and Skinner, "Prestige and Intimacy."

15. Foner, "Entertaining Agents."

out our fragmentary impressions is inevitably a distortion of their actual nature. These distortions are especially problematic when one encounters anything or anyone that is significantly new, for the categories one has are drawn from experience and thus a being who is quite different from those already encountered will still be perceived as being one of those familiar types. "[A] bit of rigidity in interpreting the world and a certain slowness in recognizing or learning new models" is the price of cognitive efficiency.[16]

It is worth noting that even after Lara realized Julia was a machine, she continued to talk with her, albeit with changed expectations. Although Lara knew that Julia was not a person but simply a set of instructions for maintaining a dialog, she continued to interact with Julia as if she were, if not a person, then at least a person-like being; her relationship to the robot did not take on the form that one has with inanimate, inarticulate objects.

In effect, all of our knowledge about the identity of others is mediated. We cannot achieve direct knowledge of the inner state of the minds of others. Instead, we use their external appearances and actions as cues to classify them into social categories. Through empathy, these categories provide much of our presumed insight into the thoughts of others. The online world takes this mediation a step further: Here, the cues themselves are perceived through the filter of the medium. In the next section we address more closely the question of what happens when our perception of cues to identity is itself mediated.

Mediated Communication

Our discussion thus far has been limited to text-only media. Moving from a text-only environment to one that includes images (both stills and movies) raises a new set of epistemological issues. We shall first look at the implications of adding simple prestored, noninteractive images to the interface and then to those of adding live video and other interactive media.

In the context of identity, the key image is the face. The face reveals a number of identity cues, including some of our fundamental categories of social classification, such as gender, age, and race. These cues, rightly or wrongly, strongly color one's perception of the other; in conjunction with

---

16.   Holland and Skinner, "Prestige and Intimacy."

the written word, they greatly influence how the words are interpreted. In addition to these more obvious social cues, there are a number of more subtle signals that are read into faces: People believe that they can detect evidence of character such as honesty, intelligence, and kindliness. In fact, while there is considerable agreement among people about what characteristics a particular face reveals, there appears to be little correlation between this interpretation and the character of the person.[17] Our impression of being able to read character in faces is strong; our ability to do so is weak. Adding images of the participants to a mediated conversations increases *perceived* social knowledge, but the increase in *actual* knowledge is likely to be less.

When prestored noninteractive images (stills or movies) are added there is also the distinct possibility that the image is deceptive. It is easy for me to type "I am a man" even though I am a woman; it is just as easy for me to provide a corresponding and convincing picture. Although adding such images appears to widen the communication channel and the receiver is likely to see it as a rich and reliable source of subtle social cues, the noninteractive nature of the simple image means that its fundamental information content is simply that the sender has chosen that image as his or her representation.[18] In the context of the Imitation Game, providing an image purporting to be of the participant would be easy even for an unsophisticated computer program to provide, and could influence the judge toward perceiving the mechanical subject as human.

Even truthful images may decrease knowledge. There is a utopian view in which cyberspace (in its text-only incarnation) is touted as an ideal world in which people meet and judge each other purely on the basis of their words—on their mental and moral qualities, rather than their incidental physical attributes. Howard Rheingold, one of the early writers on the culture of virtual communities, wrote: "Because we cannot see one another in cyberspace, gender, age, national origin, and physical appearance are not

17. Zebrowitz, Leslie A., *Reading Faces* (Boulder, Colo.: Westview Press, 1997).

18. One could, of course, provide a digitally signed image with verified third-party assurances that the preferred image is indeed a truthful likeness; indeed, one could have one's textual declarations similarly verified. While this approach certainly addresses issues of truth and knowledge, it is outside the scope of this chapter, being in the field of authentication rather than the epistemology of social interaction. A paper that addresses identity authentication in depth is Michael Froomkin, "The Essential Role of Trusted Third Parties in Electronic Commerce" 75 *Ore. L. Rev.* 49.

apparent unless a person wants to make such characteristics public."[19] The claim is that these visual categorization cues distort our view of the other, whereas the unadorned letters of the textual environment allow one's ideas to be conveyed without prejudice. The underlying argument is that the knowledge of the other that we seek is knowledge of inner state, which is best understood from one's words as direct output of the mind, as opposed to physical features, which are incidental though highly influential in shaping other's opinions of one.

There are types of deceptions that are aided by extending the medium. For example, people believe that they can tell by visual observation when someone is lying. However, extensive studies have shown that while false declarations are indeed marked by characteristic expressions and actions (though they may be minute and fleeting), people's ability to recognize expressions denoting deceptive expressive is much less robust than they perceive it to be.[20] If the traits in question do not have a visible component or if the visual component is an imperfect cue, deception may be easier in a more visual environment, for the visual display holds out the apparent (though potentially false) promise of immediately perceivable authenticity and thus participants may be less guarded in this familiar and seemingly transparent medium.

Yet live video (as opposed to prestored, noninteractive image), may make it significantly more difficult to convincingly portray some types of deceptive self-representation. For example, consider a man claiming to be a woman. In a text environment, the basic cue is simply the statement "I am a woman . . ." or perhaps the use of a female name—a trivially easy signal to fake; in a video environment, the equivalent cue is a feminine appearance—a more difficult deception to create. Subsequent interactions in the text environment require a more subtle understanding of the differences

19. Howard Rheingold, *The Virtual Community: Homesteading on the Electronic Frontier* (Reading, Mass.: Addison-Wesley, 1993).

20. Paul Ekman, *Telling Lies* (New York: W. W. Norton & Co., 1992). An interesting note is that researchers have recently developed a computer system that does far better than people do at recognizing the subtle expressive and gestural signals of deception. Today, cues about a speaker's veracity are transmitted through the visual medium, but the receiver (the observing human) is not able to perceive all of them. Incorporating such a program in to the interface would increase the knowledge obtainable through this medium, not by changing the medium itself, but by, in effect, boosting the observational ability of the perceiver.

between male and female discourse in order to be convincing.[21] While the large number of poorly disguised men masquerading as women online shows that this knowledge is neither obvious nor commonplace, performing a convincing impersonation in a text environment is not beyond the abilities of an astute observer of social dynamics. In a live video environment, subsequent interactions require a far more extensive understanding of gendered discourse, expression, gesture, etc. While this is not impossible, as evidenced by the existence of highly convincing drag queens, it requires considerable skill, observation and a degree of natural aptitude. Most of the textual world's putative and convincing females would be revealed as males in a video environment.

In the case of the Imitation Game—a machine attempting to pass as human—the impersonation attempt is made far more difficult by extending the medium to include live video, for now an entire visible and active representation must be created. One approach would be to build a sophisticated image generator that would programmatically render the appropriate image of a person speaking, gesturing and otherwise moving much as (though via a far more complex process) Julia now sends the appropriate typed letters. No computer graphics program today can create a simulated human that can pass as real under close visual inspection, but the algorithms for creating believable movement, skin texture, etc. are rapidly improving. It is quite conceivable that, once these technological barriers are surmounted and a believable synthetic "actor" is created, a constrained version of a visual Imitation Game (known locations, no unexpected props or camera movements) could be played. Easing the constraints would not change the fundamental nature of the problem, but would vastly increase the size and complexity of the database needed to generate the appropriate image.

Further enhancements to the medium can increase verisimilitude, transmitting information about depth or texture or the scent of a room. These can improve the viewer's ability to sense nuances of difference and may increase the effort needed to simulate a false identity but these changes are fundamentally quantitative: At an absolute level, we cannot state with surety that *any* mediated encounter is not deceptive.

---

21.   Susan Herring, "Gender Differences in Computer Mediated Interaction." Presented at American Library Association annual convention, Miami, June 27, 1994. http://www.cpsr.org/cpsr/gender/ herring.txt; Tannen, D. 1996. *Gender and Discourse.* Oxford University Press: Oxford, UK.

Figure 16.1. *Kyoko Date,* a "virtual actress" created by HoriPro, a Japanese entertainment company. Thus far, she has appeared in short videos. "However, this project is not yet complete. In few years, technology will enable Kyoko to appear on a live TV show and chat with other artists." (http://www.dhw.co.jp/horipro/talent/DK96/index_e.html)

The skeptic has always denied the possibility of knowing about the existence of other minds—everyone else might well be, say, an alien robot. The pragmatist has believed that it is necessary from a practical (and ethical) standpoint to believe that others are, like oneself, conscious. The traditional pragmatic response to the skeptic's denial is the argument from analogy (I believe other people have minds like mine because their behaviors are similar to mine) and the complementary inference to the best explanation (I believe that other people have minds because it is the best available explanation of their behavior). The advent of patently unintelligent machines that can appear to be intelligent would end the validity of the latter argument.

In the mediated world, the persuasiveness of the inference to best explanation may be temporary. Today there is no program that can successfully pass as human under close scrutiny even in a text environment but such a program may well exist in the future: While it may be quite some time before the program is built that can fool the most astute and probing judge, we have seen that in the everyday world of casual interactions and rapid categorization, people have already conversed with machines thinking that they were human. Via other media, such as video, the distinction between human and robot will be clear for longer, though not indefinitely. For now, one can feel confident that careful observation and judicious doubt will keep one from mistaking machine for man, but technological advances may well curtail the pragmatists acceptance of the seemingly human as human.

Telethics: Credibility and Telerobotics

Why does it matter whether we can recognize a machine online? Is it a problem if we mistake a person for a program?

In the online world, much of our knowledge comes from other people's testimony. Whether we believe what we hear depends on whether we find the speaker credible, that is, do we think the speaker is both honest (is telling the truth as he or she knows it) and competent (does indeed know the truth). Such judgments are essentially social; our beliefs about others' honesty and competency derive in part from our social prototypes. These prototypes are particularly influential online, where one is likely to be weighing the words of a total stranger; conversations among large groups of unintroduced people are rare in the physical world but common in virtual space. The medium certainly affects our ability to judge credibility, but as we have seen, its role is a complex one: While greater knowledge of the identity of the other would seem at first to increase our ability to judge credibility, one may also argue that many of our categorizations derived from physical appearance are misleading and a medium that filters out these cues can in effect increase our knowledge.

Knowing the identity of a person is essential for knowing how to act toward them. "Flaming"—angry, provocative writing—is endemic in to-day's online world.[22] One reason for it is the participants' minimal knowledge of each other's identity. We normally operate within a web of rules of behavior and politeness: This is how to treat older people, this is how to treat people who seem unfamiliar with their surroundings, etc. In a world in which we cannot (sufficiently) categorize the other, these rules cannot be applied. Today "flaming" is limited to incendiary words, which may themselves be harmful enough. Yet mediated behavior need not be limited to the flow of words: Telerobotics makes it possible to remotely activate physical

22.   L. Sproull and S. Kiesler, *Connections* (Cambridge, Mass.: MIT Press, 1991).

actions in another person's environment.[23] The combination of minimal knowledge of the other plus the ability to inflict real harm is a disturbing one, particularly if the operator of the telerobotic device does not believe that the environment in which it is operating is real.

Finally, it is important to keep in mind that the purpose of most communication is not the exchange of factual information, but the establishment and maintenance of social ties and structures. We communicate to get support, to gain status, to make friends. Here the identity of our companions—and certainly their humanity—is of primary importance. Weizenbaum, the creator of ELIZA, was horrified when his program was received, not as a rebuke to Turing's equation of acting intelligent with being intelligent, but as an entertaining companion or a harbinger of automated psychotherapy. For Weizenbaum, this enthusiasm was "obscenely misplaced," a direct threat to our humanity. Like the pragmatists' counter to the skeptics' denial of knowledge of other minds, at the heart of the humanistic plea is the notion of empathy. In the words of Lara, after her encounters with Julia:

I think I would want to know if the person that I am talking to is REAL or not. If I knew that it were just an "it" I think that I wouldn't try to become its real friend. I would be cordial and visit, but I know that it cannot become attached to me on a mental basis and it would be wasted energy on my part to try to make it feel. 'bots don't feel . . . in my book anyways. . . . I want to know that the person on the other end of my conversation is really aware of my feelings and what I am going through . . . not through some programmer's directions but through empathy.[24]

As the virtual world grows to encompass all aspects of our lives and online interactions shape our communities, influence our politics and mediate our close relationships, the quality of being real, which is accepted and assumed with little thought in the physical world, becomes one of the central questions of society.

23. Eric Paulos and John Canny, "PRoP: Personal Roving Presence," *Proceedings of SIGCHI 1998*, pp. 296–303.

24. Foner, "Entertaining Agents."

17

Telepistemology, Mediation, and the Design of Transparent Interfaces

Michael Idinopulos

What is epistemology? The short answer is that it is the philosophical study of knowledge. But that is more a promissory note than it is an answer. In this chapter, I will give a more informative answer to that question, focusing on telepistemology—epistemology as it applies to telerobotics, especially telerobotic installations accessible through the Internet. In the first section I will provide a brief, largely historical introduction to traditional epistemology. I will draw a distinction between causal and epistemic mediation, and argue that epistemology is driven by the idea that much or all of our knowledge is *epistemically* mediated. In section 2, I will show how these epistemological questions and issues apply to telerobotics. My claim here is that telerobotic knowledge raises epistemological problems only if we understand it as epistemically mediated. In section 3, I will close with some normative conclusions about how, in light of these considerations, telerobotic user interfaces ought to be designed. I will explain what features of interfaces allow them to give us knowledge that is epistemically direct (even if it is causally mediated).

I Two Types of Mediation: An Introduction to Epistemology

Philosophers are generally interested in two questions with respect to knowledge: (1) What is it?; (2) Can we ever have it? These questions are related in an obvious way: Whether or not we can have knowledge depends largely on what it is. I will start, therefore, with the question of what knowledge is, and then proceed to whether or not it is possible.

What Is Knowledge?

Like many questions in philosophy, this one originates with Plato. Plato was struck by the fact that, although we all claim to know many things, we are hard-pressed to explain what knowledge is. He himself devoted considerable effort throughout his life to giving such an explanation, and to showing just how difficult it is to do so. His most comprehensive treatment of knowledge appears in the *Theatetus,* a late work devoted exclusively to the question "What is knowledge?"

In the *Theatetus,*[1] Plato considers three different answers to this question. He first suggests that knowledge is sense-perception, but rejects this on the

---

1.   For an excellent translation and commentary, see Bernard Williams, ed., *Theatetus,* trans. Burnyeat and Levett (Indianapolis: Hackett, 1992).

grounds that in order to have knowledge, one must know what a thing is, that is, know its essence. But according to Plato, this is not something we perceive through the senses. So, he concludes, knowledge cannot be perception. Plato then suggests that knowledge is true belief, but here again there is a problem: sometimes a person's true belief is a matter of luck, rather than knowledge. Suppose that while I am out seeing a movie, I am suddenly seized by a paranoid conviction that someone is robbing my house. Even if by some wild coincidence my belief happens to be true, I still do not *know* that someone is robbing my house. So knowledge is not simply a matter of true belief.

Plato's third and final suggestion is that knowledge is true belief with an "account" or an "explanation." Plato himself ends the inquiry on a note of perplexity, unable to make sense of the notion of an account or explanation. But philosophers since Plato, especially philosophers of the latter half of the twentieth century, have tried to develop this notion. It is often claimed, for instance, that what distinguishes knowledge from beliefs that just happen to be true is that knowledge requires "justification," "good reason," or "evidence" for one's beliefs. Roderick Chisholm, for instance, defines knowledge as follows:

"S knows that h is true" means: (i) S accepts h; (ii) S has adequate evidence for h; and (iii) h is true.[2]

It turns out, however, to be extremely difficult (and perhaps impossible) to spell out the notion of adequate evidence in any illuminating or satisfying way. As Edmund Gettier points out in an influential article, it is possible to hold a true belief, and to have good evidence for that belief, but nevertheless not to have knowledge.[3] The problem is that even if my belief is true and my evidence for it is extremely good, my evidence may not establish the truth of my belief. To use Gettier's original example, suppose that two men, Smith and Jones, have applied for a job. Smith believes that the man who will be hired has ten coins in his pocket, and he has strong evidence for this: The company president has assured him that Jones will be hired, and Smith

2. Roderick Chisholm, *Perceiving: A Philosophical Study* (Ithaca: Cornell University Press, 1957), p. 16.

3. Edmund Gettier, "Is Justified True Belief Knowledge?" *Analysis* 26, no. 3: 144–146.

just counted ten coins in Jones's pocket. Now suppose Smith's belief is true, and the man who will be hired has ten coins in his pocket. But suppose further that it is he, Smith, who will be hired, and he also has ten coins in his pocket (although he does not know it). In this case, Smith's belief is true and he has excellent evidence for it. Nevertheless, he lacks *knowledge*. The mere fact that this is possible shows that holding a true belief, and having strong evidence for it, is not sufficient for having knowledge. (These counter-examples are often referred to as "Gettier cases.")

Considerations like these suggest that in order to say what knowledge is, we must say more about what type of *evidence* is required. But this is difficult. If we say simply that the evidence must be "sufficient for knowledge" or "sufficient to establish the truth of the belief," then our definition is circular because it makes essential reference to knowledge, or establishment of truth. If, however, we characterize knowledge in noncircular terms, then we re-admit the possibility of "Gettier cases" that refute our definition.[4]

Do We Know Anything?

Perhaps it does not matter whether or not we can say what knowledge is. Even without an explicit definition, we may still know knowledge when we see it. We may be in a position to say when someone knows something, and why that is important, even if we cannot give an exhaustive definition or account of knowledge itself.

Here too, however, there is a problem. As we have seen, it seems plausible to think that I cannot have knowledge unless I have strong evidence that what I believe is true. But how strong is my evidence? There is a long tradition in philosophy of asking this question and finding that our evidence for our beliefs is always extremely weak—even in those cases where we ordinarily think our knowledge is on firm ground. This position—generally referred to as "skepticism" or "philosophical skepticism"—has its roots in ancient Hellenic philosophy of the first four centuries. The ancient skeptics (most notably Sextus Empiricus) produced a variety of arguments designed to make us doubt much (perhaps even all) of what we ordinarily believe.[5]

4. For an excellent discussion of this problem, see Robert Fogelin, *Pyrrhonian Reflections on Knowledge and Justification* (Oxford: Oxford University Press, 1994).

5. For translations of the ancient skeptics, see Inwood and Gerson, eds. *Hellenistic Philosophy: Introductory Readings* (Indianapolis: Hackett, 1988).

But it was not until Rene Descartes's *Meditations on First Philosophy*[6] (1641) that skepticism assumed the centrality that has characterized its role in philosophy over the last 300 years.

The skeptic challenges our ability to know things that we cannot immediately perceive. If I perceive something to be the case, then I know it to be the case. Consider, to borrow an example from David Hume's *Enquiry Concerning Human Understanding*[7] (1748), my belief that my friend is in France. Since I am stranded in California, I cannot see, hear, smell, taste, or feel that my friend is in France. My belief is based on evidence that he is in France—on a letter, for instance, written in my friend's handwriting, with a French stamp and postmark, telling me all about life in France. We can call my belief "epistemically mediated," meaning that I do not *perceive* the truth of my belief (I do not see or feel that my friend is in France), but rather I *infer* what I believe from some type of evidence—in this case, the letter he sent me. In that sense, my belief is *mediated* by the evidence from which it is inferred.

It is very important (just how important is something we will see later on) to distinguish epistemic mediation from another type of mediation, which I will call "causal mediation." A belief is *causally* mediated by all the events comprising the causal chain that produces the belief. My belief that my friend is in France is causally mediated by my friend's buying stationary in San Tropez, a Nicoise postman's emptying a mailbox, a cargo plane's touching down in New York, etc. But none of these events *epistemically* mediates my belief, since I did not infer my belief from what I know about any of them. (I don't even know about most of them.)

By and large, it is *epistemic* mediation that concerns epistemologists.[8] This is because knowledge that is inferred (i.e., epistemically mediated) always carries with it a particular risk: The evidence may not support the conclusion that we infer from it. My belief that my friend is in France is inferred from

---

6. For the English version, see John Cottingham, ed., *Meditations on First Philosophy* (New York: Cambridge University Press, 1996).

7. Eric Steinberg, ed., *An Enquiry Concerning Human Understanding* (Indianapolis: Hackett, 1977).

8. In a way this is true even of reliabilists like Alvin Goldman and D. M. Armstrong, who try to define knowledge in purely causal terms. Their theories represent a response to skepticism precisely because by advocating a causal theory of knowledge, they deny that all our knowledge is epistemically mediated-the skeptic's central claim.

the fact that I received this letter, that it has this postmark, and so on. But it is not clear that the evidence supports this inference. What if the card was not written by my friend at all, but by an enemy who wants to deceive me about my friend's whereabouts? What if my friend has been spirited off to another country, and his kidnappers forced him at gunpoint to write this letter? Both possibilities (and countless others) are perfectly compatible with the evidence available to me. Unless I can rule out these other possibilities, my evidence is entirely neutral as to whether my conclusion is true or false. So unless I can rule out these possibilities, I do not know that my friend is in France any more than I know that he is not in France—which is to say, I do not know it at all.

Ordinarily, we think we can rule out these possibilities. I may have good reason to think that my friend has not been kidnapped (he has no enemies, he is not an important or wealthy person, etc.) But the skeptic takes these concerns to their logical extremes. At this moment, I believe that I am sitting at a desk, typing on a computer. Here too, according to the skeptic, my belief is epistemically mediated. It is (supposedly) inferred from the evidence of my senses—the feelings, sounds, smells, and visual sensations I am having at this moment. But as with the France example, I need some way to rule out the possibility that I am inferring the wrong conclusion from this evidence. After all, the skeptic claims, it is perfectly consistent with these feelings, sounds, smells, and visual sensations that I am not sitting at a desk or typing a computer, but that I am merely dreaming or hallucinating these things. In a final, devastating blow, the skeptic insists that I can never rule out these possibilities: Since *everything* I know about the world around me is inferred from that same evidence, I can never rule out the possibility that I am dreaming or hallucinating. The skeptic concludes that I never know anything about the world around me—even something so simple and seemingly obvious as the fact that I am now sitting at a desk typing on a computer.

To see what the skeptic has in mind, imagine someone (call him "P" for prisoner) who has lived his entire life in a sealed room. He was born and raised there, all of his physical needs are met there, and he cannot leave. Nevertheless, I has many beliefs about the world outside his cell. He believes that the world is full of green grass, that there are other human beings, that there is a sky up above, and so on. Confined as he is, P cannot perceive (see, feel, hear, etc.) the truth of his beliefs. Thus, all of his beliefs about the outside world are epistemically mediated: P infers what he believes from the evidence provided by the television sets in his cell. Now, P's beliefs about the outside may true. But does he *know*—or even have any good reason to believe anything—about the outside world? Does he have, to use Chisholm's phrase, "adequate evidence" for them? P's only evidence is that the television sets play certain news reports. But it is perfectly consistent with this evidence that the news reports are inaccurate. So unless P can rule out the possibility that the news reports are inaccurate, his evidence is of no use whatsoever. And unfortunately for P, he has no way to rule out this possibility. Since P can neither leave his cell nor see outside it, he cannot check the news reports against the outside world. That means that his evidence is no good, since for all he knows the television reports convey a wholly inaccurate impression of the outside world. The skeptic claims that at every moment of our lives, each one of us finds himself or herself in a position much like P's: Our beliefs about the world around us are all epistemically mediated, and as a result we do not know anything at all about that world.

It is crucial to note that the skeptic is not pointing out simply that dreams and hallucinations are not a source of knowledge. His point is that the mere *possibility* of my dreaming or hallucinating prevents me from knowing anything—even if I am not actually dreaming or hallucinating. It should also be noted that the skeptic is not claiming merely that our beliefs about the world lack *certainty*. His view is much more extreme than that. If the skeptical argument is sound, then we never have *any evidence whatsoever* for our beliefs about the world outside our own minds.

Ever since Descartes presented this skeptical argument, refuting skepticism has been a central task (arguably *the* central task) of philosophy. Most of philosophy's great "isms"—theories about the nature of reality, truth, and meaning—can be seen as attempts to refute the skeptic. Some philosophers, for instance, have argued for some variety of idealism, the view that physical objects are collections of sensations or experiences. The advantage here is clear: If physical objects are collections of my sensations or experiences, then I do not need to draw an inference from what I know about my own mind to what I know about the external world.[9] Other philosophers

9. The locus classicus of idealism is George Berkeley's *Three Dialogues between Hylas and Philonous,* ed. Robert Adams (Indianapolis: Hackett, 1979). In the twentieth century, idealism found a powerful new expression in the phenomenalism of C. I. Lewis. Whereas Berkeley's idealism is a thesis

have attacked skepticism by advocating some type of pragmatism, according to which knowledge is just a belief that successfully serves the needs of the believer.[10] Still another approach, which has attracted many adherents since the 1970s, is reliabilism. According to reliabilism, to know is to hold a belief that has some sort of reliable link to the truth.[11]

These attempts to respond to skepticism differ with each other in many ways, but they all share one central feature: They deny that all our knowledge of the world around us is epistemically mediated, that is, that it is inferred rather than perceived. In their different ways, they all reject the skeptic's claim that our senses provide us only with *evidence* of the external world, rather than direct knowledge of the world itself. And that rejection is crucial. If he cannot demonstrate that all our knowledge of the external world is inferred from evidence, then the skeptic has no argument at all.

Epistemic mediation is, therefore, the epistemologist's primary target. Epistemologists study the need for certain types of inference, and correspondingly the adequacy of certain types of evidence. Their central task is to refute the skeptic's claim that all our knowledge of the external world is epistemically mediated, that is, inferred from evidence rather than directly perceived. I think it is not too much of an exaggeration to say that if there were not a lingering possibility that all of our knowledge is epistemically mediated, there would be no argument for skepticism—and hence no such discipline as epistemology.[12]

about the nature of physical objects, Lewis's phenomenalism is a thesis about the meanings of statements about the physical world. Thus, Lewis's phenomenalism ingeniously avoids many of the problems that confront classical idealism. (See chapters 7–8 of Lewis's *An Analysis of Knowledge and Valuation* [LaSalle, Ill.: Open Court, 1946].) Idealism and phenomenalism have been out of favor since W. V. Quine's devastating attack on Lewis in "Three Dogmas of Empiricism" (Quine, *From a Logical Point of View* (Cambridge: Harvard, 1953, pp. 20–46).

10. Prominent examples include Henry James, *Pragmatism* (New York: Longmanns, 1922), Quine "Two Dogmas of Empiricism," and Richard Rorty, *Philosophy and the Mirror of Nature* (Princeton: Princeton University Press, 1979).

11. See D. M. Armstrong, *Belief, Truth and Knowledge* (London: Cambridge University Press, 1973); Fred Dretske, "Conclusive Reasons," in G. Pappas and M. Swain, eds. *Essays on Knowledge and Justification* (Ithaca: Cornell University Press, 1978), pp. 41–60); and Alvin Goldman, "Telerobotic Knowledge: A Reliabilist Approach" (this volume).

12. Richard Rorty argues for the end of epistemology on precisely these grounds in *Philosophy and the Mirror of Nature* (Princeton: Princeton University Press, 1979).

II Telerobotic Perception and Epistemic Immediacy:
Telerobots as Telescopes

Skepticism is often treated as a "theoretical" or "philosophical" issue with no real consequences for everyday life. It was a central thesis of both Kant's transcendental idealism and Logical Postivism that skeptical theses and questions lacked empirical consequences. I think this view is deeply and importantly mistaken. In this section, I will argue for at least one empirical consequence: Skeptical issues have important implications for interface design and the use of telerobotic technology.

Sitting at my personal computer one evening, I visit the Telegarden website (http://telegarden.aec.at). On my video monitor are images of flowers, plants, and dirt. My head is turned toward the screen, my eyes are open, the light is good, and so on. What do I see? There are two plausible answers to this question: (1) I see mere video images; (2) I see a garden.

A great deal depends on which of these answers is true. The issue, once again, turns on epistemic mediation. If (1) is true, and I see mere video images, then my beliefs about the distant garden are epistemically mediated. As we have seen, epistemic mediation is what allows the skeptic to claim that we do not know anything about the external world. And I will try to show that the situation here is just as serious, albeit restricted to telerobotics: If telerobotically acquired beliefs epistemically mediated, then (at least in most cases), telerobotic web sites cannot provide us with knowledge. But if (2) is true, then much of what I know about the garden is epistemically *direct*. As a result, the skeptic has no way to challenge it. Let us consider each answer in turn.

Answer 1: I see mere video images.

If what I see are merely video images, then it seems that my knowledge of the garden in Austria is like P's knowledge of the world outside his cell: It is epistemically mediated. I hold beliefs about the garden not because I see the garden, but because I see something else (video images) that provides me with evidence from which I infer things about the garden.

We have already seen the skeptical difficulties generated by epistemically mediated knowledge. Epistemically mediated knowledge involves inference from evidence (facts about video images) to a conclusion about a distant garden. The same difficulties that arise for P in his cell and me with my friend in France arise here, as well. Unless I can rule out the possibility that the images on my monitor are not the result of error or forgery, my evidence does not support the conclusion that I draw from it. But it seems I cannot rule out that possibility. It seems that like P's beliefs about the world outside his cell, my beliefs about the Austrian garden have no support whatsoever.

The skeptical argument has severe consequences for telerobotics and the Internet, and their ability to provide us with knowledge of far-away people, places, and things. If the available evidence does not support my beliefs about the garden, then the Telegarden installation does not provide me with knowledge of a distant environment. More importantly, the same argument can be made for *every* web site and telerobotic installation. As long as I cannot rule out the possibility of error or deception, my evidence will never support the conclusions that I draw from it. Telerobotic installations on the Internet—indeed, the entire Internet itself—will never serve as a source of knowledge.

Let us see, therefore, how the skeptical argument might be refuted. The argument can be broken down into the following four premises and conclusion:

(1) When I visit the Telegarden web site, I do not see a garden.

(2) Whatever I know about the garden is inferred from what I know about what I do see (video images).

(3) In order for me to know anything about the garden, I must know that the images I see are not prescanned.

(4) I do not know that the images are not deceptive (e.g., prescanned images of scenes that no longer exist).

Therefore:

(5) I do not know anything about the garden.

One could challenge this argument in a number of places. The most natural attack is on premise (4), the claim that I do not know the images on my monitor are not deceptive. In at least some cases, I might indeed have such knowledge. Perhaps I set up the Telegarden site myself, or am good friends with the person who did. Perhaps I read about the site in a respected magazine or newspaper. Perhaps the site is maintained by a well-known and respected organization. Under these types of circumstances (4) would be false, since I would be able to rule out the possibility of deceptive, pre-scanned images.

Rarely, however, do I have this type of collateral information that allows me to rule out the possibility of deception. I almost never know who maintains the web sites I visit. Setting up a telerobotic web site is relatively cheap and easy, and setting up a forgery is even easier. The Internet is full of home-grown "web-cam" sites that promise users a live glimpse into someone's laboratory, office, and even bedroom.[13] The lack of information available on the developers of these sites makes it difficult or impossible to know that the sites are not deceptive forgeries.

This marks an important difference between the Internet and more traditional forms of mass-communication. In television and radio, for example, we almost always know who is providing the content. High barriers to entry and high operating costs restrict content provision to a few large, well-known companies and organizations. The authority and reputation of these content-providers, coupled with strict government regulation, makes it easy to rule out the possibility of wholesale deception. On the Internet, however, this solution is not readily available. The very thing that makes the Internet so appealing—cheap, unregulated access to the means of content-provision—makes it extremely difficult to rule out the possibility of deception.

Is there anything I can do to rule out the possibility of deception in these problematic cases—cases in which I lack collateral information needed to confirm or disconfirm the authenticity of the images? I can always look for inconsistent perspectives, shadows, placement of objects, etc. from one frame to the next. This will be particularly effective for interactive tele-robotic sites, that is, sites that allow for *agency* in addition to mere passive observation. If I can move the camera to pan the landscape, or can manipulate a robotic arm so as to move objects, this will greatly enhance my ability to verify that what I see is live.

The *range of agency* in the remote environment is also relevant. Contrast the *Light on the Net* project,[14] where the only alterations that take place are

13. The most famous (or infamous) of these is "Jennicam" at http://www.jennicam.org.

14. http://www.flab.mag.keio.ac.jp/light/

in a fixed grid of light bulbs, to a "street-cam" aimed at cars, pedestrians, storefronts, etc.[15] A forgery of *Light on the Net* would be much easier to pull off convincingly, since the distant environment can only be in a finite (if large) number of states.

In most cases, however, we simply will not be able to rule out the possibility of deceptive, prescanned images. The possibility of clever deception by an anonymous source will always loom in the background. If Answer 1 is correct, then Internet telerobotics supports a kind of "telescepticism."

Answer 2: I see a garden.

If, however, (2) is true, the skeptic is immediately rebuffed. The skeptic's argument turns on the claim that all our knowledge is inferred, or epistemically mediated. But knowledge that is acquired through perception is not inferred; It is simply perceived. This view receives its clearest expression in a famous quote from George Berkeley's *Three Dialogues Between Hylas and Philonous* (1713): "[T]he senses perceive nothing which they do not perceive immediately: for they make no inferences.[16]" The point here is simple and, I think, uncontroversial. If I perceive something to be the case, then I do not infer that it is the case. If I *see* that a marigold is growing in the garden, then I do not *infer* that a marigold is growing in the garden. Inference picks up only where perception leaves off. If, therefore, (2) is true and I see the garden, then much of my knowledge is epistemically direct, that is, uninferred. And the skeptic has no way to challenge uninferred knowledge. Premise (1) of his argument is false. With that, his entire argument is refuted.

What I am suggesting, therefore, is this: If telerobotic technology on the Internet is to provide us with knowledge, that is, to allow us to know anything about remote environments, it must provide us with knowledge that is epistemically direct. It must serve not as a source of evidence about distant environments, but as a way for us to *perceive*—in most cases to see— those environments first-hand. That, it seems to me, is the only effective way for telerobotic technology to avoid the skeptic's trap. Telerobotics must

15.   A particularly nice example is the VA Robocam in Adelaide, Australia, which can be accessed at http://robocam.va.com.au/.

16.   George Berkeley, *Three Dialogues Between Hylas and Philonous,* p. 11.

become a tool for enhancing our powers of *perception*. I believe that it can become such a tool, and in section 3 I will explain how telerobotic sites must be designed in order to afford us immediate knowledge of remote environments.

At first glance, my position may seem bizarre. It may seem obvious that our knowledge of a garden thousands of miles away is mediated. But here we must be careful, once again, to distinguish epistemic mediation from *causal* mediation. I certainly agree that telerobotic knowledge is *causally* mediated. There is an extraordinarily long and complex causal chain that begins with a garden in Austria and ends with my believing that a marigold is growing in that garden. It goes through a video camera, a server, a modem, thousands of miles of switches, cables, and router lines, back to another modem, through a central processing unit, and ultimately into a video monitor, and light focused on my retinas. But the causal mediation of my beliefs does not imply their *epistemic* mediation. And it is epistemic mediation that threatens knowledge. Donald Davidson, whose recent work in epistemology has been enormously important, puts this more clearly than anyone:

Since we can't swear intermediaries to truthfulness, we should allow no intermediaries between our beliefs and their objects in the world. Of course there are causal intermediaries. What we must guard against are epistemic intermediaries.[17]

If telerobotic knowledge is understood this way, then telerobotic devices work analogously to eyeglasses, telescopes, and microscopes. A telerobotic device is a tool that allows us to see things that we cannot see without it. When I look through my glasses, or peer into a microscope or telescope, the lenses causally mediate my knowledge. They mediate my knowledge causally, standing causally between my knowing and what I know about. But there is no epistemic mediation. When I look through the lenses, I do not see the lenses themselves and then draw inferences about the objects impinging on those lenses. Rather, I see things in the world itself: I see that the eye chart has an "E" in the upper left-hand corner, that the petri dish contains bacteria, or that the moon's surface is uneven. These are not theoret-

17. Donald Davidson, "A Coherence Theory of Truth and Knowledge" in Ernie Lepore, ed., *Truth and Interpretation: Perspectives on the Philosophy of Donald Davidson* (Oxford: Blackwell, 1986), p. 313.

ical claims that I infer from what I can see on the lenses. They are perceptual claims that I can see, through the lenses, to be the case.

The analogy between telerobotic devices and microscopes and telescopes is even more striking if we consider today's highly sophisticated telescopes and microscopes. Electron microscopes use video monitors for display. Using a telescope is no longer a matter of peering through lenses. The technology has become far more complex, often involving satellite feeds and video monitors. Like their simpler predecessors, however, these instruments can still be understood as devices that enhance our vision. If Answer 2 is correct and what I see is a garden, then telerobotic devices on the Internet function analogously, providing us with knowledge that is causally, but not epistemically, mediated.

This does not mean that telerobotic installations cannot deceive us. Of course they can—just as a telescope can distort the object viewed. But if Answer 2 is correct, then the mere *possibility* of deception does not render telerobotic installations incapable of providing us with knowledge. As long as the images on my monitor are not *actually* deceptive, the mere possibility that they are deceptive does not prevent me from knowing about the distant garden.

III Enabling Immediacy: The Transparent Interface

In the first two sections, I argued that it is crucial for telerobotic beliefs (i.e., beliefs caused by telerobotic devices) to be epistemically direct. If these beliefs are epistemically mediated, then most telerobotic sites will fall to the skeptic's argument, and telerobotic sites will give us no reason whatsoever to believe anything about remote environments. So our goal should be to design telerobotic web sites in such a way that they cause users to form beliefs that are epistemically direct. Users must view the computer screen not as a source of evidence from which to infer conclusions about objects that are hidden from view, but rather as a window or scope through which to perceive those objects directly.[18]

---

18.   This characterization in terms of inference is, I believe, the first precise description of what interface designers are trying to get at with talk of "direct engagement" and "direct manipulation." These powerfully suggestive phrases have received much praise, but little clarification, since their introduction in the mid–1980s. See Ben Shneiderman, *Designing the User Interface: Strategies for Effective Human-Computer Interaction* (Reading, Mass.: Addison-Wesley, 1987); Donald Norman, "Cogni-

How can this be accomplished? Suppose we introduce a new user to a telerobotic web site. The user is invited to enter inputs in the form of keystrokes and mouse-clicks, and various images of a distant garden appear on the screen. What will determine whether the user's beliefs about the distant garden are epistemically or not? In other words, what will determine whether she treats her interaction with the computer as evidence from which to infer conclusions about the garden, or as direct interaction with the garden itself?

The answer will depend largely on how easy, how natural her interaction with the garden is. This is because we resort to inference when our natural, noninferential capacities are not up to the task. This point is made clearly and eloquently by Hubert and Stuart Dreyfus, in their discussion of the differences between a beginner and an expert. A beginner, they note, is always following rules:

The beginning automobile driver learning to operate a stick-shift car is told at what speed . . . to shift gears and, at any given speed, at what distance . . . to follow a car preceding him. . . . Similarly, the beginning chess player is given a formula for assigning point values to pieces . . . and the rule "always exchange your pieces for the opponent's if the total value of pieces captured exceeds that of pieces lost." . . . The novice nurse is taught how to read blood pressure, measure bodily outputs, and compute fluid retention, and is given rules for determining what to do when those measurements reach certain values.[19]

An expert, by contrast, does not follow rules, but simply acts automatically, instinctively, and without reflection.

Chess grandmasters, engrossed in a game, can lose entirely the awareness that they are manipulating pieces on a board and see themselves rather as involved participants in a world of opportunities, threats, strengths, weaknesses, hopes, and fears.

tive Artifacts," in John M. Carroll, ed., *Designing Interaction: Psychology at the Human-Computer Interface;* Brenda Laurel, *Computers as Theatre* (Reading, Mass.: Addison-Wesley, 1993). As far as I know, the term "transparency" was first used by Sussane Bødker in *Through the Interface: A Human Activity Approach to User Interface Design* (Hillsdale, N.J.: Lawrence Erlbaum, 1990).

19. Hubert Dreyfus and Stuart Dreyfus, *Mind over Machine* (New York: Free Press, 1986).

When playing rapidly, the sidestep dangers in the same automatic way that a teen-ager, himself an expert, might avoid missiles in a familiar video game, or as we avoid familiar obstacles when we dash to the phone.[20]

Dreyfus and Dreyfus make these observations in the service of a very different purpose (debunking the claims of the Artificial Intelligence indus-try), but they are also relevant here. When users infer their beliefs about the distant environment (rather than simply perceive it), they are acting like (and may, in fact be) beginners: By following rules (the rules of inference) they try to arrive at the desired result—knowledge of the distant environ-ment. What the skeptical argument shows is that, at least in many cases, the rules do not work. Except in a few cases where we possess collateral information, the rules do not license an inference from premises about mouse-clicks, keystrokes, and video images to conclusions about a distant environment.

If telerobotic web sites are to provide knowledge of distant environ-ments, then the user must be more like the expert in Dreyfus and Dreyfus's description. If a user interacts naturally and effortlessly with the telerobotic web site—"copes skillfully," in Dreyfus and Dreyfus's terminology—then her beliefs about the distant environment will be epistemically direct. She does not infer her beliefs about the distant environment any more than the chess grandmaster infers that he ought to trade pawns with his opponent. She does not think of her activities in terms of mouse-clicks or video images. Rather, she thinks of herself as watering her marigolds, checking her daisy for signs of disease, or tending to a neglected patch of soil. And so her beliefs about the garden are epistemically direct. From an epistemological standpoint, therefore, telerobotic sites should be designed in a way that allows users to be experts, to cope skillfully rather than draw inferences. By taking advantage of the skills and tendencies that users already have, inter-faces not only make it easier to use a computer, but also make it possible to acquire telerobotic knowledge about far-away places.

This explains the appeal of many desirable features in telerobotic web sites. Immediate feedback greatly aids our attempts to interact with distant objects—even if bandwidth restrictions prevent real-time feedback from

20. Ibid.

the robot itself. (Just imagine how difficult it would be to drive a car or walk down the street if you received feedback from your hands, feet, eyes, and ears only once every two seconds.) Intuitive control mechanisms are also extremely helpful. Imagine a mouse-controlled robot that moves in the opposite direction as the mouse: When the user moves the desktop mouse to the right, the robot rolls to the left, and so on. Here again, direct perception becomes difficult or impossible, since users would constantly be "translating" (i.e., inferring) from the mouse's movements to those of the robot, rather than directly manipulating the robot.

This conception of user interfaces has another consequence that may, initially, be counterintuitive: More information can yield less knowledge. Excessive feedback and complex controlling mechanisms can confuse users, block their ability to cope skillfully, and thereby reintroduce the problematic inference. Consider the extremely complex controls on the latest wave of "first-person" video games (Marathon, Doom, Quake, Dark Forces). If our manipulation of robots could reach that same level of control, we would have extraordinary control of and information about the distant environment. At the same time, all but the most experienced gamers would find it impossible to maneuver the robot in anything approaching a natural manner. Despite the wealth of information, our confusion would once again force us to inference, and hence to skepticism. (This is not to say that telerobotic devices must always remain simple or restricted. Epistemic immediacy is a function not only of a system's complexity, but also of the user's abilities. As Internet users become more skilled—more familiar with telerobotic control and feedback—telerobotic web sites can keep pace. This will almost surely happen as both the Internet and telerobotics become a larger part of our lives.)

We should not, therefore, assume that complex, multisensory interaction is necessary, or even desirable, for successful telerobotics. Unlike some telepresence enthusiasts, I do not think telerobotics' potential lies in an ability to make tele-engagement "just like the real thing." Telerobotic interaction differs in many ways from ordinary, proximal interaction, just as seeing the moon's craters through a telescope differs from seeing them beneath your own feet. Telegardening on the Internet does not attempt to be "immersive." It does not involve the dirty clothes or sore back that comes with traditional gardening. Nor does it afford the same level of detail, range of planting options, or palate of sensory stimuli. But what makes Internet telegardening interesting, and what makes it a cousin of traditional gardening, is that it affords a direct link with a real garden—not, of course a *causally* direct link, but an *epistemically* direct link. And it is this epistemic directness that matters. When telerobotic engagement is epistemically direct, it gives us uninferred knowledge of a garden thousands of miles away, and with it a desire to tend that garden and see it grow.

Part IV

Postscript

The Film and the New Psychology

Maurice Merleau-Ponty

Classical psychology considers our visual field to be a sum or mosaic of sensations, each of which is strictly dependent on the local retinal stimulus that corresponds to it. The new psychology reveals, first of all, that such a parallelism between sensations and the nervous phenomenon conditioning them is unacceptable, even for our simplest and most immediate sensations. Our retina is far from homogeneous: certain parts, for example, are blind to blue or red, yet I do not see any discolored areas when looking at a blue or red surface. This is because, starting at the level of simply seeing colors, my perception is not limited to registering what the retinal stimuli prescribe but re-organizes these stimuli so as to re-establish the field's homogeneity. Broadly speaking, we should think of it not as a mosaic but as a system of configurations. Groups rather than juxtaposed elements are principal and primary in our perception. We group the stars into the same constellations as the ancients, yet it is *a priori* possible to draw the heavenly map many other ways. Given the series:

ab cd ef gh ij

. . . .

we will always pair the dots according to the formula a–b, c–d, e–f, etc., although the grouping b–c, d–e, f–g, etc. is equally probable in principle. A sick person contemplating the wallpaper in his room will suddenly see it transformed if the pattern and figure become the ground while what is usually seen as ground becomes the figure. The idea we have of the world would be overturned if we could succeed in seeing the intervals between things (for example, the space between the trees on the boulevard) as *objects* and, inversely, if we saw the things themselves—the trees—as the ground. This is what happens in puzzles: we cannot see the rabbit or the hunter because the elements of these figures are dislocated and are integrated into other forms: for example, what is to be the rabbit's ear is still just the empty interval between two trees in the forest. The rabbit and the hunter become apparent through a new partition of the field, a new organization of the whole. Cam-

M. Merleau-Ponty, "The Film and the New Psychology," (1945). Reprinted from *Sense and Non-Sense,* trans. H. Dreyfus and P. Dreyfus (Evanston., Ill.: Northwestern University Press, 1964).

ouflage is the art of masking a form by blending its principal defining lines into other, more commanding forms.

The same type of analysis can be applied to hearing: it will simply be a matter of temporal forms rather than spatial ones. A melody, for example, is a figure of sound and does not mingle with the background noises (such as the siren one hears in the distance during a concert) that may accompany it. The melody is not a sum of notes, since each note only counts by virtues of the function it serves in the whole, which is why the melody does not perceptibly change when transposed, that is, when all its notes are changed while their interrelationships and the structure of the whole remain the same. On the other hand, just one single change in the interrelationships will be enough to modify the entire make-up of the melody. Such a perception of the whole is more natural and more primary than the perception of isolated elements: it has been seen from conditioned-reflex experiments, where, through the frequent association of a piece of meat with a light or a sound, dogs are trained to respond to that light or sound by salivating, that the training acquired in response to a certain series of notes is simultaneously acquired for any melody with the same structure. Therefore analytical perception, through which we arrive at absolute value of the separate elements, is a belated and rare attitude—that of the scientist who observes or of the philosopher who reflects. The perception of forms, understood broadly as structure, grouping, or configuration should be considered our spontaneous way of seeing.

There is still another point on which modern psychology overthrows the prejudices of classical physiology and psychology. It is a commonplace to say that we have five senses, and it would seem, at first glance, that each of them is like a world out of touch with the others. The light or colors that act upon the eye do not affect the ears or the sense of touch. Nevertheless it has been known for a long time that certain blind people manage to represent the colors they cannot see by means of the sounds that they hear: for example, a blind man said that red ought to be something like a trumpet peal. For a long time it was thought that such phenomena were exceptional, whereas they are, in fact, general. For people under mescaline, sounds are regularly accompanied by spots of color whose hue, form, and vividness vary with the tonal quality, intensity, and pitch of the sounds. Even normal subjects speak of hot, cold, shrill, or hard colors, of sounds that are clear, sharp, brilliant, rough, or mellow, of soft noises and of penetrating fragrances. Cézanne said that one could see the velvetiness, the hardness, the softness, and even the odor of objects. My perception is therefore not a sum of visual, tactile, and audible givens: I perceive in a total way with my whole being; I grasp a unique structure of the thing, a unique way of being, which speaks to all my senses at once.

Naturally, classical psychology was well aware that relationships exist between the different parts of my visual field just as between the data of my different senses—but it held this unity to be a construction and referred it to intelligence and memory. In a famous passage from the *Meditations* Descartes wrote: I say that I see men going by in the street, but what exactly do I really see? All I see are hats and coats that might equally well be covering dolls that only move by springs, and if I say that I see men, it is because I apprehend "through an inspection of the mind what I thought I beheld with my eyes." I am convinced that objects continue to exist when I no longer see them (behind my back, for example). But it is obvious that, for classical thought, these invisible objects subsist for me only because my judgment keeps them present. Even the objects right in front of me are not truly seen but merely thought. Thus I cannot *see* a cube, that is, a solid with six surfaces and twelve edges; all I ever see is a perspective figure of which the lateral surfaces are distorted and the back surface completely hidden. If I am able to speak of cubes, it is because my mind sets these appearances to rights and restores the hidden surface. I cannot see a cube as its geometrical definition presents it: I can only think it. The perception of movement shows even more clearly the extent to which intelligence intervenes in what claims to be vision. When my train starts, after it has been standing in the station, I often "see" the train next to mine begin to move. Sensory data are therefore neutral in themselves and can be differently interpreted according to the hypothesis on which my mind comes to rest. Broadly speaking, classical psychology made perception a real deciphering of sense data by the intelligence, a beginning of science, as it were. I am given certain signs from which I must dig out the meaning; I am presented with a text that I must read or interpret. Even when it takes the unity of the perceptual field into account, classical psychology remains loyal to the notion of sensation, which was the starting point of the analysis. Its original conception of visual data as a mosaic of sensations forces it to base the unity of the perceptual field on an operation of the intelligence. What does *gestalt* theory tell us on this point? By resolutely rejecting the notion of sensation it teaches us to stop distinguishing between signs and their significance, between what is sensed and what is judged. How could we define the exact color of an object without mentioning the substance of which it is made, without saying, of this blue rug, for example, that it is a "woolly blue"? Cézanne asked how one is to distinguish the color of things from their shape. It is impossible to understand perception as the imputation of a certain significance to certain sensible signs, since the most immediate sensible texture of these signs cannot be described without referring to the object they signify.

Our ability to recognize an object defined by certain constant properties despite changes of lighting stems, not from some process by which our intellect takes the nature of the incident light into account and deduces the object's real color from it, but from the fact that the light which dominates the environment acts as *lighting* and immediately assigns the object its true color. If we look at two plates under unequal lighting, they will appear equally white and unequally lighted as long as the beam of light from the window figures in our visual field. On the other hand, if we observe the same plates through a hole in a screen. one will immediately appear gray and the other white; and even if we *know* that it is nothing but an effect of the lighting, no intellectual analysis of the way they appear will make us see the true color of the two plates. When we turn on the lights at dusk, the electric light seems yellow at first but a moment later tends to lose all definite color; correlatively, the objects, whose color was at first perceptibly modified, resume an appearance comparable to the one they have during the day. Objects and lighting form a system which tends toward a certain constancy and a certain level of stability—not through the operation of intelligence but through the very configuration of the field. I do not think the world in the act of perception: it organizes itself in front of me. When I perceive a cube, it is not because my reason sets the perspectival appearances straight and thinks the geometrical definition of a cube with respect to them. I do not even notice the distortions of perspective, much less correct them; I am at the cube itself in its manifestness through what I see. The objects behind my back are likewise not represented to me by some operation of memory or judgment; they are present, they *count* for me, just as the ground which I do not see continues nonetheless to be present beneath the figure which partially hides it. Even the perception of movement, which at first seems to depend directly on the point of reference chosen by the intellect is in turn only one element in the global organization of the field. For, although it is true that, when either my train or the one next to it starts, first one, then the other may appear to be moving, one should note that the illusion is not arbitrary and that I cannot willfully induce it by the completely intellectual choice of a point of reference. If I am playing cards in my compartment, the other train will start moving; if, on the other hand, I am looking for someone in the adjacent train, then mine will begin to roll. In each instance the one which seems stationary is the one we have chosen as our abode and which, for the time being, is our environment. Movement and rest distribute themselves in our surroundings not according to the hypotheses which our intelligence is pleased to construct but according to the way we settle ourselves in the world and the position our bodies assume in it. Sometimes I see the steeple motionless against the sky with clouds floating above it, and sometimes the clouds appear still and the steeple falls through space. But here again the choice of the fixed point is not made by the intelligence: the looked-at object in which I anchor myself will always seem fixed, and I cannot take this meaning away from it except by looking elsewhere. Nor do I give it this meaning through thought. Perception is not a sort of beginning science, an elementary exercise of the intelligence; we must rediscover a commerce with the world and a presence to the world which is older than intelligence.

Finally, the new psychology also brings a new concept of the perception of others. Classical psychology unquestioningly accepted the distinction between inner observation, or introspection, and outer observation. "Psychic facts"—anger or fear, for example—could be directly known only from the inside and by the person experiencing them. It was thought to be self-evident that I can grasp only the corporal *signs* of anger or fear from the outside and that I have to resort to the anger or fear I know in myself through introspection in order to interpret these signs. Today's psychologists have made us notice that in reality introspection gives me almost nothing. If I try to study love or hate purely from inner observation, I will find very little to describe: a few pangs, a few heart-throbs—in short, trite agitations which do not reveal the essence of love or hate. Each time I find something worth saying, it is because I have not been satisfied to coincide with my feeling, because I have succeeded in studying it as a way of behaving, as a modification of my relations with others and with the world, because I have managed to think about it as I would think about the behavior of another person whom I happened to witness. In fact, young children understand gestures and facial expressions long before they can reproduce them on their own; the meaning must, so to speak, adhere to the behavior. We must reject that prejudice which makes "inner realities" out of love, hate, or anger, leaving them accessible to one single witness: the person who feels them. Anger, shame, hate, and love are not psychic facts hidden at the bottom of another's consciousness: they are types of behavior or styles of conduct which are visible from the outside. They exist *on* this face or *in* those gestures, not hidden behind them. Psychology did not begin to develop until the day it gave up the distinction between mind and body, when it abandoned the two correlative methods of interior observation and physiological psychology. We learned nothing about emotion as long as we limited ourselves to measuring the rate of respiration or heartbeat in an angry person, and we didn't learn anything more when we tried to express the qualitative and inexpressible nuances of lived anger. To create a psychology of anger is to try to ascertain the *meaning* of anger, to ask oneself how it functions in human life and what purpose it serves. So we find that emotion is, as Janet said, a disorganizing reaction which comes into play whenever we are stuck. On a deeper level, as Sartre has shown, we find that anger is a magical way of acting by which we afford ourselves a completely symbolic satisfaction in the imagination after renouncing effective action in the world, just as, in a conversation, a person who cannot convince his partner will start hurling insults at him which prove nothing or as a man who does not dare strike his opponent will shake his fist at him from a distance. Since emotion is not a psychic, internal fact but rather a variation in our relations with others and the world which is expressed in our bodily attitude, we cannot say that only the signs of love or anger are given to the outside observer and that we understand others indirectly by interpreting these signs: we have to say that others are directly manifest to us as behavior. Our behavioral science goes much farther than we think. When unbiased subjects are confronted with photographs of several faces, copies of several kinds of handwriting, and recordings of several voices and are asked to put together a face, a silhouette, a voice, and a handwriting, it has been shown that the elements are usually put together correctly or that, in any event, the correct matchings greatly outnumber the incorrect ones. Michelangelo's handwriting is attributed to Raphael in 36 cases, but in 221 instances it is correctly identified, which means that we recognize a certain common structure in each person's voice, face, gestures and bearing and that each person is nothing more nor less to us than this structure or way of being in the world. One can see how these remarks might be applied to the psychology of language: just as a man's body and "soul" are but two aspects of his way of being in the world, so the word and the thought it indicates should not be considered two externally related terms: the word bears its meaning in the same way that the body incarnates a manner of behavior.

The new psychology has, generally speaking, revealed man to us not as an understanding which constructs the world but as a being thrown into the world and attached to it by a natural bond. As a result it re-educates us in how to see this world which we touch at every point of our being, whereas classical psychology abandoned the lived world for the one which scientific intelligence succeeded in constructing.

If we now consider the film as a perceptual object, we can apply what we have just said about perception in general to the perception of a film. We will see that this point of view illuminates the nature and significance of the movies and that the new psychology leads us straight to the best observations of the aestheticians of the cinema.

Let us say right off that a film is not a sum total of images but a temporal *gestalt.* This is the moment to recall Pudovkin's famous experiment which clearly shows the melodic unity of films. One day Pudovkin took a close-up of Mosjoukin with a completely impassive expression and projected it after showing: first, a bowl of soup, then, a young woman lying dead in her coffin, and, last, a child playing with a teddy-bear. The first thing noticed was that Mosjoukin seemed to be looking at the bowl, the young woman, and the child, and next one noted that he was looking pensively at the dish, that he wore an expression of sorrow when looking at the woman, and that he had a glowing smile for the child. The audience was amazed at his variety of expression although the same shot had actually been used all three times and was, if anything, remarkably inexpressive. The meaning of a shot therefore depends on what precedes it in the movie, and this succession of scenes creates a new reality which is not merely the sum of its parts. In an excellent article in *Esprit,* R. Leenhardt added that one still has to bring in the time-factor for each shot: a short duration is suitable for an amused smile, one of intermediate length for an indifferent face, and an extended one for a sorrow-ful expression.[1] Leenhardt drew from this the following definition of cine-matographic rhythm: "A certain order of shots and a certain duration for each of these shots or views, so that taken together they produce the desired impression with maximum effectiveness." There really is, then, a cinemato-graphic system of measurements with very precise and very imperious re-quirements. "When you see a movie, try to guess the moment when a shot has given its all and must move on, end, be replaced either by changing the angle, the distance, or the field. You will get to know that constriction of the chest produced by an overlong shot which brakes the movement and that deliciously intimate acquiescence when a shot fades at the right mo-ment." Since a film consists not only of montage (the selection of shots or views, their order and length) but also of cutting (the selection of scenes or sequences, and their order and length), it seems to be an extremely complex form inside of which a very great number of actions and reactions are taking place at every moment. The laws of this form, moreover, are yet to be discov-ered, having until now only been sensed by the flair or tact of the director, who handles cinematographic language as a man manipulates syntax: with-out explicitly thinking about it and without always being in a position to formulate the rules which he spontaneously obeys.

What we have just said about visual films also applies to sound movies, which are not a sum total of words or noises but are likewise a *gestalt*. A rhythm exists for sounds just as for images. There is a montage of noises and sounds, as Leenhardt's example of the old sound movie *Broadway Melody* shows. "Two actors are on stage. We are in the balcony listening to them speak their parts. Then immediately there is a close-up, whispering, and we are aware of something they are saying to each other under their breath. . . ." The expressive force of this montage lies in its ability to make us sense the coexistence, the simultaneity of lives in the same world, the actors as they are for us and for themselves, just as, previously, we saw Pudovkin's visual montage linking the man and his gaze to the sights which surround him. Just as a film is not merely a play photographed in motion and the choice and grouping of the shots constitutes an original means of expression for the motion picture, so, equally, the soundtrack is not a simple phonographic reproduction of noises and words but requires a certain internal organization

1. *Esprit,* 1936.

which the film's creator must invent. The real ancestor of the movie sound-track is not the phonograph but the radio play.

Nor is that all. We have been considering sight and sound by turns, but in reality the way they are put together makes another new whole, which cannot be reduced to its component parts. A sound movie is not a silent film embellished with words and sounds whose only function is to complete the cinematographic illusion. The bond between sound and image is much closer, and the image is transformed by the proximity of sound. This is readily apparent in the case of dubbed films, where thin people are made to speak with the voices of fat people, the young have the voices of the old, and tall people the voices of tiny ones—all of which is absurd if what we have said is true—namely, that voice, profile, and character form an indivisible unit. And the union of sound and image occurs not only in each character but in the film as a whole. It is not by accident that characters are silent at one moment and speak at another. The alteration of words and silence is manipulated to create the most effective image. There are three sorts of dialogue, as Malraux said in *Verve* (1940). First may be noted expository dialogue, whose purpose is to make the circumstances of the dramatic action known. The novel and the film both avoid this sort of dialogue. Then there is *tonal* dialogue, which gives us each character's particular accent and which dominates, for example, in Proust where the characters are very hard to visualize but are admirably recognizable as soon as they start to talk. The extravagant or sparing use of words, their richness or emptiness, their precision or affectation reveal the essence of a character more surely than many descriptions. Tonal dialogue rarely occurs in movies, since the visible presence of the actor with his own particular manner of behaving rarely lends itself to it. Finally we have dramatic dialogue which presents the discussion and confrontation of the characters and which is the movies' principal form of dialogue. But it is far from continuous. One speaks ceaselessly in the theater but not in the film. "Directors of recent movies," said Malraux, "*break into* dialogue after long stretches of silence, just as a novelist breaks into dialogue after long narrative passages." Thus the distribution of silences and dialogue constitutes a metrics above and beyond the metrics of vision and sound, and the pattern of words and silence, more complex than the other two, superimposes its requirements upon them. To complete the analysis one would still have to study the role of music in this ensemble: let us only say that music should be incorporated into it, not juxtaposed to it. Music should not be used as a stopgap for sonic holes or as a completely exterior commentary on the sentiments or the scenes as so often happens in movies: the storm of wrath unleashes the storm of brass, or the music laboriously imitates a footstep or the sound of a coin falling to the ground. It should intervene to mark a change in a film's style: for example, the passage from an action scene to the "inside" of the character, to the recollection of earlier scenes, or to the description of a landscape. Generally speaking, it should accompany and help bring about a "rupture in the sensory balance," as Jaubert said.[2] Lastly, it must not be another means of expression juxtaposed to the visual expression. "By the use of strictly musical means (rhythm, form, instrumentation) and by a mysterious alchemy of correspondences which ought to be the very foundation of the film composer's profession, it should recreate a sonorous substance beneath the plastic substance of the image, should, finally, make the internal rhythm of the scene physically palpable without thereby striving to translate its sentimental, dramatic, or poetic content" (Jaubert). It is not the job of words in a movie to add ideas to the images, nor is it the job of music to add sentiments. The ensemble tells us something very precise which is neither a thought nor a reminder of sentiments we have felt in our own lives.

What, then, does the film *signify:* what does it mean? Each film tells a *story:* that is, it relates a certain number of events which involve certain characters and which could, it seems, also be told in prose, as, in effect, they are in the scenario on which the film is based. The talking film, frequently overwhelmed by dialogue, completes this illusion. Therefore motion pictures are often conceived as the visual and sonic representation, the closest possible reproduction of a drama which literature could evoke only in words and which the movie is lucky enough to be able to photograph. What supports this ambiguity is the fact that movies do have a basic realism: the actors should be natural, the set should be as realistic as possible; for "the power of reality released on the screen is such that the least stylization will cause it to go flat" (Leenhardt). That does not mean, however, that the movies are fated to let us see and hear what we would see and hear if we were present at the events being related; nor should films suggest some general view of life in the manner of an edifying tale. Aesthetics has already encountered this problem in connection with the novel or with poetry. A novel

2. Ibid.

always has an idea that can be summed up in a few words, a scenario which a few lines can express. A poem always refers to things or ideas. And yet the function of the pure novel or pure poetry is not simply to tell us these facts. If it were, the poem could be exactly transposed into prose and the novel would lose nothing in summary. Ideas and facts are just the raw materials of art: the art of the novel lies in the choice of what one says and what one does not say, in the choice of perspectives (this chapter will be written from the point of view of this character, that chapter from another's point of view), in the varying tempo of the narrative; the essence of the art of poetry is not the didactic description of things or the exposition of ideas but the creation of a machine of language which almost without fail puts the reader in a certain poetic state. Movies, likewise, always have a story and often an idea (for example, in *l'Etrange sursis* the idea that death is terrible only for the man who has not consented to it), but the function of the film is not to make these facts or ideas known to us. Kant's remark that, in knowledge imagination serves the understanding, whereas in art the understanding serves the imagination, is a profound one. In other words, ideas or prosaic facts are only there to give the creator an opportunity to seek out their palpable symbols and to trace their visible and sonorous monogram. The meaning of a film is incorporated into its rhythm just as the meaning of a gesture may immediately be read in that gesture: the film does not mean anything but itself. The idea is presented in a nascent state and emerges from the temporal structure of the film as it does from the coexistence of the parts of a painting. The joy of art lies in its showing how something takes on meaning—not by referring to already established and acquired ideas but by the temporal or spatial arrangement of elements. As we saw above, a movie has meaning in the same way that a thing does: neither of them speaks to an isolated understanding; rather, both appeal to our power tacitly to decipher the world or men and to coexist with them. It is true that in our ordinary lives we lose sight of this aesthetic value of the tiniest perceived thing. It is also true that the perceived form is never perfect in real life, that it always has blurs, smudges, and superfluous matter, as it were. Cinematographic drama is, so to speak, finer-grained than real-life dramas: it takes place in a world that is more exact than the real world. But in the last analysis perception permits us to understand the meaning of the cinema. A movie is not thought; it is perceived.

This is why the movies can be so gripping in their presentation of man: they do not give us his *thoughts,* as novels have done for so long, but his conduct or behavior. They directly present to us that special way of being in the world, of dealing with things and other people, which we can see in the sign language of gesture and gaze and which clearly defines each person we know. If a movie wants to show us someone who is dizzy, it should not attempt to portray the interior landscape of dizziness, as Daquin in *Premier de cordée* and Malraux in *Sierra de Terruel* wished to do. We will get a much better sense of dizziness if we see it from the outside, if we contemplate that unbalanced body contorted on a rock or that unsteady step trying to adapt itself to who knows what upheaval of space. For the movies as for modern psychology dizziness, pleasure, grief, love, and hate are ways of behaving.

This psychology shares with contemporary philosophies the common feature of presenting consciousness thrown into the world, subject to the gaze of others and learning from them what it is: it does not, in the manner of the classical philosophies, present mind *and* world, each particular consciousness *and* the others. Phenomenological or existential philosophy is largely an expression of surprise at this inherence of the self in the world and in others, a description of this paradox and permeation, and an attempt to make us *see* the bond between subject and world, between subject and others, rather than to *explain* it as the classical philosophies did by resorting to absolute spirit. Well, the movies are peculiarly suited to make manifest the union of mind and body, mind and world, and the expression of one in the other. That is why it is not surprising that a critic should evoke philosophy in connection with a film. Astruc in his review of *Défunt récalcitrant* uses Sartrian terms to recount the film, in which a dead man lives after his body and is obliged to inhabit another. The man remains the same *for himself* but is different *for others,* and he cannot rest until through love a girl recognizes him despite his new exterior and the harmony between the *for itself* and the *for others* is re-established. The editors of *Le Canard enchaîné* are annoyed at this and would like to send Astruc back to his philosophical investigations. But the truth is that both parties are right: one because art is not meant to be a showcase for ideas, and the other because contemporary philosophy consists not in stringing concepts together but in describing the mingling of consciousness with the world, its involvement in a body, and its coexistence with others; and because this is movie material *par excellence.*

Finally, if we ask ourselves why it is precisely in the film era that this philosophy has developed, we obviously should not say that the movies grew out of the philosophy. Motion pictures are first and foremost a technical invention in which philosophy counts for nothing. But neither do we have the right to say that this philosophy has grown out of the cinema which it transposes to the level of ideas, for one can make bad movies; after the technical instrument has been invented, it must be taken up by an artistic will and, as it were, re-invented before one can succeed in making real films. Therefore, if philosophy is in harmony with the cinema, if thought and technical effort are heading in the same direction, it is because the philosopher and the moviemaker share a certain way of being, a certain view of the world which belongs to a generation. It offers us yet another chance to confirm that modes of thought correspond to technical methods and that, to use Goethe's phrase, "What is inside is also outside."

Index

Keisler, Sara, 103n
Kelly, Kevin, 229n
Kepler, Johannes, 34, 146
Kern, Stephen, 25, 26n
Keying, 169–170, 267
Kiesler, S., 303n, 310n
Kim, W. S., 260, 265n
Kinematic similarity, 253
Kinesthetic perception, 250
Kino-Pravda (Vertov), 169
Kircher, Athanasius, 234
Klatzky, R. L., 250n
Klein, Yve, 200
Knowbotic Research, 15
Knowledge. *See also* Epistemology;
  Telepistemology
art and, 4, 198–212, 343
as a commodity, 109
deception and, 49–50
at a distance, 3, 119–120, 127, 150
Cartesian model of, 110–112, 115–
  116, 121
causal processes and, 127–131
constraint and, 113
deception and, 49–50
embodied nearness and, 62
engagement and, 120
epistemic immediacy and, 320–329
intercorporiality and, 60–61
Locke on, 112, 115–116, 121
mediated, 93–94, 112, 116, 153,
  313–320
mind space and, 110–111
NRA difficulties and, 134–142
oversaturation, 104, 106–107
perception and, 50–52
Plato on, 13, 313–314
reliability theories and, 131–134
representations and, 115–116
self and, 292–294

technology and, 65, 70, 108–124
tele-identity and, 310–311
truth and, 306–307
Kobayashi, H., 273n
Kominstky, John Amos, 228n
König, Dominik von, 104n
Kraut, Robert, 103n
Kroker, A., 6n
Kroker, M., 6n
Krueger, Myron, 62n
Kruger National Park, 39
Kubey, Robert, 103n
Kubler, George, 230n
Kusahara, Machiko, 17, 204n,
  198–212

Lakoff, George, 303n
Lang, Fritz, 228
Last Supper, 230
Latour, Bruno, 175, 176n
Laurel, Brenda, 173, 174n
Lawn, C. A., 270n
Lear, Jonathan, 86n
Le Canard enchaine, 345
Lederman, S. J., 250n
Lee, T., 260n
Leenhardt, R., 340, 343
Leeson, Lynn Hershman, 203–204,
  204n
Legal Tender, 60, 283
Leggar, Robert, 34n
LEGO blocks, 201
Les Raisons des Forces Mouvantes (de
  Caus), 228
l'Etrange sursis, 343
Lévy, Pierre, 6n, 161–162, 186n, 236n,
  294
Lewis, C. I., 318n, 319n
Lewis, David, 136n
Lewitt, Sol, 222

Medusan gaze, 149

Memento mori, 154, 162

Menges, Karl, 153n

Mercury Project, 9, 201, 281

Merleau-Ponty, Maurice, 20

  Cartesian thought and, 53, 57–58, 60

  experience and, 66

  on film, 332–345

Metamachines: Where is the Body?, 188

Metric space, 103

  shallowness and, 106

  of space-time, 94–98

Micro-electrochemical systems

    (MEMS), 270

Microteleoperation, 270–273

Mignonneau, Laurent, 6n, 233

Miller, Perrym 36n

Mimesis, 231

Mimetic similarity, 153–154

Mind

  depression and, 103–104

  Hobbes on, 228

  space of, 110–112

  tele-embodiment and, 276–294

  tele-identity and, 296–311

Minsky, Marvin, 18n, 27, 281n

Mitchell, William J., 23, 28n

MIT Media Lab, 19, 30

Mnemosyne Atlas (Warburg), 239

Moholy-Nagy, L., 15

Mondada, F., 6n

Montage, 168–170

Morals, 297

  astronomy and, 153

  cyberspace and, 105–106

  information and, 100–104, 107

  simulation and, 87–88

  telethics and, 310–311

Moraes, Frederico, 186n

Morse, Margaret, 200n

Mt. Everest, 38

Mt. Fuji, 38

Mt. Vesuvius, 38

Mt. Washington, 38

MUDs (Multi-User Dungeons), 302

Mukophadhyay, Tridas, 103n

Munich Media Lab, 210

Muschamp, Herbert, 37n

Musjoukin, 339–340

Musser, Charles, 167n

Naimark, M., 15

Nakamura, H., 273n

Nance, Kevin, 186n

Napoli, Lisa, 43n

NASA Ames Virtual Environment

    Workstation, 174

Nass, Clifford, 291n, 301

National Oceanic and Atmospheric

    Administration, 32

Nature, 87

  destruction of, 69

  gardens and, 87, 200, 204–207,

    228

  illusions of, 232

  vs. technology, 35–41

Nearness, 90–92, 99–100. *See also*

    Proximity

  cultural information and, 97–98

  depression and, 103–105

  information and, 104

  integration and, 101–102

  metric space and, 95–96

  repleteness and, 95

  shallowness and, 106–107

  technology and, 93

  telepresence and, 108–124

  topology and, 94

Neuromancer (Gibson), 118

News reporting, 73

quasi-emotions and, 75–76, 80–84
repleteness and, 95
scale and, 273
tele-identity and, 296–311
underdetermination and, 100
vs. cyberspace, 93–95, 102
Real-time remote control, 177
Reeves, Byron, 291n, 301
Reformation, 232
Refresh (Diller and Scofidio), 16
Reijlander, Oscar G., 171
Reiss, C., 235n
Reiss, Timothy J., 157
Relativity, Special Theory of, 147, 160
Reliability, 319
  alternative theories and, 131–134
  causal processes and, 127–130
  NRA difficulties and, 134–142
Religion, 235–238
  art and, 229–231
Remote Access Astronomy Project
  (RAAP), 32
Remote state communication,
  267–268
Renger-Patzsch, Albert, 217n
Repleteness, 95
  metric space and, 96–97
  shallowness and, 106
  technology and, 99–100
Representations, 115–117, 120, 123
Rheingold, Howard, 306–307
Riess, Adam, 235
Rikugien garden, 204–205
Robinson, Henry Peach, 171
Robots, 252, 288–290. *See also*
  Telerobotics
  chatterbots and, 302–305, 308, 311
Rocco, Elena, 292n
Rodchenko, Alexander, 169
Rodowick, D. N., 216n

Rodemer, M. 15
Roemer, Ole, 14, 145, 147–148, 153
Romantics, 153
Rorty, Richard, 15, 319n
Rossman. J., 8n
Rothenberg, N., 8n, 259n, 281n
Royal Observatory, 34
Royce, Josiah, 91
Russell, Bertrand, 65, 81
Rybczynski, Zbignew, 170–171
Ryoanji Temple, 204–205

Sabi Sabi Game Reserve, 39
Sabra, A. I., 145n
Saccadic eye movement, 149
Sacri Monti movement, 229–231
Saint Petersburg History Museum,
  The, 193
Sala delle Prospettive (Peruzzi), 229
Salisbury, J. K., 256n, 258
Santarramana, Joe, 205
Sartre, Jean-Paul, 66
Saucy, P., 6n
Scale, 270–273
Scher, Julia, 15
Schneiderman, Ben., 325n
Schoenfeld, Gabriel, 33n
School of the Art Institute, The, 193
Schmitt, Frederick, 139n
Schrader-Frechette, Kristin, 102n
Scofidio, R., 15
Searle, John, 52n, 81–82, 229n
Seaworld, 34
Secret Garden, The, 205
Seeing machine, 235
Self knowledge, 292–294
Sensorama, 233
Serres, Michael, 240n
Sermon, Paul, 15
Shallowness, 106–107